THE ONE YEAR®

EXPERIENCING
GOD'S LOVE

DEVOTIONAL

THE ONE YEAR®

EXPERIENCING GOD'S LOVE

DEVOTIONAL

SANDRA BYRD

TYNDALE
MOMENTUM™

The nonfiction imprint of
Tyndale House Publishers, Inc.

For my husband, Michael Byrd, MDiv.
Thank you for halving my grief and doubling my joy
for better than thirty years.

"For we are co-workers in God's service."

1 CORINTHIANS 3:9

Introduction

Happy New Year!

January opens with breathtaking freshness, and opportunities beckon us forward. I can't wait—can you? Thank you, dear reader and fellow believer, for joining me for twelve months of deepening our understanding of what it means to experience the love of God.

When I reflect on the people I'm the closest to and the most intimate with, in whom I place the most trust, it's those people I spend a lot of time with. These are the people who are present in our lives for each up and down, the people we don't have to "catch up" with, because they are near-constant presences, the ones we're knit together with. I know them, and I sense when they are feeling blue or want to share some victory. They know me and understand my frailties and come alongside with a card, a hug, or an encouraging word.

No matter how close we are with other people though, they can't always be with us. A spouse may work or have other interests, and eventually he or she will pass away. Our closest friends have other interests and friends too. Our children grow up and move on to lives of their own. Small groups and Bible studies switch up over the seasons; we may change churches several times during our lives.

Only one person never changes and is always with us: our Lord. With God, we can be more intimate than with any other because he is omnipresent— always with us. "So do not fear, for I am with you," he pledges in Isaiah 41:10. "The LORD your God goes with you; he will never leave you nor forsake you," Deuteronomy 31:6 promises. I have long known that God loves me and loves you. But I long to experience it each and every day.

To experience something is to live it, to encounter it, to understand it, to explore it with our hearts, minds, and souls as well as with the five physical senses and our God-given spiritual ones. It means to join him in doing his work and to be the recipient of it too. In every action we do with and for God, every good day and bad day when we walk hand in hand with God, we experience him.

Through these daily devotions (six days each week plus the opportunity to put new insights into practice in a hands-on way on the seventh), I pray that this year you will experience the love of God in powerful and deeply personal ways. "May you experience the love of Christ, though it is too great to understand fully. Then you will be made complete with all the fullness of life and power that comes from God" (Ephesians 3:19, NLT).

Ready? Let's go!

Sandra

JANUARY

The Payoff for Practice

My New Year's resolution: coax music out of the mahogany piano which sits, pretty but mute, in our living room. In fact, the only time the strings sound is in a reverberating response to my husband's infamously loud sneezes.

Beethoven would not approve.

As a girl, I never liked practicing, and that hasn't changed. Tackling a new piece, note by note, over and over, seems tiring and somewhat repetitive—unfulfilling, as it is often done alone. But that measure-by-measure practice is foundational to all the seamless, rewarding music that follows. In his book *Outliers*, Malcolm Gladwell says, "Practice isn't the thing you do once you're good. It's the thing you do that makes you good."

So often we want the reward, the pleasure, before putting in the time with drills. Practice, though, builds muscle memory, and muscle memory will kick in almost without thought when needed. For example, when stage fright threatens to wreck a piano performance, the oft-practiced piece will obey the rhythmic, expected motion of the hands till the fear settles down. The hands will automatically do what they have been trained to do even if the brain isn't consciously directing them.

January 1 is a good time to settle what *spiritual* practices you'd like to reestablish too. Trusting God for small things will trigger an automatic faith response when the larger challenge arrives. When a difficult circumstance arrives unannounced, we often don't have the presence of mind to tell us what to do to lean on God in that moment. If we've "practiced" the disciplines of prayer, dependence, and courage, they will kick in without conscious thought when we most need them to.

Additionally, in happier circumstances, being trained to sense the leading of God will allow your spiritual muscle memory to learn how to play the new songs he's created for your life, even when you're afraid. Inevitably, I find peace in prayer and direction in reading the Bible, even when I didn't feel like doing either at first. Habits enable us to do what is right and trust that supportive feelings will follow.

What spiritual discipline is the Holy Spirit leading you to practice this year, so you and he will make beautiful music together?

Physical training is good, but training for godliness is much better, promising benefits in this life and in the life to come.   1 TIMOTHY 4:8, NLT

Beyond Expectation

Come, thou long-expected Jesus,
born to set thy people free;
from our fears and sins release us,
let us find our rest in thee.

Charles Wesley wrote those words in 1744, and while they may provide comfort to the believer, they may also provide pain. The Jesus who *is*, is not always the Jesus we long for or expect.

Jesus is a healer, and we expect that he will heal. He often does, but many times he does not. If we have prayed for a fellow believer who has gone to be with the Lord, we can comfort ourselves with the fact that our loved one is out of pain and in his presence. Still, there is sometimes disappointment that the Jesus who heals did not do so here on earth when it mattered to us.

Jesus is a provider, but for those who struggle with unemployment or homelessness or hopelessness, it can be difficult to be content with the Jesus who holds their hand in the dark but does not immediately change the circumstances.

When the Lord first appeared on earth, the Jewish community had been expecting a Messiah that would free them from the political and physical oppression they suffered under the Romans. Jesus' priority, though, was the souls of people. He came to carry out the most important charge his Father had given him: to die for our redemption. The way he acts and does not act was, and still is, sometimes bewildering even to those who love and follow him. Even his cousin John, who had recognized Jesus by leaping while still in his mother Elizabeth's womb, had a moment of doubt while imprisoned. "Are you the one?" he asked of Jesus in Matthew 11:2-3 (esv). "Or shall we look for another?"

The first-century Jewish community was expecting someone to solve their immediate problems, and when Jesus didn't do that, some grew disappointed in him. In time, though, Jesus promises he will make all things new and dry every tear. In your present circumstance, what kind of savior are you expecting? Can you find rest and release in Jesus as he truly is and does? He is righteous and good. You need look for no other.

I know whom I have believed, and am convinced that he is able to guard what I have entrusted to him until that day. 2 Timothy 1:12

Inspired

I sat in the family room, chick flick on in the background, inflating a floating mountain of balloons in preparation for a celebration.

I was also worrying about post-Christmas and health-care bills.

As the balloons expanded, I thought about how what filled them often defined the little orbs. Filled with water? Water balloons. Ready to soar skyward? Hot-air balloons. Huffing and puffing, I thought these would certainly be Sandra balloons—filled with air that had come from inside me. The balloons, though filled, drooped on the floor as if in confirmation of my weighed-down spirit. It put me in mind of Scripture.

Genesis tells us, "The LORD God formed the man from the dust of the ground. He breathed the breath of life into the man's nostrils, and the man became a living person" (2:7, NLT). When we were filled with his breath of life, that was our defining moment as humans. We are filled with him, which is who we are meant to be.

That verse is directly where the word *inspiration* comes from. We are animated, filled, and defined by what is inside us.

The book of Acts shows Barnabas to be a good man, filled with faith and the Holy Spirit. After Saul had approved of the stoning of Stephen and the ravaging of the church, he left for Damascus to do more damage. Then Saul saw Christ in a vision and was saved. Barnabas found Saul and brought him back to Jerusalem. While many believers were understandably filled with fear at the sight of Saul, Barnabas was filled with faith. I imagine, like the other believers, he had that choice: be filled with fear or be filled with faith.

We, too, as modern-day disciples, have that same choice when faced with troublesome situations, large or small: faith or fear. What fills us, defines us? God tells us that he does not give us a spirit of fear but of himself—power, love, and self-control. Because he loves us, we each have the choice every day to be filled with the Spirit. Which do you choose? He wants to breathe peace and life into you today!

God gave us a spirit not of fear but of power and love and self-control.
2 TIMOTHY 1:7, ESV

Minty Fresh

The first week of the year is a time when most of us hope to make a fresh start, a new beginning. It's a biblical concept—our Lord is a God of fresh starts and do-overs. The psalmist pleads, like we do, "Create in me a clean heart, O God, and renew a right spirit within me" (Psalm 51:10, ESV).

A dieting trick I picked up some years ago was to brush my teeth immediately after I'd finished a properly-sized portion or any time I was tempted to overindulge. Most of the time it worked, because it gave me two minutes to consider the commitment I'd made to my health.

In our Christian walk, it also feels good to be clean, and when we are spiritually shipshape, there's hesitation to mess that up. The price of "getting clean" spiritually is much costlier than a couple of minutes in front of the sink and a tube of toothpaste. It cost the Lord his very life.

I had a friend who refused to drive another friend's expensive convertible because she was afraid she'd wreck it. She had no trouble driving my old Toyota, though. First Corinthians exhorts us, "Do you not know that your body is a temple of the Holy Spirit within you, whom you have from God? You are not your own, for you were bought with a price. So glorify God in your body" (6:19-20, ESV).

When I consider the cost to Christ for his relationship with me, I remember and experience his love for me in a fresh and energizing way. Recognizing anew the price Christ paid to purchase me, I'm compelled to consider my own devotion to being his disciple. When I sin, now, I not only ask for forgiveness and a fresh start, I prove my intentions by planning ahead, like that tooth brushing. When I sin, I pray, confess, repent, and text a friend and admit it. It's much harder than it seems, but it works, because who wants to do that multiple times a day and seem like a spiritual slacker? Not I. Being accountable and knowing how expensive this convertible was to my Savior lessens the desire to mess up.

Do you have a plan to avoid your temptations? You can succeed!

Submit yourselves, then, to God. Resist the devil, and he will flee from you. Come near to God and he will come near to you. JAMES 4:7-8

The Gentle Cycle

I arrived at the gym in the late afternoon, just after school let out—a mistake. Half the pool was cordoned off for swimming lessons, which meant that all free swimmers would have to cram, like proverbial sardines, into the other half of the water. I looked out over the crowd. Many bathers did not have room to stretch their arms without whacking someone else, much less enjoy the water. The pool was over capacity.

I determined to come back another time, another day, but I mused on overcapacity all the way home. I wasn't sure my packed schedule allowed for another visit soon.

Sometimes I stuff too much into my washing machine in an attempt to get everything clean in one load. Only problem—nothing gets clean when the washer is over capacity. I'd recently read of a party on a college campus. Not only were there many revelers, but too many of them had also spilled out onto a tiny balcony designed for two plus a little grill, to tragic results. The balcony collapsed and took the students down with it.

Too many plugs in the socket leads to a blackout wherein nothing gets juice. So, too, when much is asked of anything or anyone, above and beyond their designed capacity, uselessness, poor performance, lack of joy, and even disaster may result.

We often think of self-control as stopping ourselves from participating in something harmful. But often, self-control means moderating the amount of good we take on. Self-control means saying no to two ministries so that we might do one well. Self-control means not taking on too many hours at work to the detriment of the body. Self-control means carving out time for rest, reflection, and pleasure in a society which often equates value with busyness. Things and people regularly running at overcapacity eventually break down, black out, or collapse. When I pack my life (or allow others to pack my life) with stuff to do, there is very little time to be: be Sandra, be still, be with Jesus and experience his presence and provision that day. Even the Lord withdrew from ministry, his work, to rest and recharge (see Luke 4:42; 5:16).

What might you trim back to do, be, and enjoy what remains? Your body and spirit deserve to be treated gently.

Like a city whose walls are broken through is a person who lacks self-control.
PROVERBS 25:28

In Need of a Little Christian-ease

So often we Christians exhort others to "have faith." Have faith that the situation will be resolved in the right way. Believe that all will end well, although current events seem to be careening out of control. Trust that shattered relationships will be restored, that God is bigger than any situation or circumstance that we face and can overcome for and with us. Our advice is true and biblical. After all, we walk by faith and not by sight, as 2 Corinthians informs us. We're so used to saying "just have faith," though, that it's become *Christianese*, something we casually reference but don't practically facilitate.

I'm here to tell you, it's not "Christian-ease" to have faith in difficult times; it's "Christian-hard."

We rejoice and praise together when times are good, but we must persevere and lean into faith in both God and his faithful followers when times are tough. God has promised that he will never leave nor forsake us, but as a child once said, I sometimes wish I had Jesus with skin on him, right here and right now, in my house.

That little child's prayer can be answered. The word *encourage* means to inspire courage or confidence in someone. People who need courage are facing a daunting, tiring, or worrisome situation. We are to help them be brave, to hold them up as it were, as they stand or fight. We experience the love of God in an unmatchable, powerful way when we act as his agents, on his behalf, offering that love to others. To "go and do likewise" (Luke 10:37) to someone who is disheartened is a marching order from Jesus Christ to all who believe.

To whom, today or this week, can you bring a little "Christian-ease" by your loving, helping presence? Having a "Christian-hard" week, yourself? Be brave. Reach out to a loved one and ask for help and hugs.

Let us hold unswervingly to the hope we profess, for he who promised is faithful. And let us consider how we may spur one another on toward love and good deeds, not giving up meeting together, as some are in the habit of doing, but encouraging one another—and all the more as you see the Day approaching.   HEBREWS 10:23-25

Experiencing the Love of God

The amazing thing about giving to others is that it gives back to us, and almost immediately. "Give, and it will be given to you"—the mysterious economy of our wonderful God.

Today, right now, think of three or four people who could use a little lift and then reach out and encourage them. It works best if you target their particular need. Someone who is suffering from physical pain might benefit by your sharing a meal you prepare or buy, or rubbing their feet and hands. Someone who is discouraged might be encouraged by a funny card. In a day of e-mail, receiving an actual card in the mail shows care and concern. Or poke a plastic pink flamingo in their front lawn. Do you know parents who need an evening out? Send a gift card.

For the friend who needs prayer, offer to pray every day this week, and then set a calendar reminder and let them know once or twice after you've followed through.

Another friend might like a quick walk with you if weather allows. You can leave positive reviews online for your favorite authors, musicians, and even doctors and dentists.

Now—the harder part. Reach out and ask for help yourself. Text a friend when you need prayer. Admit your marriage is in trouble or your child is wandering, and get help. Ask on social media for a book recommendation that will lift your spirits. Join a Bible study—many new groups form at the start of the year. Lift others, and let them lift you, too.

We all experience God's love when we're holding hands.

The people I will reach out to, and how:

The people I'll ask for help, and for what:

Give, and you will receive. Your gift will return to you in full—pressed down, shaken together to make room for more, running over, and poured into your lap. The amount you give will determine the amount you get back.
                                                      LUKE 6:38, NLT

Only One Voice

I write for a living, which involves direction and suggestion from lots of people. Everyone from editors to friends to readers lets me know what I've done right— and wrong—and tells me what I should do next. My family even pitches in. When my young son read one of my books for tween girls, he told me exactly where I'd gone wrong. "No submarines," he said. "That's why they're not selling. You don't have any submarines in your books."

I'll bet your job is like that too, whether it be your career, your ministry, your mothering, or whatever else you undertake. Someone always knows how you should be doing it differently. Though there may be dozens of voices trying to direct me, I aim to satisfy primarily one person—my editor, my boss.

When he directs me, it is for our common goal. When he signs off on the project, he's saying, "Well done." No other voice ultimately matters.

Overall, most of us are tempted to be people pleasers. But Scripture is clear that we cannot have two masters. It's easy for the noisy one in the same room to win out over God's still, small voice.

When the Lord compares us to sheep, it is not exactly a compliment. Sheep are prone to "sheep pleasing." In fact, if one sheep panics and runs toward the edge of a cliff, the entire flock might thoughtlessly follow her; she'll lead them all to their deaths. A good shepherd will guide the sheep away from areas of danger, using his voice, his staff, and his dog to usher his flock to areas of good grazing and water so their wool can grow thick and rich. He does not allow strange animals or robbers to distract, waylay, or mislead his sheep. For this to be successful, though, the sheep must follow him and not one another or some other "boss."

I'm praying today that God will open my eyes to the places where I still want to please people, to look good in front of them, instead of listening to his quiet, leading voice. Will you join me?

Am I now trying to win the approval of human beings, or of God? Or am I trying to please people? If I were still trying to please people, I would not be a servant of Christ. GALATIANS 1:10

Three Points of Contact

Recently, we had our house painted. It's a tall house with a steep drop-off, and I watched in wonder as the painters confidently scrambled up what seemed to be shaky, thin ladders stabilized only by tiny metal feet.

I recalled the lesson my husband taught our kids when they were young and liked to climb rocks. "Three points of contact," he drilled into them. Two feet must be firmly planted, along with one hand gripping the point of contact, before the second hand could reach forward. Or, both hands held firmly to whatever was being climbed and one foot braced while the other took a step forward, backward, or down. In this way, a person could move forward, make progress, grasp, and reach. Those three points provided a stable and safe base.

The Christian has three points of constant contact in the Trinity. One of the beautiful mysteries of our faith is that, while we serve one God, he expresses himself in three unified persons. Each person of the Godhead reaches, teaches, and loves us in a unique manner, and we can hold on to all three at once.

God the Father, who calls us his children, so loved the world he created that he adopted us into his family. He called us and dearly loves us and receives our prayers. He made everything and made the way for everything. Even adults need a daddy, and in God the Father, we have that place of safety, protection, and refuge.

Jesus, the Son, is our savior, the mediator between us and the Father in salvation and in everything that comes after. He is our advocate still, our brother, friend, husband, and our model for life. "Follow me," he said.

Jesus told us that it would be a wonderful thing for us to receive the Holy Spirit, the third person of the Trinity. The Spirit is a counselor to us at all times; he helps us recall Scripture and spiritual lessons. He convicts us of poor courses of action and affirms and urges us toward wise ones.

Are you excited to climb, walk, reach, and grasp the delightful life God has gifted you from your stable, safe base of love?

May the grace of the Lord Jesus Christ, the love of God, and the fellowship of the Holy Spirit be with you all. 2 CORINTHIANS 13:14, NLT

He's Made Us Fast

Among the most motivating movies for Christians to watch is *Chariots of Fire*. It tells the story of two world-class runners, including Eric Liddell, a Scottish man born to Christian missionaries in China.

Liddell was selected to run in the 1924 Olympics. When he was scheduled to run his race on Sunday, he declined, saying he would not run on the Sabbath, though he was pressured by many to ignore his convictions. It's been claimed that an American Olympic team masseur slipped a piece of paper into Liddell's hand with this quotation from 1 Samuel 2:30: "Those who honor me I will honor."

Liddell withdrew from the 100-meter race to avoid running on the Sabbath and instead ran the 400-meter event on another day. The 51st Highland Brigade played their pipes outside the stadium before Liddell ran, to give him courage and national pride. Liddell ran—and won the gold, setting an Olympic record. Liddell's fidelity to his Christian convictions made him famous at the time, and even better, put his faith and ours front and center.

So often we feel that our best ministries are those that are traditionally defined—pastor, preacher, missionary, Sunday school teacher. Mostly, though, our strongest testimonies come through when we decide, with a moment's notice, to live the faith we claim. Eric Liddell's family honored God as missionaries, and he himself returned to missionary work after the Olympics. What the family is best remembered for now is not that traditionally defined Christian ministry, but Liddell's spot decision to honor God with his life in the nonreligious details. He said, "I believe that God made me for a purpose. . . . But he also made me fast, and when I run, I feel his pleasure."

Where do you feel God's pleasure?

Those who honor me I will honor.   1 SAMUEL 2:30

Abiding Love

I've spent the past couple of years losing weight, slowly but successfully, after not having been able to do that for some time. I've found a new way of eating that works for me and have incorporated the changes gradually, one by one. I'd heard the adage, "It took you X years to put this on; it's not going to come off overnight." But somehow, with the effort put forward, it seemed like things were moving too slowly.

Our world loves to promote successes: overnight financial successes, start-ups that make a billion dollars with no college required, houses flipped for instant profit, fifty pounds lost in fifty days. The hare always seems to come out as the media winner, and the tortoise, rarely even acknowledged. But as we know, the tortoise wins in the end because of perseverance.

I mentioned the slow progress to a mentor, who told me, "Plateaus are good for the health. They give us time to adjust at each level, each change in habit, before moving on to the next." They allow us to remain and to abide.

This, too, is true for our spiritual health. We read the Word, or listen to a speaker or a pastor, and glean a new and exciting insight that we immediately apply, and it changes us. Then, time goes by before the next epiphany. Our walk seems slow, routine, unexciting. These seem like spiritual plateaus; in fact, they are. But they allow us time to incorporate each new truth, each new insight given, into our daily life. We experience increased understanding of the Lord when we reach a new height in our spiritual lives, but we experience a new depth in his abiding love when we remain on plateaus. We are not designed to incorporate many new habits at once. When we try that, often none of them stick. Perseverance wins the day.

The human body, and the body of Christ, both grow toward health with steady forward progress. Is there somewhere you feel like you're not making progress quickly enough, but in truth, you're moving at just the right pace for permanent change?

I have loved you even as the Father has loved me. Remain in my love.

JOHN 15:9, NLT

Lean on Me

Social media can be the fount of many ills, but it has also been a force for good. From the privacy of home, we meet new friends and brothers and sisters in Christ, people we may never have met while here on earth. One such friend, Robert Cook, underwent the most severe tragedy a parent can imagine. As he crept through that trial on his knees, he taught all of us, near and far, what it means to trust God.

Robert's son was undergoing some extreme difficulties, and when Robert was called to his son's hospital bedside, he went to social media and asked all of us who believe to pray. I knew Mr. Cook was a brother in Christ and a parent, and my heart went out to him as did many hundreds if not thousands of other hearts. We prayed for his son, and we prayed for Robert. Despite the best medical efforts and all those prayers, Robert's son passed away, into the arms of Jesus. Robert was crushed, and so were all of us who had come alongside him. He showed grace and dignity during the situation, and he also showed vulnerability in reaching out for help when he needed it—not putting on a stoic face but living an honest life of faith.

The moment in which I learned the most from Mr. Cook was after his son had been buried. Speaking of his Christian faith, his relationship with Jesus, Robert said, "I'm continuing my walk, just with a limp." He was willing to experience the love of God, both in his deep love for his son and in the crushing loss of his son. Who better than Jesus to lean on when our walk is unsteady?

Has there ever been a stronger, truer, more encouraging testimony? If we live long enough, each of us will take a bat to the shins, perhaps many times over. What does that do to our walk? Are we paralyzed? Do we turn away from Christ? Or do we keep walking, slowly, with the one who holds us up when we stumble?

Take his hand. Take mine. It's okay to limp. We all limp sometimes. Let's just keep walking.

Brothers and sisters, we do not want you to be uninformed about those who sleep in death, so that you do not grieve like the rest of mankind, who have no hope.　　　　　　　　　　　　　1 Thessalonians 4:13

Sense and Sensibility

Our son-in-law, a new believer at the time, had a big concern and voiced it to us. "How do I hear from God? I want to hear his voice, but I'm not sure how to understand what he's telling me about everyday things."

Many of us, no matter how long we've been Christians, would agree that we long to hear from the Lord, directly or indirectly. "If God would just tell me what to do, I'd do it," has escaped my lips every year. With our son-in-law, we discussed reading Scripture and paying attention to the leading of the Holy Spirit—good teaching, covering all the basics. But one way the Lord speaks to us, every day, is often overlooked.

God has given us five senses, sensibility, and the Holy Spirit to help us discern. He's asked us many times in Scripture to observe and then draw conclusions.

How do I know if someone is a safe person to be in a relationship with, learn from, befriend, or marry? Jesus says, "A good tree cannot bear bad fruit, and a bad tree cannot bear good fruit. . . . Thus, by their fruit you will recognize them" (Matthew 7:18, 20).

How do I know that you'll care for me, Lord? "Consider the ravens: They do not sow or reap, they have no storeroom or barn; yet God feeds them. And how much more valuable you are than birds!" (Luke 12:24).

Do you see my needs, Lord? "Consider how the wild flowers grow. They do not labor or spin. . . . If that is how God clothes the grass of the field, which is here today, and tomorrow is thrown into the fire, how much more will he clothe you?" (Luke 12:27-28).

When I'm lonely, and he nudges someone to call me, I know he's listening to my heart, and I "hear" from him in the voice of my friend. When I see someone who can't provide a birthday party for her child, and he reminds me I'm good at baking cakes, he's speaking to me and asking me to speak for him, through a cake. I love to read the Word and listen to it taught. But how sweet it is, indeed, to see and hear and taste and touch him at work all around us every day, when we have eyes to see!

Ears that hear and eyes that see—the LORD has made them both.

PROVERBS 20:12

Experiencing the Love of God

Training our senses, both physical and spiritual, to sense and see God at work around us takes practice. But it can be done and is well worth the effort to communicate with him in this manner every day. When we learn to discern his hands at work and act as his hands at work, we experience his love—and our partnership with him—in a deeper, more meaningful way.

Scripture tells us that "whatever is good and perfect is a gift coming down to us from God our Father (see James 1:17, NLT), so that's a great place to start. Got something good going on? Thank you, Lord!

Scripture also tells us that "for whom the LORD loves He chastens" (Hebrews 12:6, NKJV). Had a gentle (or not so gentle!) correction lately, one that sent you in the right direction? Thank you, Lord!

I have always had a thing with pennies, between God and me. When I see one I remember what is stamped on it, "In God We Trust." It reminds me to trust him. When I'm feeling weak or worried, I often find a penny on the floor or on the ground, and I know he's drawn my eye to it.

One day I was under a lot of stress, and I asked the Lord, "Please reassure me." I walked into the dry cleaner, which is owned by Christians, and heard a lovely praise song. I just knew that was from God! And then, as I paid, my eyes were drawn to a huge cup FILLED with pennies. "Need one? Take one!" it said. My eyes filled with tears. That was from him too.

How do you see God's work in your life in the natural world around you this week? Don't skip past this. Stay here, prayerfully, until you can list at least five ways.

1.

2.

3.

4.

5.

Whatever is good and perfect is a gift coming down to us from God our Father, who created all the lights in the heavens. JAMES 1:17, NLT

Keep Humble and Hustle Hard

A nearby store was selling coffee growlers that I knew my son would enjoy. The bottles were stamped with "Keep Humble and Hustle Hard." My son is a tech entrepreneur, and among entrepreneurs, the need to hustle—to move quickly, effectively, and keep pushing forward—is a byword for success. After college, he told us he was going to bootstrap his new company; we heartily affirmed him but reminded him that we'd invested in his college, so it was his *own* bootstraps that needed to be used to pull himself up. He knew. Having skin in the game keeps you hungry and hustling.

His energy and commitment remind me of a story I watched about a woman starting her own flower business. She purchased a decommissioned food truck and traveled her small town in it, selling bouquets. An entrepreneurial friend told her that she should buy more flowers than she thought she could sell as a way to risk, push forward, look for creative techniques, and not rest on her laurels. Her flower business was a blooming success!

Investors lend seed money, or startup capital, as an indication of faith in the idea and anticipated return on investment. In the end, though, it is up to the entrepreneur to maneuver the company to success. In the same way, the Lord has "seeded" us with spiritual giftings which we are to use, in conjunction with him, for the benefit of other Christians. The ministry is handed to us, with our human skin in the game, in an indication of the faith God has in us and our ability to creatively and persistently work out that calling.

Like any investor, God can add or remove gifts depending on how they are stewarded. The parable of the talents in Matthew clearly shows that the Lord expects us to wisely invest the talents he's given us for a good return. How do we do that? We fan those gifts into flame through an intentional blend of dependency, intention, and action. What has the Spirit gifted you with that you can invest in Kingdom work?

Stay humble and hustle hard!

I am reminded of your sincere faith, which first lived in your grandmother Lois and in your mother Eunice and, I am persuaded, now lives in you also. For this reason I remind you to fan into flame the gift of God.

2 TIMOTHY 1:5-6

Beauty Marks

A month after our first baby was born, I stood in front of a mirror wondering if my body would ever return to its pre-baby form. (The answer is no!) While I was pregnant, my skin had stretched and stretched to accommodate a growing baby. I felt changed, different, maybe even damaged. No amount of cocoa butter or expensive potions would take away those icicle-like pink and silver streaks across my abdomen.

After a few months, though, I began to take pride in them. My skin had stretched, as required, to accommodate a baby. The goal had not been to have perfect skin, after all. I'd nurtured a child, and I was filled with joy by his presence.

Stretching, and the attendant marks, were required to accommodate that new life and growth.

This happens in our spiritual lives too. Often a situation pushes us to do new—and sometimes uncomfortable—things. A friend who had become a Christian left her live-in boyfriend; she felt convicted and decided she could no longer live with him, unmarried. Her loneliness was a stretch mark of faith. Another woman was led to speak to her women's group, but her voice trembled, and people looked away in embarrassment, causing her regret and awkwardness for weeks afterward—stretch marks of belief that she'd done what she was supposed to do. A man left a job which required him to do things "under the table" and lost his house because of it—stretch marks of trial in trust.

In time, though, the first woman married a godly man, the second heard from others who'd been touched by her words, and the man moved to a new town and took a new job and started fresh. Accommodating new life in our faith journey stretches us, but part of experiencing the love of God is the stretching that brings new growth and life to ourselves and others. Scripture says in 2 Peter 3:18, "Grow in the grace and knowledge of our Lord and Savior Jesus Christ."

Don't be afraid of the changes brought about by stretching and growing. In Kingdom terms, they're beauty marks!

Whenever a woman is in labor she has pain, because her hour has come; but when she gives birth to the child, she no longer remembers the anguish because of the joy that a child has been born into the world.

JOHN 16:21, NASB

Badge of Honor

As we discussed in yesterday's devotion, there are stretch marks. But there are also scars, which are something different altogether. Scars come about not by growth but by injury. On the body, they are a manifestation of tissue harmed and then healed.

While walking one day, my husband and I passed another couple. The man had no hair on his head, and his entire face was white and pink, no whiskers. My husband, who had interned in a hospital burn unit, told me later that the man's face was nearly completely covered with postburn scar tissue and skin transplants.

While it had been initially startling to look at the scarred man, the way he held his head up in pride, the affection with which he held his wife's hand, and the steady confidence of his smile lingered in my memory. They silently proclaimed, "I have come through the fire, and I have survived."

Scars are often used as defining marks when identifying people, and that is not a bad thing. The battles we've fought and won, the fires we have come through, define us. If we let them, they proclaim gravitas and victory.

It's difficult to read the portions of Scripture that describe the horror of huge nails being driven through the Lord's feet and hands. The mind's eye wants to look away when he is pierced through with a spear. Yet he underwent those sufferings for us; the scars are a permanent emblem of his deep love for us. His crucifixion and resurrection from the dead marked him; they identify him and what he did and who he is, forever.

Your scars may be in your heart or in your spirit, unseen and yet still defining. Those fires, walked through, also make us who we are. They give us tender spirits for the suffering, compassion for those in pain, and motivation to reach out to the lonely. God will use every injury for his good and ours, if we believe that he can, and will, redeem our pain in service to others while healing us and bringing us a promised, future joy.

What scars identify you? You made it through! Well done.

Jesus came and stood among them and said, "Peace be with you!" Then he said to Thomas, "Put your finger here; see my hands. Reach out your hand and put it into my side. Stop doubting and believe." JOHN 20:26-27

Unlimited Resources

A friend was going on a short-term mission trip to India, and to fund the trip, she'd set up an account on a popular crowdfunding website. By typing in our city name, I hoped to bring up her account and donate to the very worthy cause.

I found her page and donated. But as I scrolled, I was overwhelmed by the number of other requests—pleas, even—from others in my town.

Some of them brought a smile: a man who was getting married and would have to sell his boat to pay for it. Get used to it, buddy. You're an adult now!

But most of the requests were heartbreakingly difficult to read. They'd been penned by people who could not afford to host a funeral or bury a loved one. People who needed cancer treatment but did not have the funds to afford it. Families who needed basic sustenance while the breadwinning member was ill. People whose house had burned down (I knew those people!). Children who needed wheelchairs and children who needed speech therapy—or school clothes—were all listed.

I closed the website, a little overwhelmed by the number of needs. Truthfully, I wished I'd won a lottery and could give some to each. But I hadn't, so I couldn't. I prayed and asked the Lord if there was some way I could help any of them with my limited resources. My spirit was touched with the answer of what I did have to offer.

Prayer.

Scripture tells us that when righteous people pray, great things happen. "All things you ask in prayer, believing, you will receive" (Matthew 21:22, NASB). There was no limit on how much I could pray. And so I began. I've made prayer lists for loved ones and friends, but there was an amazing power in my new understanding that I could be a force for good in the lives of people I'd never met, but who needed mercy.

It's been said that prayer is like a set of buckets; when prayers rise to the Lord, he sends down mercy in return.

Send your bucket up! Watch what he sends down.

The prayer of a righteous person has great power as it is working.
JAMES 5:16, ESV

Through the Glass, Darkly

There's a certain kind of quiet to winter where I live. The landscape is frozen, dormant, and silent. Nothing grows except the most cunning plants—moss, for example, and that in fits and starts. Animals are bedded down till spring, and night visits early and stays late.

It can seem like a season of sadness, but to me, it is a season of waiting. I know that there are bulbs, long since planted in softer ground and on warmer days, storing up the strength to burst forward. There is no evidence of them yet. But they are there. The promise remains even in what seems to be barren silence.

When I was researching one of my novels, the Lord directed my eyes and mind to the stained glass windows in a magnificent, old church. The winter day was dark, and the glass was dimmed. The portrait of the Lord was barely visible. I could not see him. I would not have known it was him if I hadn't known he was there. When I later returned to the church on a glorious spring day, the light shone through the panes bringing the image of Jesus magnificently to life.

I have thought, *Lord, in the darkness is when I need to see you, to hear from you, but it's there you often seem hidden and mute.* But he is not hidden or mute. He is waiting, in his all-encompassing goodness and foreknowledge, for the right moment, the best time, to reveal himself and his plan in the glorious light, because he *is* light. Even when we cannot see him, can't quite make him out, he is there and will shine brilliantly again soon. I sometimes cannot see him; that does not mean he is not there. We experience him in faith during a blind season by remembering that what we can see is only the smallest part of what is happening.

Do not worry when you come upon a season of quiet, of dark, of waiting. All will be fully revealed and made right; some things here on earth, some things in the hereafter. Seasons of waiting *are* longer than seasons of harvest, but that's the process in all fruitful living.

For now we see through a glass, darkly; but then face to face: now I know in part; but then shall I know even as also I am known.

1 CORINTHIANS 13:12, KJV

Eyes to See

I have no idea who came up with the idea of Mr. Potato Head and his wife, the lovely and fleshy Mrs. Potato Head, who comes with button earrings. The creative genius, I've thought, must have taken a long riff on the fact that potatoes have eyes that need to be removed before they can be eaten.

Stripped down, the plastic potato is just a bulbous head. Eyes need to be added, and my kids had great fun positioning the eyes and then allowing the formerly blind Mr. Potato Head to see what was in the room with his new set of eyeballs. Next, ears could be added or removed, depending on if you wanted Mr. Potato Head (or Mom!) to hear what was being said in the room. I made a great joke of taking off his lips if they spoke something sassy. I hoped my stern face and comments made a point with my children . . . but no. They just had Mr. Potato Head say the mischievous things that they didn't think they could get away with. Finally, after his face was complete, Mr. Potato Head was given arms to hug with.

God brought me a lesson to use then, and it has stuck with me all these years. *Someone* had to give Mr. Potato Head the eyes to see; without them being applied, he could not. Until his ears were affixed by a benevolent sovereign—my five-year-old, who chortled at her newfound power—there was nothing that Mr. Potato Head could hear whether he wanted to or not.

His lips, given to him by Mom, were for speaking words of praise and honor and lifting others up, not tearing others down. Hebrews reminds us, "Through Jesus, therefore, let us continually offer to God a sacrifice of praise—the fruit of lips that openly profess his name" (13:15).

Ears and eyes are given to all humans, but only Jesus can turn them into useful tools that allow us to spiritually comprehend what he is doing. Each person is born with lips, and through Jesus, we can use them to offer a sacrifice of praise, even when the situation doesn't seem praiseworthy.

What God-happenings do you see and hear today, through the eyes and ears given you by Christ? You've got the power!

Blessed are your eyes because they see, and your ears because they hear.
MATTHEW 13:16

Experiencing the Love of God

The perfect dinner for a cold winter's evening, whether or not you indulge in a round of Mr. Potato Head first (see yesterday's devotion), is what the British call jacket potatoes.

Americans refer to them as baked potatoes, and I think they're very tasty if they are stuffed and then baked twice—you can even add a few black olive slices to add buttons to the potato jacket!

Russet potatoes work best. If you choose potatoes about the same size, they will bake at about the same rate. Look for ones that are fleshy and bulbous, like Mr. and Mrs. Potato Head.

Lightly scrub the potatoes, and leaving their skins (or "jackets") on, bake in a 350-degree oven for about an hour, depending on the size of the potato. Poke a skewer clear through each potato to make sure they are soft.

Take them out of the oven, and while still warm, slice vertically and lightly split each potato. Scoop out the flesh, and in a bowl, mix with sour cream, shredded cheese, salt, pepper, and crumbled bacon if you wish.

Restuff the potatoes, pull the jacket tight, and apply the sliced olive buttons. Place back into the oven till warmed through.

Warm meals are best enjoyed with warm hearts. A baked potato bar is a fun way to share a Sunday meal with a group of friends, a small group, or family members. Ask each person to bring one of the toppings, and you can provide the baked potatoes. The conversation might revolve around a lesson shared at church or at a Bible study in which your eyes were opened and your ears heard something new. End with a prayer thanking God for the provision of a hot meal on a cold day!

They devoted themselves to the apostles' teaching and to fellowship, to the breaking of bread and to prayer.   Acts 2:42

A Journey from Death to Life, Again

Some years ago, a model for understanding the emotional processing people go through when they survive the death of a loved one was introduced by psychiatrist Elisabeth Kübler-Ross. While the death of a loved one can be the most difficult of all deaths, we each face "deaths" on a regular basis: the death of a dream, a job, a hope for good health, a beloved stage of life, a marriage. Kübler-Ross's five-stage model is helpful to navigate those "little deaths" that arrive, unwelcome but regularly, to us all.

Denial. First, we deny that it is happening. We understand the situation wrong, we ignore the symptoms, we write off what our logical mind informs us is going on and replace it with a less painful, possibly believable alternative. Eventually, though, we must face that the thing we wish were not happening, truly is. God helps open our eyes so that we can face the truth of any situation, because accepting the truth will set us free.

Anger. Why me? Why us? Why now? This is unfair! We tend to lash out at anyone we believe has the power to change the situation, including God. He can take our anger, our emotional honesty with him and others, though he instructs us not to sin in our anger, which is an important requisite for intimacy.

Bargaining. We offer to God, or our boss, or our spouse, options and propositions to get them to change their mind, to use their power to bring about what we want to bring about. Sometimes this may indeed be effective, but when the loss is definite, bargaining leaves us feeling powerless and perhaps even humiliated. It helps to remember that God tells us to come and reason with him. He wants to hear what we have to say, even if the circumstances don't change.

Depression. We bog down into what feels like, in John Bunyan's famous book, the slough of despond. Will we ever be or see light again? God will send other people and his Spirit to show us that we have hope for the future.

Acceptance. We understand that the death, the circumstance, or the situation is resolved, but not as we had wished. At that point, we are resigned to a new reality, and if we let him, God will give us his supernatural peace.

What "death" is your Lord waiting to comfort you through?

I will not leave you comfortless: I will come to you.   JOHN 14:18, KJV

A Healthy Gain

It's three weeks into the new year. How goes your new eating and exercise plan?

Me, too.

A few years ago, I started a group for Christians who wanted to lose weight. I named it I Must Decrease after John 3:30, "He must increase, but I must decrease" (ESV). I knew to decrease in weight I had to increase the control the Spirit offers.

Swapping entrenched (and often beloved) habits and weaknesses for fresh and healthy ones was nearly impossible on my own. To succeed, I'd have to confront temptations with the power of the Lord behind me. In my flesh, I am weak, but in the Spirit, I can be strong.

The idea of John 3:30 is the concept of replacement. To introduce something new into something that is already solid, something would have to be dislocated. When you get into the bathtub, the water must move to make room for you. To remove an old habit, I would put a new one in its place, replacing the bad with the good. Overeating was replaced by reading, short naps, lovely long baths, chats with friends, and a monthly massage. My walking shoes replaced my evening TV and couch. Something had to decrease for something to increase, because there were still those same twenty-four hours in the day.

Likewise, when we leave bad spiritual habits and ways of thinking behind, we have space to replace them with healthy, godly ones. Rather than depending on ourselves and our own efforts, we replace our grasping hands with our knees, in prayer. When I diminished the discretionary income I would have spent on myself, I gave to charities I care for. For him to increase in me, making me more like him, I had to decrease. Funny, though, when I did that I became more like Sandra, as she was designed to be, than I ever had been before.

What do you need to decrease so he may increase in your calling, in your health, in your life? It's so worthwhile.

"My thoughts are nothing like your thoughts," says the LORD. "And my ways are far beyond anything you could imagine. For just as the heavens are higher than the earth, so my ways are higher than your ways and my thoughts higher than your thoughts." ISAIAH 55:8-9, NLT

God Is Not a Micromanager

Recently, my family watched a movie that recounted the story of Moses. As the movie progressed, God's plan for Moses became clear. He was the chosen instrument to lead the Israelites out of bondage and into freedom.

God often spoke to Moses, which must have been a great comfort. But the task was daunting and, from a human point of view, guaranteed to meet with disaster. Pharaoh and his armies were powerful, and the children of God had not been able to free themselves for hundreds of years. In Exodus 14, God tells Moses where to camp—in a somewhat risky area—and the Egyptians would be emboldened to move on the seemingly trapped Israelites. Yet God promised victory.

The Israelites grew nervous and accusing. Moses sought to reassure them but seemed to experience a moment of fear and doubt himself. In the movie, he paces while asking God once more if he is doing the right thing. God does not answer. Moses must move without hearing another direct command. He draws on his experience, what he knows of God, what he's been told, how he's been created, and then moves forward in faith. That time of silence is not as clear in Scripture, but in Exodus 14:15, the Lord does seem to rebuke Moses for asking directions again.

Our God is a good and great commander in chief; he does not raise people to positions they are unqualified for. Once he gives them a position, he trusts them with it. He is not a micromanager. He had prepared and commissioned Moses. His silence, however long it lasted, was a vote of confidence because Moses had stayed in a close relationship with God. God was saying, "You know what to do. I trust you. Go do it!"

Now when God seems silent, I do not take it as a rebuke. I take it as a vote of confidence in me and what he has commissioned me to do. He has chosen and prepared me, and you, too.

You know what to do. He trusts you. Go do it!

The LORD said to Moses, "Why do you cry to me? Tell the people of Israel to go forward. Lift up your staff, and stretch out your hand over the sea and divide it, that the people of Israel may go through the sea on dry ground."

EXODUS 14:15-16, ESV

One Good Thing

One of the beauties of living in the digital age is that there is a lot of information readily available on nearly every topic we can think of, to help us live right. The downside, of course, is that we can become swamped by that same information. There is information on everything you might want to do and know to live a healthier, happier, more fulfilling life, and we're prompted to do it all, all the time.

Sometimes I feel like I have failed because I can't do it all, not every day. I do not have time to lift weights for fifteen minutes followed by a forty-five-minute walk, floss twice a day, drink sixty-four ounces of water, tithe my time, reach out to my neighbor, and make healthy meals—while holding down a job and helping my family and getting eight hours of sleep. But I can do each of them sometimes. God doesn't expect perfection from me; he knows that I, beloved, am made of dust and clay.

A friend who is a member of Alcoholics Anonymous shared one of their mottoes: Just for Today. It can be difficult for a recovering addict to think about refusing to imbibe or indulge in their destructive habit for the rest of their life. So they pledge to make that one right choice just for today, as well as choosing to do one good thing just for today.

Of the hundreds of commands I am supposed to execute to live a Christian life, I can be purposeful about doing one or two each day, and in so doing, experience and share his love.

Don't allow my heart to be troubled (see John 16:33).
Go the second mile with someone (see Matthew 5:38-42).
Fear God, but not man (see Matthew 10:28).
Feed his sheep in some way (see John 21:15-16).
Be on my guard for covetousness (see Luke 12:15).
Pray for more to spread the gospel (see Matthew 9:37-38).
Love my neighbor (see Matthew 22:39).
Be a cheerful giver (see 2 Corinthians 9:7).

None of us is promised tomorrow, but all of us have received today. What would you like to do—just for today?

Do not worry about tomorrow, for tomorrow will worry about itself. Each day has enough trouble of its own.					MATTHEW 6:34

Our Deliverer

When I was in junior high, I was attacked by a group of bullies. It still gives me a little tremor to remember it. I'm sure some of you quivered just a little when you read that opening line too. Bullying is universal and doesn't end when childhood does.

A group of girls decided they did not like me, and they stalked me in the halls and made my life miserable, until one day they cornered me outside of school. All the buses drove away, and I was left there, alone. One of them took my head and pushed it into the brick wall. And then, someone intervened.

Not a teacher, but a very powerful, popular girl whom I had never met and did not know. She moved forward, and the others parted to make way for her. She took my hand and looked at the rest of them and said, "This will never happen again."

And it didn't.

I do not know why she decided to save and protect me, to be my strong defender when I most needed it, but she did. I was never beaten up again, nor cornered, nor taunted. It did not mean I was universally loved, but I was safe.

I was not a Christian then, but later, after thinking back on this, I thought how much like the Lord that girl was. She was a rock and a fortress to me— her power protected me, and none dared go against her. I took refuge in her, and she shielded me. Maybe God sent her. I know he's sent me to help others since then.

Life hands down some bad moments when we are cornered. Scary times. There are bullies, and we all have enemies. God is your strength, though, and he wants you to take refuge in him. He also wants you to offer refuge to those who need it, in his name.

Call upon him, right now, to save you from your enemies, whomever or whatever they may be. He will do it.

I love you, O LORD, my strength. The LORD is my rock and my fortress and my deliverer, my God, my rock, in whom I take refuge, my shield, and the horn of my salvation, my stronghold. I call upon the LORD, who is worthy to be praised, and I am saved from my enemies.

PSALM 18:1-3, ESV

Just in Time

When my husband worked in quality control, they utilized an inventory method called Just in Time. It meant that they did not stockpile too many resources, parts and such, ahead of time. If they had, they would not have been able to take advantage of new technology, having too much of the old. Just in Time allowed them to be good stewards of their resources and provide their customers with exactly what was needed at a given time.

Corrie ten Boom, the beloved Dutch Christian woman who was interned in a concentration camp for sheltering Dutch Jews, wrote of her fear of death. She asked her father about it, and he reminded her that he gave her a train ticket just as she was about to take her journey. Just in time, he provided her what she needed as she was about to board the train—not too far in advance where it might be lost or the journey might change. Her dad was telling her, God will provide the courage to face death just when you need it—not too far in advance.

Fear tells us that we must anticipate every situation that lies ahead so we can prepare for it and ensure that we can face the task. No one, though, besides God, knows what lies ahead tomorrow or next week. Not being able to predict the circumstance, we must instead rely on the trustworthiness of the one who knows all.

God will provide everything you need. God provided food for Joseph and his family during the famine; God provided a husband for Ruth and a protector for Naomi. God provided a fish for Jonah and a welcoming shelter for Saul. Finally, God provided the lamb for the sacrifice for Abraham, and the Lamb for all of us, in the person of Jesus Christ.

He can be trusted to provide exactly what is needed exactly when it is needed. He means to free you from worry about the future, which he holds firmly in his good hands.

What do you need to release into those hands today?

God says, "At just the right time, I heard you. On the day of salvation,
I helped you." Indeed, the "right time" is now. Today is the day of salvation.

2 CORINTHIANS 6:2, NLT

Experiencing the Love of God

One year, when my husband was in seminary and money was very tight, we approached a gift-giving occasion with no money to buy gifts for each other or our kids. We knew that family would give things to us and were grateful for that. But we wanted to buy something for our kids.

At a meeting one night, I silently lifted that prayer up to God but said nothing aloud to anyone. The very next day someone had put an envelope in our mailbox with thirty-five dollars. Someone had been listening to the prompting of the Holy Spirit, and the money had arrived just in time.

I have been both the recipient of and the giver of the "just in time" gifts that the Lord prompts. Because he knows we need to feel love from people with skin on them, God often sends people to be the hands that reach out with his love. It's a powerful way we can each experience and offer his love—a little like that old game "Pass It On." We can listen for the Lord's still, small whisper of love and then pass it on to someone else.

The other day, a friend was laid on my heart, and I texted, "How are you?" Her answer? "Thank you for listening to the prompting of the Lord, sister. I needed to know someone cared right now."

Stop now, and pray. Wait for that still, small voice, and when you hear it, don't second-guess. Who can you reach out to, just in time? Do you have something you'd like to ask for too?

We loved you so much that we shared with you not only God's Good News but our own lives, too.   1 THESSALONIANS 2:8, NLT

You Are Here

One cold day we went to the mall to get some errands done. This was a mall that wasn't very close to our house, and we do a lot of our shopping online, so I wasn't too familiar with it. My husband and I had planned to divide and conquer the chores, but we had no idea where any of the stores we needed to visit were located.

As is true for most malls, there was a small billboard that showed where each store was, along with a list and a map of the others. In one corner was an arrow that proclaimed, "You Are Here."

"Wave," my husband suggested. I had no idea why he'd said that, but I did, and then turned toward him.

"What was that all about?"

"I was looking on the map to see if I could see where we were."

Ha.

We found where we needed to go, and I halfheartedly set about doing my section of the errands. Maybe it was the gray day, but my heart was also heavy with a decision I had recently made, one which had not turned out for the best. If I could have, I would have undone it, but it could not be undone, and I had to live with the consequences. "I wish I could take it back," I said in my heart to the Lord. How did he answer me?

You are here.

I needed to stop second-guessing what I'd done, what I may have done differently. I was where I was, now. Instead of having further regrets, I needed to ask him, "What's next? What now?"

We are all prone to mistakes, and even when we don't make a mistake, we often must choose between two equally good or bad paths. It's a waste of energy, a distraction from the future, to second-guess. I take great comfort in God's sovereignty, knowing that no matter what I do I cannot derail his ultimate plans for my life or for others.

I am here. And he is here with me.

I am certain that God, who began the good work within you, will continue his work until it is finally finished on the day when Christ Jesus returns.
PHILIPPIANS 1:6, NLT

Marked Out for Victory

Recently, I watched some running races on TV. I'm not a huge sports buff, so I hadn't paid a lot of attention to track and field throughout my life, but something caught my eye this time. The runners did not start at the same place—some were farther ahead than others, and the final racer seemed to be starting from way behind. Their starting spots were staggered.

It seemed unfair.

I looked it up, and the staggering was actually a means to make the race *fair*. Each runner's race was marked out, and by staggering the lanes, it ensured that the runners on the outside did not have to run farther than those on the inside.

So often, I look toward others and (I admit) think: something is unfair here. Sometimes I am moaning about my own life, over which I think someone has an advantage based on family of origin, or financial resources, or networking. But then I compare those who live in my home country with poorer nations and realize how hard many people must work just to have a home and food and clean water.

If we let ourselves, we can get bogged down in the fairness or unfairness of life. It's a godly impulse; God is a God of justice, and we, created in his image, feel that desire for justice. We can do what's in our power to help in this world—donate to a food bank, help build a house, support a child overseas—but we also need to trust that God will see justice done.

My lane is not your lane—I may seem to be starting out ahead of you, but my lane is just as long as yours, though you may not see my conflicting circumstances. I am only to run my race, and by looking left or right, I am unnecessarily slowing down or distracting myself. I must run the race set for me, not the one set for you or for a sister in China.

What race must you run this week, this month, this year?

Since we are surrounded by so great a cloud of witnesses, let us lay aside every weight, and the sin which so easily ensnares us, and let us run with endurance the race that is set before us. HEBREWS 12:1, NKJV

A Benediction for January

Every week at the close of the service, our pastor asks us to raise our hands toward the Lord while he prays a benediction over us. I love the music at my church, and its many ministries, and I am fed from the Word there every week. But the thing that touches my heart the most deeply is this blessing. Many of us long to be blessed by others; we are thirsty for it, but it rarely comes.

A benediction is simply a prayer asking for God's favor over another; it's a reassurance of his constant affection, attention, protection, and guidance. On Sundays at 11:45, my entire congregation is lovingly blessed and commissioned for the week ahead. At the close of each month's devotionals, I'd like to offer a traditional benediction from the Bible for you, to bless and commission you for the new month—and new *year*—ahead. "See, I am doing a new thing! Now it springs up; do you not perceive it?" (Isaiah 43:19). God loves you and wants you to be blessed.

Consider reading the words aloud—there's something about hearing the words as well as reading them that makes them doubly powerful. Then spend a few moments meditating on the passage and on God's desire to bless you. Perhaps you might even choose to bless someone else by speaking the Scripture into their lives too.

Through these pages and the power of Scripture, I reach my hands out to and over you, as your sister in Christ, and pray . . .

Now may the God of peace, who through the blood of the eternal covenant brought back from the dead our Lord Jesus, that great Shepherd of the sheep, equip you with everything good for doing his will, and may he work in us what is pleasing to him, through Jesus Christ, to whom be glory for ever and ever. Amen.　　　　　　　　　　HEBREWS 13:20-21

FEBRUARY

Trash Talk

Driving home the other day I saw a couple in bright orange vests walking up the side of the narrow, wooded road that leads to our neighborhood. They were picking up trash.

Some of the bits were small—crunched cans and wilted papers, cigarette butts and even dangerous hypodermic needles. Some pieces of trash were huge—tires, which they worked hard to drag to the side of the road. Hours later the thoroughfare was clean, safe, and attractive once more. Deer browsed the greenery. Kids walked with their parents.

I do not know that man and woman, but I admire that they saw ugliness and quietly tried to make it right.

Our world is going through a troubled time right now, and there are lots of people "trashing" not only their neighbors but also people they don't know. They accuse people of motivations, actions, and thoughts that they have no proof of those people having. Sometimes people gossip about those in their family or social circles. Sometimes we stand by and say nothing, even if silently disagreeing. None of us are completely innocent of the sins of the mouth, as we're each human and subject to our pride and flesh.

Our beloved Bible does not speak well of slandering others. It's called bearing false witness, and we're commanded not to do it, whether it be toward an individual or an entire group. We are not to gossip, either, though all are tempted, because words of gossip are tasty morsels (see Proverbs 18:8). We must tame our tongues because we can't praise the people God created while simultaneously speaking ill of them (see James 3:10).

I so admire that couple who was busily, quietly picking up the trash and doing it for the good of all. It inspired me to reach out to others and offer a simple hug or a kind word or a welcoming invitation to begin to clean up the trash that our world, and sometimes our own circle, so easily hurls. It's not enough just to avoid trash talk—though that's a good start. Let's begin the healing our communities need by loving our neighbors as ourselves.

He has shown you, O mortal, what is good. And what does the LORD require of you? To act justly and to love mercy and to walk humbly with your God.　　　　　　　　　　　　　　　　　　　　　Micah 6:8

Rainy Days and Sunshine

The day was filled from start to stop with what we call "Seattle sunshine." Yep—rain. It should be no surprise: the months from early November till the Fourth of July are dominated by clouds and rain. Sometimes that rain falls as a steady, gentle mist, and sometimes it comes down in sheets. But if you choose to live in the Pacific Northwest, you're choosing to live in an area in which the ground is mostly soggy.

That rain canceled my outdoor walk, so I headed to the YMCA and got on a treadmill. I faced out—toward the parking lot—and watched the stream of people flow in and out as I walked. As my time was nearly completed, I saw a young boy and his dad exit the Y and head toward the car. The little boy ran out into the parking lot and, as little boys will do, found every single puddle.

Once he located them, he jumped, splashing himself and his dad with water. And the good dad did not reprimand his son. He jumped too. They went from puddle to puddle like a big and little duck, splashing in the water and laughing in the rain. Their shorts were wet. Their legs ran with water. And they held hands and laughed.

Warm, inside, I laughed too. Their joy was my true Seattle sunshine.

We each have years that seem to be wall-to-wall rain, one difficult situation followed by another. Yet we know that no one promised life on earth would be easy. Our Lord himself told us that in this world, we will have trouble, but then he exhorted us to take cheer. He has overcome. And we can rejoice while we await his return. It doesn't have to be, as C. S. Lewis said, always winter and never Christmas. It can be both cold and fun.

As I left the Y that day, caring not a fig for the laundry, I splashed in three or four puddles. Smiling. Because of Christ, his victory, his resurrection, his attention to every detail and his overcoming, I can have joy in the midst of gray clouds.

Thank you, young lad, for teaching me how to have joy even when I live in a land with lots of rain. Find a puddle today. Splash. Laugh. Overcome!

The hope of the righteous brings joy.　　　　　PROVERBS 10:28, ESV

Pull the Chute

Throughout my Christian life, I've often used the words *trust* and *believe* interchangeably, almost without thinking about the difference. We've had a set of challenging circumstances lately, though—situations which made trust difficult for me.

I came to understand, to some extent, that I *believe* in the light but I must *trust* in the dark.

My husband is former infantry, and although he was not airborne, he shared with me the training he went through before jumping out of an airplane. They made a practice jump into a sawdust pit to perfect their form. They were reassured that experts had packed their chutes and the soldiers would land safely once the chutes were safely deployed. Intellectually, he'd agreed that all would be well.

Once on the plane, though, doubts seeped in. Who had packed this chute, and was he or she qualified to do that? What if a mistake had been made? From five thousand feet, nothing looked as it should, and there was no time to hesitate. He'd be midair before he found out if the trust he had put into the masters proved true. Trust is not an intellectual endeavor, like belief; it's a leap of faith.

My belief in Christ is mostly built in the light. I have studied the Scriptures; I have seen God work in my life. He has repeatedly proved true, and his principles are at work around the world whether the world understands that or not.

My trust, though—my faith—is built mostly in the dark. I must rely on those truths and beliefs even when I cannot see how it will all work out—and often, it doesn't work out in the way I'd expected. My trust is put to the test when I must jump from the plane, because there are no other options. And yet each time I trust, there is a new piece of intellectual knowledge to add to my belief: the chute deploys, I drift down, the view is amazing.

Is God asking you to trust him today, to realize that he has packed your chute with care and has trained you for what you must do? Head confidently into the dark requirements of trust from the bright light of belief.

Now faith is the substance of things hoped for, the evidence of things not seen.　　　　　　　　　　　　　　　　　HEBREWS 11:1, NKJV

Experiencing the Love of God

When I'm in a dark period in my life, what brings me the most comfort and joy is the intimate, personal way God and other people reach out to me. The Lord often illuminates a familiar Scripture passage in a way that is perfectly suited to my situation, and I'm reminded that the Word is living and active, relevant for any circumstances I find myself in. However, I must get into the Word for that to happen. If I've memorized some Scripture, the Spirit can draw on my muscle memory for application. Holding fast to comfort and courage in times of darkness is a discipline every believer must practice.

One of the loveliest parts of a dark winter is the soft light candles cast from the early afternoon onward. Many candles also have delightful scents, whether floral or earthy or homey. Unlike electric lights, candles feel intimate and personal.

Psalm 18:28 tells us that God illumines our darkness, and a candle in the room where you're relaxing or working can bring that Scripture to mind as well as the things he's taught you in the light. On your next stop to the store, pick up a pretty candle for yourself, and maybe one for a friend to bring that Word of hope and encouragement to her life too.

What Scripture brings you peace in dark circumstance?

What times can you recall in which the Lord brought hope just when you needed it?

You, LORD, keep my lamp burning; my God turns my darkness into light. With your help I can advance against a troop; with my God I can scale a wall. PSALM 18:28-29

My One True Love

February is often thought of as the month of love as it is centered around Valentine's Day. Valentine's Day was once the holiday used to celebrate the affection between romantic partners, but it has expanded to include friends, parents, children, and others.

Scripture is clear that God is the source of all that is good, and not only is he the source of love, it tells us that God *is* love. Simply put, to know God is to know love. To not know God is to not know love. There is no other way.

When I first became a Christian, I was encouraged to put my name into John 3:16, to personalize that verse in a way that brought home the intimate nature of God's love for me. *For God so loved Sandra that he gave his only begotten Son, that Sandra should not perish but have eternal life.* It did make me feel loved to put my name in there.

For the next week or so, let's put God's name in the familiar verses of 1 Corinthians 13 to personalize, in an intimate way, who he is, as Love.

Often this 1 Corinthians passage is used to illustrate and teach us how we are to love others. We're exhorted to read it as it shows us what our love, in action, should look like. Let's look at this familiar and—dare I say it—much-"loved" passage to understand how, exactly, God is love, as he himself is the perfect embodiment of that affection.

You may have a sweetheart, or you may not. You may have a child, or you may not. You may wish you had more friends to love or to love you. You may not have parents to love you any longer; perhaps you never did. But this is true: God loves you. My prayer for you as you begin this series is that by the time February 14 draws near, as Ephesians promises, "you, being rooted and grounded in love, may have strength to comprehend with all the saints what is the breadth and length and height and depth, and to know the love of Christ that surpasses knowledge, that you may be filled with all the fullness of God" (3:17-19, esv).

God loves you. He really does. Let's look closer at what that means.

God is love.   1 John 4:8

Tying Shoelaces

God is patient; God is kind.

At an indoor event, a man and his young son sitting on the nearby bleachers caught my attention. Action and crowds swirled around them, and yet they seemed to have blocked out the world and were focused on only one task at hand.

Teaching the little guy to tie his shoes.

The dad very patiently held the boy's hands while he weaved and looped the lace over and over, not quite getting it for a few minutes. The look of pure bliss on his face when the task was mastered brought a smile of delight to my own. And that was the father's look of bliss, not the son's! He beamed too.

A less patient father might have grown irritated by the need the child had. He could have quickly tied the shoe for the boy. He could have allowed him to wear slip-ons—forever. But he saw the need his child had and with patience and kindness led him to the next step in maturity.

I'm reminded of when Jesus fed the five thousand. He had important work to do—his years to convey his teachings were limited compared to the vast expanse of time which came before and after them. He could have let the people go hungry for a few hours, feasting on the Bread of Life, if not bread. And yet he was moved with compassion, seeing they had a need that they were unable to solve for themselves. Gently, kindly, he provided for their physical needs as well as their spiritual ones, expecting nothing in return but modeling for us, as he did.

In Luke 8:49 we read, "While Jesus was still speaking, someone came from the house of Jairus, the synagogue leader. 'Your daughter is dead,' he said. 'Don't bother the teacher anymore.'" Jesus spoke gently to Jairus and interrupted his teaching to tend to the girl. It was not a bother to him. In his patience with and kindness toward us, he displays his abiding love.

We often wonder if God tires of teaching us the same lesson over and over—loop and hook, weave through the eye. But even more than the dad with the little boy and his sneaker, our Father is patient and kind. He rejoices with us when we take the next step toward maturity. Thank you, Father.

Love is patient, love is kind.   1 CORINTHIANS 13:4

You Are His Beloved

God does not envy or boast.

One of the first lessons good parents teach their children is not to desire or grab what doesn't belong to them. We all sometimes want what others have, discontented that someone else has what we do not. It may be as big as coveting a neighbor's wife or as small as coveting the extra cherry in the fruit cocktail your brother is eating (a particular sin of mine as a child!).

Coveting is yearning for that which does not belong to you.

I've seen people squirm when taught that God is a jealous God. Jealousy seems so petty, so human, so ungodlike. But the word used in Exodus 34:14 to describe God as jealous isn't the same as the word used for envy or covetousness. In fact, the word *qannâ* is used in Scripture only to describe the jealousy God feels for what is rightfully his.

It isn't wrong for a spouse to feel jealous for her husband—his affections are due to her and her alone. That is different from coveting the affections due another woman—wanting her neighbor's man. God doesn't covet what doesn't belong to him. He jealously yearns for what's rightfully his.

What is rightfully his? In Mark 12, Jesus points out that the Roman coins have Caesar's image on them. When the religious leaders ask if they should pay taxes, Jesus tells them to render to Caesar that which bears his image (a coin), but to God that which bears his image (us—our hearts, our worship, our loyalty).

Boasting, too, comes naturally to humans. When we feel insecure, we point out our achievements—money, a good job, an award, our children's accomplishments—as a way of reassuring ourselves that we matter. What a pleasure, though, when we learn to let our work speak for itself or to let the lips of others speak our praise rather than our own. God set the example for us; his works and people speak for him (see Psalm 19:1; Matthew 5:16).

Whether we want to point out our accomplishments to others or steal a brother's cherry, we must understand that both envy and boasting stem from discontentment—an emotion alien to our God. He has provided everything you need and everything he needs too. Rest easy that we worship someone worthy of our devotion.

Love does not envy or boast.   1 CORINTHIANS 13:4, ESV

Lead like Jesus

God is not arrogant or rude.

People watch and listen to us not only to see how Christians respond but how they would expect Christ to act and speak. Scripture tells us that teachers are judged more heavily because of that weighty responsibility. In this world, we are all examples, teachers in one way or another.

We have all known leaders who humble-brag about accomplishments, who pretend to turn down the seat of honor while "relenting" soon enough. They are superficial, not genuine, and have little time for those without influence or money or anyone who can't advance them in some meaningful way.

Most of us have also known people who serve from a pure heart, who do not call attention to themselves: people who, as the Lord instructs, sit at the foot of the table until they are invited up. These servants are the ones who have modeled their lives after our serving Lord.

Isn't it interesting that the disciples, steeped in their religious traditions and living in a religiously focused society, had to ask Jesus to teach them how to pray? It's not that they hadn't seen and experienced prayer from rabbis—of course they had, regularly. But Jesus was a game changer—he was clearly different, and they knew they had to change directions to truly understand God and then teach and lead others to him.

Jesus did not call attention to himself. He taught with a focus on the Father but was never condescending, nor did he seek out those with money or influence. When he prayed, he withdrew to a private place.

Arrogance comes from thinking we are better than others. Scripture tells us that Jesus, "who, being in very nature God, did not consider equality with God something to be used to his own advantage; rather, he made himself nothing" (Philippians 2:6-7). An arrogant mind-set leads to rude actions; it's why the two are twinned in Scripture.

We follow Jesus' example when we sit under, follow, and then lead like leaders who lead like Jesus: humble in attitude, polite in action, and honoring of others even when offering a strong, necessary rebuke. Jesus' example of leadership is also a clear example of how to honestly love those under our care. As the teacher is, so the student becomes.

[Love] is not arrogant or rude.   1 CORINTHIANS 13:4-5, ESV

Party Preparations

God does not insist on his own way.

Once, when growing up, one of my children was making a series of bad decisions that I could see leading to painful consequences. I stepped in a few times but ultimately had to let the situation run its course. I said, "I can reach out and catch you, hold you, stop you, while you're running headlong toward the cliff, but eventually I will not have room to do that, and you'll go hurtling over it if you so choose."

That child tripped quite a few times and hurtled over a few cliffs. It was painful for both of us. I have run over a few cliffs myself, and not only as a child.

Then, and now, it reminded me of the story of the Prodigal Son. This son is often portrayed as an ingrate, or as selfish, and perhaps that is true. But perhaps he was confused and searching. He made some outrageous demands, among them that his father liquidate some of his holdings and give him his inheritance right then and there. It was understood that the son was saying, "I'd be better off if you were dead."

Although he'd have had every right to disinherit his son, to give him nothing, to force him into compliance, the father did not do that. The father did not—this time, anyway—grab and hold him to keep him from hurtling over the cliff. He let the young man fall, pick himself up, and return home, where he met his son with open arms, tears, and a party.

Our society likes to portray our God as a "my way or the highway" kind of God. Instead, God portrays himself as the prodigal's dad: providing the right thing—salvation—in the right way—Jesus—but allowing for choice. He woos, he offers, he desires, he holds out his hand in love. But he does not insist; he allows us to choose.

Which of us has not been a prodigal son or daughter? Which of us has not returned after falling off the cliff, with bloodied knees and filled with tears, hoping for that embrace and party?

He did not insist. But he was there, waiting and hoping, then. He is here now, too.

[Love] does not insist on its own way.　　　　1 CORINTHIANS 13:5, ESV

Unlimited Cool Water

God is not irritable or resentful.

I know wonderful people in the "helping" professions: doctors, nurses, teachers, chaplains, caregivers, and so on. They all have in common the desire to assist others, to come alongside with support and counsel, intervention and help. The downside is their proclivity to burn out. A teacher my husband once sat under warned him that when you're giving others a drink from a cup of cold water, do not break that cup (yourself) into pieces and give that away too. Burnout leads to irritation toward and resentment of those we are called to help.

But God, of course, has unlimited emotional resources. He does not burn out, his cup never breaks, and he himself is the water we drink (see John 4:14). We can come to him again and again, and he will never be tired, irritated, or resentful of our many needs.

When the woman with a hemorrhage sneaked up to Jesus and clutched his robe, he did not resent the fact that she was slowing him down on his journey or, in essence, robbing him of some of the power he felt leaving him when she did. He did not resent that a woman whom society considered unclean had now made him unclean by her touch. Instead, he turned and gently told her that her faith had healed her. Her need was not an interruption in his agenda.

Jesus, as a Jewish man, was a member of a people oppressed by the Romans. The Romans represented unfairness, difficulty, cruelty, and subjugation for the Jewish people. Jesus had every reason to feel resentful toward them. Instead, when the Roman centurion approached Jesus to inform him that his servant lay suffering and paralyzed, Jesus offered to come and heal the servant. Jesus did not resent that the one who had badly treated him and his people then turned to him in his hour of need.

Sometimes we humans feel so needy—sending out one prayer request after another, careful not to post too many on social media or ask for prayer too many times in a small group or Bible study. But we can be sure that the one who receives all our prayers, the one to whom they are directed, is never burned out by our needs.

What do you need to ask Jesus for today? He's listening patiently and with love.

[Love] is not irritable or resentful.　　　1 CORINTHIANS 13:5, ESV

Experiencing the Love of God

As mothers of young children, my friends and I joked about which were the "three little words we longed to hear." Among the contenders:

Let's Eat Out
Stay in Bed
You Look Great
Kids Are Asleep

What the phrase "the three little words we long to hear" refers to, of course, are the words "I love you."

Wanting to hear those words is not in any way limited to romantic love. We want to hear them from our parents, our children, our friends, and mostly, of course, our God.

Notice that we want to "hear" those words. It's not the three little words we long to *read*. Yet while the Holy Spirit can speak to us through our hearts and inner impressions, the only voice we have of God, for the moment, is through Scripture.

Just like we as people can be "Jesus with skin on," one good way to hear and experience God's love is to listen to the Bible in an audio edition. My husband prefers a version narrated by David Suchet, of Poirot fame (*The Complete NIV Audio Bible*). My favorite is narrated entirely by African American actors (*Inspired by…The Bible Experience*). Audio programs such as Audible allow you to listen to a sample before purchasing, and many e-book programs offer the option of having the books read aloud by a speaker.

Choose a program during this month of love to listen to God whisper and shout and declare those three little words over and over again.

The word of God is alive and powerful. It is sharper than the sharpest two-edged sword, cutting between soul and spirit, between joint and marrow. It exposes our innermost thoughts and desires.　　HEBREWS 4:12, NLT

Private Conversations

God does not rejoice at wrongdoing, but rejoices with the truth.

Every year the world becomes more connected and intimate. It's easy to sit at our computers or on the couch with our tablets or phones and carry on conversations. In some ways, this is a blessing because we can interact with and reach out to people we might otherwise never have.

Sometimes digital connectedness can be poorly used. Some take the platform not for Christ but to use as a megaphone to publicly shame, blame, and condemn, believing they are upholding righteousness and holiness.

The Bible speaks about gently correcting others—in private (see Matthew 18). In John 8, the religious leaders were preparing to stone a woman for adultery—clearly a sin, then and now. They made a public display of what they considered their own holiness and purity and seemed to delight in shaming the woman in their keep. They asked Jesus, "This woman was caught in the act of adultery. In the Law, Moses commanded us to stone such women. Now what do you say?"

Jesus asked for the one who had never sinned to throw the first stone, and, of course, her accusers melted away. When the mob had fled, Jesus gently and privately told her he was not condemning her, but she should go and sin no more.

He did not shame her or blame her or hold her to public ridicule, even though her behavior was sinful. He won't do that to you or me either, and those who would are not acting as *he* would. In fact, if anyone has the right to condemn sinners, it is Jesus, and he did not come to condemn the world but to save it (see John 3:17). Jesus did not do away with the truth—he held the woman to it. His response, even in a situation in which sin was clearly evident on a number of levels, was the embodiment of love. He didn't rejoice or take part in the wrongdoing that the religious rabble had been ready to publicly inflict upon her; they were sinners just like she was. He did not shame or condemn them, either.

He will correct us gently—privately, too, when need be, through his Spirit and through loving but convicting words of others, freeing us to ignore those who act otherwise.

[Love] does not rejoice at wrongdoing, but rejoices with the truth.

1 CORINTHIANS 13:6, ESV

For the Joy, For the Win

God bears all things, believes all things, hopes all things, endures all things.

I had to be induced to give birth to my first child. I arrived at the hospital early in the morning, with my little travel case, holding my husband's hand. We were escorted to our birthing suite, and while we waited to go in I could hear a woman down the hall screaming.

"Get this thing out of me!" she shouted and then groaned loudly once more.

I turned to my husband, eyes wide and threatening to spill tears. He smiled and squeezed my hand. "No turning back now," he said, patting my very large belly.

Near midnight, after many hours of travail, I gave birth to our son. Seeing him turn his little head toward me as I called out his name erased the hours of agony that had preceded that moment.

There is a reason we call it *bearing* children. The word is also used to describe situations that seem unbearable. Or that we must bear up under travail. The verb *bear* conveys that something must be done that causes great pain and difficulty.

And yet mothers give birth as they always have, knowing it will be difficult but understanding the joy that lies just ahead.

Jesus "bore" us, his children, into eternity, with an unimaginable amount of travail and pain. Just before his crucifixion, he, understanding what lay ahead, asked God, "'Father, if you are willing, take this cup from me; yet not my will, but yours be done.' An angel from heaven appeared to him and strengthened him. And being in anguish, he prayed more earnestly, and his sweat was like drops of blood falling to the ground" (Luke 22:42-44).

No turning back.

Hebrews 12:2 tells us that "For the joy set before him he endured the cross." Jesus knew what lay just beyond that terrible, heavy burden. He could look past that to the results—his eternal relationship with you and me.

There is nothing that Jesus would not bear for you, believing it to be right, hoping for the eternal future he knew his father would bring to pass. For that future, together with us, he endured all things.

How great a love he has for you (see 1 John 3:1)!

Love bears all things, believes all things, hopes all things, endures all things.

1 CORINTHIANS 13:7, ESV

Our Forever Valentine

God never ends.

We recently applied to refinance our mortgage, and the first thing anyone would do before they would discuss rates, options, or payments, was to pull our credit history. Why? It's been said that the best predictor of the future is the present and the past. If we were currently paying our bills responsibly, it was likely that would continue. Once we proved that we have a long history of doing what we said we would do, people trusted us to continue to do the same long into the future.

Time has been said to be a dot on a line stretching infinitely into the past and infinitely into the future. God has always existed and will always exist. And yet he is here for us today, right now. He is right next to us today at this point on the line.

All our career decisions, our ministry choices, the ways we raise our children, and how we conduct our lives are based on God: obeying him, pleasing him, working out what we hope is his will.

And yet, though we've never met in person, we know so much about him. He speaks to us through his Word, through his creation, through his people, through his Spirit.

"Jesus Christ is the same yesterday, today, and forever" (Hebrews 13:8, NLT). No matter where or when in our lives we meet him, no matter what we are faced with at that point, he will prove true then and from then on. He is the same God who rescued his people from Egypt. He is the same God who fed Elijah in the wilderness. He will meet your needs too.

We do not know what the future holds, but the best predictor of whether God will always be present, always be loving, always be faithful to us no matter what comes is the past. He did not leave Elijah to starve in his bewildering wilderness; he will not leave you.

What difficulties are you facing today—now? Do not fear. God is your refuge and strength—a very present help in our time of trouble, no matter where on the line of time that trouble falls.

His love for you is infinite, backward and forward. It will never end.

Love never ends.   1 CORINTHIANS 13:8, ESV

After God's Own Heart

God desires to be loved by his beloved, too.

How do we do that?

Scripture gives us a direct answer. Jesus tells us, "If you love me, you will keep my commandments" (John 14:15, ESV). In Acts 13:22 we read, "God testified concerning him: 'I have found David son of Jesse, a man after my own heart; he will do everything I want him to do.'"

What made David a man after God's heart? He would do everything God wanted him to do. And what did God want David to do? First Samuel 13:14 tells us, "The LORD has sought out a man after his own heart and appointed him ruler of his people."

To our human ears and eyes, the idea that obedience is the preeminent way we can express our deepest affections and love seems strange. I think it's because we are used to loving our equals. Scripture tells us that we are children of God, and it is not at all odd to expect children to obey. Good parents ask their children to do only things that are for their own good, for the good of the family, for the good of others, and to achieve the good work that must be done. The book of 1 John, written by the beloved disciple, gently reassures us that "His commandments are not burdensome" (5:3, ESV).

Like any good parent, God wants his children to love one another. Nothing makes me happier than seeing my adult children enjoy one another's company and pull together when one of them has a need. John elaborates, "If anyone says, 'I love God,' and hates his brother, he is a liar; for he who does not love his brother whom he has seen cannot love God whom he has not seen" (1 John 4:20, ESV).

God is love, and he demonstrates that lavish love to us in multiple creative ways every day. The hoped-for response from us? "You shall love the Lord your God with all your heart and with all your soul and with all your mind. This is the great and first commandment. And a second is like it: You shall love your neighbor as yourself" (Matthew 22:37-39, ESV).

It all ties together. He loves us, and he commands us to love him and others in return because the greatest power in the universe is love.

Now these three remain: faith, hope and love. But the greatest of these is love.   1 CORINTHIANS 13:13

Attagirl!

When I pray, coincidences happen, and when I don't, they don't.
WILLIAM TEMPLE

We are created in God's image, and therefore a sense of compassion and justice is embedded into our sensibilities. The needs of our neighbors and family are well beyond our ability to resolve for them—at least on our own. God can work his will and has unlimited resources. We say we believe this, right? Why then do we pray so little, relatively speaking, to ask him to bring about victory and relief?

Perhaps it's because, deep down, we don't believe God will act. Most of us believe he has the power to act in response to our prayer. But because so many prayers seem to have been unanswered, or answered too slowly, or answered not in the way we'd wished, we wonder if he has the *will*.

One of my mentors told me that we need ten "attaboys" just to overcome the memory of one put-down. I wonder if it might likewise be true that our minds cling so tenaciously to the one prayer for which the answer seemed to tarry that we forget the nine that were resolved?

Maybe it's just that we spend too much time worrying instead of praying.

I'd been telling a friend about a situation that had the potential to cause harm to my family. At some point, though, God gave me the strength, and the words, to acknowledge his kind sovereignty. "The situation is completely out of my hands now," I told her. "So I'm not wringing them."

Just then, I heard it, deep in my spirit. God was saying, "Attagirl!"

The situation was in his good hands. Rather than wringing mine, I could unclench them and put them together in prayer.

You know what? I'm still waiting for the answer to that prayer, the solution to that situation. But in the meantime, many others have been swiftly resolved. I either believe, or I don't. God tells me that my prayers matter, that he is listening, and that they are powerful and effective. "I love the LORD because he hears my voice and my prayer for mercy. Because he bends down to listen, I will pray as long as I have breath!" (Psalm 116:1-2, NLT).

Try it. Yep—right now. What would you like to ask our good God for today?

The prayer of a righteous person is powerful and effective.   JAMES 5:16

Sojourners

Within the past few months, several of my friends have made important life decisions. A few have moved. Some have changed jobs. Some have left unhealthy relationships or churches and begun to pursue wholeness and health. It all sounds good—in principle. But practically speaking?

It's always scary to go.

When we leave something, whether it be unsatisfying or even harmful, or whether it is something wonderful, we know exactly what it is we are leaving. We have sometimes mastered or can manage the situation. Sometimes we just plain like what we've got. It takes a real act of faith to put on our shoes and walk.

I think about Abram, a relatively old man with no children. For his own reasons, God chose to bless Abram and build his nation and his people from him. It started, though, with a lonely walk.

God asked Abram to leave his town and his tribe. God promised rewards in return: "I will make you into a great nation, and I will bless you; I will make your name great, and you will be a blessing. I will bless those who bless you, and whoever curses you I will curse; and all peoples on earth will be blessed through you" (Genesis 12:2-3).

But these were promises for the future (in some cases, a future very far off). Nothing at that moment showed that things would be all right.

And yet Abram left.

I often wonder: I confess my faith with my mouth, and I surely believe in my heart, but do I believe with my feet, too? Will I leave a job I love if God calls me to something else? Will I leave a town that I love if he insists I was simply sojourning there for a time? Will I leave a relationship if it's clear it's not healthy, or habits or affections that are no longer beneficial?

The proof of the pudding, as they say, is in the eating. Perhaps the proof of my faith is in my feet. Abram followed immediately, without question, and was beloved for it. The next time I'm asked to walk, I will put one foot in front of the other. How about you?

> The LORD had said to Abram, "Go from your country, your people and your father's household to the land I will show you. . . . So Abram went, as the LORD had told him.
> GENESIS 12:1, 4

Experiencing the Love of God

Faith is stepping out when you sense you're supposed to, not always knowing what the first step will lead to or how long the path will be. It's simple confidence in the one who calls us forward.

I have always wondered, what was Lazarus's first thought when, from the grave, he heard Jesus call, "Lazarus, come out!"? Whatever he thought, he came out.

"Step in and the waters will part" is a lesson found in Joshua 3. That's just how faith works.

Our desire for security sometimes makes us want to stay put. If that's where God has called us to remain, then that's exactly what we must do. But fully experiencing his love also requires us to walk in faith—sometimes with a little fear—when we sense him beckoning us forward. Striding into the unknown need not threaten our security if that security is grounded in our certainty in his love, not in keeping our circumstances static. Stepping out can be an adventure.

Today, why not take some time to prayerfully consider the following questions:

What is God calling you to leave?

To run toward?

To set aside or step into?

To embrace?

Don't wait another day—what if Lazarus had tarried, for heaven's sake. God intends life for you. Step forward! The water will part!

As soon as the feet of the priests who were carrying the Ark touched the water at the river's edge, the water above that point began backing up a great distance away. . . . And the water below that point flowed on to the Dead Sea until the riverbed was dry. Then all the people crossed over near the town of Jericho.   JOSHUA 3:15-16, NLT

Loving Otters as Well as Yourself

Growing up in the Pacific Northwest, my kids learned early on about seagoing creatures. My son's first and favorite stuffed animal was an orca (sometimes known as the killer whale, very appealing to my son), and my daughter cherished otters. She saw them at the many aquariums we visited, and I must agree they are adorable.

Otters live together for comfort, companionship, and protection. Their community (called a raft, because they float!) might be as large as many dozens or as few as two or three. Large or small, one of the most charming things about otter rafts is that the animals hold hands—all of them—while they sleep, so they don't drift apart. They've also been known to lightly entangle themselves in the long vegetation growing up from the seafloor, so they don't drift away from their home base.

Every year the demands on our time increase. We are supposed to be at work every hour of the night and day—connected electronically—and supposed to respond to things deemed too important to wait. We have increasing civic responsibilities, parental responsibilities, or responsibilities for aging parents. Saturday has become a day to do chores. Sundays? Well, some Sundays I just want to sleep in. Or I want to skip small group.

But mostly I don't. My otters are waiting.

Remaining connected to other believers, floating in a world that is truly deep water with scary creatures about is an important way to keep my sanity, joy, and anchor in this world. We all have coworkers, family, and neighbors, but those true sisters-of-the-heart are other believers.

Do you make time for fellowship and fun with other believers? I know, I know, they are imperfect, and so are you and I. But in rough waters, they will hold your hand to make sure you don't drift apart, and wrap you in seaweed when it looks like you might be heading in the wrong direction.

Two are better than one, because they have a good return for their labor: If either of them falls down, one can help the other up. But pity anyone who falls and has no one to help them up. Also, if two lie down together, they will keep warm. But how can one keep warm alone? Though one may be overpowered, two can defend themselves. A cord of three strands is not quickly broken. ECCLESIASTES 4:9-12

Massage Envy

Every month my friend would text me about her massage appointment, and I would text back politely, a little envious. Finally, I was convicted that if I wanted to see a massage therapist too, I should stop envying my friend, cut another expense, and make it happen.

I sit most of the day, doing work. At the end of the day, I'm kind of like a folding chair: stiff pieces that don't bend so much as collapse into each other. I feel knots in my neck, and my legs are not limber.

I made it happen. I signed up.

For the first sessions, the masseuse gently began to work out the kinks. It was rather relaxing. But once all the surface issues had been resolved, she had to do deep tissue massage, addressing the base—long-standing complications deep in my muscles, which were the source of most of my pain. It didn't feel good. I started thinking, *Hey, I was paying for a nice, relaxing massage with a little calming lavender oil!* Instead, I was grimacing and popping and could feel knots roll out and away under my skin.

But week by week, I began feeling better. I enjoyed my work more. I enjoyed my life more.

I had a friend who once told me, regarding working through emotional pain, when it starts to feel worse, it's getting better. It's coming to the surface and washing away.

When we first meet Christ we are, of course, transformed. But sanctification and wholeness come with time. At first, gently, Jesus works on our surface issues, sustaining us as he does. Then, as we grow in confidence and courage, he seeks to work out those deeper knots, the ones which are the source of our most constant, most impactful pain. And it hurts, until suddenly, it doesn't.

Jesus is willing to allow us to hurt on the way to healing, but he will never harm us. You know that friend, the one you envy because she is filled with joy and praise? Well . . . you and I can get there too. Give the master free reign over your pain and be transformed by his healing power.

The LORD sustains them on their sickbed and restores them from their bed of illness.   PSALM 41:3

Safe Base

My adult daughter called me on a Sunday afternoon to tell me she was having some health challenges and was going to urgent care. She texted that she was okay, but eight hours later her husband called to say things were much worse and asked if we could meet them at the emergency room.

My husband and I hopped into the truck and drove over; by the time we arrived, they were already waiting. We sat in the hospital lobby waiting for her to be seen, and she held her husband's hand on one side and leaned her head on my shoulder on the other. I patted her on the knee.

"When you're a kid," she said, "you know that no matter what happens or who is coming after you, Mom is 'safe base.' Nobody can get you and nothing bad can happen if you're holding on to Mom."

I stroked her hair. Even when kids are all grown up, they still need a loving parent and are reassured by his or her presence, attention, and protection. Knowing that someone who represents power and goodness and care is in your life provides comfort even when the situation seems dire or is not immediately resolved.

Jesus taught mainly through "teachable moments" as life was happening. In Matthew 18, with children nearby, Jesus took a moment to teach his followers that they had to become like children—entirely trusting, honoring, dependent, and innocent if they were to enter the Kingdom of Heaven.

Most of us reading this devotional are adults and carry on as such most of the time. But when we are sick or worried or harassed or tired, we need a strong hand to hold on to and a shoulder to lean on. Our Father's hand and shoulder are always available. He's got us covered; he's got our back: "You hem me in behind and before, and you lay your hand upon me" (Psalm 139:5).

He, truly, is our only safe base.

He called a little child to him, and placed the child among them. And he said: "Truly I tell you, unless you change and become like little children, you will never enter the kingdom of heaven. Therefore, whoever takes the lowly position of this child is the greatest in the kingdom of heaven."

MATTHEW 18:2-4

A Good Sense of Direction

We Christians talk about being Spirit-led—that is, letting the third person of the Trinity, the Holy Spirit, guide us from the inside. The fact that we have God living inside us is a singularly amazing miracle and a tremendous honor.

What does it feel like to be led by the Holy Spirit? Sometimes it's sensing a wall going up when you step in the wrong direction. Acts 16:6 says, "Paul and Silas traveled through the area of Phrygia and Galatia, because the Holy Spirit had prevented them from preaching the word in the province of Asia at that time" (NLT). Sometimes it's doors and windows opening . . . or sometimes slamming shut.

We don't want to think of the Spirit leading us into difficult situations; it can make us second-guess if we've understood his intentions correctly. I find it comforting that even Jesus, filled with the Spirit as well, was led by the Spirit. "Jesus, full of the Holy Spirit, left the Jordan and was led by the Spirit into the wilderness, where for forty days he was tempted by the devil" (Luke 4:1-2).

Maybe like a visitor to a foreign land, we need someone to guide us to a place we have not yet been and do not know how to get to, or to a place we need to be even though it's scary for a time. Maybe when we're lost or in the dark or recalcitrant or weary, we just need someone to nudge us forward toward the best path.

Occasionally, but not often, it is a loud inner voice that says, "No" or "Don't go" or "Move!" Mostly, though, I think it's like following the car ahead of you—you have a sense of the direction but are comfortable following the lights and the lead, through Scripture or an inner push. Often the Spirit leads by giving us divine insight, according to 1 Corinthians 2:10: "These are the things God has revealed to us by his Spirit."

Like anything else, learning to discern his voice comes with attention and practice. How do you sense the Spirit leading in your life? Making ourselves more sensitive to his guidance, gentle or firm, will build intimacy and confidence in his direction.

Those who are led by the Spirit of God are the children of God.

ROMANS 8:14

A Gentle Whisper

If it's true that the Holy Spirit leads us by an inner voice, it's imperative that we learn to discern his voice.

I came across some printed plates of games that the Victorians played to while away the long winter days. I stopped on the print that showed blindman's bluff, because it was so beautifully painted that you could see the emotions on the faces. The emotions of the one who was blindfolded were distress and confusion. She was stopped in her tracks.

There were many voices calling out to her from different directions. Sometimes it feels like blindman's bluff inside my head. Is that God speaking to me? Or is it Satan?

When you don't know, do what the woman on the print did—pause. Stop till it's clear.

What we know of God's character, and of Satan's, will help us determine the source of the voice. God does not lie, he does not taunt, he does not condemn his own (see Romans 8:1). He came to give us life abundantly; he loves us without end. He created us and finds us beautiful. He urges us forward toward holiness and sanctification. When we take a step in the direction he is leading, we feel peace and calm, even though we may have taken the step tentatively.

Satan is the father of lies; he slanders, deceives, condemns, and tempts. His voice is never kind. When you take a step toward his voice, you feel an inner sense of wrongness, conviction, and a compulsion to turn back.

Learning to discern between the two is imperative, and the Spirit will help you do just that if you wait for his guidance. Following God, who works openly, will lead to strength, joy, and fulfillment. In 1 Kings 19:12, we're reminded that he speaks in a gentle but spiritually discernible whisper. Satan tends to work in darkness, his taunts and temptations undermining us like a stream of water running underground, doing damage until the ground above it collapses.

Does the voice you hear lead to godliness and peace, or to condemnation and indulging the flesh? Pause, pray, and seek wisdom till you can take the blindfold off and confidently walk forward.

When the Spirit of truth comes, he will guide you into all the truth, for he will not speak on his own authority, but whatever he hears he will speak, and he will declare to you the things that are to come. JOHN 16:13, ESV

Gold-Medal Girls

There's a road by our house that is a long downhill slope, and it's very easy to speed on it. It runs next to a church, a park, a volleyball pit, and a picnic area. These are places where there are lots of kids all the time, and kids are prone to dashing into the street. Because of that, our city put up a speed meter most of the way down the hill. It's large, and it flashes big, red numbers urging you to slow down.

One day we were driving down the road when we noticed a young girl, perhaps about nine years old, running down the side of the road. She was pumping her arms and ran with a purpose. We were some ways behind her, the only car on that stretch of road. She raced down the hill, looking up as she did, at the speed reader.

When she reached the foot of the hill, she jumped up and down triumphantly and pointed at the meter. It read, "24." She shouted toward her mother at the top of the hill, clearly thinking that she had been running twenty-four miles an hour.

I don't know if her mother told her the truth later: it was our car that had triggered that speed for the future Olympic sprinter. But it heartened all of us in the car, and I'm guessing her mother, too, to see her persistent, joyful spirit.

I can do anything if I set my mind to it and work hard!

Well . . . that's what we tell our kids and other people's kids. We believed that ourselves once, maybe, a long time ago before difficulties ground the essence out of us like a mortar and pestle.

The girl's can-do spirit powered her; yours can power you, too. Can't find it? God will renew it!

Our car triggered her happiness, and her spirit triggered mine. I felt that can-do spirit bleed into my own like sunlight on a gray February day. I can do it. God is with me. I am fearfully and wonderfully made. I have strength, endurance, and power in the Spirit of the Lord.

So does she. So do you!

They who wait for the LORD shall renew their strength; they shall mount up with wings like eagles; they shall run and not be weary; they shall walk and not faint. ISAIAH 40:31, ESV

Experiencing the Love of God

What long-held dream have you given up on that you are not ready to say good-bye to? It can be something large or small, but it must be something that you can work toward (i.e., not "winning the lotto")!

One thing I've noticed: as we get older, we may get wiser, but we also grow more cynical and less hopeful. We focus more on making it day to day than on making someone's day or trusting that someone will make ours.

I love to bake, and on my birthday I like to make my own cake. I think about it for months ahead of time, searching through recipes and purchasing high-quality ingredients. On the big day, I set aside time to make a special cake for me—and I enjoy the process.

One time, a friend who hadn't known me very long felt bad that I was making my own cake, but truly it brings me great satisfaction to plan for and then bring into being my own special treat.

There's a lesson here. Can you bake your own cake (or fulfill whatever dream is in your heart)? You bet you can. Don't wait around for anyone else to do it for you. Pray for guidance, sustenance, and encouragement, and then "Ready, set, go!" Experiencing the love of God means acknowledging that he has set dreams within your heart.

Come on. Be brave. Write down your dream today and then set it to repeat on your calendar so you'll go the distance. *Tell someone* you're going to pick up that instrument again or apply for the job or start writing a book or reach out to find someone to date. Find your dream—again—and then pick it up. If nine-year-olds can do it, we can too. Right?

(This year's cake was cherry chip, by the way!)

Delight yourself in the LORD, and he will give you the desires of your heart.
PSALM 37:4, ESV

My Favorite Fruit

February, at least in much of North America, is a month of scarcity. There are no new plants growing. The roads are slick with ice or wet with rain, and the sun doesn't appear very often or for very long. It's been a long time since the joy of Christmas, and it's quite some days until summer. It's hard to be hopeful, and late winter can sometimes seem to be a slog.

There are seasons in life like that too, when joy and resources and hope seem scarce. It's easy to be generous or hopeful when there are ready resources at hand. It's harder when the pocketbook and heart are almost empty. And yet . . . our God often uses scarcity to show his powers and bestow his blessing, because then it's clear it can only be him at work.

In Genesis 18:14, God reminds Abraham and Sarah about his promise to them, that he would bring them a child from Sarah's womb. They disbelieved, and God asked, "Is anything too hard for the LORD? I will return to you at the appointed time next year, and Sarah will have a son."

Hannah had the affections of her husband but not the esteem of her friends and relatives because of her barrenness. In 1 Samuel 1:19 we are told, "the LORD remembered her."

It was not the rich young ruler with his wealth who was admired. Nor was it the man who had stored his wealth in a barn—and whose life was shortly to be demanded of him. No, it's the simple widow's mite that spurs us to faith.

God used famine in Egypt and an emotionally crushing set of years to prepare Joseph for the tasks ahead. In this way, God used Joseph to bring Jacob and his family to Egypt, where they grew into the large, mighty nation of Israel—his chosen people.

It was not David's superior career training, wealth, or mentoring that brought about his calling and career, but the very scarcity of those things when partnered with his faith in God.

When God brings fruit from a seemingly barren field, he displays his attentiveness and power, which builds our faith.

He is watching! He is listening! He will provide in a way only he can.

I am the LORD, the God of all mankind. Is anything too hard for me?
JEREMIAH 32:27

Universal Donor

A friend asked us to pray for her daughter-in-law, who was having major surgery. The operation had gone fine. Then she was found to have internal bleeding and had to be rushed back into surgery to seek and stem the source of that loss. In the meantime, she would need a blood transfusion.

Blood transfusions, the transfer of blood from one person to another, happen when someone is in desperate need of healthier blood, more blood, or clean blood. When there is not enough blood flowing through the tissues, they rot, and death sets in. When there is not enough blood pumping, the heart can fail. Infected blood spreads disease throughout the body.

Blood transfusions depend on the generosity of others. Someone donates blood, which will take weeks or months to build back up and comes at a personal cost, so someone else who would die without it may live. My husband has type O negative blood, which is referred to as the universal donor; all blood types may use his as a substitute. Because of that, he donates often.

From the very first sin in the Garden of Eden, a life was required to remove the fatal, terminal infection of sin (God killing an animal for its skin, to cover Adam and Eve). Tracing blood sacrifices through the Bible, from the intended sacrifice of Isaac through the substitutionary sacrifice of the Passover lamb and right on up to Christ, the true Paschal Lamb, it's clear that blood—not a brain or a heart or a head—is what represents and preserves life. Leviticus 17:14 tells us, "the life of every creature is its blood."

Interestingly, Leviticus is the book in which God teaches about his holiness.

Believers have all been the recipients of a most generous blood transfusion, one that came at a high cost, the death of Jesus Christ. Christ's blood becomes our life; our sinfulness is paid for by his holiness; he is the ultimate universal donor. His blood for us. His life for ours. We celebrate this somberly, regularly, and gratefully with Communion.

My friend's daughter-in-law was completely healed, and so are you as you live in the health and wholeness that Christ's blood provides.

Jesus said to them, "Very truly I tell you, unless you eat the flesh of the Son of Man and drink his blood, you have no life in you." JOHN 6:53

A Benediction for February

Please let me offer a benediction for the end of February, the month of love; my prayer is that you would understand how very much God loves you. "See what great love the Father has lavished on us, that we should be called children of God! And that is what we are!" (1 John 3:1). I hope that you have experienced his love in fresh ways and that you sense him beside you, day and night, encouraging, exhorting, disciplining, and enjoying you.

A benediction is simply a prayer asking for God's favor over another; it's a reassurance of his constant affection, attention, protection, and guidance. As this month draws to a close, I'd like to offer a traditional benediction from the Bible for you, to bless how you've grown closer to God in the month that has passed, and to commission you for the exciting, challenging month ahead.

God loves you and wants you to be blessed. Take a few moments right now to meditate on God's great love for you, and receive his blessing. Do you sense him speaking to you, drawing near as you draw near to him? I find that when I speak the blessing aloud, whether over myself or someone else, the Scripture takes on even more power. You might consider speaking or texting or e-mailing these words of truth to a friend today to bless him or her with the love of the Lord.

As for me, through these pages and the power of Scripture, I reach my hands out to and over you as your sister in Christ and pray . . .

I pray that you, being rooted and established in love, may have power, together with all the Lord's holy people, to grasp how wide and long and high and deep is the love of Christ, and to know this love that surpasses knowledge—that you may be filled to the measure of all the fullness of God.

EPHESIANS 3:17-19

MARCH

Self-Care

An uncomfortable part of early Christian history was the practice of self-flagellation. To experience what they thought Christ must have experienced prior to his crucifixion, some would lash themselves with metal-tipped whips until their backs shredded and bled. One part of their bodies—their hands—was inflicting damage on another—their backs. While one might admire their devotion, the method and results caused lasting damage.

And yet today we use parts of our bodies to damage other parts. If a person drinks too much alcohol, he or she does grave damage to the liver and capillaries. Smoking cigarettes, held by a hand, permanently damages skin, lungs, teeth, and gums. Overeating with the mouth stresses out the heart, metabolism, and every joint.

The body is damaging itself.

The body can also heal itself. Feet are willing to walk off that extra weight. The body regenerates cells to replace damaged ones. Scabs are part of the body's self-healing system. Bones merely need to be set straight to knit themselves together. A doctor told me once that the best medicine is often simply aligning the circumstances so that the body can mend itself.

As the body of Christ, when we harm other believers, we harm ourselves—but we can be a part of the repair. We can arrange circumstances so that the atmosphere is conducive to helping the sick, suffering, or weary parts of the body get the health, well-being, and rest they need.

We make time for exercise, rethink what we eat and drink, and see doctors and dentists when we need to. We are stewards of our physical bodies. But we are also stewards of the body of Christ. We experience the love of God corporately, so let's treat that body with gentleness and care too.

Maybe it's okay not to argue the points that might best be left to grace and individual decision. It's fine to allow for difference in theology and worship style. As for healing? Some are poor in spirit; we can cheer them. Some mourn; we can comfort them. Some are hungry and thirsty; we can feed them.

God has put the body together. . . . If one part suffers, every part suffers with it; if one part is honored, every part rejoices with it.

1 CORINTHIANS 12:24, 26

A Community Table

A few weeks ago, our small group held our monthly dinner. The hostess did not assign courses but just instructed us, "Let's have a true potluck. Everyone just bring something, and we'll make a good meal out of it."

It was fun to see what everyone showed up with. When given latitude, most people bring something they are proud of, that they'd love to share, and everyone's offering was different from everyone else's but contributed to a richly unique, wildly enjoyable whole.

A recent spate of newspaper articles has covered the heartbreaking divisions troubling our country. One man had an idea—he held a community dinner in which all parties, from many races and areas of town, came together, bringing food—their unique offerings—to share. By all reports, it was a great success. People got to know one another as individuals, not members of "them" or "us." People listened to those sharing a table with them, and new friendships were made.

One of my favorite songs as a child was "He's Got the Whole World in His Hands." God doesn't just have me in his hands; he's got you in his hands, sister. God doesn't just have me in his hands; he has you in his hands, brother. We are in this together, church family.

A great mystery of Christianity is the Trinity—how God can be eternally three persons and yet one whole. Jesus explains that he not only hopes but he *prays* that his body—those people who believe in him and call on his name— will be one in the same manner. Not divided but always united, as closely aligned in affection and purpose as the Father and Jesus and the Spirit are. He says we will be known by our love for one another. Right now, we seem to be at a non-engaged arm's length.

It's compelling that our Savior so desires our oneness that he prays for it. Can we sit still and do nothing, knowing that?

I pray also for those who will believe in me through their message, that all of them may be one, Father, just as you are in me and I am in you. May they also be in us so that the world may believe that you have sent me.

JOHN 17:20-21

A Sympathetic Searchlight

Most of us believe that we have no prejudicial thoughts against anyone who is different from us—denominationally, culturally, socially, racially, regarding income, profession, or education, or any other category we can splice ourselves into. Yet despite our highest desires, the sin nature is buried deep within all of us and especially asserts itself when we are hurt, insulted, threatened, or frightened for ourselves or someone we love.

For many years, I would unabashedly have said I had no unhealthy biases. And yet, challenged by a social media post by another believer, I prayed, and God opened my eyes to subtle ways I occasionally viewed people through a wrong, sinful, prejudging lens. Repenting and reorienting my heart set things to right again. I know this will be a continual process of asking God to help me see people through his unbiased perspective. "If you prepare your heart, you will stretch out your hands toward him. If iniquity is in your hand, put it far away, and let not injustice dwell in your tents" (Job 11:13-14, ESV).

Would you be willing to join me in asking God to illuminate anywhere you might be harboring wrong thoughts or allowing impulsive reactions? I have found God to be gentle and restorative when I ask him to do so. Let's not be hard on ourselves or others, but let's quietly search ourselves and ask God to search our hearts, as David did.

Think how good it feels when the clouds lift and the sun shines. If we, as the body of Christ, are to be one in the way he wishes us to be, the first step is to ask him to bring the truth to light so we might not walk any longer in the darkness. His Word tells us that once we are in that light, we can walk in fellowship with one another—but not before (see 1 John 1:6-7).

Dear God,

I mean well, but I am flesh and blood. Would you please have your Spirit recall places where I am thinking wrongly? Please show me, and I promise to react with repentance and change.

Your child, _____.
Amen.

Search me, O God, and know my heart! Try me and know my thoughts!
PSALM 139:23, ESV

Experiencing the Love of God

It's all very well and good to say we desire something, but it's important that our actions meet our intentions. God is very intentional in his love for us—from before the moment humankind first sinned (see Ephesians 1:4) he had a plan in place to reconcile us to himself, and even to others, at a great cost to himself. He had not only the sentiment but a plan and the will to put the plan in place. Experiencing his love can often mean acting like he does, because then we are one in him (see John 17:21).

After asking God to search your heart, is there one way you can reach out to someone this week, someone who might feel that he or she is isolated from or has been hurt by the body of Christ or an individual believer? Is he lonely or new? Does she feel rejected by the church or by society? Just plain old left out with few friends or family?

It can be a series of smiles at strangers, a phone call, a job offer or an internship, support for a charitable organization, a donation to a cause, an invitation to coffee or a welcoming seat at your table—anything at all.

You might have an idea right now, but the week will soon crowd it out. Write it on your calendar, make a sticky note, and don't take it down till you've completed the action—or just act right away.

I'm reminded of the Good Samaritan—he married intentions with immediate action, in contrast to the priest and the Levite, who noticed a problem but passed by without acting. May we aim to be like the Samaritan.

A despised Samaritan came along, and when he saw the man, he felt compassion for him. Going over to him, the Samaritan soothed his wounds with olive oil and wine and bandaged them. Then he put the man on his own donkey and took him to an inn, where he took care of him. The next day he handed the innkeeper two silver coins, telling him, "Take care of this man. If his bill runs higher than this, I'll pay you the next time I'm here."

LUKE 10:33-35, NLT

One Step at a Time

My husband grew up in Colorado, in the mile-high city where the air is thin. When he arrived in Kentucky—the lowlands—for boot camp, he ran faster and farther than almost anyone there. "Where are you from, son?" his drill instructor asked, having observed that Michael never seemed to tire.

"Colorado," my husband answered. "What do you do with all the extra air you have down here?"

"It'll catch up with you," the drill instructor said. And it did.

By the time boot camp was nearing the end, the weather had turned hot and so humid that one could see the moisture clouding in the air. The young future soldiers were tired. They had a long run ahead of them, and there was no backing out. Drill instructors are not known for their gentleness, but they understood the daunting task that lay ahead in the long, timed run, and they ran alongside the recruits, speaking words of encouragement and endurance.

"Don't think about the whole distance," they'd call out. "Just run to the next light pole, and then run past it, and then keep going. Don't quit. You'll get there."

When we first start our walk with God, we are excited, enthusiastic, and fresh. Nothing seems daunting—until life begins to wear on us once more. The circumstances get hotter, and all that extra "air" we had at first is used up.

Then the Holy Spirit comes alongside us, encouraging us to go one more step, one more hour, one more day. He reminds us that we can run in such a way that we might win—that is, one step at a time, never giving up, never losing hope.

It's good to remember that the drill sergeants did not send those soldiers out on their own—they ran alongside them right through the finish line. No matter how difficult the circumstance, how long the road ahead, how daunting the task, God is right here with you. He's speaking encouragement to you, light pole to light pole. Can you sense him?

Forgetting what is behind and straining toward what is ahead, I press on toward the goal to win the prize for which God has called me heavenward in Christ Jesus.   PHILIPPIANS 3:13-14

A Call to Jubilee

A family who is dear to us had a cascade of difficulties crash down upon them like bricks. Years spent pursuing education had left them cash poor and steeped in student loan debt. Worse, medical and dental bills had built up, and it became an unmanageable load when one of their children had a hospital bill nearing $100,000. Finally, unable to meet basic needs in addition to keeping the payments on the bills going, they had to declare bankruptcy.

Financial bankruptcy is a legal declaration that you can no longer handle your obligations on your own and need help to start over—a clean slate. It wasn't very long ago that those who could not pay their bills were thrown into a Dickensian workhouse—or worse. Remember the parable of the debtor in Matthew 18? A creditor was owed money, and when it could not be repaid, that creditor ordered the debtor's family to be sold to pay the debt. This was a legitimate solution at the time.

This family's bankruptcy—and ultimately freeing redemption—reminded me of salvation in Christ. Through a combination of events we have no control over, such as original sin or the consequences of others' sins, plus our own sinful choices, humankind finds itself stuck and unable to redeem itself. In a financial bankruptcy, someone—the creditor—through no fault of his or her own, must take on the responsibility for the unpaid debt. It causes a real loss for that creditor.

Likewise Jesus, through his sacrifice, paid our debt in full, redeeming us from the growing, suffocating bondage of sin which we were unable to escape on our own.

Many good people find themselves in financial situations from which they cannot escape on their own. All people find themselves bound in sin from which they cannot escape on their own. As we consider our debt that has been paid by a most blessed Redeemer, he teaches us not to judge whatever circumstances cause someone to cry out for relief and to freely do so ourselves, whether it be financial, relational, or otherwise. He, after all, hears every call and offers a chance to begin anew.

God made you alive with Christ. He forgave us all our sins, having canceled the charge of our legal indebtedness, which stood against us and condemned us; he has taken it away, nailing it to the cross. Colossians 2:13-14

Clean Slates and Fresh Starts

Once you begin anew, the real work begins, whether it's with a clean slate spiritually, financially, or relationally. A family who declares bankruptcy must learn to budget, cut back on extras, and live within their means lest they find themselves back in trouble. People who have to start over with their relationships need to understand what they contributed to the breakdown of earlier ones. If they do not, they might find themselves mired in another unhealthy bond.

There is that saying, "Wherever I go, there I am." What is the cure? A new "I" to bring to a new situation. Second Corinthians tells us that "the Lord—who is the Spirit—makes us more and more like him as we are changed into his glorious image" (3:18, NLT).

I once worked for a man who declared bankruptcy every seven years—as soon as he was allowed. And yet he always drove new cars and had monogrammed shirtsleeves. Everyone understands needing a fresh start. People also understand, though, when grace is exploited. We don't want to exploit creditors, people who love us, or the sacrifice made by our Lord, which covers every sin.

Our fresh start spiritually begins at the moment of our salvation. We begin, as the Bible says, as babes in Christ, drinking milk—easy teachings—and progressing toward meat—that which needs more chewing and time to digest. It's tempting to return to the habits and decisions which got us into trouble in the first place.

Peter tells us in 1 Peter 1:14-15, "Don't slip back into your old ways of living to satisfy your own desires. You didn't know any better then. But now you must be holy in everything you do, just as God who chose you is holy" (NLT).

Salvation removes our debt of sin, but it does not remove our propensity to sin. We can learn to spend wisely, relate wisely, and walk wisely in the Spirit and not in the flesh. We are in training, and day by day, decision by decision, we are made new in Christ. Hurrah!

Not that I have already obtained all this, or have already arrived at my goal, but I press on to take hold of that for which Christ Jesus took hold of me.
PHILIPPIANS 3:12

An Invitation

One year a new family moved in next door. We struck up a few conversations, and they invited us to dinner. Of course, we accepted!

When I asked what I could bring, the wife assured me I should bring nothing at all. My husband and I arrived at the appointed hour, but there were only two settings at the dinner table. They indicated that we should sit down and they would serve us. "Won't you be eating with us?" I asked. "No," she replied. "It is our custom to serve our guests. We will eat when you leave." It was a little awkward, but their intentions and hearts were so good we loosened up right away.

The next week, my husband saw a long string stretching across the man's garage. From the string hung meat, which dripped down like beefy icicles from the eaves. "What is that?" he politely inquired. "Oh," our new neighbor said. "In my country, this is how we dry meat." My husband was about to inform him about homeowner associations and other local regulations, but the Lord pressed him to hold his tongue.

Instead, we invited them to dinner.

After a lovely meal—all four of us at the table this time—the man asked about the rules regarding the meat. My husband gently let him know what was permissible and what was not. Over time, they asked us about our Christianity, and we were delighted to answer those questions too.

The Lord taught us a lesson then that we have carried forward. In our Christian culture, we often observe things that seem wrong to us but do not seem wrong or odd to our family, friends, and neighbors. It might not be dried meat, of course; it might be habits or lifestyles. In their "culture" these things are perfectly normal, and everyone they love agrees. Nowhere does Scripture tell us to lecture or bully or belittle or holier-than-thou our neighbors. Instead, the onus is on us to love them unconditionally, wait for them to ask, and have an answer prepared. Because if we do love unconditionally, they *will* ask, and we will not only have an answer prepared, but we will have earned the right to speak it gently.

If someone asks about your hope as a believer, always be ready to explain it. But do this in a gentle and respectful way.　　1 PETER 3:15-16, NLT

The Abundant Life

When my daughter was a young girl, she came to us one day and asked when she got to be a dult. "A dult?" we asked. "Yes," she said. "The dults have all the fun. They stay up late; they eat what they want; they go shopping; they drive cars. I want to be a dult."

Ah, to be a child is to want to be an adult. To be an adult is to wish for the carefree life of a beloved child! Our daughter is an adult now—one with a job, a marriage, financial responsibilities, and sometimes serious health challenges. She also enjoys late nights and fun foods! I know she's having a good time, but it's not quite the nonstop party she had expected as an envious preschooler.

Spoken or unspoken, we expect that things will go perfectly well when we grow up, when we get a new job, when we are married, when we lose weight. But we can get sick and lose jobs. We can be at an ideal weight, and life can still have painful potholes. There's a moment when we all become adults, and it's not when we hit eighteen. It's when we realize that life is beautiful, but life is sometimes hard, too.

There are hours of joy, and they are sometimes salted with moments of pain. Once we stop looking for every day to be better than the one before, stop telling ourselves that we can be happy when . . . then we begin to enjoy life. "There is nothing better for a person than that he should eat and drink and find enjoyment in his toil. This also, I saw, is from the hand of God" (Ecclesiastes 2:24, ESV).

Jesus told us that in this life we would have troubles; he was orienting our expectation to adulthood. Expecting constant calm and happiness is a recipe for steady disappointment. Here's what he tells us we can expect: an abundant life, a very present help in time of trouble, mercy, patience, rescue.

Unending love.

Redemption. Fellowship. Beauty from ashes.

Thank you, Lord, for the richness of a full life.

"I know the plans I have for you," declares the LORD, "plans to prosper you and not to harm you, plans to give you hope and a future." JEREMIAH 29:11

One Heart

Flipping through channels one night, my husband and I stopped at a news report that showed a most festive occasion—a wedding. The Middle Eastern groom and bride were filled with joy, and their friends and family had formed a big circle around them, and they were all dancing. The wedding music almost, but not quite, covered the sound of the bombs going off in the background. The detonations were close enough that I, a world away, flinched.

This is not an unusual circumstance in that area of the world. A recent report in the paper also discussed the celebration of a wedding, this time in Syria, and the music there, too, was punctuated by the sounds of warfare. "There is war, and then there is life," said best man Omar Hretani. "We have two hearts in this country—one for sorrow and one for happiness. Everything has its own story."[1]

Not long after, I saw an image of a baby being baptized in a church in that area of the world, where people have been baptized for nearly two thousand years. What history, what hope! Yes, the world is on fire. But Jesus was, is, and will be, and this child being presented was being claimed for him.

People who prevail at living life by enjoying the moments they can and living with hope—getting married and baptizing babies—have a lesson to teach those of us who live in comfortable situations. Joy must be taken by the power of the will. Happiness must be wrenched from difficult situations. And it can be!

We may not live in a war zone, but Ephesians 6:12 makes it clear we are in the midst of our own war, "against evil rulers and authorities of the unseen world, against mighty powers in this dark world, and against evil spirits in the heavenly places" (NLT). We know that no matter what bombs are being dropped around us, in Christ we ultimately win. Your story, my story, may have sorrow in it, but ultimately, it is one of triumph, both now and then. He has one heart for us, filled with love.

Always be joyful. Never stop praying. Be thankful in all circumstances,
for this is God's will for you who belong to Christ Jesus.

1 THESSALONIANS 5:16-18, NLT

---

[1] Declan Walsh, "On the Ground in Aleppo: Bloodshed, Misery and Hope," *New York Times*, April 30, 2016, http://www.nytimes.com/2016/05/01/world/middleeast/syrian-city-torn-by-war-shows-jarring-resolve-to-try-to-live-normally.html.

Experiencing the Love of God

I'll bet you've had some difficulties this week, this month, this season of life. I have. Although we don't live in a war zone, our difficulties might still have been unexpected and heart-wrenching. Or they might have been a monthlong slow drip of irritations—the kind of constant drip that can wear a stone into a pebble or a smile into a sigh.

And yet, the ability to celebrate is in our hands. We do not have to wait until . . . we are married, we get a new job, we feel better, this trial or trouble or year passes. In fact, we *cannot* wait. We can celebrate right now, even for just a moment. We must choose it. And then we must do it!

Choose a way to celebrate—today. Find something to celebrate and the reason behind it. Christmas, Easter, Passover, Communion are all focused celebrations. I'm not just going out, I am declaring a feast of remembrance, I am celebrating friendship, love, a fallen comrade. Do it today, because if you don't plan or do it now, it will slip to the bottom of the to-do list where it will rot, forgotten, like greens in the back of the fridge.

Why not go out for ice cream? Make hot chocolate and watch a movie you've been putting off till you had more time. Invite a friend over for dinner, or even better, ask a friend or two if they'd like to do a progressive dinner. Read a book. Plan a trip.

Solomon encourages us "that everyone should eat and drink and take pleasure in all his toil—this is God's gift to man" (Ecclesiastes 3:13, esv). That is a wedding gift from your groom, Jesus, to you, his bride. *That* is something to celebrate.

I recommend having fun, because there is nothing better for people in this world than to eat, drink, and enjoy life. That way they will experience some happiness along with all the hard work God gives them under the sun.

ECCLESIASTES 8:15, NLT

Knight in Armor

I had the pleasure of mentoring a wonderful young writer named Brianna. One day we were having dinner, and she was talking about the heroes that are written into books, especially romance books or fantasy books of epic battles. We both agreed that we loved a happily ever after at the conclusion of a book. After all, we know our own story, as believers, has a happily ever after. Our conversation then turned to heroes, and we agreed we liked them strong but loving and real. Then she brought up an excellent point about traditional heroes:

"I don't get it," she said. "You don't want a knight in shining armor, really, do you? Shining armor, after all, means it has never been worn; it's never been tested. If you're a woman, or a soldier, or someone whose world is being attacked, you want a knight whose armor is dented."

See why she's going to succeed? She's brilliant. And generous. I asked if I could share that with you all, and she said yes.

Our hero, our commander in chief, does not have shining armor. He is wise, he is generous, he has been tempted, and he has prevailed. He has fought, and he has sacrificed. He is courageous, and he is the general.

Feel confident that your knight—your Lord, your King—and his tested armor are well prepared to protect you here and in the hereafter. He has the power, the courage, and the will to bring the victory.

I saw heaven opened, and a white horse was standing there. Its rider was named Faithful and True, for he judges fairly and wages a righteous war. His eyes were like flames of fire, and on his head were many crowns. A name was written on him that no one understood except himself. He wore a robe dipped in blood, and his title was the Word of God.

The armies of heaven, dressed in the finest of pure white linen, followed him on white horses. From his mouth came a sharp sword to strike down the nations. He will rule them with an iron rod. He will release the fierce wrath of God, the Almighty, like juice flowing from a winepress. On his robe at his thigh was written this title: King of all kings and Lord of all lords.

REVELATION 19:11-16, NLT

Uniquely Designed

It's easy to look around and think how much smarter, better, richer, or more successful others are.

But the voice inside your head, the one that repeats how miserable or undeserving or inadequate you are, is not the voice of God. How could it be? Would he question how you were made or how you turned out—after all, he made you—wonderfully. Psalm 139:14 encourages, "I will praise You, for I am fearfully and wonderfully made; marvelous are Your works, and that my soul knows very well" (NKJV).

Perhaps, then, his is the voice that says you are not prepared or talented or gifted enough for the works God would like you to tackle? Well, no. Ephesians 2 tells us that God prepared those works in advance for you to do. I do not believe that he would prepare something uniquely for you unless he knew you were uniquely designed, by him, for success at that task.

The shepherd David was certainly not traditionally prepared and readied for war—if he had been, he'd have been there fighting instead of delivering food to his brothers. And yet God designed and called him to meet and defeat Goliath. Saul would have seemed to be the better fit. But Saul had failed. In fact, when David tried to wear Saul's gear, David knew it would cause him to fail too.

David had the tools designed for David, prepared for David's skills and David's task. Living as Saul would have meant failure.

Whatever situation you are facing, do not try to fight in someone else's armor. You and your skills, talents, and indeed, armor, were uniquely designed by God for the glorious works he designed just for you. You cannot be anyone else, but more importantly, no one can be you. You are fearfully and wonderfully made!

Saul dressed David in his own tunic. He put a coat of armor on him and a bronze helmet on his head. David fastened on his sword over the tunic and tried walking around, because he was not used to them. "I cannot go in these," he said to Saul, "because I am not used to them." So he took them off. Then he took his staff in his hand, chose five smooth stones from the stream, put them in the pouch of his shepherd's bag and, with his sling in his hand, approached the Philistine. 1 SAMUEL 17:38-40

Undercover Boss

Several years ago, a television show was broadcast in which senior management dressed up as entry-level employees. The bosses went on location as everyday workers in their stores, businesses, restaurants, and other firms and worked alongside the other employees—no special privileges.

Day in and day out, the bosses saw the kinds of conditions and challenges their employees were subject to. Also, because no one knew they were executives, they got to see who was slacking off on the job, bad-mouthing the boss, or stealing from the firm. They also got to see who went above and beyond, often without recognition.

After a week or two, the boss was revealed to the employees. In some cases, the employees were shocked and disbelieving; in some cases, dismayed; and in some cases, pleased. The employees were coached, praised, or fired accordingly. The show, wildly successful on many continents, was called *Undercover Boss*.

In a way, Jesus was our undercover boss. He arrived in the skin of the lowliest human, a needy baby. He grew up, like we did, and struggled with temptation like we do. I experience his love in a fresh way when I remember that he did those things for you and me. He had a job. He took pleasure in his friends and family. He faced disappointment with those he loved. He saw some of the religious leaders slacking off or taking advantage of "the boss." He also found servants who were faithful and true.

In Luke 20, Jesus relates the parable of a farmer who had leased his land out to tenant farmers. The tenants treated the owner's servants unfairly, though, so the farmer sent his son to collect the owner's share of the crops. He assumed, wrongly, that the tenants would treat his son with respect. They did not, and Jesus showed that God had some strong words in response.

Jesus has now been openly declared as the owner's son. During his time living as a man, he walked in our shoes; he understands the difficulties and challenges of our day-to-day life, but he's still the boss. He's just no longer undercover.

If he shows up at my workplace today, will I be found faithful?

It was necessary for him to be made in every respect like us, his brothers and sisters.　　　　　　　　　　　　　　　HEBREWS 2:17, NLT

Just Walk Away

Three times in the book of Acts the Lord performs a miracle to free his imprisoned disciples. I noticed as I read that despite the miraculous removal of their chains, the believers were still expected to act.

In Acts 5, the Lord opened the doors and brought the disciples out, but then told them to go and preach. In Acts 12, as Peter's life was in danger from Herod, an angel appeared and struck Peter. He told him to get up, dress himself, put on his sandals, wrap his cloak around him, and walk out of prison. In Acts 16, Paul and Silas were set free but had to immediately step in to save the life of their jailer, then follow him out and to his home, where they ministered directly after.

The point? God takes off the chains, but I must walk away from prison.

When the Lord Jesus saved us, he freed us to eternal life by grace alone. After that salvific moment, though, he partners with us in the business of becoming holy. He has taken off the chains; I must walk away. I must walk away from the fears that paralyze me, from the sins that enslave me, from the habits that keep me down. So often I call out to him to save me from those, and it's not that he doesn't help. He does. But most often he whispers, "I took off the chains, but you must walk away."

Sometimes I find it's easier to be angry with him for not helping enough, but really, it's that he's given me the power to move. Is there something the Lord is calling you to walk away from? Go ahead. You're not shackled anymore!

"The Spirit of the Lord is upon me, because he has anointed me to proclaim good news to the poor. He has sent me to proclaim liberty to the captives and recovering of sight to the blind, to set at liberty those who are oppressed, to proclaim the year of the Lord's favor." And he rolled up the scroll and gave it back to the attendant and sat down. And the eyes of all in the synagogue were fixed on him. And he began to say to them, "Today this Scripture has been fulfilled in your hearing."　　　　LUKE 4:18-21, ESV

Thin Skinned

I have a health condition that requires regular blood draws. I also have squirrely veins, which means my one compliant vein was used over and over and over again for the procedure. After some years, though, the skin over that vein grew tough and calloused because it had been breached so many times. It had grown thick to protect itself from repeated needle punctures. It didn't want any more pain, and it was building a hardy defense to make sure that didn't happen again.

A new vein was located. Blood must be drawn from a place that is not calloused and on which there are not thick scars. I had to offer up new, tender skin on an arm that was pockmarked with past trauma. To yield life, we need to be thin skinned.

I'm old enough now and I have been in the ring enough times that I can feel a little battered from the blows I've sustained from the fists of life, and I sometimes shy away from new fights. When I see a situation that calls for me to intervene, but that I know might cause pain, I can't help but hold back. I don't want any more pain or scars.

Yet while I cannot avoid pain, I can redeem it. The only way to redeem it is to turn my painful history into a salve for others. We cannot become calloused to the pain of others or allow our scars to interfere with helping others. Jesus' pain was redeemed by the knowledge that his suffering was the redemption for mankind, as well as the provision of abundant life for them here and now.

Which vein are you being asked to offer up on behalf of someone who needs life? How can your pain be redemptive for others? Perhaps a willingness to revisit a difficulty in your own life to shepherd a person through that same difficulty in her own will be painful, for a moment. But joy at your usefulness and her relief will surely come in the morning!

He comforts us in all our troubles so that we can comfort others. When they are troubled, we will be able to give them the same comfort God has given us. For the more we suffer for Christ, the more God will shower us with his comfort through Christ. 2 CORINTHIANS 1:4-5, NLT

Committee Members

When I first moved to the town I now live in (and love) I was invited to be on the auction committee of a local charity. Barb, a friend from church, invited me to participate. She is a wonderful person and a few steps ahead of me in life, so in many ways she's also been a mentor.

Within the committee itself were subcommittees assigned to recruit catering, do marketing, or decorate; a friend and I solicited donations from local businesses. We were asked not to veer into one another's territory, so potential donors were not inadvertently overwhelmed or asked twice.

One day at lunch with Barb, the conversation turned toward personal matters. I told her that my adult children were making their way through, shall we say, "situations," and I wasn't sure what advice to offer them.

She gently redirected me back to our recently completed auction. "Whenever I had an idea that was not in my area, I would simply keep quiet unless asked and remind myself, 'I'm not on that committee.'"

I grinned at her delightful, kind, and yet pointed advice. I've raised those kids. They are adults making their own decisions, and I am no longer on that committee—just available to offer advice when it's solicited. I'm also not on the committee to tell my neighbors how to keep up their house, nor the one that points out weaknesses in friends or pastors or programs my church undertakes.

I *am* on some committees, and there, I'm to speak.

The illustration reminded me of a time when my family was making chili. I added some spice, and then not knowing it, my husband added some spice. Later, my son didn't think it smelled right and added some too. It was too hot to eat or enjoy, and we learned a lesson. We proved the adage "too many cooks spoil the broth," or in this case, the chili!

Keeping busy with what is legitimately my concern not only keeps me busy enough, it keeps me from being a busybody.

Make it your goal to live a quiet life, minding your own business and working with your hands, just as we instructed you before. Then people who are not believers will respect the way you live.

1 Thessalonians 4:11-12, NLT

Experiencing the Love of God

I want to share the very best things with my friends, including the love of my Lord, recipes, and meals! Two of my friends shared these recipes with me, and I want to share them with you, my reading friend. (I'd cook the chili for you too, if it were practical!)

RED CHILI
From Rhonda LeClerg's Kitchen

1 pound ground beef
1 pound ground sausage
   (Note from Rhonda: kielbasa
   is also a good addition!)
1 onion, chopped
1 can chili beans

1 can pinto beans, drained and
   rinsed
1 can beef broth
1 can tomato sauce
1–2 tablespoons chili powder
   (to taste)

Brown the meats and sauté the onions together in a large pot and drain off the fat.

Return meat and onion to the pot and add all the rest of the ingredients. Let simmer for 30 minutes (or cook on low all day in the slow cooker). Add more chili powder as needed.

WHITE CHILI
From Kirsten Erickson McElroy's Kitchen

1–1.5 pounds boneless, skinless
   chicken breast
1 tablespoon olive oil
2 tablespoons garlic, minced
2 cups onion, chopped
1 4-ounce can green chilies

3 16-ounce cans Northern white
   beans
2 14-ounce cans chicken broth
2 teaspoons cumin
2 teaspoons oregano
¼ teaspoon cayenne pepper

Ahead of time, poach or bake the chicken breasts.

In a large pot, sauté the onions and garlic in olive oil. Once fragrant, add the green chilies (with liquid), beans (with liquid), and chicken broth. Cube the cooked chicken and stir into the liquid mixture.

Add the cumin, oregano, and cayenne pepper. Heat to boiling. Enjoy!

They should be rich in good works and generous to those in need, always being ready to share with others.　　　　　1 TIMOTHY 6:18, NLT

The Life Changer

To complete his chaplain's training, my husband did rotations through various departments in the hospital. The one that he found most difficult was the pediatric intensive care unit. At the same time, we had a good friend who was a police detective. He had to rotate through departments too, and the one everyone dreaded was the department that investigated crimes against children.

"How do you deal with it?" we asked. After having investigated and then spent time with traumatized children, he had to come home to his own kids. "The only way I can deal with it," he said, "is to remind myself that no matter what they have been through, once I arrive on the scene, things are only going to get better. I promise that to myself and to them. Once I step into the situation, things change."

It was a thoughtful answer from a man who does work most of us couldn't face. He did not deny that those kids had been abused and traumatized. He simply ensured that life would look better going forward. They now had a protector intervening on their behalf.

Scripture tells us that once we belong to Christ, we have eternity with him to look forward to. "I give them eternal life, and they will never perish" (John 10:28, NLT).

We usually think of eternal life as what lies in the future, after we die, but eternity does not start later; it has already started. It's now. Jesus tells us that he has come to bring us life abundantly, or as translated below, a rich and satisfying life, even while suffering, here on earth, is still spliced in.

All of us still experience some pain. There is, ultimately, no complete and satisfying answer to "Why doesn't God intervene every time, and earlier on?" He does promise to be with us in the here and now, to give us a rich and satisfying life no matter what deep waters we walk through together from time to time. He also parts the deep water sometimes, and he promises that the life to come has no such fears or tears.

Today, he's stepping into your situation. Things are going to change.

The thief's purpose is to steal and kill and destroy. My purpose is to give them a rich and satisfying life. JOHN 10:10, NLT

Homesick

As a teenager, I had the great fortune to be able to spend part of two summers living abroad. I ate the foods that locals normally ate—which were different from those at home—and I enjoyed almost all of them (except for boxed milk!). My life was immeasurably changed for the better by my hosts' generous hospitality.

One night in Germany I tried to dial my family back home and did not realize that Germans cross their sevens. So they appeared to my American eye as ones with a wee tail in the front. With the time zone change, I tried dialing out all night, 0-7-7 instead of 0-1-1, which is the code to connect with the United States. I missed my family, but we couldn't connect.

Another year, in France, I went to a local salon and asked for a haircut but ended up with a very curly perm instead. The following week, I had a wonderful time climbing the Alps, but late that night, as teenagers will, I missed home. I read and reread the one English language periodical on hand, a *Time* magazine, in the almost-dark of my tent.

When it was time to fly back to the States, I packed up some wonderful items—there was delighted shock and awe when I returned with Nutella, which had not yet made it to US grocery stores—and a bottle of French champagne for my parents. I'd had two remarkable experiences, but I was ready to be home.

I was homesick.

As I write this devotional, I am preparing to return to a city I love, London, which always provides an amazing time among people I love and places we so enjoy. But when it's time to return home, I'll be ready for my own bed, my own town, and the embrace of my family. East or west, home is best.

We are to enjoy the rich and satisfying life God has given us here, but pleasures await us in heaven, too, our true home after this earthly sojourn. I'm eager to see him in person and enjoy his love face-to-face in the home he has prepared for us. Feel a little weary of this world? It's perfectly natural. Maybe you're just homesick!

This world is not our permanent home; we are looking forward to a home yet to come.
HEBREWS 13:14, NLT

Well Traveled

In preparing for our trip to London, we're looking for especially good walking-tour guides. Having some very specific research needs, we need an expert to guide us to the correct locations, give us the right direction, and provide trustworthy insight. As I thought about guides, I remembered some of the last words my friend Jane spoke to me.

A few days before she died, she told me that she'd been suffering a lot of fear of death at night. Then, one night, she had a dream in which Jesus appeared to her. They were climbing a mountain together, and Jesus was, of course, leading. "Can't I sit and rest awhile?" she asked him, but he shook his head and held out his hand and directed her forward, safely.

A few days later she died. He had led her forward, safely, through all the days of her life and preceded her into God's Kingdom.

When Jesus called his disciples, he bade them, "Follow me." We, too, are his disciples, and the call has not changed. They did not always know where they were going or where he was leading. Nor do we. For sure, he is going to direct us to some rocky places, areas where we need to walk slowly and get a sturdy foothold. Just like when we visit new countries, we will travel into territory that is unfamiliar to us. But he will lead faithfully, give us good direction, provide just the right insight . . . and lead us to magnificent views and understanding that can be gained no other way.

I'm very excited for my forthcoming trip: for the adventures we'll enjoy, the new people we'll meet, the narrow trails we'll manage, and the amazing things we'll see.

In the end, what we want is a guide with well-worn shoes, who is well traveled, wise, and reliable. That would be Jesus and those he sends to guide us.

Are you enjoying your lifetime trip with Jesus as your trustworthy guide?

As you received Christ Jesus the Lord, so walk in him, rooted and built up in him and established in the faith, just as you were taught, abounding in thanksgiving. COLOSSIANS 2:6-7, ESV

Angels among Us, Part 1

A few years ago, our family was in London for a holiday—for work and pleasure—and we'd rented a tiny flat with a lovely view of the Thames but in an area my daughter declared to be teetering on the "edge of sketch."

After a day's sightseeing, we deposited our teenagers at the flat while my husband and I set out for a stroll. There was a hole-in-the-wall restaurant not too far away, I explained, that I'd read had wonderful "takeaway" food. We could bring some back for dinner. We set out walking, and walking, and walking, and it wasn't too long till we realized we were blindingly lost.

We had a small map, which didn't do much once we were in the thinner arteries of the city, in a less-traveled neighborhood, where we were clearly recognized as not of its own. There were few people walking, even fewer loitering on door stoops, smoking as they warily eyed us. We stood in an empty intersection, turning this way and that, wondering what to do next and praying for help. After nearly completing a clockwise spin, my husband turned back from looking down an empty street and was surprised to find a small, elderly man with a neat, white beard appear from nowhere; he stood in front of a locked and barred door which had just been vacant.

Approaching my husband, he asked in a thick Scots accent, "Which way are ye going?" "That way," my husband said hesitantly, pointing west. "That's where I'm going too," the stranger replied. "No," I said, turning back around, certain that the restaurant was in another direction. "That way." I pointed southeast. "That's where I'm going too," the Scotsman said.

My husband and I exchanged a glance above the stranger's head. Didn't he know where he was going either? I explained that we were Americans; he grinned—clearly he could already guess this by our accents. We wanted to locate a restaurant I'd read about online but which had become a challenge to find.

"Follow me," he commanded. "I know the place."

We hoped he would be able to lead us in the right direction, that his guidance would be a provision from God. Have you experienced an uncanny provision of God's grace?

I am sending an angel ahead of you to guard you along the way and to bring you to the place I have prepared. EXODUS 23:20

Angels among Us, Part 2

You'll remember from yesterday's devotion that my husband and I were lost in London and an old Scotsman offered to show us the way to our destination. I was nervous following him, but what choice did we have? I looked him over and noticed my husband did too. The man was slight, perfectly dressed in an expensive navy wool coat with a tartan scarf wrapped around his neck and a blue felt hat on his head. Because the man was smaller, my husband could "take him" if need be.

I glanced at the man's shoes. They were well worn, almost falling apart, a distinct contrast to his well-cared-for clothing. I wrote it off to Scots frugality, and we followed him. Within a minute or two, he was leading us down an alley, which appeared to be completely deserted. *Was he leading us somewhere to be jumped?* I wondered. It was off the beaten path, and the buildings were so high on either side that we would be completely hidden from view. I glanced at my husband, who was between us and making light, awkward conversation with the man, and he nodded.

After a few minutes of twists and turns, we arrived at the start of a long street, nearly abandoned, with business after business on either side shuttered and barred off, which eventually met with a busy crossroad about a half mile down.

We stood in front of the restaurant we had been looking for, and the man nodded. "Here you are, then." He looked down the long street. "When you've finished, you walk straight and quickly till you come to the main road, and then turn right." He had not asked us to where we were returning, so I did not know how he knew which way we should go. I realized we hadn't even mentioned the name of this restaurant!

He spoke up again. "Do not go back the way you came," he said in a strong voice. "It's nae safe for you." We nodded and, still somewhat bewildered and stunned, said nothing, just stepped inside the restaurant. Within a second I said to my husband, "Oh! We forgot to thank him!" I turned and went outside, but he was gone.

Warnings are meant to be helpful, aren't they? But they can rightfully scare us too. Can you recall a time when the Lord sent a compelling warning your way? How did you respond?

He will command his angels concerning you to guard you in all your ways.
PSALM 91:11

Angels among Us, Part 3

Yesterday's devotion ended with our Scotsman showing us safely to our destination. But just as he left our company, I remembered that I hadn't thanked him. As soon as that realization hit me, I stepped out of the restaurant to say thank you, but the man was no longer in sight. I hurriedly walked several steps in one direction, and then the next, but there were no breaks in the walls of businesses, and none of the surrounding buildings were even open; our Scotsman was nowhere to be found. Within the previous few seconds, he had completely disappeared.

My heart quickened, and I felt wrapped in a holy hush; within my spirit, I knew. He'd been sent to help us, presented in a way that would make us feel safe and comforted, but in the well-worn shoes of someone who had walked many miles in service. We bought our delicious food and walked toward the road, as we'd been instructed. It was true, then, what Scripture promised. Angels are sent to guard our way, to guide us, to serve, protect, and be messengers of God: our Scotsman's warning, "Do not go back the way you came, it's nae safe for you," is timeless truth for all who walk the path of faith, is it not?

Angels are not just for "back then" and not just for others, but for all of us, here and now, those of us who will inherit salvation.

Billy Graham, in his book *Angels: God's Secret Agents*, recalls a similar situation wherein a group of American troops trapped up north during the Korean War were freezing, starving, and lost. After prayer and praise, they found themselves suddenly confronted with an English-speaking South Korean who led them through the mountains to safety behind their own lines. "When they looked up to thank him," Graham writes, "they found he had disappeared."

I read this account some years after our London encounter, but it resonated with me. Life can be difficult; we can become lost, bewildered, confused, and in dangers of various sorts. God, however, promises that he will never leave us; he is a very present help in times of trouble. Sometimes, to our unexpected pleasure, that help arrives in angelic form, of which we mostly, at the time, remain unaware.

Are not all angels ministering spirits sent to serve those who will inherit salvation?   HEBREWS 1:14

Experiencing the Love of God

Have you ever had an experience that you thought might have been an encounter with an angel? Are you open to others' stories of their belief? We are sometimes too quick to dismiss anything that doesn't seem perfectly rational to us.

And yet our entire faith is built on the supernatural—Virgin Birth, Incarnation, Resurrection from the dead. That's part of the holy mystery of God. He is most assuredly *not* like humanity, and his other creations are not all alike either.

I admit to having been a skeptic when I first encountered angelic intervention (see the devotions for March 22–24). I almost think that the Lord allowed me this experience so I could teach it with confidence, as it was clear to me that he wanted that understanding passed on. In these troubled times, and always, he helps us in many and varied ways. Our true touchstone, though, is not experience but the Bible. Did you know that angels are mentioned nearly three hundred times in Scripture, from Genesis to Revelation?

God shows us his love in natural ways. He provides shelter, food, water, and clothing. He sends people to love us and tend to our relational needs. He provides for our spiritual needs too—our salvation through Jesus Christ and our ongoing maturity through the Spirit, the Word, and other forms of teaching.

I love when the Lord reaches out to me in *super*natural ways—for example, through our situation with the angel, or when he places me on a friend's heart at exactly the right time. While we should always be quick to ascribe every good work to the Lord, both natural and supernatural, we get a true sense of his mighty power and his great affection for us through these heavenly encounters.

Have you or someone you love observed God at work supernaturally?

In what ways do you see the Lord at work supernaturally in Scripture?

Do you believe that Jesus is the same yesterday, today, and forever (see Hebrews 13:8)? With that in mind, is it likely that he is still at work supernaturally?

What supernatural situations do you struggle to believe?

It expands my faith to know that God is not limited to working in ways I can understand. Let's be like the Bereans in the passage below—open minded, but searching Scriptures to verify.

The people of Berea were more open-minded than those in Thessalonica, and they listened eagerly to Paul's message. They searched the Scriptures day after day to see if Paul and Silas were teaching the truth. ACTS 17:11, NLT

Bespoke

Although we share a common language, I discover some wonderful new words whenever I am in England. One of my very favorite new words is *bespoke*.

Bespoke has a sense of the upper class about it; it means something, anything, that is designed and created with a specific person in mind. No buying clothes off the rack—I'm going to have a bespoke dress, one designed just for me. (One dress. The rest of my clothes are bought online.) My husband loves hats (he says all balding men do!), and when we return to London in a few months, he's going to have a cabby hat made just for him.

Bespoke.

Despite the cool clothing that *bespoke* can refer to, one reason to truly love the word is that it reminds us of God's specific, direct, and personal love. Genesis tells us that God spoke, and it was done. Romans reminds us that God "calls into being things that were not" (4:17). Psalm 33:9 pronounces, "He spoke, and it came to be."

Although he spoke the world and some creatures into being, when God saw that the man was lonely, he created a companion for the man in a unique way. He took one of Adam's ribs, something part of the man, and fashioned a woman out of it. He created someone perfectly suited for Adam. Not just any woman, not spoken from the void or created from the ground. Custom made for the man himself.

It's a reminder to us of the sacred nature of marriage, but it also reminds us that God created all of us, his children, especially for himself. He knew what he wanted; he always does. He knows how to meet those desires; he is God. When he created you to think and feel and respond and work, he created you exactly as he wanted you, his beloved, to be. He calls us his bride, after all.

You are just right. He "bespoke" you for himself!

The LORD God caused a deep sleep to fall upon the man, and he slept; then He took one of his ribs and closed up the flesh at that place. The LORD God fashioned into a woman the rib which He had taken from the man, and brought her to the man. GENESIS 2:21-22, NASB

No Armchair Christians

It's fun to be an enthusiastic armchair traveler. Sometimes it's by necessity—it's too expensive to visit in person so we must visit through books or movies. Sometimes it's a choice—I'd rather sit on my soft couch in sweatpants than board an airplane, don a rucksack, and engage in the challenging experience of exploring.

Sometimes, however, we're fortunate enough to travel.

When I was in the plane circling London just before my first visit, I closed my eyes and prayed. I was there with my beloved husband and my children, but the real exultation was to be there with God, sensing his love as I prepared to experience London with him in spirit. So many times he had been with me in my reading and virtual visits—long before I knew my husband or had my children—just the two of us. "We are here! Together!" I whispered to him.

When I am in a foreign country, I am an ambassador for Americans. I may be the only American many people meet. They may have met Americans who did not leave a good impression. They may have come to understand Americans only through distorted media portrayals. I can change their perspective by what I say and do, if I display an even temperament, respect for their traditions, and a friendly disposition, and keep a good sense of humor!

"We are strangers before You. We are just staying here for a time," 1 Chronicles 29:15 (NLV) reminds us. We are all travelers in this world, visiting for a time, and we have an opportunity to be an ambassador for our Lord, as 2 Corinthians 5:20 teaches, by what we say and do during our earthly sojourn.

Sometimes it's tempting to be an armchair Christian and stay parked on my couch in my sweatpants. We're called, however, to dig in to the hard work of the gospel. Ephesians 6 exhorts us to pull on, like shoes, the readiness of the gospel of peace. Shoes, of course, imply we'll take that gospel somewhere and do something with it. Walk!

How will you "do" the gospel today? Can you hear his whisper to you? "We are here! Together!"

Be doers of the word, and not hearers only . . . being no hearer who forgets but a doer who acts, he will be blessed in his doing. JAMES 1:22, 25, ESV

Traveling Companions

A pleasant traveling companion helps us on our journey as much as a carriage. JONATHAN SWIFT

One of the best things about traveling—about life in general—is enjoying it with other people. When you travel abroad, the entire journey is more pleasant, and even safer, when you travel in numbers. In the March 22–24 devotions about angels among us, I shared how my husband and I were lost in London. I would have been even more frightened had I been alone. Many people travel with prearranged group tours, so they know they are appreciating and discussing sights with like-minded travelers. They can fill one another in on the history of the area, keep one another company on the adventure, and best of all, enjoy their time together.

Traveling companions, of course, need not only be for far-flung trips.

A friend and I are planning to hike a local mountain as soon as weather allows. We've picked a trail we know will include wildflowers, which we both enjoy. We can remind each other to bring blister-guard bandages and to drink enough water while hiking.

Another friend is an adventurous eater—I'd ask her to come with me to try squid or oysters. Ecclesiastes 8:15 encourages, "I commend the enjoyment of life, because there is nothing better for a person under the sun than to eat and drink and be glad. Then joy will accompany them in their toil all the days of the life God has given them under the sun."

Now when traveling in new areas, I always try to reach out to a local friend for advice. This helps me enjoy the time I have there "like a local" and helps me avoid dangerous areas on the "edge of sketch"—unless God calls me to go there. Ecclesiastes also reminds us that "two are better than one, because they have a good reward for their toil. For if they fall, one will lift up his fellow" (4:9-10, ESV).

We will have days of pleasure and days of travail on our earthly sojourn. Who have you chosen to be your traveling companions? Do you need to expand a regular twosome or threesome into a full-blown tour group? Might be fun!

I am a companion of all who fear you, of those who keep your precepts.
PSALM 119:63, ESV

Fishing . . . and Catching

Late last March my husband, son, and son-in-law went on a daylong fishing trip. They'd been planning the trip since Christmas and had prayed and prepared. We ordered wet gear for everyone. They woke up early, doughnuts and coffee in hand, and drove to meet the fishing guide.

They spent the day laughing and talking and drifting down the river. However, they caught no fish. There was lots of wildlife to see—eagles and otters and hawks—but only one fish, and it was unsuitable for eating. At the end of the day, the guide was embarrassed, although the men had had a good time. "That's why they call it 'fishing,' not 'catching,'" my husband reassured him.

This trip with the sons was markedly different from the first time my husband took our son fishing. Our son was about five years old, and they visited a local pond so stuffed it was practically a fishbowl. The pond was regularly stocked and the fish kept hungry. To no one's surprise, my son hooked a fat fish, which they cleaned and we ate.

We are all disciples of the Lord Jesus, and he told us that we would become, at his commissioning, fishers of men. Sometimes, though, we plan, prepare, pray, and give a ministry our best effort only to catch . . . nothing. Fishing, not catching.

Sometimes I speak with someone, hurriedly and offhandedly, neither truly paying attention nor intending to have the conversation evolve into matters of faith, when suddenly that person is shown to be very hungry for what I have to offer—Jesus.

We don't always know where he is going to bring the fish; sometimes your Father leads you to a stocked pond, and sometimes the fish are thin in the water. We do know that if we're in the boat with mended nets, day after day, when Jesus brings the fish we'll be ready to catch them!

When he had finished speaking, he said to Simon, "Put out into the deep and let down your nets for a catch." And Simon answered, "Master, we toiled all night and took nothing! But at your word I will let down the nets." And when they had done this, they enclosed a large number of fish, and their nets were breaking. LUKE 5:4-6, ESV

911

We once lived in a lovely old-fashioned neighborhood of vintage homes. One night we awoke to the sound of the people across the street calling for help. They were sitting, au naturel, on the large eave of their house, outside their bedroom window!

We called 911 and the police came; we later learned that our neighbors were asleep in their house when they sensed, and then heard, someone creeping down their hallway toward their room. The only route of escape was out their window, and there was no time to waste.

The criminal was later caught. He had used a woodpile stacked in the backyard to climb into a window, open to let in the summer's breeze. It hadn't taken much to give him a foothold—a stack of wood from which he leveraged himself into their home, endangering their lives.

In a very real sense, allowing the devil a foothold is a house break-in; Satan is breaking into your "home," the temple that is your body. The word *foothold* reminds me of the concept of a beachhead. In wartime, if the invading force can land on, and hold, one beach, they can spread their forces throughout the land, conquering it foot by foot, acre by acre. If the defenders can push them back into the sea, they can prevent the invaders from getting a secure beachhead—foothold—and can keep their land safe.

A beachhead is just a tiny little square, yet from it, the invading force can spread quickly and do tremendous harm. It can be any weakness we have toward temptation to sin—or the sin itself, once indulged. In Ephesians 4 we are commanded not to give the devil a foothold. The order is surrounded by verses to help us know what to look out for, including:

- "Put off falsehood and speak truthfully" (verse 25).
- "In your anger do not sin: do not let the sun go down while you are still angry" (verse 26).
- "Anyone who has been stealing must steal no longer, but must work" (verse 28).
- "Do not let any unwholesome talk come out of your mouths" (verse 29).

It's not meant to be an inclusive list. Most of us know what our temptations and sins are. Thankfully, we can call 911 (*Dear Lord—help!*), and in his love for us, he does help us—he helps us to repent and turn away, loosening the devil's foothold and pushing Satan back into the sea.

Do not give the devil a foothold.   EPHESIANS 4:27

A Benediction for March

Please let me offer a benediction as you leave March, which is sometimes said to go out like a lion. Lions can scare us, and so can situations in life that Satan uses to provoke fright. Thankfully, the Lion of Judah, our Lord Jesus Christ, has triumphed over every circumstance, mild and mighty. "Do not weep! See, the Lion of the tribe of Judah, the Root of David, has triumphed" (Revelation 5:5).

I'm so gratified to know that the Lord is near to all who call upon him, whether it's for help in a small matter or a full-on 911 situation! I feel blessed, and in turn, want to offer his blessing to others so they may share in his love, care, and affection.

A benediction is a kind of blessing, a prayer asking for God's favor over another; it's a reassurance of his constant affection, attention, protection, and guidance. At the close of this month, receive this traditional benediction from the Bible, and reflect on how you've grown closer to God in the month that has passed—looking toward the exciting, challenging month ahead.

God loves you and wants you to be blessed. After you've experienced his blessing, you might consider speaking words of blessing over someone else.

Through these pages and the power of Scripture, I reach my hands out to and over you, as your sister in Christ, and pray . . .

Now may the God of peace himself sanctify you completely, and may your whole spirit and soul and body be kept blameless at the coming of our Lord Jesus Christ. He who calls you is faithful; he will surely do it.

1 THESSALONIANS 5:23-24, ESV

APRIL

Experiencing the Love of God

As a boy, my husband delighted in practical jokes. His favorite target? His long-suffering mother. She was in the habit of pulling down the passenger-seat mirror in the car as the family took trips together and saying, "Oh, what a pretty lady!" to her reflection. One April Fools' Day, my husband cut out a picture of a monkey and taped it to the mirror. When his mother pulled down the mirror she started, "Oh, what a—" and then quickly shouted her surprise—which brought a burst of laughter from behind her.

It was a fun and harmless joke between mother and son, but truth be told, my mother-in-law had a healthy approach to how she looked—pretty—and she modeled it well for the three kids in the back seat.

More often, we bemoan how we look. Our sparse eyebrows, dull skin, small eyes, crooked teeth, fuzzy hair, or whatever it is that we decide to pick on ourselves about. This week, turn April Fools' on its head. Copy the verse from Song of Solomon below onto some small cards or slips of paper, and tape one to the bottom of your bathroom mirror. And then tape one to the automobile mirror for someone you know and love. It might be a spouse, or a child, or a friend . . . or even yourself.

God created you exactly as you are, and he loves you with an everlasting love that isn't dependent upon looks, performance, wealth, status, or any other human criteria. This knowledge allows us to know with certainty that we are beautiful to the one who matters most.

You are altogether beautiful. You really are—no foolin'!

You are altogether beautiful, my love; there is no flaw in you.
SONG OF SOLOMON 4:7, ESV

Intimate Companions

I find comfort and encouragement in reading the Psalms. They are easy to relate to and understand because David holds nothing back—not his anger or fear or distress or desire for revenge. He also doesn't hold back on his praise, worship, trust, and joy. Just like we do, David struggled some days to trust the God he knew so well. He's honest; he asks questions; he turns back to faithfulness.

I admit, though, that I mostly do not get from fear and anger to resignation and trust as quickly or as often as David does. It has sometimes seemed unreachable, how quickly he changes emotional—and spiritual—gears, and that used to discourage me. But an insight freed me.

Time *occurs* much more slowly than it is *read*.

Psalm 143 was written by David during the war with his son Absalom; it is a nervous plea to God. The next psalm, 144, is a song of praise for deliverance. Although those two psalms may take us ten minutes to read, the time covered between them might have been more than one year. Time to worry, and then time to see victory.

David was given time to process his life and his emotions and to grow in faith as he saw—over time—God's strength and care revealed in his life and difficult circumstances. The situations David was subject to took time to live and process. But because the Psalms are read quickly, it may seem that David didn't take long to return to faith from suffering. In truth, the events of his own life and their attendant emotions and faith took time to resolve . . . just like in our lives.

Don't be afraid to bring every emotion to God or to share your life with others. God created us for intimacy, and our testimony is never stronger than when it's honest. If you feel like life is giving you a thrashing right now, hold on. Victory is just over the horizon; it might be months or a year away, but it is coming. When it does, don't forget to praise!

LORD, hear my prayer, listen to my cry for mercy; in your faithfulness and righteousness come to my relief. PSALM 143:1

A Tender Healer

A few months ago, our dog had a growth cut off her flank. The vet wasn't sure if it was cancerous or not (thankfully, it wasn't), but it needed to be tested. Afterward, her skin was stitched up, and the area needed to be protected until it was healed. You know what that means. The vet fitted her with what many dogs believe to be their worst nightmare—the cone of shame.

The cone was a constant source of irritation to her. She couldn't eat or drink normally. She took corners wrong, awkwardly bumping into things she couldn't sense. Worse, it was clear to us that she knew she looked different. She wanted that cone off, and we were sorry for her dilemma, but we would not take the cone off until her stitches were completely healed—for her own good.

The protection is necessary because the dog will lick her wound over and over until the stitches are broken open and the injury reexposed and made vulnerable once more. Dogs without human guidance won't leave the sore alone, and sometimes it never heals. New stitches must be placed, and the process must begin again.

As I watched her pouting, I thought how very much like dogs we can be. When I have a wound—for example, someone hurts me, or I'm left out of something, or I make a mistake—do I simply shake it off and let it go? Sometimes. But mostly, I'm tempted to lick that wound over and over. I rehearse in my mind what I should have done, what the other person should do to make it right, or how upset I am. Constantly revisiting it ensures I don't get past the situation; my feelings don't heal, and I don't feel happy and well.

Our dog has us to care for her wounds and ensure she mends, even when it feels wrong or awkward. In a like manner, our "master" has only our best interests in mind. In his love for us, he may allow, or even bring us to, painful situations when they are required for our growth and well-being. He promises to heal us if we trust his methods, which might be uncomfortable, rather than our own, which might be familiar but inflict more harm. He is the Great Healer!

He heals the brokenhearted and binds up their wounds.   PSALM 147:3

The Greatest Story Ever Told

As readers, we often don't think about the elements that make a novel work, but they are there, just like the framing that hides behind a house's siding. For example, in a book's structure, the big idea and the inciting incident come in the first third of the book. In our faith, we might consider those to be God's creation of the world and our subsequent fall into sin. In the second section of a novel, our hero is moving forward but progress is blocked. He or she does not, however, give up, despite what seems to be a worsening situation. In Scripture, God provided the law, love, care, and protection, but humanity was both unable and unwilling to meet the way of life that God required.

About three-quarters of the way through the book comes what writers refer to as the black moment. It seems all is lost. The disciples at the moment of Christ's crucifixion undoubtedly felt all was lost. It was, perhaps, the darkest moment in human history. And yet . . . our Hero had not given up. Instead, he'd willingly sacrificed himself for our good and rose again.

At a story's end, the main characters (that would be us, too, in faith) are living now in their true identities, in our case made possible by our Redeemer.

In life, we want smooth water and happy times. In a book, though, if there is no struggle, a reader will soon abandon the book. Christianity is wholly true and still the greatest story ever told. It's a blessing to know that our hero—Jesus—was tested in all ways, as we are, and he prevailed!

Guess what? In your story, the heroine is you!

Do not be disheartened if your story includes struggle; it's in the struggle, after all, that our mettle is tested. You will meet roadblocks, and there will be dark moments. But the victory is assured. Our hero has carried the day and delivered our happily-ever-after ending.

Your eyes saw my unformed substance; in your book were written, every one of them, the days that were formed for me, when as yet there was none of them. PSALM 139:16, ESV

In the Garden Was a Snake, Part 1

I was speaking with a friend who was trying to come to terms with the horrible abuse she had suffered as a child. "Why did it even have to happen?" she asked. "Why didn't God just stop it from happening?"

We all wish we had the answer to that question. If God has the power to stop pain and suffering from happening, why doesn't he? As I prayed about it, the Lord spoke an understanding to me through a long-ago situation with another friend, Cindy.

Cindy lived in the high desert. One day her family was making ice cream on the front porch when she heard a piercing scream from her two-year-old son. As they ran to him, they saw a coiled rattlesnake nearby; then they saw his hand had been bitten. As Cindy and her son took off for the hospital, Cindy's sister, Jennifer, ran behind the ambulance, crying and screaming. Cindy knew just what her sister was overwrought about; she had the same fears.

At the hospital, the black marks up and down the boy's arm became emboldened, and the poison arced in a visible line toward his heart. The doctors continued to inject ampoules of antivenin.

They applied the antitoxin to his wrist, and then his arm, and then his shoulder. Finally, the shot given to him just before his heart stopped halted the spread of the poison. Her son told her later that the little birds had taken him to where the children were, but he cried and asked to be returned to his mommy. Cindy's toddler would live.

At that moment, she did not ask why that had happened to her son, why she had not foreseen that this might happen, or why God had allowed him to be bitten at all, although they were all valid questions. She was simply glad that there was an antidote for the snake's venom, and although pain was involved at every level, the antivenin had saved her boy's life. Not every boy's life had been saved, though, as we'll see tomorrow. Because of God's constant love and presence, he will be there for the good and the bad—and both fall into every person's life.

I have told you all this so that you may have peace in me. Here on earth you will have many trials and sorrows. But take heart, because I have overcome the world.　　　　　JOHN 16:33, NLT

In the Garden Was a Snake, Part 2

My friend Cindy's sister, Jennifer, arrived at the hospital just after Cindy's snake-bitten son began treatment, overwhelmed and overjoyed that her nephew would live.

His life carried special meaning for Jennifer. A little less than two years earlier, both Cindy and her sister had birthed baby boys just two weeks apart.

While Cindy's son was healthy, Jennifer's son was not. Three months after his joyous birth, despite people around the world praying for his life and health, Jennifer's son died. She handed him from her own arms into the arms of Jesus, for safekeeping till she would see him once again. The little birds did not return her son to her.

When Jennifer saw her nephew heading toward the hospital with a mortal wound, she feared the worst: her sister's son would soon follow her own son to heaven. Of course, she rejoiced when he survived the snakebite, and today he holds a special place in her heart and affections, the cousin to her own son, who did not live.

Why did one child die and the other child live? Why were prayers answered affirmatively one time but not the other? Why did my other friend have to suffer? Why does anyone?

The answers to these questions are frustratingly out of reach sometimes. But given a choice between the answer to the question and the antidote to that which would kill body and soul for all time, most of us choose the antivenin. Here on earth, God doesn't always offer an explanation to us. But someday, we will understand all. There will be no more death, and God will see justice done. Paul tells us in 1 Corinthians 13:12 that "now we see in a mirror dimly, but then face to face. Now I know in part; then I shall know fully, even as I have been fully known" (ESV).

And while the Lord doesn't always offer the answer right now, he immediately offers the life-saving antivenin against the one who seeks to harm and destroy us—the snake, Satan. That antidote is Jesus Christ.

Jesus said to her, "I am the resurrection and the life; he who believes in Me will live even if he dies."
JOHN 11:25, NASB

Wisdom Is as Wisdom Does

A friend and I discussed a difficult personal situation she'd found herself in. She knew what to do; she just didn't want to do it. It was easy for her to make suggestions and offer advice, even exhortations, to others, she told me. It was so much more difficult to apply good advice to her own life. Having found myself in a similar place time and again, I agreed.

But in the end, it's no sense having wisdom if you don't use it. Just ask Solomon.

Scripture recounts in 1 Kings 3 a story with which most of us are familiar. God was pleased with Solomon and told him to ask for what he wished. Solomon asked for discernment—wisdom—and God agreed, telling him he would give him a wise and discerning heart such as had never been, nor ever will be, seen. Unfortunately, even with God-given wisdom, Solomon made some bad choices.

Deuteronomy 17 instructs that kings must not acquire great numbers of horses or make the people return to Egypt to get them. A king is told not to take many wives, lest his heart be led astray. Solomon disobeyed both instructions. First Kings 10 shares that Solomon's horses were imported from Egypt. First Kings 11 tells us that Solomon loved many foreign women. He knew what God's Word said, but he didn't listen. In 1 Kings 11:9, Solomon turned to other gods. And so, "The LORD became angry with Solomon because his heart had turned away from the LORD."

In consequence, God told Solomon that he would tear Solomon's kingdom from him and give it to one of his subordinates—but worse, perhaps, he would take it away from Solomon's son. And then God raised up an adversary against Solomon. I don't know about you, but I would not like to face an adversary that God raised up against me. To appreciate the love he has for us, we need to put to good use the wisdom he has lovingly given us.

We have the wonderful riches of Scripture at our fingertips and in our earbuds; we can watch teaching on TV and the Internet, and attend a Bible study every night of the week if we wish. But in the end—what do we do with it? I dearly want to follow the wisdom imparted to me, not merely dispense advice.

Behold, I give you a wise and discerning mind, so that none like you has been before you and none like you shall arise after you. 1 KINGS 3:12, ESV

Experiencing the Love of God

Wisdom is a gift from God, and like all good givers, God offers this gift with the specific needs and desires of the recipient in mind. Most of us would be reluctant to say, "No thank you" to the Lord for anything he chooses to show or impart to us. And yet so often I let my Bible go unread or teaching go unheeded or godly wise advice go disregarded for the time being. The receipt of wisdom is tied to the walk of the person who receives it. Is there something you know you should do, is wise to do, that you would clearly advise someone else to do, but which you are not doing?

Don't condemn yourself. Life is hard. Making good decisions is hard, and when we know what to do and don't do it, it's usually because we're afraid.

Is there something you know you need to do—something that's the right, godly thing to do—but you aren't doing it? Can you gently probe your heart and mind and ask yourself, *Why am I not doing this right now?*

A situation in which you know you need to act:

Why you aren't acting:

Your commitment to act—what will you do, and when?

Don't be afraid. God promises in Proverbs 2:8, "He guards the course of the just and protects the way of his faithful ones." His affections never fail, and he has you covered. Make a commitment today to do the right thing. Can you ask someone to hold you accountable?

The LORD gives wisdom; from his mouth come knowledge and understanding. He holds success in store for the upright, he is a shield to those whose walk is blameless. PROVERBS 2:6-7

Arm in Arm

We were on a road trip, driving from our relatively urban home through and to another part of our state, which is wide, open, and agricultural. As the miles rolled by, the land sloped down from the edge of mountains to patchwork fields of green and gold. Mostly, the land was flat, and I noticed that on the homesteads of those patches were strategically planted stands of trees.

With no mountains or structures to interrupt, the wicked winter winds could pick up speed and do real damage. Stands of trees would be a natural barrier, protecting the houses from the elements, saving energy costs, and shielding the residents from outside forces. Stands of trees, clumped together in the middle of the fields, provided necessary shade for the livestock. At the edge of the fields, long rows of untended trees provided welcome coverage for wildlife.

Later, I stood near one of those fields and noticed the irrigation system. There was row after row of long pipes with sprinkler heads every several feet. "In a dry and parched land where there is no water" (as the psalmist puts it in Psalm 63:1), water needed to be brought in to encourage and nurture life from the crops. With acre upon acre of potential crop, one or ten or one hundred sprinkler heads standing alone could not do the job of drenching the fields. When the heads were linked and working together, they provided a steady spray, nurturing the harvest the farmer desired as his yield.

Perhaps that's how we work together as a body. One of us standing alone is easily overcome, but Christians standing arm in arm, working together, can block malevolent forces and protect ourselves and others from the elements. Joining in ministry we can water the world with the Living Water (see John 4:14), producing fields that are white and ready for harvest (see John 4:35, ESV). We can't do it alone, and we do want to present to our farmer the yield he desires.

Have you linked up with brothers and sisters? Who has your back, and whose do you have? Who are you working with side by side in the field?

Though a man might prevail against one who is alone, two will withstand him—a threefold cord is not quickly broken. ECCLESIASTES 4:12, ESV

Custom Engraved

Recently, one of my friends told me that for Mother's Day, arriving in a month, she had requested stacking name rings. The rings are fashioned into the names of each one of her children, facing out, and then stacked on her right ring finger. It's a way to keep her children close to her. "And to remind me to pray for them every day," she said.

Super cool. I think I'm going to copy her.

When my daughter was a teenager, she would write reminder notes to herself on her lower arm. "Ever heard of paper?" we would tease. At that point, she had note-taking apps on her phone but didn't use them, either. "I can't forget it this way," she said. "I know I'll remember because I can't look down without seeing what I need to do."

Just a year or two ago, a new associate pastor at our church told us that we shouldn't be startled when we saw him walking around with a word written on his wrist. It was to prompt him each day, he explained. The word might be *peace* or *trust* or whatever he felt he needed to be reminded of in his faith life that day.

Wearing a word or a name in an area visible to all is a public declaration. It tells people who you are, what you need to do, and who is important to you. I was delighted when I discovered the verse that says God has not only *written* me on his palm but *engraved* me there.

Engraving can't be washed off; it permanently alters the object upon which it is carved. It's a forever declaration. Not only are we engraved upon his palm, he tells us in the verse just before it the reason he does that. He loves us more than a human mother does. Even she might forget her child, which seems so unlikely, but he never will.

He's made a permanent, public declaration of his love for you. What a thought to start—or end—your day!

Can a woman forget her nursing child, that she should have no compassion on the son of her womb? Even these may forget, yet I will not forget you. Behold, I have engraved you on the palms of my hands.

ISAIAH 49:15-16, ESV

May I See Your Badge?

I looked in my rearview mirror, and my heart beat a little faster. But why? I wasn't on my phone, wasn't speeding, and to the best of my knowledge, none of my lights were out. At a stop sign, I got a better look at the driver of the car behind me.

I must be getting really old, I thought, because the young lady driving the police car behind me looked very young, too young to be an officer. I pulled over, and the car passed me. It was definitely black and white and had the extended mirrors and front bumper of a police vehicle . . . but was a little dinged up. My taxes at work? But there was no emblem declaring the city's authority. I later learned it was an old, retired police car sold to the public, and I was not only a little embarrassed but duped. I'd been fearing the wrong "authority" all along!

False authority. It was the representation of power and authority and the implied right to question and perhaps detain me that brought on a racing heart when I saw that car. It wasn't anything I had done wrong. But the young lady wouldn't have had authority to question me, despite initial appearances.

Satan, too, tries to intimidate us. The Bible calls him the accuser, the father of lies, and a deceiver. He does have influence in this world but only what God allows him to have, and we're reassured that Satan has been disarmed.

He has no ultimate power or authority. He's riding around in an old, decommissioned car under no one's authority.

No need for your heart to beat faster when he comes around, accusing, lying, and trying to hold you to his account. You've been declared righteous by the one who *does* have authority: Jesus Christ.

He forgave us all our sins, having canceled the charge of our legal indebtedness, which stood against us and condemned us; he has taken it away, nailing it to the cross. And having disarmed the powers and authorities, he made a public spectacle of them, triumphing over them by the cross. COLOSSIANS 2:13-15

The Last, Victorious Word

Many victories begin as a temporary defeat; a job is lost but leads to a better job. A child loses a good friend, but a healthier friendship grows in its place. There is no greater seeming defeat than death, and it's hard to see how it could be a victory of any kind. Unavoidably, death comes to all: once each personally, but in painful multiples counting those we love. As the years pass, the emptiness that grief hollows beneath the rib cage, the inability to sleep or even breathe well after a loss, becomes unwelcomely familiar.

One week, cancer stole the vibrant life from the teenage son of a family friend. A few days later, a close friend texted me in tears over the loss of the sweet three-year-old daughter of a young Christian couple. That very night my husband and I happened upon neighbors lifting a spotted fawn, just struck and killed, from the road. Her mother, the doe, followed in bewilderment, and yes, you could see the grief on her face. She knew.

Although the children who'd passed away were clearly more important, seeing the bewildered doe was the final straw and brought me to tears. Death! Why so much of it, so often, even to the very young? The doe lives in dangerous territory—in the same locale, she found green foliage and also the car that struck her young. Likewise, the same world that provides nourishment and affection and goodness and pleasure also delivers death and disease to our children and to us.

There is deep comfort in the truth that proclaims, "O death, where is your sting?" (1 Corinthians 15:55, NLT). Death is rendered as a personal pronoun in this verse because it feels, and is, very personal indeed. The longer we live, the heavier the death debt.

And yet the verse also reminds us that death does not have the last word—Jesus does. Although it may tarry, the victory has absolutely been won. Christ's final triumph was over death. Weeping may endure for a nighttime. But joy will absolutely reign in the morning. In his love, God has removed from us, inevitably and eternally, the deepest cut of all.

On this mountain he will destroy the shroud that enfolds all peoples, the sheet that covers all nations; he will swallow up death forever. The Sovereign LORD will wipe away the tears from all faces. ISAIAH 25:7-8

April Showers

April, a month of rains, reminds me of Elijah. In 1 Kings 17, Elijah prophesied a severe years-long drought over the land of Samaria, ruled by wicked King Ahab and his wife, Jezebel. Later, in 1 Kings 18:1, it says, "After many days the word of the LORD came to Elijah, in the third year, saying, 'Go, show yourself to Ahab, and I will send rain upon the earth'" (ESV). So Elijah showed himself to Ahab, even though he feared him.

Circumstances had led Elijah to fear what was in front of him, perhaps as much as or more than he trusted God. The familiar story of the defeat of the prophets of Baal occurred, after which Elijah told Ahab he heard the sound of rain. Elijah then told his servant to look for the rain, but the servant didn't see any, though he was sent six times. Elijah confidently sent him back, and on the seventh journey, a tiny cloud appeared, promising rain. And rain it did.

What struck me was Elijah's absolute confidence in God despite what he could or could not see, which hadn't always been the case. He'd fled in fear when facing Jezebel, although the Lord had been with him. By the time the rain came, however, Elijah wasn't looking at circumstances present or past to intimidate or reassure him. There was nothing in the sky to indicate the great rain just ahead; he trusted solely in the word of God even before any evidence of its coming to pass was presented. In fact, he "heard" the rain before the tiniest cloud, the size of a man's hand, had appeared.

All of us who walk with God sometimes waver in belief when the circumstances are fearsome or the evidence of the fulfillment of God's promises doesn't quickly appear. But what he promises, he brings to pass. Scripture is full of stories reminding us that whenever God claimed something would happen, it did. A review of my own life proves his faithfulness as well, even when he hasn't always brought about the circumstances I wanted in the time frame I wished for. As Jesus said when he was facing his death, "Nevertheless, not my will, but yours, be done" (Luke 22:42, ESV).

The seventh time he said, "Behold, a little cloud like a man's hand is rising from the sea." 1 KINGS 18:44, ESV

Beauty Reset

A friend of mine inherited a cache of jewelry from her great-aunt. Most of the pieces had been designed nearly one hundred years earlier, and while they were pretty, they looked dated. The metals were tarnished, and the rocks didn't sparkle as much as they might; they'd been dirtied by contact and use.

"Can you wear any of it?" I asked. "I hope so," she said. "It's worth a lot and has sentimental value, not only for me but for my whole family." She took a necklace and put it on. "I remember this," she mused. "I wore this when I was a girl."

She brought the jewelry to a local craftsman, and he cleaned everything up and then placed many of the jewels in appropriate settings.

Some people teach that we had little or no worth before we met the Lord and followed hard after him. But Scripture clearly declares that untrue. "Before I formed you in the womb I knew you, before you were born I set you apart," Jeremiah 1:5 tells us. While we may have been born into original sin, we were also formed with great love. Before we knew him, God valued us to an unimaginable end. "God showed his great love for us by sending Christ to die for us while we were still sinners" (Romans 5:8, NLT).

We were precious stones but perhaps in need of the right setting. When my friend updated her treasures, she was able to keep the sentiment, the history, and the family line, but repurposed.

When you became a Christian, you did not lose the essence of who you were. God made you just as you are; he only cleaned off the tarnish and reset the jewels in a way that would set them to their best advantage. You are who you are; you will always be who you are. Only now, you have been reclaimed as a treasure by the master craftsman. You, too, re-higher-purposed, are a pearl of great price.

We are God's masterpiece. He has created us anew in Christ Jesus, so we can do the good things he planned for us long ago.   Ephesians 2:10, NLT

Experiencing the Love of God

I love the idea of recycle, reuse, and repurpose, just like resetting precious gems. What parts of your life can be repurposed?

If you've overcome addiction, you have a unique ability to guide someone who suffers from addiction issues. Have you suffered abuse? Have you come through the pain of a divorce? Been let go at work and unemployed? You have a unique platform to take what was painful and craft it into wisdom for someone else.

I've "repurposed" several things in my life. I've taken a picture frame that held a photo of a painful time of life, "distressed" it, and replaced the old picture with a photo of a new era which brings me joy.

DISTRESSING AN OLD PHOTO FRAME

1. Find a frame that is made of wood. It doesn't matter what kind of condition it's in, as you'll be painting it.
2. Find one color of paint (if you want the original stain to come through) or two, if you want layers.
3. Paint the frame your base color. If you're going to use only one color and the original wood, skip the next step.
4. After the base color is dry, paint the second color on.
5. After the paint is dry, take petroleum jelly and lightly coat the areas of the frame you want to be distressed. Paint with the second color once more. After it's dry, use a nail file, sandpaper, or a steel wool pad to "distress" the areas you spread the petroleum jelly over. Don't worry if it's not exact; the scraping and scratching will still go through. You can create deeper grooves by using a knife or a screwdriver if you so wish.
6. After the frame is as distressed as you'd like it, and completely dry, spray a glossy or matte paint sealer over the top. Voilà!

This means that anyone who belongs to Christ has become a new person.
The old life is gone; a new life has begun! 2 CORINTHIANS 5:17, NLT

Get Your Blinders On!

Although I'm an urban girl, I do love visiting our state fair, which is held in both autumn and spring. I love the scones and the home crafts and the onion burgers and the animal exhibits. Our spring fair begins in April, and I took my kids when they were little. Now, I just wander through and enjoy it with friends.

I have several horse-loving friends, so besides stopping by the Swifty Swine Racing Pigs, we always view the horse events. Not being a horsewoman myself, I'd always wondered what the little pieces of leather attached to the bridles were. To the inexperienced eyes—mine—it looked like they were blinding the horses. Quite the opposite, a friend shared. Because horses' eyes are to the sides of their heads, they have great peripheral vision. That also means, though, that if not forced to look forward they can become easily distracted and quickly wander offtrack. The blinders are not to "blind" them but to help them keep clearly focused on the path they're meant to follow.

Do you find yourself looking left and right too often? I do. I compare myself to my friends, coworkers, family members, and neighbors. Then I'm tempted to envy their circumstances or blessings, and when I do that, I start wandering off the path that the Lord has carved out for me. Deuteronomy 5:33 instructs us to "stay on the path that the LORD your God has commanded you to follow" (NLT).

I know when I arrive in heaven and the Lord gently asks me to answer for my life, he's not going to ask me to compare myself to others, or to compare my ministry, family, or stewardship to others'. He has, after all, created me to be who I am, with my unique gifts and abilities. He isn't asking me to be anyone else; he'll want me to account for how well I managed the gifts he gave to me to accomplish for him. The best way I know to do that is to put on blinders to block out all that tempts and distracts me—even if I am not a horse!

Let your eyes look directly forward, and your gaze be straight before you. Ponder the path of your feet; then all your ways will be sure. Do not swerve to the right or to the left; turn your foot away from evil.
PROVERBS 4:25-27, ESV

Broken Beauty

My most trusted kitchen appliance is my stand mixer because I bake a lot. I tend to crack eggs on the edge of its bowl, but then broken eggshell pieces drop into my batter.

A friend told me a trick—use a piece of broken eggshell to "attract" the pieces that have fallen inside the bowl. Eggshell bits are notoriously difficult to fish out of the gel-like egg whites they float in. If you hold a piece of the shell near the bit you want to fish out, though, it almost magnetically attracts the piece you need to recapture.

Last week was an anxious, painful, tear-soaked time, which led to distraction and more dropped eggshell bits than normal. I started thinking about that: the only thing that could reach in and rescue those broken bits was another shell—like attracts like. There is something instantly comforting about people like us. When I travel abroad, it's always fun to spot other Americans. When someone moved to my new town from my old town, we found it easy to reminisce. More somberly, when we discover someone who has undergone a similarly difficult situation to one we've undergone, there is a special kind of bonding and understanding.

When Jesus came to earth, he set aside the fullness of his glory for a time. He identified with us—was born as a baby, was hungry and tired like we are, grieved like we do, laughed like we do, was tempted as we are. Psalm 8 tells us that humans were made a little lower than the angels, and Hebrews 2 tells us that Jesus, too, was lessened to be a little lower than the angels. He was a human, for a time, as we are. And just like we are, he was broken.

Scripture reminds us in 1 Corinthians 11:23-24 that "the Lord Jesus on the same night in which He was betrayed took bread; and when He had given thanks, He broke it and said, 'Take, eat; this is My body which is broken for you; do this in remembrance of Me'" (NKJV). His brokenness was beautiful. Without that brokenness, our salvation could not have been won.

Jesus understands us, he identified with us, and he reached down to rescue us. He is near to us especially when we are broken and is ready to lift us out of despair.

The LORD is near to the brokenhearted and saves the crushed in spirit.
PSALM 34:18, ESV

Rose of Jericho

April is when I begin to think seriously about my garden. It's time to dig out the weeds that are just starting to shoot evil roots. They are easy to remove now because the ground is wet and yielding. When planning what to add to my yard, I consider placing plants with biblical meanings, because this keeps the Lord before me even when I am outside. I consider the rose of Sharon, lilies, and others; one unique plant I just became familiar with is the resurrection plant.

The original plant is found in the Holy Land, in the Judean desert, and is called the rose of Jericho. It is a low-growing plant that, after spreading its seeds, curls up like a fist and dries up completely. It resembles a little tumbleweed. Unlike a tumbleweed, though, which is dead and disconnected from its roots, only a few drops of water will resurrect the rose of Jericho, or its seeds. It lies dormant, waiting for someone or something to sprinkle a few drops of water on it. Then it comes gloriously back to life.

There's a resurrection plant much like it that grows on my side of the world too. When missionaries first arrived in the New World, they used it to illustrate the concept of being born again. In John 7:37, Jesus tells us, "Let anyone who is thirsty come to me and drink."

I became a Christian as an adult, so I can remember what it was like to be thirsty for the hope, affection, and reassurance that salvation brings. The thing is, I didn't know that I was curled up in a dry ball until someone showed me the Way. I'm so glad my spiritual parents, who led a Bible study at my college, risked my affections to tell me so. I was dead in my transgressions and, after I was saved, reborn into vibrant life.

Is there someone you would be willing to risk telling about life-giving water? It only takes a few drops.

As for you, you were dead in your transgressions and sins. . . . But because of his great love for us, God, who is rich in mercy, made us alive with Christ even when we were dead in transgressions—it is by grace you have been saved. EPHESIANS 2:1, 4-5

Sleeper, Creeper, Leaper

Well, it seems I could hardly have a garden of biblical plants without including a fig tree! It's not hot here very often, and fig trees mostly grow in desert climes. Plus, I must admit, I was a little worried that if it did not produce fruit I might think it had been cursed (see Mark 11), and I didn't want that in my garden!

However, we love figs with goat cheese, and we love fig jam. So during a stroll through my favorite nursery last year I saw a fig tree for sale and stopped. Okay, "tree" is a hopeful, positive spin on what I'd spied. It was a slender stalk in a pot. No foliage. Nothing that looked like it might grow and produce fruit. I read the tag, and it promised that another fig lover had propagated this plant to grow in our area. Not only would it fruit, but the promise was for twice-a-year fruiting!

I could not resist. I bought it, and my husband planted it.

By the end of that first season, the plant had two hands' worth of lush, green palms. It had grown about six inches. I remembered the gardener's adage: first year, sleeper; second year, creeper; third year, leaper. So my tree's hopeful little display of forward motion was sure to be multiplied in the years to come. I believe! In three or four years, I'll be making fig jam—twice a year!

Isn't that very much like the model for many precious things we hope for and hold dear? It certainly seems to be how we begin a new endeavor. We start with a slender stalk of desire, but it's an idea or desire with potential. God is an experienced gardener, and he has "propagated" me for the climate in which he expects me to bear fruit, and he tends me as I grow. Our projects and endeavors, our prayers, are well known to him ahead of time! It's okay if you start out weakly. Remember—first year, sleeper. Just start. Before you know, whatever it is you've undertaken together, you'll be creeping, then leaping. You've been designed for success!

I am the vine, you are the branches. He who abides in Me, and I in him, bears much fruit; for without Me you can do nothing.   John 15:5, NKJV

Sample Ladies

When I take myself out to lunch in the middle of the day, I do it in style. I leave my desk, work undone, and head to the big-box store nearby that offers free samples.

I always try a thing or two I know and have eaten before, such as mini hot dogs or chicken on a skewer. But mostly, I've experimented with new cuisine, like edamame hummus or cheddar with embedded blueberries. The reason the store gives away these little nibbles is that it wants to introduce us to food it believes to be tasty (and almost always is!) but with which we are unfamiliar. The hope, of course, is that we'll pick up a package or two and take some home. I've heard that the samplers get a bonus based on how many of the packages of whatever they are sampling sell that day.

The woman handing out that cheese and caramel popcorn sample should be taking home a hefty check thanks to me. I did not like cheese and caramel corn mixed—until I tried that brand!

As Christians, we are commissioned to spread the Good News, to bring the hope that Christ offers to others near and far. Many of the people we meet will have already heard of Christianity. Many will claim to have tried it and perhaps found it to "fail." Christianity doesn't fail, of course, although Christians, as humans, often do. Perhaps you could offer a savory nibble so they might reconsider? A small gift, a word of encouragement, true friendship, or a bit of neighborly help? Because the world is becoming more globally mixed, some of your coworkers or neighbors might have little introduction to Christianity at all—kind of like edamame hummus for me. When I sampled it, though, I found it to be delightful.

Wherever you are, whomever the Lord brings to your life for an hour or a year or more, consider offering them a little taste of the Lord's love, grace, and affections by your words and deeds. Be a sample lady. It might lead to a full meal later!

Walk in wisdom toward outsiders, making the best use of the time. Let your speech always be gracious, seasoned with salt, so that you may know how you ought to answer each person. Colossians 4:5-6, ESV

Wedding Cakes

The phrase for "window shopping" in French is literally "licking the windows."

Before my daughter's wedding, we visited several bakeries looking for a perfect wedding cake. We walked by one nearby bakery after it was closed, and that seemingly peculiar French phrase suddenly made perfect sense. The cakes inside were so beautiful and looked so delicious, my daughter and I practically "licked the windows."

We made an appointment to visit shortly after that, and as we walked into the salon room with those beautiful cakes, we looked at them close-up. The icing was hard and kind of cracked. Some of the cakes had dust on them!

"You won't want to eat one of those," the baker teased. "They are made of cardboard, cement, and other materials and are for display only." In other words, they were cakes that look pretty but don't taste good. Not what was promised through the windows, hoped for, or even expected.

Sometimes, in our desire to introduce others to our wonderful God, we tell them only the best parts without mentioning the suffering that is sure to come. There is persecution, harassment, and hardship. Discipleship is rewarding but not easy. Because we know that believers undergo these things, it's only fair that when we discuss the miracle of grace, the inestimable gift of eternal life, and God's deep and abiding love that we explain some difficulties, too. We're asking them to make a considered commitment.

Later, with a smile, the baker brought out *real* cakes, and they tasted so much better than I had even expected.

Jesus says in Luke 14:28-30, "Which of you, desiring to build a tower, does not first sit down and count the cost, whether he has enough to complete it? Otherwise, when he has laid a foundation and is not able to finish, all who see it begin to mock him, saying, 'This man began to build and was not able to finish'" (ESV).

Let's make sure we share our wonderful Lord and the life he gives but relay honestly the sweet and savory parts of the delightful life that lies ahead for those who choose it. That way they can count the cost for themselves before choosing to become his bride.

Whoever does not bear his own cross and come after me cannot be my disciple. LUKE 14:27, ESV

Experiencing the Love of God

Yesterday's devotion shared how something may look good but, upon closer inspection, isn't what you'd expected it to be. Some of us may have had friends who didn't share the full experience of the Christian life—fearful, perhaps, of turning us away from the saving grace of Jesus.

Jesus, however, said the truth will set us free, and the truth includes the difficult truths of discipleship as well as the exhilarating truths of his unconditional love and constant presence. Don't be afraid to share the truth of Christianity. Invite your friends to investigate God—to taste and see that he is good!

If you're going to take time to make a cake from scratch for your friends, why not start with what the Norwegians named the World's Best Cake (*Verdens Beste*)? This recipe from Crystal Johnsen's website, *Little Bit Funky*,[2] really delivers.

WORLD'S BEST CAKE

10 ½ tablespoons butter, room temperature
1 ⅔ cups sugar
1 ⅓ cups flour
1 teaspoon baking powder

5 large eggs, separated
⅓ cup milk
¼ cup almonds (sliced or slivered)
1 cup heavy cream
1 teaspoon vanilla

Preheat the oven to 350°F, with a rack in the middle position. Line an 8 x 12 inch baking pan with parchment paper.

Beat the butter and 2/3 cup of the sugar in a large bowl with an electric mixer until light and creamy, about 3 minutes. Add the flour and baking powder and mix well. Mix in the egg yolks and milk. Scrape the batter into the baking pan. It will be thick.

In a large, clean bowl, beat the egg whites and the remaining 1 cup sugar until it forms soft peaks. Spread on top of the cake layer. Sprinkle with the almond slices.

Bake for 30 minutes, or until the meringue is golden brown and puffed. Cool on a wire rack in the pan. Transfer to a cutting board.

When the cake is cool, put the cream in a medium bowl and add vanilla. Beat with an electric mixer until it forms soft peaks.

Cut the cake in half crosswise with a serrated knife. Place one half of the cake, meringue side up, on a serving tray and cover meringue with the cream. Place the other half, also meringue side up, on top.

Let the cake sit for 1 hour in the fridge before serving.

Taste and see that the LORD is good. Oh, the joys of those who take refuge in him!
PSALM 34:8, NLT

---

[2] "World's Best Cake," *Little Bit Funky*, http://www.littlebitfunky.com/2014/04/worlds-best-cake-verdens-beste-in-norway.html. Permission granted.

Free to Be Me

One day when my daughter was eight years old, she and I had a disagreement. She desperately wanted to do something, and I would not give her permission to do it. She wheedled and pleaded and begged and bribed and cajoled. I did not think the thing she was asking for was in her best interest, so I continued to calmly refuse. She went silent, and I thought she had finally accepted my verdict. About a minute later, though, she said something that shocked me.

"I hate you." I was so taken aback that I didn't answer. I don't know that anyone else had ever told me that they hated me—at least not since I'd been a girl myself. In my stunned silence, though, I soon heard another noise: tears of sorrow and resignation.

I sensed the Lord comforting me from the pain of hearing my child's honest expression of emotion, and I didn't respond to her right then. My daughter, with whom I have always had a loving relationship, felt free to be honest with me because of the intimacy of our relationship. I was a safe place for her to express herself without a filter. I was the person to whom she needed to tell the truth, the whole truth, and nothing but the truth.

She viewed me as having the power over what she needed and wanted, and I had denied it to her. She didn't understand why, and thwarted and in pain, she'd struck out. Later, after we'd talked, she cuddled next to me and said, "Mommy, I love you."

"I know you do," I told her.

"I'm sorry," she said. I knew she was.

God, the best and most loving parent in the world, often tells us no. We might plead or cajole or beg, and sometimes he still says no. We don't understand and can become angry with him. I have been angry with him when he wouldn't stem my hurt or fix what I thought he should. Then I return to him and love him and ask to reestablish intimacy. I think he loves that I trust him enough to talk honestly with him—respectfully so—because he says he wants us to.

"Come now, let us reason together," says the LORD.   ISAIAH 1:18, ESV

From Red to Black

I'll admit publicly that the first thing I do when I wake up in the morning is reach for my phone. I could say that I don't want to wake my husband by getting out of bed before his alarm goes off. And that's true. Mostly.

I scan e-mails and a few other necessities, and then I check in with my bank. We live on a relatively tight budget. Occasionally, I've taken my eye off balancing the online checkbook, and the first thing I see in the morning is that I'm close to being overdrawn, which is not a cheerful way to greet a new day.

Then I must figure out how to move some money from savings or business so that checking is covered. Normally, that is a wake-up call that I'm overextending. I'm trying to do too much with too little, and I need to cut back. What do we need? What do we want? What is not necessary, really? I move money so we're covered, and then my husband and I talk so we can comfortably live within the provisions the Lord makes for us.

Finances are an easy way to take my temperature, because a red bank balance indicates a personal imbalance. In truth, when I'm overextended in one area it's likely because I'm overextended elsewhere, too; I'm trying to spread one small tablespoon of peanut butter over two slices of bread, which makes an unsatisfying sandwich for everyone. I might have taken on too much work, too many volunteer opportunities, or maybe I'm having too much fun! Whatever it is, when I'm stretched, I must take resources from one area to meet the lack in another. That leaves something depleted and me, tired, unless and until I say no.

I'm happy to report I'm committed to living within the resources God provides. In his love, he provides everything I need and many of the things I want. If I were to long for more than that, I might be expressing dissatisfaction or a lack of trust in his gracious provisions. Have you mastered the fine art of saying a gracious no to self and to others? I'm working on it!

Not that I am speaking of being in need, for I have learned in whatever situation I am to be content. I know how to be brought low, and I know how to abound. In any and every circumstance, I have learned the secret of facing plenty and hunger, abundance and need. PHILIPPIANS 4:11-12, ESV

The Whipping Boy

One of my kids' favorite books, when they were young, was a thin novel about a little boy who took the punishment for all the naughty things his higher-born master did. You can see why it was a favorite, right? Do what you want—never get in trouble yourself. The young lad taking the pain was the whipping boy.

The whipping boy was an actual person in history, one who "stood in" for a misbehaving prince. Because the right of royalty was thought to be derived from God himself, the only person who could rightly punish a prince was a king—who was not always on hand.

Therefore, a young boy about the prince's age was selected, a lower-born companion, and when the prince would misbehave the whipping boy would get the discipline. The hope was that the prince would become so attached to his friend, whom he had grown to love, that he would keep in line so his friend didn't get flogged very often.

After we had read the book, the kids and I would discuss how the whipping boy stood in and took the punishment he didn't deserve, just like Jesus did for us. Christ took the punishment for our transgressions and paid the price for us because the King, God himself, required his rules upheld, even for his own children.

Just like the historical prince would be encouraged not to misbehave, because of his love for the one who took his punishment, we, too, should be humbled, grateful, and forewarned. Our sins cost someone—Jesus—significant pain when he paid for them on our behalf. Romans 6:1-2 refers to this when it asks and answers, "What shall we say, then? Shall we go on sinning so that grace may increase? By no means!"

I'm so grateful Christ stood in for me to take the ultimate consequence for my transgressions. I'm working hard to appreciate this by showing him that I won't abuse the privilege.

He was wounded for our transgressions, he was bruised for our iniquities: the chastisement of our peace was upon him; and with his stripes we are healed. ISAIAH 53:5, KJV

Daddy's in the Emergency Room

Recently I spent some time in the emergency room, a congregation of misery. People were in physical pain; the mothers of hurting children seemed to be in as much agony as their children. They tried to make the kids, big and small, comfortable on hard, sterile chairs and clucked over them soothingly with words I was certain they believed.

I have been in the hospital with a very sick child. My husband had to restrain our son, an infant screaming in pain, while the nurses inserted an IV into our baby's throbbing head. It was the only place with a vein big enough to be accessed.

Our daughter was once so ill with asthma that they weren't sure her breathing could be restored. Though no one said the word *death*, the absence of palpable hope spoke for itself, as did talk of intubation. I made her as comfortable as I could and then went into her hospital bathroom to silently heave out cries, a place where she couldn't see me, but God could.

The only person to call out to at a time like that is God, because he is the only one who is always loving and always present. He calls himself by many names, including Judge and Consuming Fire. But he also calls himself Abba, Daddy.

He tells us that he cares for us and brings us to safety as a good mother would. When I am down or fearful or ill or in distress of any kind, he watches over me like a mother does her sick child. He is never too tired or fearful to turn his eye away from the situations we are undergoing—he never hands us off. Scripture reassures us that he is near to the brokenhearted. He doesn't back away from us, even when we are in an emergency room of any kind: physical, emotional, mental, or spiritual.

No matter what trial you or a loved one is undergoing, you can take comfort in this: his affections and attentions, his comforts and his protections never fail. Even when one of his children doesn't physically recover, we can be certain he is taking each one up and carrying him or her safely away.

Like an eagle that rouses her chicks and hovers over her young, so he spread his wings to take them up and carried them safely on his pinions.

DEUTERONOMY 32:11, NLT

For the Love of Radar

My sister-in-law and her husband are dog lovers. One year they decided to adopt a rescue dog. The little fella's name was Radar, and he'd been badly abused, mostly by men. One day after Radar came to live with Mark and Val, my father-in-law sneezed while standing behind the dog. The noise was so shocking and scary that the pup jumped off the porch in a self-protective measure.

Radar had also been neglected. No one had ever played with him. One day, Mark took him outside to play and jumped toward him in a happy gesture. Radar was afraid. But day after day, Mark kept on in a friendly, loving manner, playing with him and loving him gently. One day, Radar let out a little, excited bark and then quickly looked around him to see where that sound had come from. He hadn't felt excitement like that before, nor felt safe to express it. What was that little bark, anyway?

He'd soon find out—he came to love playing and love barking, and he felt safe. He'd always felt safer with Val, a woman, but for him to trust a man, even when he'd been abused by other men in the past, took a giant leap of doggy faith. That faith was made possible by the constant, loving, gentle presence of a man who understood what he'd been through and was committed to bringing joy to the rest of his days.

Many of God's children have been neglected in some way, harmed by others, hurt, and perhaps even abused. God, in his unlimited love and affection, won't leave us there. Paul tells us in the book of Romans that Christ became a servant for us, and Paul blesses us in Romans 15:13: "May the God of hope fill you with all joy and peace in believing, so that by the power of the Holy Spirit you may abound in hope" (ESV).

I'm so sorry for the hurt you have suffered at the hands of others. Please understand that there is one who understands that you are reluctant to trust again. But he is patient and worthy and wants nothing more than to coax you into a good life. Won't you let him?

Like a shepherd He will tend His flock, in His arm He will gather the lambs and carry them in His bosom; He will gently lead the nursing ewes.

ISAIAH 40:11, NASB

Local Customs

Christ said, "I am the Truth"; he did not say "I am the custom."
Saint Toribio

In the Bible, like now, customs relate to the habits, backgrounds, and behaviors of societies and people.

Sometimes those customs are bad: "Keep my requirements and do not follow any of the detestable customs that were practiced before you came and do not defile yourselves with them. I am the Lord your God," Leviticus 18:30 indirectly commands us.

Customs—routine and almost unquestioned behavior—can clearly be good as well: "Jesus then left that place and went into the region of Judea and across the Jordan. Again crowds of people came to him, and as was his custom, he taught them" (Mark 10:1).

Whether discussing a society or an individual, how we customarily behave and react can become a characterizing part of our identity. When I first read the quote above, my mind went to the society around me, which is not characterized by Christlikeness. One cannot watch TV without running into coarse language and vulgar situations—and it reflects our society's customs. Upon further reflection, though, I wonder if the quote is more likely directed to you and me? Instead of wishing the culture looked like Christ, which is unlikely to happen, I wonder if my life and the tiny portions of society I can influence are customarily characterized by Christ.

When I enter a conversation, a situation, a committee, or a task, do I bring selfish ambition or envy? Am I annoyed when things do not go my way? Do I subtly promote discord (see Galatians 5:20-21)? Or, when I enter the room, do I usher in joy and kindness, gentleness and self-control?

Christ will never be the custom of the world. The Bible tells us that Satan is the god of this world (see 2 Corinthians 4:4), and the world is going to act like its god. The bigger question is, are we acting like our God? We can influence whatever portion of this world and age that God allows us to, by letting him shine out of us habitually, customarily, reflexively, taking ground inch by inch, drawing those trapped by the darkness toward the light.

Let's make it our custom!

The fruit of the Spirit is love, joy, peace, forbearance, kindness, goodness, faithfulness, gentleness and self-control. Against such things there is no law.
Galatians 5:22-23

Experiencing the Love of God

Most people love to offer a helping hand to those in need. Because God gives selflessly of himself, we are like him when we offer others love, affection, financial gifts, a word of praise or blessing, or anything else with no strings attached. I find myself feeling gratitude for people more often than I actually express my thanksgiving. Sometimes I assume they know how much they mean to me, but when I don't express it openly, I can't be sure.

It takes only a moment to thank someone—usually much less time than it took for him or her to plan and execute the care offered me.

Has someone ministered to you lately, or even long ago, in a way that sticks in your memory? Take a moment to call, write, e-mail, text, or message that person to tell him or her, even now, how much that blessing meant. Sometimes people, especially giving people, don't hear how much their affection and attentions mean to those of us who receive them. Cards sent through the mail are especially meaningful in this digital age. Next time you bake cookies, bake an extra dozen and deliver them to someone who needs encouragement. When you're at the grocery store, pick up an extra candy bar for someone sweet.

Is there someone you know who is hurting? Is there a clever, kind, and immediate way you can refresh him or her? My friend Teresa calls herself the "Secret Gardener," and she shows up and plants and weeds people's gardens for them—secretly. Part of God's mechanism for refreshing others after we've been refreshed is to partner with us as his tools. Don't wait!

Every time I think of you, I give thanks to my God.   PHILIPPIANS 1:3, NLT

A Benediction for April

Please let me offer a benediction for the close of April, the month where new life begins to spring forth into May, where it grows and flourishes, as I hope you will too. "Speak to the earth, and it will teach you. . . . Which of all these does not know that the hand of the LORD has done this?" (Job 12:8-9).

If the weather allows, take a moment today to sit or stand outside for a moment. In that quietness, drink in the eternal peace and goodness of our Lord, who blesses us every day in ways we can see and many ways we won't comprehend until we're with him in heaven.

Until then, let me offer a blessing and benediction to you. Perhaps you'll want to bless a friend too by speaking some Scripture to her, whether in person or in writing. As we come to the end of another month, I offer this prayer from the Bible for you, as a reminder that God loves you and wants you to be blessed.

Through these pages and the power of Scripture, I reach my hands out to and over you, as your sister in Christ, and pray . . .

My God will meet all your needs according to the riches of his glory in Christ Jesus. To our God and Father be glory for ever and ever. Amen.

PHILIPPIANS 4:19-20

MAY

Standing Firm

A friend from another country and I were talking about the tradition of children circling beribboned maypoles, originally instituted on May 1 for May Day. The custom reminded me of tetherball, and I was surprised to learn that she had no idea what tetherball was!

In case you're reading this from a country where kids don't play tetherball, or it's just been a few years since you've been on a playground, I'll explain a wee bit. In the center of the tetherball circle is a tall pole, like a maypole, affixed to the ground with concrete. At the top of the pole is a long rope, and at the end of the rope swings a lightweight ball, like a volleyball. Two players stand on either side of the pole and whack the ball back and forth against each other until the ball slips by one of them and the rope wraps completely around the pole. Someone will always win if the players don't quit, because the ball is "tethered" by the rope. It cannot roll or blow away.

Sometimes I feel like that ball—battered first from one side and then the next, with very few slow moments in between. Circumstances arise which whack us to and fro, back and forth. As believers, we are fortunate that we can never go completely off course if we are securely tethered to the Lord. We must wrap ourselves in prayer and praise. We must read the Word. We must engage in fellowship. We know the basics, but if you're like me, sometimes an entire day escapes without engaging in any of them.

When we mature in Christ it doesn't matter who tries to push us forward or hold us back; we will be grounded in the Word, steady. Ephesians 4:14 promises, "Then we will no longer be infants, tossed back and forth by the waves, and blown here and there by every wind of teaching and by the cunning and craftiness of people in their deceitful scheming."

No matter what circumstances are battering you today, this month, this year, keep your mind tethered to your Lord, and he will bring you peace.

You keep him in perfect peace whose mind is stayed on you, because he trusts in you. ISAIAH 26:3, ESV

Ready to Listen

A few days ago, a friend texted that she'd stopped by to see if I wanted to walk with her, but since I didn't answer the door, I missed out. The problem? I'd been home that whole morning! I didn't hear her ring the bell at all. Sad about the missed opportunity, I investigated what might have gone wrong. The issue was likely one of four things. I hadn't heard the doorbell ring because . . .

1. It had been disconnected.
2. There had been too much noise going on in my house to hear it.
3. I'd been too far away to hear it.
4. The chimes were set too soft.

How alike the situation is to my feeling that God has been silent in my life. Sometimes he is silent. Sometimes we can't hear his voice because we haven't repented of a sin. Other times, he guides by silence, provoking us to go deeper and deeper in prayer . . . or to wait. But sometimes, maybe, we can't hear him because . . .

1. We are disconnected—not going to church, hanging out with other Christians, attending a Bible study, or reading and listening to the Bible very often. "Let us not neglect our meeting together, as some people do, but encourage one another, especially now that the day of his return is drawing near" (Hebrews 10:25, NLT).
2. There is so much noise going on in our lives that we can't hear beyond the demanding human voices calling out for immediate attention. "Jesus often withdrew to lonely places and prayed" (Luke 5:16).
3. We've been too far away. Sometimes we're angry with God and don't seek fellowship. Maybe we haven't made him a priority. Maybe sin has come between us. I don't like that far-away feeling. I identify with the psalmist when in Psalm 27:9 he begs, "Do not hide your face from me, do not turn your servant away in anger; you have been my helper. Do not reject me or forsake me, God my Savior."
4. He sometimes speaks in a still small voice, as he did to Elijah. Do I tarry long enough to hear it? "After the fire a still small voice. And it was so, when Elijah heard it" (1 Kings 19:12-13, KJV).

Got the doorbell fixed. I don't want to miss out next time!

I will listen to what God the LORD says.　　　　　　　　　PSALM 85:8

129

Leaving the Better for the Best

One heartbreaking story in Scripture is that of the rich young ruler. The young man seemed to have it all—but he was wise enough to understand that Jesus was offering the one thing of which he did not feel assured. Mark 10:17 recounts, "As he was setting out on his journey, a man ran up and knelt before him and asked him, 'Good Teacher, what must I do to inherit eternal life?'" (ESV). Jesus recounted some of the commandments, and the ruler agreed, happily, that he had kept the commandments from his youth.

The next portion of Mark touches my heart because of the first seven words. "*And Jesus, looking at him, loved him*, and said to him, 'You lack one thing: go, sell all that you have and give to the poor, and you will have treasure in heaven; and come, follow me.' Disheartened by the saying, he went away sorrowful, for he had great possessions" (verses 21-22, ESV).

The young man would not give up what comforted and kept him in this world for what he could have in the next. He would not risk what reassured him now for the better solution later.

Often we Christians recount this story by cluck-clucking or tut-tutting. We would certainly not choose his path. Perhaps that is an easy conclusion for us to reach, though, because most of us aren't rich nor do we rule. But what about the choices we do make in the day to day?

I began to think about ways I make a poor trade by keeping what comforts me in the immediate against the better thing the Lord offers just around the corner. I often choose worry over his offered gift of peace. I choose control over his offered gift of provision. I choose works over his stated desire for worship.

I'm not so different from that rich young man. May the Lord help you and me make those choices, giving up the good for the better, the better for the best, every day.

Jesus, looking at him, loved him, and said to him, "You lack one thing: go, sell all that you have and give to the poor, and you will have treasure in heaven; and come, follow me."   MARK 10:21, ESV

God's Long Game

Writing devotionals is, in a way, speaking in God's stead, a holy calling, and a privilege. Don't write devotionals? You probably speak to others about the Lord, or teach or admonish or pray together. Same thing! I'm attentive to the admonition in James 3:1, "Not many of you should become teachers, my fellow believers, because you know that we who teach will be judged more strictly." That makes me a little fearful. But I also am mindful that "the one who calls you is faithful, and he will do it" (1 Thessalonians 5:24).

As I began this book, the Lord summoned a memory to my mind. I was a young girl of ten in a family that did not follow Christ. I had somehow found a copy of *The Way*, often considered the world's first user-friendly Bible. It had a paper cover with what looked like young, hip, smiling people on the front. The cover claimed that it was a Living Bible; I didn't know what that meant, but it sounded promising. Early in the pages was a list of questions a person might have and direction to the Scriptures that answered them.

Hungry, thirsty, I read for hours.

It was the first time I was drawn to God and his Word, and it was a devotional format that did it. Do you know who published *The Way*? Tyndale House, the publisher of the book you're reading right now, the publisher of all my devotionals.

In summoning that memory from deep storage, God showed me that he'd always had a plan for my life, and he'd been steering me toward the good works that he had prepared in advance for me to do. I need not be fearful of anything he brings my way.

When you look back on your life, where has God been present and active? How did he use and draw you when you were young, and how does that connect with your life now? Seeing his steady hand while looking backward gives us courage and confidence when moving forward, seemingly into the dark. Take courage. He is the only Way.

God is working in you, giving you the desire and the power to do what pleases him.   PHILIPPIANS 2:13, NLT

Iron Sharpening Iron

Recently, I received an e-mail from someone in ministry, explaining how to minister to people going through tough times. She described the wrong approach as offering suggestions or advice. Just sit, listen, and hug.

On the surface, that all seems okay. Which of us wants to be the friend known as the one always there at 3 a.m.? Which of us wants to be known as the bossy know-it-all? The answers? All of us, and none of us. And yet . . .

We are not called to be marshmallows sharpening marshmallows. Marshmallows are soft and sweet and comforting, but they don't effect change in any way. Second Timothy 4:2 exhorts us, "Be prepared in season and out of season; correct, rebuke and encourage—with great patience and careful instruction." Iron is neither soft nor sweet, but when another piece of iron is rubbed up against it—even carefully, gently—both are changed forever. Sharpened. Readied.

I think what truly bothered me was the implication that we are to be vessels, receptacles, for others to share their feelings and emotions, but we are to remain mute if not solely affirming. What that says is, "It's not really important for *you* to be here. Anyone who will listen will do." It's inviting someone to a potluck but not desiring to enjoy their contribution. You know how when you bring your favorite salad, you look to see if others are enjoying it? And if no one chooses it, you feel like your offering is somehow less than, not desired.

Wanting a specific person to be present—you, me, a next-door neighbor—implies that our particular insight, gifts, advice, comfort, offering, and presence are wanted. Not just anyone to dump on so the dumper feels better and we feel worse when it's over. When it's our turn to need a listening ear, we're to desire iron to sharpen our iron rather than a bowl to simply receive what our jug pours out.

Be a kind and loving friend; look for kind and loving friends. Just don't be, or require, a marshmallow. Your friends can make a wonderful, individual, unique contribution to your circumstances and life if you let them speak freely. Speak freely to your friends too. Life, like potlucks or salads, is best made up of many differing ingredients that add to a tasty whole, which would be sadly lacking without one key ingredient—you!

As iron sharpens iron, so one person sharpens another. PROVERBS 27:17

Experiencing the Love of God

I love that my friends are both similar to one another and different from one another in many ways. It's what my Australian friend, Dotti, calls a mixed bouquet of lollies. I agree—and my friends are just as sweet. I benefit from the different perspectives they bring to my life, the fun we have together, and the wisdom-filled talks we have. I pray that I can bless them as much and as often as they bless me. Do you have a mixed bouquet of lollies for friends? Why not invite them all over for something else just as sweet?

This salad is sometimes called Friendship Salad because each friend can bring an ingredient, or sometimes it's called Ambrosia Salad because it tastes heavenly! It's a delicious way to welcome spring with your friends.

FRIENDSHIP SALAD—WITH MARSHMALLOWS!

½ cup heavy cream
1 tablespoon sugar
4 ounces sour cream (soft cream called crema agria is best)
6 ounces mini marshmallows, approximately 3 cups (try multicolored!)
1 cup mandarin oranges, drained
1 cup canned pineapple pieces
½ cup coconut, grated
1 cup fresh green grapes, halved
1 cup pecans, chopped and toasted
½ cup maraschino cherries, drained

Have each friend bring one of the ingredients in the list above. When you're all present, whip the cream and sugar together and fold in the sour cream. When it's well blended, fold in the remaining ingredients. Let sit in the fridge for 45 minutes or so while you eat lunch, and serve your heavenly salad for dessert!

The wisdom from above is first of all pure. It is also peace loving, gentle at all times, and willing to yield to others. It is full of mercy and the fruit of good deeds. It shows no favoritism and is always sincere. JAMES 3:17, NLT

Follow the Leader

We were in town a few days ago, enjoying the spring blossoms, and we saw a couple walking their dog. The dog was at a perfect heel. The heel is important because it allows the master to lead and requires the dog to follow. Dogs that pull at their leashes are anticipating where their masters are going and are running ahead, thinking they know the right direction when perhaps they do not. The master may be choosing a new, unknown, and unanticipated path.

Dogs also try to control their masters by coming off the heel. This time, they're not anticipating where their masters are going—they are insisting on leading the way. If a dog is somewhat fearful, she may shy away from where her master is leading and head in another direction, not trusting him to pick her up or see her safely through.

The dog who walks comfortably alongside her master, though, is at peace. She looks to the master to see which way he is going, and she follows. She stops when he stops, trusting that there is a good reason, and doesn't tug to move along again before the master is ready. She looks to him for direction.

I am not a dog! But I do tug at my lead sometimes. Mostly, it's because I'm eager. I do believe that the Lord loves our enthusiasm, but I don't want to be heading left while he's trying to guide me right. Sometimes I want to control the situation. I see where he is leading, but I don't want to go that way. I try to lead, and soon enough I see how misdirected that was. I am also, from time to time, afraid. I am learning to rest in confidence that my Lord and Master will see me safely through.

What do I do, now, Lord? Where do we go from here? is a plea I often speak, and I know my brothers and sisters in Christ do too. My obedient canine buddies have the answer. If God stops, I stop. If God keeps walking, I keep walking. I am most likely to experience his loving protection and see exciting new sights when I follow his lead!

Since we live by the Spirit, let us keep in step with the Spirit.

GALATIANS 5:25

I'll Fly Away

In Washington State, where I live, salmon are very important and in the next few months will be preparing to spawn. One of the most interesting things about salmon is that they return, mysteriously, to their birthplaces to spawn. Even if the journey is hundreds or thousands of miles, and even if they had not been there since birth, they are somehow guided back.

Another creature in God's Kingdom that always returns home is the homing pigeon. Because they can find their way back even after having traveled long distances, or having been gone for a considerable amount of time, they have been used as message carriers for thousands of years. A little silver container is affixed to one of their legs, with a short, scrolled message inside. When let free, they fly to one who awaits them, to deliver the message within.

For a long time, carrier pigeons could only fly one direction—home. Then they were trained, by reward, to be able to fly in both directions—out to a chosen location and then back again. This made them especially useful in times of war.

Perhaps because my last name is Byrd, I feel a special affinity with those birds. In a way, you and I are homing pigeons too. We will eventually fly away, as the spiritual song promises we will, to our true home with Jesus: "Some bright morning when this life is over / I'll fly away / To that home on God's celestial shore / I'll fly away." But till then, he has sent us out with a message—a message to be delivered, perhaps, in the midst of a war-torn world.

Deliver the message! This was his last earthly charge to us before he, too, returned to his home with the Father. Acts 1:8 promises, "You will receive power when the Holy Spirit comes on you; and you will be my witnesses in Jerusalem, and in all Judea and Samaria, and to the ends of the earth."

Someday, we *will* fly away home. Till then, let's faithfully fly outward with the message with which we've been entrusted.

We are citizens of heaven, where the Lord Jesus Christ lives.

Philippians 3:20, NLT

You Are His Beloved

In Scripture, Jesus often refers to God as his father, but we don't see them mentioned together very often. That's why the moment in Mark 1 when Jesus is baptized and the entire Trinity is present is particularly touching. The Father, in his interactions with his Son, models for us as parents, spiritual parents, or parental figures the critical elements we should offer those under our care: affection, affirmation, and approval.

Affection: *You are my beloved.* There is nothing quite as life-giving as being told you are loved—directly, publicly. To know that he or she is *beloved*, which implies being pulled close in love, is what every child desires from a parent. I am worthy. I am valuable. I am liked and likable. I am loved!

Affirmation: You are my beloved *Son.* To know that we belong to someone, that our status is secure and immovable, that we are claimed, is something every person longs for. God the Father affirmed to Jesus, and to the world, that Jesus was his son with all the privileges, responsibilities, and honor that implies. Sonship and daughterhood cannot be removed from God's children, no matter what. God says, "I will never leave you nor forsake you" (Hebrews 13:5, ESV).

Approval: *With you I am well pleased.* Every child longs to hear that he or she is favored. *Way to go! Excellent effort! Your persistence paid off! You have a tender heart/a caring spirit/great integrity. I am proud of you.* There is no one from whom a child yearns to hear an endorsement more than his or her parents.

God, of course, is the perfect parent. Most of us were not parented by perfect parents, nor are we perfect parents ourselves. But he willingly fills the gaps where those gaps are present and active in our current lives. Listen! Do you hear your perfect, loving Father proclaiming his affection for, affirmation of, and approval of you, his beloved?

In those days Jesus came from Nazareth of Galilee and was baptized by John in the Jordan. And when he came up out of the water, immediately he saw the heavens being torn open and the Spirit descending on him like a dove. And a voice came from heaven, "You are my beloved Son; with you I am well pleased." MARK 1:9-11, ESV

Stepping Up and Out

I'm a little wary when people claim to take a step of faith, though I know we're all required to take them. In John 14:12 Jesus tells us, "Very truly I tell you, whoever believes in me will do the works I have been doing, and they will do even greater things than these, because I am going to the Father." He also commends the woman with the hemorrhage, saying her faith has made her well (see Mark 5:34). Faith was required in both situations and of course in many others.

It's clear the Lord empowers us to step out and act on our faith. But sometimes our own desires get in the way, and we step out in presumption, not faith, in order to do things *we* want to see done, even though we're not convinced God wants them to be done. When we put the "step of faith" stamp on personally motivated actions, we claim God's power and blessing over something we may desire but which is not motivated by his priorities.

There's a fine line between faith and presumption, and I don't want to cross it. Using the Lord's name and his cover for our own desires is, after all, taking his name in vain. Yikes!

Faith is a conviction in God that brings about our willing submission to doing his will, to seeing him glorified and his Kingdom strengthened. Acting in faith, then, is stepping toward what is clearly known about God's character and desires, and is always in compliance with his stated instructions—Scripture.

Presumption is based upon what we believe to be true about ourselves and is therefore what we deserve—what we're owed, what is our will, not God's. It's hard not to rationalize our own desires, though, isn't it? We can convince ourselves what we want might really be what God wants to happen.

We must ask:

1. Does what I am stepping out in faith for resonate with the stated will of God?
2. Do Scripture and other mature believers support my actions?
3. Would I feel disobedient or working against what I perceive to be his will in my life if I did not step out?
4. Will God be glorified in this, or will I be?

Pass the test? Then step right out!

Whatever you ask in my name, this I will do, that the Father may be glorified in the Son.
JOHN 14:13, ESV

Semicolon Strength

I don't have any tattoos, though some of the people I love best in this world do. I've just never felt like I wanted one. There is a faith-based movement of tiny semicolons tattooed on the inner wrist, though, that might be meaningful for almost all of us, even if only in consideration.

A semicolon (which looks like this ;) divides a sentence with two complete clauses, one on either side. The clause before the semicolon and the clause after it are closely related and equal. One is not subordinate to or lesser than the other. Why is this important? The semicolon tattoo was begun by people who had survived a suicide attempt or the desire to self-harm.

Later, it expanded to include people who had survived abuse or depression or other forms of considerable suffering that provoked hopelessness—which might be everyone alive! What the tattooed proclaim with this quiet little punctuation mark on their wrists is, *I have survived. I am still here. I will not quit. What comes after what happened to me, what I went through, is as important as what preceded it.*

It's a statement of strength and faith.

A friend once shared a truly profound statement: time doesn't heal all wounds, but God does. God understands and is present with us in our pain. He doesn't shy away from our pain or his own. He suffocated to death for us, after all. That's hard to think about, and graphic. But we must recall that if we want to fully realize that he does understand what it is like to suffer, to be reviled, to be spat upon, to be the scapegoat, to be harmed through no fault of his own.

What preceded the Crucifixion was so important—the birth of Christ was prophetic fulfillment. But his resurrection, what came after, allowed for new, abundant, and eternal life for all who believe. That's you and me!

Don't quit. Don't give up, give in, sink, or dwell on the darkness. What is coming ahead in your life is at least as important as what brought you here. Tomorrow will be bright and powerful. You'll see!

See, I am doing a new thing! Now it springs up; do you not perceive it? I am making a way in the wilderness and streams in the wasteland.   ISAIAH 43:19

Roses Have Thorns

For the first birthday I celebrated with my now-husband, he bought fifty roses at a discount stand. After returning to his apartment, he spent the night watching Westerns and clipping off thorns so he could present me with a huge bouquet of divinely perfumed—and painless—roses.

I said "yes" just a few months later. Wouldn't you have?

It was a beautiful way to begin our life together, but the truth is, the ensuing thirty years have never again delivered even a week without thorns such as illness, unemployment, loss of relationships, loss of homes, and rejection.

And yet, the years delivered roses, too, with their distinctive perfume that lingers hours after the flowers themselves have gone. At about the same time as the birth of Christ, an ancient Roman poet named Ovid said, "The sharp thorn often produces delicate roses."

Prickles guard the new bud, the blossoming flower, and finally, the rose hip that will spark new life with its death. They protect the flower from being overharvested, quickly used up, or treated less than gingerly, carefully, lovingly.

The apostle Paul relates, "In order to keep me from becoming conceited, I was given a thorn in my flesh, a messenger of Satan, to torment me. Three times I pleaded with the Lord to take it away from me. But he said to me, 'My grace is sufficient for you, for my power is made perfect in weakness'" (2 Corinthians 12:7-9).

Paul's weakness required him to be humble and dependent on God and others. The thorn protected his ministry. Conceit would have rendered him useless, as Proverbs 8 teaches that God hates pride and arrogance. He did not allow Paul to slide from either effectiveness or affection, and I don't want God to allow me to slide from his favor either.

It's the start of the rose season now, in May. God brings the roses. In his love and wisdom, God also brings the thorns.

[Job's] wife said to him, "Are you still maintaining your integrity? Curse God and die!" He replied, "You are talking like a foolish woman. Shall we accept good from God, and not trouble?" In all this, Job did not sin in what he said.

JOB 2:9-10

Experiencing the Love of God

Roses are the quintessential flower. When we think of flowers, roses often come to mind first. When my daughter played a nun in *The Sound of Music*, one of her favorite parts was having her daddy bring a bouquet of roses to her after her performance. One of the things I most love about roses is that they are useful and beautiful at the same time. Roses are often given to new mothers; they also show up at the celebration of life for a loved one who has passed away. I, too, desire to be useful all of my life, especially to bring the fragrance of Christ wherever I may travel. Let's celebrate roses—and life!

It's spring, the time for fresh life to come forward, and no flower smells more delightful, is more useful, than a rose. If you have a pot or a patch of land, find a rose plant that grows well in your area. Some of them have engaging names:

Suffer from headaches? How about an *Aspirin Rose*?

Like royalty? *Princess Diana* rose is stunning.

Love to cook? Why not plant a *Julia Child* rose? Bon appétit.

If you have no place to plant a new rose, you needn't miss out on the fun. Buy some rose water and use it to wash your face. Divine and sleep inducing! Try a tea made from rose hips—the spent buds—and add a little honey to sweeten the deal. Perhaps you might deliver a rose or two to a young person who is performing at school this season.

Do roses have thorns? Of course they do. God brings them both, with a good purpose to each. The potential for sorrow is no reason to avoid love or life or risk. The presence of thorns is no reason to avoid roses.

For everything there is a season, a time for every activity under heaven.
A time to be born and a time to die. A time to plant and a time to harvest.
ECCLESIASTES 3:1-2, NLT

Baby's Breath of Life, Part 1

Whenever I think of roses, I think of baby's breath, the flowers with tiny tips of white pearl budding at the ends of their stems. They're often tucked in alongside roses in bouquets. When I think of baby's breath, I think of a real baby I never knew, and the breath of life given her, unexpectedly, and the faith it breathed into me unexpectedly too.

We were a family in disarray, like a loosely held bunch of pickup sticks when the hand that has clasped them lets go. Our young daughter was seriously ill—again. Months before, she'd been rushed to Children's Hospital, where, after eleven hours of constant asthma treatment and a near miss admission to the ICU, her lungs finally broke open. Six months later here she was, down again, missing two more weeks of school as doctors searched their experiences and resources to help. We pleaded with God for an answer, for relief, for help. Help seemed long overdue in coming, if at all. God remained silent.

Our son, overlooked during the acute phases, was putting on a good face, but his schoolwork and attitude began to fray. My work was pushed aside and began to pile menacingly at my desk. My husband had permanent ashen circles under his eyes from many sleepless nights. Still, my daughter's waxy complexion and complete lack of energy reminded us: she's not well. We needed a break.

After two months, she seemed to turn a corner. Some kind friends offered us the use of their beachfront condo for a long weekend, and we'd been planning on it for months. Well, wouldn't you know, my daughter came down with a fever the day before we were supposed to go. We *needed* this break. We wrestled with whether we should go. In the end, after prayer, my husband and I both felt that we should go, no matter what.

So, we drove.

On the way down the coast, I prayed, *Lord, I can step forward in faith here. I don't need to hear from you, but I'd like to.*

I heard nothing. In my hour of need—silence. Have you had a time when you needed to hear from God but only heard . . . silence? Over the years I've trained myself to sense his love in the silence, knowing that while it may seem he's not there, he is acting on my behalf behind the scenes. The same is true for you!

LORD, you have seen this; do not be silent. Do not be far from me, Lord.

PSALM 35:22

Baby's Breath of Life, Part 2

God moves in a mysterious way / His wonders to perform; / He plants His footsteps in the sea / And rides upon the storm.   WILLIAM COWPER

In yesterday's devotion I began the story of a trip we took in the midst of some health issues our daughter was having. A few hours into our drive we stopped for dinner. Our daughter still looked wan and lethargic; I wondered, again, if we'd made a mistake in coming. She occasionally smiled, chattered with her brother, and then fell asleep. We continued our drive south. We were going a new way—with directions printed out from the Internet, in the days before GPS—because it was supposed to be safer, but perhaps a bit longer. After driving for some time, I asked my husband, "Should we get a map and make sure we're okay?" At this point, it was 9 p.m. He agreed, and we pulled into a highway-side Chevron in a dimly lit one-horse town.

My husband went into the gas station. Within seconds, two young people came flying out of the same station, crying and gripping one another's hands. They ran toward a van parked in the side parking lot. I tried, from my own vehicle, to see inside the gas station. I could see no one. No attendant, no customers, no husband! All the heads I could see minutes before had disappeared. Had everyone been thrown to the floor? Minutes dragged by. I couldn't leave my kids alone in the car and go see what was happening. We locked the doors. And then we prayed and prayed and prayed!

Suddenly, an ambulance screamed up. A fire truck roared in. Emergency workers poured out like ants and raced into the store. Through the window, now, I could see my husband standing, so I breathed easier. Next, I saw other heads, a woman, clutching a baby to her chest, being ushered into the back of the ambulance. A minute later my husband emerged from the store, and a young man in his early twenties pumped my husband's hand before getting into his car and following the ambulance.

As my husband got into the car, we all shouted, "What happened?"

Isn't it amazing how quickly, sometimes, life changes? I'm learning to trust God and rest in his love when things change in an instant.

Hear my cry, O God; listen to my prayer. From the ends of the earth I call to you, I call as my heart grows faint; lead me to the rock that is higher than I. For you have been my refuge, a strong tower against the foe.   PSALM 61:1-3

Baby's Breath of Life, Part 3

As I tell in the previous two devotions, a tense situation arose when we stopped to ask for directions in the middle of a family road trip. As soon as my husband walked into the store, a dad held out his baby to him and said, "Can you save my baby?" The baby's mother sat on the floor, crying inconsolably. The dad quickly told my husband that the baby wasn't breathing. My husband had been trained in all forms of CPR. He knelt, gently extended the baby's neck, opened her mouth, and began to treat her. At each moment, he felt the Lord guiding him. Soon, the baby's feather breaths responded to his. By the time the ambulance arrived, the baby was crying. *This* time, a crying baby was a good sign!

The father later told my husband the baby had had a seizure in their van on the way up from California: the first one the baby had ever had and the parents had ever seen.

As we drove away and it got quiet again, I felt the Lord speak to me. "There's your answer," he said to my heart. And I knew what he meant. Hours earlier, I had prayed, *Lord, I can step forward in faith here. I don't need to hear from you, but I'd like to.* He'd been silent then, but not for long. He'd answered me in the most compelling way. In this world, there will always be sickness and sorrow, trouble and problems. We are not in heaven yet; sickness steals upon us all and sometimes dominates our lives for a time.

But God knows the number of that baby's days, and not one of them will be snatched from her before his exactly appointed time. He made sure to get us there to keep her safe that night. In the same way, my own daughter will have health issues to manage throughout her life because we're not in heaven yet. But I can rest easy, knowing God alone has appointed her days, and he alone will make sure that she lives the full measure of them.

If he cares so much for that baby girl to direct my husband way out of our way to save her life, I know he cares for my daughter, too, and directs others to help her.

My daughter's fever was gone the next day, and we had a wonderful time. We never did get a map. But we found our way just fine.

Be on the lookout for the amazing, unusual ways God answers your prayers. When he does that, it builds our faith because we know there could have been no solution but him!

A person's steps are directed by the LORD. How then can anyone understand their own way?　　　　　　　　　　　　　　　　Proverbs 20:24

You, the Good Samaritan

Sometimes the goodness of a so-called Good Samaritan is found in seemingly trivial matters, but those small bits of grace are so important. Decent little deeds restore folks' faith in humanity.

Recently, distracted by the many things tumbling into and off the margins of my to-do list, I stopped in town to buy gas and then drove across the toll bridge to buy groceries. When I arrived, I realized—*I do not have my wallet.*

Then a slow horror crept over me. I had set my wallet on the roof of my car while I'd pumped gas but had never taken it back off!

I drove back across the bridge to the gas station. My wallet was nowhere on the ground. I slowly drove up and down all the streets again, looking to the sides. No wallet.

No money, no credit cards, no identification.

I drove back out the country road to my home—a good twenty minutes from town. I was about to call the banks and cancel my cards when a car pulled in to my driveway. A man knocked on my door. I opened it, and he looked at me, and then looked at a card in his hand—my driver's license. "Yup," he said. "It's you."

He'd seen my wallet fly off my car and had turned around himself, at his own expense of bridge fees and time lost to pick it up. Then he'd driven way out of town to return it and would have to drive way back into town to pick up where he'd left his day. He would take no money for his efforts but just asked that I pass the goodness on.

That's what the Lord is asking us to do as Good Samaritans. This Bible story shows a man who was severely wounded and a kind person who saw that the injured man was cared for. We don't need to wait for something big to do good—we can look for someone each day who could use a pat on the back, an encouraging word, a cup of coffee, or a friendly neighbor. Go and do likewise, passing along the good he has done for us, the good people do for others, little things even more often than big ones.

Pass it on!

"The next day he took out two denarii and gave them to the innkeeper. 'Look after him,' he said, 'and when I return, I will reimburse you for any extra expense you may have.' Which of these three do you think was a neighbor to the man who fell into the hands of robbers?" The expert in the law replied, "The one who had mercy on him." Jesus told him, "Go and do likewise."

LUKE 10:35-37

Doing the Impossible

In yesterday's devotion, we discussed being a Good Samaritan in small ways. Other times, the deeds of a Good Samaritan are huge. I've always been struck by how many hospital systems reflect roots in Christianity; in fact, one of the largest hospital systems near my house is Good Samaritan, named for . . . guess who!

My own medical care is a part of the Franciscan system, named for the Franciscan Brothers, founded by Saint Francis of Assisi. Dr. Tom Catena, an American Catholic missionary, is the only doctor at a Sudanese hospital with more than four hundred beds. It's named the Mother of Mercy.

In general, mainstream media is not kind to topics informed by faith, but sometimes a person's good deeds are so extraordinary that they become impossible to ignore. Such are the merciful, good deeds of an incredible Good Samaritan, Dr. Tom.

The *New York Times*, in an article titled, "He's Jesus Christ," relates that Dr. Tom works for about $350 per month with no retirement plan. He is off the electrical grid. There is often no running water. He delivers babies and helps heal those damaged by war wounds. "'I've been given benefits from the day I was born,' he says. 'A loving family. A great education. So I see it as an obligation, as a Christian and as a human being, to help.'"[3]

The village elder, a Muslim, is credited for the title of the article. In a quote from the *Times*, he said in referring to Dr. Tom, "He's Jesus Christ," because the doctor emulated consistently the care, concern, love, and healing of Jesus.[4]

Sometimes we're called to be Good Samaritans to our neighbors, and sometimes we're called all the way around the world.

Where has God called you? He *has* called you, you know. He said he has prepared good works for us in advance (see Ephesians 2:10). Your works can only be fulfilled by you. You have a unique gift to offer, a heart to reach people who can be touched only by you and your ministry. Francis of Assisi said, "Start by doing what's necessary; then do what's possible, and suddenly you are doing the impossible."

When you enter a town and are welcomed, eat what is offered to you. Heal the sick who are there and tell them, "The kingdom of God has come near to you."

LUKE 10:8-9

---

[3] Nicholas Kristof, "He's Jesus Christ," *New York Times*, June 27, 2015, http://www.nytimes.com/2015/06/28/opinion/sunday/nicholas-kristof-hes-jesus-christ.html.
[4] Ibid.

Our Perfect Pioneer

In my own devotional time, my eyes were opened to how many mentions there are of angels in the Word. While researching, I discovered something I had not consciously realized: Scripture seems to indicate that fallen angels, unlike humans, cannot be redeemed.

We're all familiar with the Fall in the Garden, how Adam and Eve sinned, thereby condemning all humanity to the consequences of sin. Because God created humans in his image and his likeness and calls them his children, he provided a means for their redemption.

Angels, however, are not created in God's image and likeness. They were created to be holy, but some angels followed Satan, a powerful angel, in sinful rebellion. Scripture tells us in 2 Peter 2:4 that some angels fell and God has damned them for their disobedience: "God did not spare angels when they sinned."

According to Psalm 8:4-5, we humans are lower in status, for a time, than the angels. "What is mankind that you are mindful of them, human beings that you care for them? You have made them a little lower than the angels."

But then our stature is clarified "and crowned them with glory and honor. You made them rulers over the works of your hands; you put everything under their feet" (verses 5-6).

Angels are messengers and servants. They worship and serve God, and he has commanded them to serve us humans as well. Hebrews 1:13-14 says, "To which of the angels has he ever said, 'Sit at my right hand until I make your enemies a footstool for your feet'? Are they not all ministering spirits sent out to serve for the sake of those who are to inherit salvation?" (ESV).

Unlike the angels, God planned to rescue us from our fall, with a most costly solution, an inestimable gift, the death and resurrection of Jesus Christ. Ephesians 2:8 reassures, "For it is by grace you have been saved, through faith—and this is not from yourselves, it is the gift of God."

In times of trouble, of difficulty, of deepest concern, we rally all our resources toward those we love. God certainly did. Can we ever doubt that he loves us?

In bringing many sons and daughters to glory, it was fitting that God, for whom and through whom everything exists, should make the pioneer of their salvation perfect through what he suffered. HEBREWS 2:10

Experiencing the Love of God

As Christians, we are called to reach out and help other people. This is a good and godly impulse, but sometimes I get tired of *doing.* I've told my husband more than once, "I don't feel like being a parent today." Some days I don't feel like reaching out, not because I don't love people or want to help them, but because I'm tired and kind of wish someone would take care of me!

That's when I need to do something to fill up my cup again. It might be taking a nap, going for a walk, reading, or baking. It also helps me to remember that not only does God help me and send other people to help me but he has also designated angels to care for me—and for you and for all who believe.

The next time you're tired of helping, it's okay to take a time-out and do something you love. You might start by baking this delicious cake! Homemade angel food cake tastes so much better than store bought. Serve with heavenly "clouds" of whipped cream!

ANGEL FOOD CAKE

1 ¾ cups superfine baker's sugar
¼ teaspoon salt
2 teaspoons cream of tartar
1 cup bleached cake flour

12 jumbo egg whites, warmed on the counter for about an hour
⅓ cup warm water
1 teaspoon almond extract

Preheat oven to 350°F.

In a large mixing bowl, use the whisk attachment of an electric mixer to blend the egg whites, water, and almond extract. Whip until the whites come to medium peaks. They should be semifirm but still lean a little bit when the whisk is removed.

In a separate bowl, blend the sugar, salt, cream of tartar, and flour with a hand-held whisk. Use a rubber spatula to gently fold the dry ingredients into the whipped whites, folding over and over until the dry ingredients are just incorporated.

Carefully spoon the mixture into an ungreased angel food cake pan. Bake for about 40 minutes before checking for doneness with a wooden skewer. When the cake is ready to be removed from the oven, it will not have a noticeable jiggle, and a skewer poked in the center will come out dry.

Cool upside down by placing the center opening of the cake pan on a tall bottle, so it hangs freely and allows air to circulate.

Once the cake is completely cool, run a knife around the side and center openings of the pan to loosen. Place the cake on a plate and serve with whipped cream and berries.

Angels are only servants—spirits sent to care for people who will inherit salvation.   HEBREWS 1:14, NLT

Tall Enough Now

When my children were young, we had step stools all over the house. When they wanted to "help" in the kitchen, they could stand on the stool and reach the counter. A bathroom stool allowed them the autonomy to brush their teeth on their own—without Mom holding them up, squishing their tummies in the process. They could step up and put their own clothes in the drawer, or step nearer to the bookshelves and select on their own what they would like to read.

My kids are grown-ups now. Adults. They definitely do not need step stools anymore! In fact, if I were to offer one to them to brush their teeth, stir the pasta sauce, or put some clothes away, they'd look at me as if I needed a nap. I'd be minimizing what they are now capable of on their own, indicating a lack of confidence in their competence.

They don't need that step up. They can stand on their own two legs and do what they need to do.

Sometimes I think I'm waiting around for someone "official" to tell me what to do, or what ministry I've been called to, or to affirm the direction I'm taking before I step up and step out on my own. I'm waiting for them—someone, anyone (who?)—to verify, to help, to lend me a hand, not because I need one, but because I want their authority to lend credence, height, to what I'm about to do. I wait till someone joins me, lifts me up, and affirms me before I reach for something new.

But you know what? I don't need that step up anymore. I did at one time, but I am no longer a babe in Christ. God has trained me, and I don't always need an assist, since I am, as Ephesians 6:10 says, "strong in the Lord and in the strength of his might" (ESV).

He speaks to me directly; he has commissioned me for his work. I can walk and lift and reach and love, "and having done all, to stand firm" (Ephesians 6:13, ESV).

We are more than conquerors, friend. Step up to the challenge!

Now get up and stand on your feet. I have appeared to you to appoint you as a servant and as a witness of what you have seen and will see of me.

ACTS 26:16

Love like Jesus Loves

Part of experiencing the love of God is to encounter it through the people in our lives. However, not every relationship is healthy. Just like a physical body needs to cure or remove unhealthy parts, our relationships need to be cured or, when there are no other options, be amputated. Otherwise, the infection poisons healthy "heart" tissue too.

Author Ellie Lisitsa, writing on the Gottman Institute's website, states, "The Four Horsemen of the Apocalypse is a metaphor depicting the end of times in the New Testament. They describe conquest, war, hunger, and death respectively. Dr. Gottman uses this metaphor to describe communication styles that can predict the end of a relationship."[5]

"The first horseman of the apocalypse is **criticism**." This is different from commenting on a project or an idea—this is a personal attack against you: how you think, look, speak, or act.

Gottman's second horseman is **contempt**. "When we communicate in this state, we are truly mean—treating others with disrespect, mocking them with sarcasm, ridicule, name-calling, mimicking, and/or body language." Contemptuous people don't care if this hurts you. According to them, you deserve it.

The post continues, "The third horseman is **defensiveness**. . . . This horseman is nearly omnipresent when relationships are on the rocks. When we feel accused unjustly, we fish for excuses so that our partner will back off." A healthy relationship will not require us to remain anxiously readied to defend ourselves.

Finally, Dr. Gottman's fourth horseman is **stonewalling**. "Stonewalling occurs when the listener withdraws from the interaction. . . . Stonewalling is when one person shuts down and closes himself/herself off from the other." The silent treatment is a power move with no heed to the other person's feelings.

Jesus tells us that we are to love others as he has loved us—the perfect model of a healthy relationship. Do you find anywhere that Jesus attacks his family, friends, coworkers, or followers through criticism and contempt, is defensive, or stonewalls others? No. He treats others with care and respect. You have every right to expect to be treated with love too.

This is my commandment, that you love one another as I have loved you.

JOHN 15:12, ESV

---

[5] Ellie Lisitsa, "The Four Horsemen: Criticism, Contempt, Defensiveness, and Stonewalling," *The Gottman Institute*, April 24, 2013, https://www.gottman.com/blog/the-four-horsemen-recognizing-criticism-contempt-defensiveness-and-stonewalling/. Used with permission.

A Careful Craftsman

When a person buys a home, she does a walk-through with an inspector. An inspector, though, can't find every potential problem in just two hours of observation. Some things can be concealed, and we have been disappointed to find hidden faults in homes we have purchased. Not with our current house, though. This time we had an extra measure of confidence.

We knew the craftsmanship would be top-notch, the tools and materials of the highest quality, and extra care put in both where it could be seen and where it would be unseen. You see, no one builds a house for his own children and makes it unsafe. The couple who built our house from the ground up built it to be their family home.

I worked my way through college, in part by being a nanny. I did this because I did—and still do—love children. But as much as I cared for and about those children I nannied, I did not love them with the undiluted devotion with which I love my own children.

It's only natural for us to feel the deepest, strongest connection to those we call our own. Your family may be your blood family, or your family of friends, or your sisters and brothers in Christ. They are your family, and those are the people you go the extra mile with, do without a meal for, or sacrifice your vacation time to care for.

There is no upgrade Jesus could have provided for you but did not. He built his house with you in mind. In John 14:2 he reassures us, "My Father's house has many rooms; if that were not so, would I have told you that I am going there to prepare a place for you?"

You, my friend, are the dearly beloved of God. You are his bride, his child, his sister, and his friend. He has loved you and carefully built you. You are, after all, the temple of his Holy Spirit.

Don't you realize that all of you together are the temple of God and that the Spirit of God lives in you?　　　　　　　　　1 CORINTHIANS 3:16, NLT

Pioneer Girls

When I was a new gardener, I was tickled to learn that there are such things as volunteer plants. I envisioned them raising their hands in the garden shop and calling out, "Here I am! Send me!"

This is the time of year when we are working on our yards and gardens, and the idea of volunteers to help that along is delightful. A volunteer plant is, essentially, one that is not specifically planted or sown into the ground by a gardener. Instead, the seed arrives via bird droppings, or clings to the pant leg of someone striding in the garden, or floats in on the wind. Sometimes they are bulbs that naturalize—they spread on their own, under the ground. In any case, they're spreading to grow and glow and claim a territory as their own, without a lot of work being put into them. I loved finding some California poppy volunteers in my own garden.

Another plant type I love is the pioneer. In case that word brings visions of women in prairie bonnets and men driving teams of horses, that's not far off. Pioneer plants are particularly hardy and are often used to repopulate areas devastated by fire or new construction or even overeager deer. They go in first, take firm hold, and make the environment safer for their shrinking daisy cousins.

I believe that God is speaking to me in my garden—after all, a garden was the first home he provided for people. Am I a volunteer? Am I able to work on my own without a lot of prodding and tending? Do I naturalize where I'm planted, making it my own? Can I be depended upon to pioneer in an area that is relatively untouched by the love of God? That most often means not in a far-off land where Christianity is unknown but in a nearby heart that has not recognized the gentle touch of God's love or one that has been scorched bare by pain and cannot, on her own, find the courage to grow again.

Are you a volunteer? A pioneer? Both?

As we have opportunity, let us do good to everyone, and especially to those who are of the household of faith. Galatians 6:10, esv

Mothers-in-Law

For a long time, I didn't discuss or teach on Proverbs 31, or if I did, it was done with a little puff of a sigh that resonated with my friends too.

I am more likely to dress in yoga pants and a T-shirt than in strength. I have never purchased a field, and I don't have any maidens to provide for. In essence, it was another place I felt I didn't measure up. The world was giving me enough comparisons; I didn't need one in Scripture, too!

Then I figured out it was a man's mother writing about the kind of woman her daughter-in-law should be (see Proverbs 31:1). More puffs of air.

I'm reminded of the joke about a young man who brings home three women and tells his mother, "I'm going to propose to one of these ladies. At the end of the night, tell me if you know which one she is." At the end of the night, his mother chooses the one who sat on the far right. The son replies, "How did you know?" His mother answers, "She was the only one I didn't like!"

And yet I now find the roles somewhat reversed. I am not only a daughter-in-law who understands on a fresh level the hopes my husband's mother had for the woman her son would marry; I understand as a mother the hopes I have for the woman *my* son will marry. Because my son is one light of my life, I want that young lady to be someone who will be an equal partner with him.

I love my daughter and my son-in-law and want them to be the best for each other. I don't favor one over the other; I favor them together. Proverbs 31 was written by a mother who saw that her son would have a tremendous role in life—king!—and wanted a suitable partner for him in sickness and in health, in youth and in old age.

I think I *like* King Lemuel's mother now. I think I *think like* her now too!

Charm is deceitful, and beauty is vain, but a woman who fears the LORD is to be praised. Give her of the fruit of her hands, and let her works praise her in the gates. PROVERBS 31:30-31, ESV

Plucked Petals

I had been struggling with some decisions and kept second-guessing myself—aloud and by text—to my family. Soon after, my son purchased some Chinese prayer lanterns for me. I was to write a brief note to the Lord on a small piece of paper and then tie it to the lantern with the light string. It could be a prayer request or a promise to release a situation or circumstance to God for good.

I decided to try it out. I tied my prayer to the string and lit the wick on the lantern, and the heat from the flame powered it skyward. It rose to perhaps twenty feet, and then the lantern was consumed, along with the prayer request and my fears. Once the whole package burned up, it was gone. I could not gather and reassemble the ashes, could I? It was a public acknowledgment that I had permanently given the situation to my Lord.

First Peter 5:7 encourages us, "Give all your worries and cares to God, for he cares about you" (NLT). I do give him my cares and worries repeatedly, I really do. It's just that I snatch those worries and cares back later when I can't see his hand at work quickly enough.

If you don't have lanterns, a lovely spring flower with pretty petals will do the trick. Pluck the petals out and place them in your palm. After you've prayed, blow the plucked petals out of your hand and let them fall where they may. We must do that with much of life, mustn't we? Let things fall where they may. We have control over almost nothing. But God has control over everything. Hebrews 1:3 reassures us, "He upholds the universe by the word of his power" (ESV). Even in the great power of that majesty, his eye tarries on the smallest of us. "Are not two sparrows sold for a penny? And not one of them will fall to the ground apart from your Father" (Matthew 10:29, ESV).

All circumstances are in the firm control of God's good hands. Let your prayers and promises and hurt and pain fly heavenward, and he will receive them, and us, into his steady care.

The king's heart is a stream of water in the hand of the LORD; he turns it wherever he will.
                                                            PROVERBS 21:1, ESV

Experiencing the Love of God

"Let not your heart be troubled," His tender word I hear,
And resting on His goodness, I lose my doubts and fears;
Though by the path He leadeth, but one step I may see;
His eye is on the sparrow, and I know He watches me.
CIVILLA D. MARTIN

I love thinking about the fact that our great God, with so many details to keep track of, is attentive to the smallest things, like sparrows or the number of hairs on our heads. It reminds me that no matter how difficult my circumstances are, I am not alone. He cares for those "lesser" creations with diligence and affection, so how tenderly and attentively will he care for us, made in his image?

One of the most beautiful salads can also be one of the most surprising—a salad that has been sprinkled with lovely flower petals! One of my favorite salad flowers is the viola. These flowers are so pretty, with their wide-open "eyes" that remind me of God's caring, constant gaze.

A quick Internet search will turn up many other flowers that have edible petals, and some are certain to grow near you. Pansies are first to appear, and then as the season progresses I love rose petals, which taste sweet as you might imagine. (They can also be sugared or candied easily, if you'd like a bit of sweetness in your salad.) Later in the season come the fragrant petals of carnations, and I adore peppery red and gold nasturtium blooms mid to late summer.

If you serve the salads to family and friends, they may be surprised at first, but pleasantly so after tasting them. A simple oil and vinegar dressing works best, with any kind of greens, so the power of the petals shines through.

Are not two sparrows sold for a penny? And not one of them will fall to the ground apart from your Father. MATTHEW 10:29, ESV

A Welcome Refreshment

There is no flavor that says, "Summer is coming" more clearly than mint. It's fresh, green, and bright, just like the season ahead. A neighbor once gave me a cutting from her own plants.

"Will this really take hold?" I asked, holding up a feeble four-inch stem with a tangle of venous roots. "Oh, yes," she assured me. "In fact, if you're not careful, it will cheerfully overrun your garden." I looked at the wan little straggler. Hardly seemed possible!

I soon found out my friend's words about mint were true. I'd kept it moist, at first, and then got busy and unintentionally ignored it. No matter—it refused to be ignored! As Jeremiah 17:8 proclaims, "They will be like a tree planted by the water that sends out its roots by the stream. It does not fear when heat comes; its leaves are always green. It has no worries in a year of drought and never fails to bear fruit." The mint grew vigorously, to my initial delight. But then it started to cross over its own boundaries and worm its way into space intended for other plants, choking them out. Now *they* were the wan stragglers. Mint is delightful, but it became greedy, wanting to place itself and its sweet taste and refreshment everywhere, claiming every open spot of land.

My neighbor came back and nodded, then smiled. "Mint is like a well-intentioned but overly involved friend," she said. "If you don't keep it potted, it will soon take over."

I asked her if she was, er, referring to the present company, and she cheerfully reassured me, no. But there are times when all of us can overshare, overask, overdemand, even overvisit. I like for my kids to respond to my texts quickly. I love their presence on all holidays. I enjoy seeing my friends often. But our friends and children all have busy lives too, and as much as we like them to text, call, or spend time with us, it's important to mind our boundaries, so they have open spaces available for others who love them.

This can be true too when it comes to sharing the spiritual wisdom and insights we've learned along the way. A word of wisdom now and then is welcome; too much direction might become bossy and preachy.

I'm working on keeping good boundaries, personally and spiritually. That way, I'll be a welcome refreshment and not a well-meaning menace!

Don't visit your neighbors too often, or you will wear out your welcome.

PROVERBS 25:17, NLT

Follow Me

My husband and I spent a recent Memorial Day on a day trip. We drove by Fort Casey, once used to guard the Puget Sound. It remained an army installation until after World War II.

Driving by the old fort brought back memories for my husband, a former infantry officer. "There's old Splinter City," he teased as we drove by the sparse barracks. "They called it Splinter City because that's what you got cleaning the place: splinters."

I began to express my dismay at the conditions the men and women who protect our country face, but he stopped me. "No, it's important to break future soldiers of their civilian comforts. That's part of what makes them a soldier, helps them keep their eyes on the mission at hand and not on themselves." He smiled at me. "No one expects boot camp to be comfy. We're preparing to be hit—it's not if, it's when."

I spent some quiet time on that drive wondering if I had grown too needy of "civilian comforts" to take on the mission God has for me, which is bound to have difficult, troubling times too. Jesus cares for us more than the sparrows; he tells us not to worry about what to eat or drink or wear. He is our defender and protector, our advocate.

But he also calls us soldiers. We're not here on earth solely to enjoy the abundant life. He commissioned us with these words: "You will receive power when the Holy Spirit comes upon you. And you will be my witnesses, telling people about me everywhere—in Jerusalem, throughout Judea, in Samaria, and to the ends of the earth" (Acts 1:8, NLT). Will we have opposition to this? Absolutely. Jesus teaches, "If the world hates you, keep in mind that it hated me first" (John 15:18).

Are we waiting till everything seems perfect and comfortable before moving forward? Does the confirmation of a calling mean that everything has neatly lined up and everyone approves? That may never come. The United States Infantry motto is Follow Me. That's exactly what our ultimate commanding officer has charged us to do, many times over, even when people disagree or circumstances look uncertain.

Join with me in suffering, like a good soldier of Christ Jesus. No one serving as a soldier gets entangled in civilian affairs, but rather tries to please his commanding officer. 2 TIMOTHY 2:3-4

Morning Breaks, Eternal

What then of death? Is not the taps of death but the first call to the reveille of eternal life?   GENERAL GEORGE S. PATTON JR.

Memorial Day is the day when we show honor and respect to those who have fallen while serving the country as members of the military. Cemeteries are visited and flags displayed. In many places, there is a roll call of honor. My church recognizes those fallen in the military but also takes the occasion, on a near Sunday, to read the names and show the photos of those in our congregation who graduated from earth to heaven in the previous year.

That always reminds me of Hebrews 11, often called the "roll call of the faithful," as the author of Hebrews reminds his readers, and all of us, of many who walked the path of faith before us, holding them up as examples. That section ends with Hebrews 12:1, reminding us that we "are surrounded by such a huge crowd of witnesses to the life of faith" (NLT).

Patton's quote is a good reminder that all of us have a limited time here, and we are to run the race or fight the battle we've been given with courage. Many are our witnesses. The three bugle calls of a soldier's life mentioned by Patton in his quote are

First call: it sounds a warning that the personnel will prepare to assemble.
Reveille: meaning *awaken* in French, it's the signal to arise.
Taps: the last, mournful bugle call of the day, it's played to signal that lights are to be extinguished and is sounded at the completion of a military funeral ceremony.

The Lord calls us (see 2 Timothy 1:9), and then we must arise (see Romans 13:11). When our mission is completed, he will call us home to be with him (see 2 Corinthians 5:8). Do not fear death. It is merely leaving the fort to return to the safety and comfort of home.

When the trumpet of the Lord shall sound, and time shall be no more,
And the morning breaks, eternal, bright and fair;
When the saved of earth shall gather over on the other shore,
And the roll is called up yonder, I'll be there.
JAMES BLACK

Wake up, sleeper, rise from the dead, and Christ will shine on you.

EPHESIANS 5:14

A Benediction for May

May is the end of spring and the beginning of the transition to summer. It's fitting, then, that we neared the end of the month with a devotional that offers assurance about our transition from this life to the next. When someone on earth dies, he or she leaves an inheritance to those left behind. Wonderfully, when a believer dies, that person comes into his or her inheritance, one which awaits us in heaven too. How delightful to enjoy both seasons in life!

As I have at the end of previous months, I'd like to offer you a benediction from the Bible, a prayer of God's favor, expressing confidence in his love and care. In your transition to a new season, I celebrate your growth and commission you for the challenges to come. I pray that you enjoy your life here on earth . . . and that you look forward to a glorious life ahead with Jesus Christ. Through these pages and the power of Scripture, I reach my hands out to and over you, as your sister in Christ, and pray . . .

Blessed be the God and Father of our Lord Jesus Christ! According to his great mercy, he has caused us to be born again to a living hope through the resurrection of Jesus Christ from the dead, to an inheritance that is imperishable, undefiled, and unfading, kept in heaven for you, who by God's power are being guarded through faith for a salvation ready to be revealed in the last time. 1 PETER 1:3-5, ESV

JUNE

Watchful and Wary

An easy mistake when learning a foreign language is to assume that a word that sounds similar to a word in English means the same thing in your new tongue. For example, in French *blessé* sounds like it should mean "blessed," but in reality it means "wounded." You wouldn't want to make the mistake of offering to *blessé* someone! *Une librairie* is a bookstore, not a library, so don't leave without paying for your novel. This concept is called *faux amis*—false friends. You think the word denotes one thing, an easily assumed meaning; instead, it means something misleadingly different.

Because I've written for young women I've become familiar with the word *frenemy*. We adults face frenemies, too: people pretending to be friends or allies but who are enemies or rivals behind the mask. False friends. In fact, as Christians, the most potent, best-cloaked frenemy we have is the devil himself.

None of us allows a known enemy to tempt us forward, to encourage us to do the wrong thing. We avoid enemies because we know, by the very definition, that they mean to do us harm. An uncloaked enemy is not a terrible threat— we see the potential peril right before us. However, Satan does not appear to us as an enemy—he comes cloaked as an angel of light—as do those who are working for and with him. Second Corinthians 11:13-15 warns us, "Such people are false apostles, deceitful workers, masquerading as apostles of Christ. And no wonder, for Satan himself masquerades as an angel of light. It is not surprising, then, if his servants also masquerade as servants of righteousness."

You can expect false friends and deceitful workers in the most unexpected, seemingly light places. So be on guard! A frenemy presents as having your best interests at heart—*Did God really say . . .*—but has your downfall in mind. Hebrews 10:24 offers one test of a true friend: "Let us consider how we may spur one another on toward love and good deeds."

Does this person, activity, or thought lead you closer to or further away from Jesus and all that he stands for?

Be alert and of sober mind. Your enemy the devil prowls around like a roaring lion looking for someone to devour. 1 PETER 5:8

ThisClose

My husband and I took a little trip away, and when I returned my dear friend Dawn texted me to say, "I hope you had a good time, but I've really missed chatting while you were away." It made my day. A different friend had a welcome-home dinner for us, and while I loved her cooking, what was the most fun was sitting around the table together, recounting our lives, sharing food, and laughing.

My husband has told me that in war, the soldiers are not fighting for home or country so much as they are for the well-being of their fellow soldiers beside them—their friends. As soldiers of Christ, there's a bit of that from time to time in our lives, isn't there? Fighting for the brother or sister right next to us. But mostly, our friends are who we share our tears and fears and laughter and time with. The people we most love to be with and to hear from. The people who always have our best interests in mind and tell us the truth when we need to hear it and love us in all our unvarnished brokenness.

After I had published a few books, one of the most amazing, awe-striking experiences I had was when I became friends—actual in-the-flesh friends—with authors whose books I had read and whose writing I so admired. I still admired their work, but now I could have lunch with them and talk with them and pray with them. What a trip for me to be a conference roommate with a writing hero. Fangirl moment! Yet what mattered to me most was our growing intimacy as friends.

Jesus has said he wants to be our friend. Friend! He's Lord, he's Savior, he's Creator, he's Master. But he also wants to be a friend. Fangirl moment! By calling us friends, he's signaling that he does not want to be far off and high up only, but nearby and *thisclose*, just like our other friends.

He takes pleasure in your company, friend. He really does.

No longer do I call you slaves, for the slave does not know what his master is doing; but I have called you friends, for all things that I have heard from My Father I have made known to you. JOHN 15:15, NASB

Experiencing the Love of God

I admit, there is one thing that makes me sad with regard to friends—it's when I am often, or always, the initiator. I love it best when I invite a friend for a walk, and she invites me for coffee next time, or we have a couple over for dinner, and then they invite us to a concert a few months later. It makes me feel as though my company is as desirable as theirs is.

When I'm the only one asking to do things or to chat or get together, I leave with a little insecurity. Is she trying to put some distance between us? Am I not as important to her as she is to me? Did I do something wrong? Am I not worth the time and effort to reach out and plan to see? I know she is busy, I'm busy, and yet . . .

Jesus knew how we'd interpret it when he called us friends—we all know what a friend means and is supposed to do. I must ask myself:

1. Do I always wait for Jesus to initiate our conversations or do I seek him regularly?
2. Do I only go to him when I need things, or am I pleased to share bits of my life with him too? Do I ask him as many questions as I talk about myself?
3. Is he verbally welcomed in my home, at my dinners, or at other activities I plan?
4. Do I have an environment (media, music, etc.) where he feels honored and welcomed?

Why not spend some time answering these questions yourself, and then decide how you will reach out to the Lord in friendship today?

You are my friends if you do what I command.   JOHN 15:14

All That Glisters

After Moses disappeared up Mt. Sinai so God could give him the Ten Commandments, the people were dismayed when he did not reappear within their comfortable timeline. They said, "Make us gods who will go before us. As for this fellow Moses who brought us up out of Egypt, we don't know what has happened to him" (Exodus 32:23). This fellow Moses' brother, Aaron, instructed them to bring all their gold so they could melt it and then form it into the shape of a calf, an Egyptian god that they could *see* and worship. The Israelites made a golden calf because that seemed godlike to them.

Gold, the human symbol of power and wealth, is but a letter away from God, who is actual power and wealth itself, but he doesn't always present that way.

Isaiah 53:2 tells us that when Jesus arrived, he was nothing to look at. "He had no beauty or majesty to attract us to him, nothing in his appearance that we should desire him." Not only that, but he did not immediately deliver freedom from oppression, nor with limited exceptions, freedom from illness or sorrow or the many other troubles that entangle us here on earth. He was not what the people thought God would look like.

This reminds me of a wonderful quote used by such notables as Chaucer, Shakespeare, Tolkien, and perhaps even in Aesop's fables: "All that glisters is not gold" (Shakespeare's version). Sometimes what *glisters*, an old English word for "glitters," is blasphemy, while real treasure is stored in simple pottery (see 2 Corinthians 4:7) or presented as a man whose appearance we do not desire.

I can't be too hard on the Israelites, upon honest reflection. So often we think our blessings will be monetary and will look like what we expect blessings to look like—health, wealth, and success. I've promised God: "If you give me a lot, I will share it!" The test of what I'll do tomorrow is what I do today. Am I sharing generously the real treasure he's given me?

I am. But I'd love to do more. We have an unlimited supply of the very best treasure to share.

Peter said, "I have no silver and gold, but what I do have I give to you. In the name of Jesus Christ of Nazareth, rise up and walk!" ACTS 3:6, ESV

No Ceiling, No Limit

Recently, I worked on a charity committee, which included both silent and live auctions. It was my first time on such a committee, and it was great fun—with a strong spiritual takeaway, as you'll see!

In a silent auction, a clipboard is placed in front of the item that is being auctioned. A person may come by and put his or her name on the list, bumping up the price in predetermined increments. The auction closes at a given time, and whoever is the highest bidder takes home the item.

A live auction is even more fun—the energy and competition cultivated by a good auctioneer make it an entertaining spectacle even if you're not bidding. Ahead of the event, the "floor" is set—the lowest acceptable bid amount—and that's where the offers begin. Bidders are handed paddles with numbers on them. When they'd like to increase the bid on a certain treasure, they lift the paddle to indicate they'll meet the new price. The auctioneer tries to drive the price higher and higher with promises and by teasing and cajoling—and the bidding can get competitive. Most bidders have a predetermined "ceiling" that they will not go beyond. No matter how much they want those football tickets, they will not pay more than $1500 for them. The item just isn't worth an additional dollar. But when something is very much desired, the person who wants that item will keep the paddle raised to ensure he or she pays the top price to take home the prize, no matter the cost.

I reflected that evening that there was no "ceiling" on the amount that God paid for us. He did not say that we were worth a ram, or a pair of doves, or a grain offering, but no more. Instead, you and I commanded an amazing fee; "God bought you with a high price" (1 Corinthians 6:20, NLT).

The next time you wonder if he loves you, remember: he withheld nothing, not even his own son, to purchase you. You are his treasure in every season, at every hour, and in every circumstance.

Since he did not spare even his own Son but gave him up for us all, won't he also give us everything else? ROMANS 8:32, NLT

Easy on the Salt

When our son was a little boy, he would sing songs from the backseat, especially on the way home from church. One of his favorites was "We salt thee, we salt thee, we salt thee, oh Lord." It was so cute to listen to that we didn't have the heart to tell him we were to exalt the Lord, not salt him.

Although we are not truly supposed to salt God, we are called to salt the world around us. In the ancient world, salt had four main purposes: to preserve food, to act as a disinfectant, to add flavor to food, and to serve as a means of payment—hence, *salary*. Salt was desirable, and the Lord told us that we were to be salt and light (see Matthew 5:13) in the world.

While a little salt is desirable, too much salt is ruinous. I made an aioli a few weeks ago, blending some pickled peppers with mayonnaise and olive oil. I forgot that the mayo was already salted, and I added salt to the blend without tasting first. It was so salty I had to throw it away, wasting good ingredients. Disinfecting a wound with salt is good until you overdo it and it begins to rub the wound raw rather than help in healing.

In Judges 9:45, after Abimelech captured the city of Shechem, he killed the people and then salted the ground, effectively killing it, too. Nothing grows from an oversalted field.

I've been blessed to walk with the Lord for many years, but I do remember when faith and its precepts were all new to me. Fed too much salt and light at one time by well-meaning, older Christians, I became overwhelmed and nearly blinded. I couldn't take it in. It was a good lesson to me to offer a bit of truth, a morsel of advice, a little guidance along with a lot of love rather than the other way around. Mark 9:50 tells us, "Salt is good for seasoning" (NLT). A little is better than none, and better, in fact, than too much.

Yes, I do want to salt people. But to exalt God in the process, I'll shake on a little at a time.

You are the salt of the earth.   MATTHEW 5:13

Keep Sowing

For the past few years, some of my plants seem to have gone haywire. Plants that should blossom only once, like my lilacs, have not only bloomed earlier but have bloomed twice. Plants that had regularly produced a vivid display of color seem tired and petered out now, offering only a small handful of sweet-smelling beauties. I don't know if it's because the climate is changing or if it's just the natural course of the earth following varying patterns, but even the apple trees in my neighborhood are off; they are blooming a few weeks late.

Those blooms, of course, are the promise of the fruit to come. The bees come and pollinate those lovely flowers, and then each pollinated flower will yield an apple from its center. No blooms, no fruit. No bees, no fruit. It's a delicate dance between varied participants, and both bloom and bee will have disappeared before the fruit appears, to the local deer's delight, in autumn. I can't control these blooms and blossoms; I can only be a good gardener.

It seems to me that is often how it is during long seasons of praying for something or someone, with no visible fruit appearing. I have prayed for years for friends and family with, it seems, little or no yield for my effort. I have asked God to fix a situation without any hope that he is tending to my requests and will bring them to the fruition I desire.

And yet . . . my husband had told me that he prayed for me many years before we met. Under the guidance of a wise youth pastor, he began praying for me when I was barely a teen and in an unbelieving family. I struggled through trials, but looking back now, I can see how God brought people to help me. Was it due to my husband's prayer? I believe so. I do not think anyone else was praying for me during those years.

One of the benefits of getting older is that it's easier for us to see the long game in the rearview mirror. Don't give up on your prayers; keep sowing to the future. In due season, the fruit will appear.

I tell you, you can pray for anything, and if you believe that you've received it, it will be yours.   MARK 11:24, NLT

Fishing for Keepers

One day my father-in-law, who was a State Patrol officer, came home and asked my husband, still a boy, to come and talk with him.

"Another patrolman saw you fishing in that, er, pond," my father-in-law said. "That's not a good idea."

My husband, confused, said, "I wasn't fishing today, only throwing rocks." His dad, visibly relieved, told him that he should not now, or ever, fish in that pond. "It's a septic pond," he said and explained what that meant. "You're not going to catch anything out of it that you want to keep."

Often, I go looking for affirmation or affection from places that are not going to offer anything to me that I can keep. Social media, for example, has great power to make us feel connected with other people, but it can also make us feel less popular, less attractive, less spiritual, less desirable. Sometimes people, even unconsciously, offer us affirmation but without clean intentions—they are manipulating us with praise to get us to agree or conform. The illustration of the septic pond has given me a whole new understanding of fishing for compliments!

Even the best-meaning people, people who love us through thick and thin, are still human and subject to the same weakness we all are. So where do we fish, then, to ensure we always catch something we want to keep? I love the line from Edward Mote's hymn, written two hundred years ago: "I dare not trust the sweetest frame, but wholly lean on Jesus' name." Money offers a temporary sense of power, but it's lost as soon as it's spent. Popularity rests on what you can do for someone rather than what they can do for or with you. "God shows his love for us in that while we were still sinners, Christ died for us" (Romans 5:8, ESV).

Cast your line toward the one who loves you unconditionally. He will always give you the affection, affirmation, love, and attention you need, and what he offers is always a keeper!

We know how much God loves us, and we have put our trust in his love.
God is love, and all who live in love live in God, and God lives in them.

1 JOHN 4:16, NLT

The Best Medicine

Everyone must go to the dentist, and most of us are not happy about it when we do. The sound of the drill, the smell of the antiseptic, that rubber dam . . . you're quaking now, aren't you? I'm going tomorrow and would be quaking except for . . .

Zakiya.

My dentist is a wonderful professional, a dental rock star, and I trust her implicitly. But the part of the visit that brings a smile to my face and some ease to my knit-together shoulders by the time I hit the chair is her dental assistant, Zakiya. Zakiya has the brightest, most wonderful laughter—the kind of laughter that resonates throughout a room and brings a reflexive smile to anyone who hears it even if they can't see her. Do you know someone with a laugh like that? I've only known a few people with that kind of laughter. It's a gift. The sound of it changes the world.

According to the Mayo Clinic, laughter will stimulate the heart, lungs, and muscles, as well as increase endorphins—happy hormones—in the brain, which improves a person's mood. The Clinic says that laughter is a great stress reliever and soothes the physical symptoms of stress.[6] Who doesn't need lots of the above? Laughter is good medicine!

Some years ago, I saw, pinned to the bulletin board in a Sunday school classroom, a picture of Laughing Jesus. It was a picture of our Lord in a full-on chuckle, a happy little sheep slung around his shoulder and children giggling nearby. I couldn't help but smile. We've all seen so many pictures of the suffering Jesus that we may perhaps have forgotten that he enjoyed life, and we should too. We may have been brought up to think that God is a stern finger-wagger, ready to judge, but he is a God of joy and love too. Just think of the fruit of the Spirit—all positives!

One of the best ways to experience the love of God is through laughter. Yes, difficult circumstances regularly present themselves. Just think about what God sees—not only our pain but everyone's. And yet he has given us laughter, too. Laughter lifts us over the "whitecaps" of life.

A cheerful heart is good medicine, but a broken spirit saps a person's strength.   PROVERBS 17:22, NLT

---

[6] "Stress relief from laughter? It's no joke," Mayo Clinic, April 21, 2016, http://www.mayoclinic.org /healthy-lifestyle/stress-management/in-depth/stress-relief/art-20044456.

Experiencing the Love of God

One of the most wonderful pieces of artwork I've ever seen (and I've been to a lot of fine museums) is a sketch of the Lord Jesus laughing. It's not often that I think of him smiling or laughing, and I don't know why not. Yes, he had a mighty task, he faced tremendous opposition, and he had plenty of sorrow. Yet he made time for pleasure and family and friends. He also created us to laugh. It brings a smile to my face to imagine him smiling, happy with his world and his people, including you and me.

When you're down, you might seek out that sketch of him on the Internet. And when there are times when you need a laugh, make time to do just that. What makes you laugh? A phone call with a good friend? A favorite comedy movie? Reading comic books? Here's an instant shot of laughter: one of my favorite videos on YouTube is a compilation of babies laughing. Go ahead. Find one and watch it and tell me if you're not laughing alongside them within a few minutes. I dare you!

Tell the Zakiyas in your life (see the devotion for June 9) how their laughter lifts you up, and spend more time in their company (except not at the dentist!). Laugh at yourself. Laugh with your friends. Laugh with the Lord and imagine him laughing along with you.

Don't wait!

God blesses you who are hungry now, for you will be satisfied. God blesses you who weep now, for in due time you will laugh. Luke 6:21, NLT

The Perfect Spouse

June is often referred to as the "marriage month," and for many, it's an anniversary celebration. However, for those who wanted to but never married, or are divorced or widowed, the marriage month can be bittersweet. Even those with seemingly happy marriages struggle through troubled times and sometimes feel misunderstood, unloved, or unappreciated, because everyone's spouse is human, imperfect, and subject to sin.

However, there is one who is perfect. He presents himself, metaphorically, as the husband of his people—Israel, and then the church. This month, let's discover the joy to be found in the tender union offered to us, married or not—in the holy pledge between the Lord and his people. He and me. He and thee. We.

Wedding vows signify a covenant—a binding agreement; a pact; a solemn, legal vow between two parties. In the Old Testament, a covenant was sealed by both parties walking between the halves of a slain animal. The implication was "So be it for me if I break this agreement"—your very life was forfeit. Touchingly, when God formed a covenant with Abraham, he precluded Abraham from walking between the animals but still committed himself. Thus, while he displayed his desire to be covenanted and his commitment to faithfulness, he also signaled his understanding of our human frailty.

And yet he still desires his imperfect people to be faithful, loving, and present. We must seek to keep up our end of the covenant. Who among us does not yearn to tell our Lord, as Ruth said to Naomi, "Where you go I will go, and where you stay I will stay. Your people will be my people and your God my God" (Ruth 1:16). That we can do, fellow Christ-lover! Traditional marriage vows are such a part of our culture that I thought it would be delightful to experience God's love and better understand how we might express our covenantal love for him through them. I hope that no matter your marital status, this exploration will bring you delight and joy.

Ready? Let's go!

I delight greatly in the LORD; my soul rejoices in my God. For he has clothed me with garments of salvation and arrayed me in a robe of his righteousness, as a bridegroom adorns his head like a priest, and as a bride adorns herself with her jewels.   ISAIAH 61:10

Fidelity

When we commit to a marriage, we forsake all others—putting every other potential romantic and life partner aside, committing exclusively before God and man to one person. Our spouse should be our primary human focus, closest friend, and ally, the person to whom our fidelity is pledged. It's a freewill choice—a marriage whereby one partner is coerced is not valid. Likewise, when we promise ourselves to God, we make a freewill choice. "Choose this day whom you will serve," Joshua 24:15 (ESV) commands. In Luke 14, Jesus asks us to consider the cost before pledging ourselves to him so that once committed we are "all in." From this day forward. No turning back.

The Lord could have rejected us, humankind. Time and again humanity turned toward idols in fear or pride, grumbled against him, and fell away. And yet because of his nature, he did not forsake us but held onto us, remaining faithful, as he still does today. "If we are unfaithful, he remains faithful, for he cannot deny who he is" (2 Timothy 2:13, NLT).

But he does, understandably, want our fidelity. "Be careful not to forget the covenant of the LORD your God that he made with you; do not make for yourselves an idol in the form of anything the LORD your God has forbidden. For the LORD your God is a consuming fire, a jealous God" (Deuteronomy 4:23-24). Most of us desire to be faithful too!

A fearless self-examination might show that the bulk of our affections, commitments, concerns, and focus go to people and places before and instead of him. Do we truly depend on him, or on our own efforts? Do we give him the best slice of our time, affections, and energies, or does something or someone else receive those? Do I express my love to God as fully as I would want my spouse to express his to me?

Join me in trying to offer that goodness to God, to have and to hold from today onward.

I will take you as my own people, and I will be your God.   EXODUS 6:7

For Better or Worse

I had taken off my high-heeled wedding shoes after my wedding reception and somehow had neglected to pack any shoes in my travel bag. The next morning, early, I dialed the number of my apartment and hoped that my roommate would pick up the phone. She did! She plucked a few pairs from our closet and brought them to me in time for my honeymoon flight.

On the plane, I told my husband I thought that was symbolic to starting our marriage—with no shoes we couldn't run anywhere, or not very fast. He laughed, and I laughed.

Our marriage has had many high notes—lovely children, comfortable homes, delightful family and friends, churches that fed our hearts and souls. But we also have had some very dark corridors to make our way down.

Infertility. Serious illness. Financial disaster. Depression. Job loss. Home loss. Churches helmed by predators. Betrayal by family and friends. School and work that was so consuming we went for days or weeks without conversation or intimacy. Sometimes those situations brought us together, but sometimes we set upon one another, looking for someone to blame.

Despite it all, we did not walk away from each other. We had times where walking away was tempting, but friends always circled back to us to remind us that we had no shoes to flee in.

When our Lord commits to us, he does so fully. He promises he will never leave or forsake us. Never. I make mistakes, I sin, I promise to learn a lesson only to have to confess, repent, and relearn it over and over. I ignore him for weeks, caught up in my busyness. Yet I find his faithfulness and love as soon as I turn to him.

We can be fickle brides, we humans. When things go wrong, instead of instantly turning to God, we sometimes turn on him. *Why did you let this happen? Why don't you fix it? How can I serve you if you won't . . . don't . . . can't . . . ?* And yet time always, always, always proves him true. For better or worse, no matter the circumstance, he will not leave you. Don't turn away from him either.

The LORD your God goes with you; he will never leave you nor forsake you.
DEUTERONOMY 31:6

172

JUNE 14

For Richer, for Poorer, in Sickness and in Health

In Job 1, Satan presents himself to God, saying he's been watching what has been happening on earth. God, rather proud of one of his own, asks him, "Have you noticed my servant Job? He is the finest man in all the earth. He is blameless—a man of complete integrity. He fears God and stays away from evil" (verse 8, NLT).

I always cringe a little reading that, knowing what must come next.

"Satan replied to the LORD, 'Yes, but Job has good reason to fear God. You have always put a wall of protection around him and his home and his property. You have made him prosper in everything he does. Look how rich he is! But reach out and take away everything he has, and he will surely curse you to your face!'" (verses 9-11, NLT).

You'll remember, Satan causes him to lose his property, his animals, and his children. Even so, Job remains faithful to God. "In all of this, Job did not sin by blaming God" (verse 22, NLT).

Satan returns in Job 2, accusing Job of being faithful only because God has preserved his health. God allows Satan to afflict Job once more, confident in his man, and Satan does. "So Satan left the LORD's presence, and he struck Job with terrible boils from head to foot" (verse 7, NLT).

Although Job's wife encourages him to curse God, Job is faithful. He responds, "Should we accept only good things from the hand of God and never anything bad?" (verse 10, NLT).

In the end, God restores Job's fortunes and health. He remains an example of a God-lover whose fidelity while undergoing disaster was so strong that God knew he could be tested and prevail.

Although Job was rich when he started, he had nothing but his faith, his love, and his knowledge of his Lord to offer God during his time of testing. And yet—that faith was what was most valuable to the Lord. Job knew God, and God knew Job. Can we be committed to our Lord in financially shaky, sick-as-a-dog times too? He'll restore us someday, and we will have given what he most desires.

I don't want your sacrifices—I want your love; I don't want your offerings—
I want you to know me.   HOSEA 6:6, TLB

To Love and to Cherish

On a recent trip, we purchased gifts for friends and family and special mementos for ourselves. Some of the gifts were durable and hardy—books, clothing, and jewelry. It seemed that my most important treasures, though, were fragile. I found an antique teacup and saucer set from the time of Queen Elizabeth II's parents; it did not have a single chip on it, and I wanted to keep it that way. How to get it safely home?

Our suitcases are soft sided. That means as the various hands drag and pull and lift and toss them onto conveyor belts and into and out of the bellies of airplanes, they are likely to hit some hard surfaces. We didn't want our gifts damaged, so we wrapped them in our clothes, carefully, thoroughly. Despite some turbulence, when we unpacked, everything was whole.

We have moved quite a bit, and my husband has perfected the art of packing. He uses reams of packing paper and rolls of Bubble Wrap, because the cardboard boxes that everything is packed into have thin skins, so it's important to protect from the inside.

I thought about this as I was displaying my tea set, something especially dear to me for its fragility. I could not transport this set to my home without its having to traverse rough air and rough handling, intended or not. So, knowing that the outside environment would sometimes be hostile, we shielded it ourselves to protect it during the journey.

So often we wonder, *If God loves me, why did he allow* _____ *to happen?* Each of us has turbulence in life. There is not one of us who has not been roughly handled, either by other people or circumstances or both.

God does not promise us an easy journey; Christ's journey was certainly not easy, and we do live in a hostile environment. He does promise to bring us, his hand-selected treasures, safely home. He shows his devotion and affection to us by wrapping us in his love, his compassion, and his protection for our journey from here to there.

I have loved you with an everlasting love; I have drawn you with unfailing kindness.   Jeremiah 31:3

Till Death Do Us Part

Just before we were to be married, my husband was required to spend six months on active military duty. The separation was difficult because just as we were to begin our lives together, we were apart. This was in the days before cell phones—and because of where he was at the time, he was only allowed to telephone occasionally. We didn't see one another at all, and communication seemed tenuous and sporadic.

We made do with occasional letters. In the final stages of wedding planning, I sometimes had to make decisions based on what I knew of him and what I thought he'd like. I didn't hear from him, so I plowed ahead, hoping I was doing it right for both of us. Although he was in a relatively safe area, other soldiers were stationed in places with more risk. I knew that their wives, fiancées, friends, and family worried not that the months would separate them temporarily but that harm—death—would part them forever.

One day a few months ago, I mused with a friend, "How strange it must seem to those who do not believe in Christ that we have arranged our entire lives around a Person we have never met face-to-face." All my goals, the way I choose to raise my children and to live my life, the friends I choose, and the ways I spend my time, my talents, and my money—are all governed by my love for my as-of-yet unseen God.

My then-fiancé and I had been temporarily separated by other duties and responsibilities. When they were concluded, we reunited once more, stronger in our love and affection for one another. Don't you think that's how it will be when we fall into the arms of our Lord, the sweetest union?

The beauty for Christians is that it never will be *till death do us part* with God. Once our earthly responsibilities have been concluded, death will usher us into an ecstatic reunion with our Lord, whom we will see, finally, face-to-face.

I am convinced that neither death nor life, neither angels nor demons, neither the present nor the future, nor any powers, neither height nor depth, nor anything else in all creation, will be able to separate us from the love of God that is in Christ Jesus our Lord. ROMANS 8:38-39

Experiencing the Love of God

Many people wear a wedding ring when they get married, a symbol that they have committed to an exclusive relationship, that they have taken vows to one person, vows they intend to keep.

Do you have any outward symbols of your commitment to the Lord? It isn't necessary, of course, nor is a wedding ring. But both are positive ways to express to those around you your affections and commitment to the Lord. Here are some ideas, if you'd like to give one a try:

- a cross necklace, or cross eternity bracelet or ring
- a crown of thorns necklace, sure to draw questions
- a plaque on your front door that reflects Joshua 24:15
- a piece of art on a wall in your house that illustrates a faith concept or Scripture
- a bumper sticker—one that invites and doesn't divide
- an embroidered pillow with a favorite verse
- a coffee mug given to a friend with a blessing inscribed on it
- a tattoo expressing your faith

What other fun ideas might you have?

If you refuse to serve the LORD, then choose today whom you will serve. Would you prefer the gods your ancestors served beyond the Euphrates? Or will it be the gods of the Amorites in whose land you now live? But as for me and my family, we will serve the LORD. JOSHUA 24:15, NLT

No More Noise

A friend and I decided to sign up for an app that would help us track our eating and exercise habits. We were feeling technologically adept until we began to get binged and dinged a dozen times a day. Apparently, not knowing we had to adjust settings, we had allowed the app to notify us each time the other added food, lost weight, logged in, or worked out. Not content to notify us only by phone, the app would also notify us by e-mails and on our tablets so that we would hear perhaps twenty noises per day. We wanted to encourage each other but didn't need that kind of racket throughout the day, so we turned off the notifications and focused on eating and working out.

My phone calendar reminds me of every appointment. When someone tags me on social media, I am alerted via e-mail. When someone e-mails, a digital heads-up is delivered. My phone company even beeps me in the middle of the night to alert me to data usage! My dentist, bless her, transmits text messages and e-mails weeks ahead of time to ensure I don't forget my appointments. I have finally started to work through them all—unsubscribe from e-mails from services and stores I no longer need, trim my social media commitments and time spent online, and silence unnecessary announcements.

We have background noise inside, too, in our hearts and minds. It alerts us when someone succeeds where we have "failed." It reminds us of things we meant to do, but didn't, and still don't have time for. It talks at us about decisions we've made, prompting us to second- and third- and fourth-guess. Sometimes that inner notification takes up so much brain space that there is no room for positive, peaceful, encouraging thoughts.

It's up to us to turn off constant, unhelpful notifications, both inner and outer, quieting the noise and bringing calm to our hearts and our environments. Seeking peace is a wonderful thing done large scale—for the oppressed and underserved. But it's a wonderful thing done small scale, too, in our own lives.

What unnecessary notifications—either inside your head or in your home— need to be turned down or shut off so you can experience God's peace?

Seek peace and pursue it.   PSALM 34:14

177

Reaching for Peace

In this world of ours, there are certain notifications, alerts, and digital inter-actions we simply can't ignore. Our world is noisy. Our health concerns, our relationships with friends and family, our finances, our jobs, our ministries—all worthy causes that crowd into the slender column of our twenty-four-hour day. When we can't cut out any more busyness and noise, we can reach upward for help.

A tree taught me that.

I live in a heavily forested region, where the land is rich with low-level shrubbery as well as soaring trees—fir trees, especially—that reach heaven-ward. Their long trunks are nearly devoid of branches from the ground up, where others crowd them. But when they break out of the pack, as it were, and stretch higher than the others around them, their foliage flourishes. That extra foliage stabilizes because it means more branches to distribute the effects of strong wind gusts. There is more photosynthesis—sustaining food. The lush tree provides better cover for others, both people and wildlife.

The truth? The trees must reach and grow and stretch to receive enough sun for those life-sustaining and life-giving effects. When they stay stunted and crowded, they remain in relative darkness. Sparse. So, when others crowd in among them, they must reach higher and higher to capture the sun.

Neither you nor I can leave the crowded life behind; it's a part of the age in which we live. God knows that! We can continue to reach higher and higher, though, seeking the Son, looking for him to shine on us, warm us, nourish us even with our roots still firmly planted within a teeming age, whose activities and technologies we sometimes do not even understand.

When we reach up, like a toddler holding his arms high toward a tower-ing parent, the Lord scoops us into his arms. We learn that, for a moment or an hour or a week, we can leave the cares and worries that call out to us like pleading street vendors and focus on the one who brings us peace.

I do not occupy myself with things too great and too marvelous for me.
But I have calmed and quieted my soul, like a weaned child with its mother;
like a weaned child is my soul within me. PSALM 131:1-2, ESV

A Certain Hope

I cherish lifelong friends not only for our long investment in one another's lives but because we know we can be honest with each other. One such friend, Hope, and I met for lunch a few weeks ago. I explained that one of my children was walking down an unexpected career path, and I was concerned. I thought maybe I'd speak up—again. She listened carefully and then asked me, "Do you have anything new to add?"

The answer was no. To bring up the topic again would be to nag, and if we get right down to the truth of the matter, it would be to try to control a situation in the life of another person—a grown adult person.

When I bring up a topic more than once to someone, I am trying to control the outcome. I may have the very best intentions, believing that I will bring about good change for the person, but the fact remains that I am trying to control it.

When I pray and turn the entire matter over to God, I am turning control over to him. The fact is, I have no idea what the best timing is for anyone's life, including my own. But God does. He knows right when my children, my friends, my husband, or my coworkers would profit best by making a change—or if, indeed, they would at all.

There's a portion of Psalm 37:7-8 that speaks powerfully to this: "Be still before the LORD and wait patiently for him. . . . Fret not yourself; it tends only to evil" (ESV). When I am still and waiting patiently for him to act, I express a vote of confidence in his goodness and knowledge. When I act out of worry—fret—I am tending toward evil, the evil of controlling others or assuming that I know better than God what needs to be done and when.

Because of Hope, I ask myself now, "Do I have anything new to add?" Because of hope, I wait upon the Lord.

I remain confident of this: I will see the goodness of the LORD in the land of the living. Wait for the LORD; be strong and take heart and wait for the LORD.   PSALM 27:13-14

Pennies from Heaven

Like many of you, I grew up hearing the little chant "See a penny, pick it up, all day long you'll have good luck." I did pick up pennies then, even when I was a little kid, tucking them into my pockets where they were soon forgotten.

When I became a Christian and came to understand that there is no "luck," but there is the will of a loving, sovereign God, I did not give up my penny-pinching, penny-picking-up habits. If anything, they increased! American pennies, thankfully, still include the words "In God We Trust." Each time I plucked a penny from the floor of a grocery store or the wet pavement outside of my car, it reminded me In Whom I Trusted. I'd spend my days praying, and he'd respond in my heart and mind, through the Word or worship music or sometimes . . . with a delightful glint of copper. Call me crazy, but it signaled to me that he was paying attention. "The LORD has remembered us; he will bless us" (Psalm 115:12, ESV).

How happy I am that I had not selected found quarters as an affectionate nod from the Lord—when people drop a quarter, they stop to pick it up regardless of luck! A gentle nudge to my heart taught me that yes, when you look for only big blessings, large interventions, significant and positive changes in circumstance, you miss most of the blessings. Most blessings are small, things that we and others might even forget or overlook, like a dropped penny.

A close-in parking spot on a wet day. A friend who asks you to walk with her. A new recipe. A chance for renewed health. A fine waived. A child's enthusiasm. I began to open my eyes not for pennies but for the small blessings that God dropped into my days, nearly every day, to speak my love language, the one that says, "I am here. I have remembered you. I will bless you."

The big gifts, rare as they may be, are from him. But so are the small ones, and if I look for them, I will see them all around me, all the time, as a constant reminder of his love.

Every good and perfect gift is from above, coming down from the Father of the heavenly lights, who does not change like shifting shadows. JAMES 1:17

Seeking What's Right

Before my husband went to seminary, he worked in quality control at a company that manufactured parts for the aerospace industry. His job was to test the pieces that would someday make their way onto airplanes, and ensure they completely conformed. The QC team trained their eyes to see every flaw, and sometimes the supervisors would be irritated when a part was rejected, but rejection was necessary.

When I am not working as a writer, I often work as an editor. It's my job to find for my clients anything and everything that could be wrong. While perfection is impossible, I look for potential errors so my clients can fix them before publication. One of the things I've had to sacrifice, though, is the enjoyment of reading. I am so busy looking for what is wrong that often I don't get to enjoy what is right—most of the book!

What's right on the job is not always right in personal relationships, though. We've all come up against people who are looking for our mistakes. Often, they are eager to point them out, "for our benefit," of course. Mostly, these people don't take the opportunity to compliment us on things they find praiseworthy. Sometimes we are our own worst enemies—seeing our flaws and pondering them over and over. But we don't see or dwell on our strong points. When we've trained our eyes to see flaws, we see much of what we seek.

My church has a motto, drawn from a seventeenth-century theologian, Rupertus Meldenius. "In essentials unity, in non-essentials liberty, in all things charity." Charity, as used in the Bible, often means love.

Could we as believers adopt this motto for life as well as faith? Let's start with charity—love—for ourselves. Let's tend, with focus, to what is essential. Let's allow ourselves and others liberty to pursue interests and a life that might look different from those around us. And when we make a mistake, we can offer ourselves charity and grace and start again.

If we train our minds to seek what is right and not what is wrong, we will find it.

Whatever is true, whatever is honorable, whatever is just, whatever is pure, whatever is lovely, whatever is commendable, if there is any excellence, if there is anything worthy of praise, think about these things.

PHILIPPIANS 4:8, ESV

You Smell Good!

One of the most wonderful things about the month of June is the lovely scent of all those flowers coming into their own in my garden. Of the five senses, when we describe things, we often mention what something looked like, sounded like, tasted like, felt like. The one most overlooked is the sense of smell.

And yet smell is one of the most powerful senses, along with touch, for evoking emotion. Do you remember the scent of your mother's perfume? Your grandmother's baking? That baby powder scent of your child's bald head right after a bath? Recently, I passed a man who was wearing the same cologne that my prom date wore many, many years ago, and suddenly I was a teenager again.

Besides the flowers, the plants that smell the best in my yard are in my herb garden. I planted it in a window box so that when the window is open and the breeze is blowing, my house smells woody, green, and zesty, like thyme, basil, dill, and mint.

My son has always been interested in culinary things, and he recently showed me something he'd learned from a cookbook—how adding torn basil and mint leaves to a salad changes its taste in a most refreshing way. Try it! My daughter has always been artistic, and she's taken to mixing flowers and herbs together in wonderful arrangements, giving a green foil to the colorful stems, and ensuring the scent is spicy and sweet at the same time. Try it!

What both of those blends have in common is the unexpected mix of tastes and scents. Unusual. And yet pleasing!

What an amazing thing, then, that we who love Jesus are said to spread the fragrance of the knowledge of him everywhere. Fragrance, which becomes buried deep in memory, which can be recalled in an instant, which takes both sweet and spicy forms, that's what we are, friend, by the grace of God.

Thanks be to God, who in Christ always leads us in triumphal procession, and through us spreads the fragrance of the knowledge of him everywhere. For we are the aroma of Christ to God among those who are being saved and among those who are perishing. 2 CORINTHIANS 2:14-15, ESV

Experiencing the Love of God

Although the idea that various flowers and plants hold hidden meanings from giver to recipient has been around for hundreds of years, the concept became wildly popular under Queen Victoria. One of my favorite herbs, which grows outside in my window box because I use it so often, is rosemary. Have you heard the phrase "rosemary for remembrance"? When placed in a bouquet, rosemary is said to help you call to mind something or someone sentimental in a way that brings hope, peace, or joy. This may be someone who has moved, someone who has passed away, or someone who simply isn't visibly present. I like to let it remind me of the Lord—always present, just not visible.

Flower language can be fun and meaningful in other ways. Want to try it out on a friend or family member? Here's what you can do. Assemble a posy or a larger bouquet, using flowers known to convey certain meanings—they can be sentiments of admiration, friendship, love, thanksgiving, hope . . . whatever! If your intended understands the language, you'll have conveyed a subtle message. If they don't understand flower language, no harm was done! They still have a lovely bouquet to share, and you can share the insight if you wish.

Here are some meanings from Victorian writer and artist Kate Greenaway to get you started. You can borrow her book from the library, or look up flower language online if you wish to have more flowers, and sentiments, from which to select! I think I'll be giving potted oak-leafed geraniums this year!

Deep red carnation: Alas! My poor heart!
Red chrysanthemum: love
White chrysanthemum: truth
Daisy: innocence
Oak-leafed geranium: true friendship
Honeysuckle: generous, devoted affection
Ivy: fidelity
Lupine: imagination
Moss: maternal love

This I call to mind, and therefore I have hope: The steadfast love of the LORD never ceases; his mercies never come to an end.

LAMENTATIONS 3:21-22, ESV

What I Treasure Most

Most first labors take some time, and the delivery of my first child was no different. For health issues, I was induced very early in the morning, and my son was not born until nearly midnight. By that time, he was tired, and I was tired, and the doctors decided to take him out by Cesarean section.

And then—he was born into a bright, unfamiliar, and perhaps scary situation. He was cold and bloody and, I'm sure, confused. There were many people in the room at the time, a true cacophony of voices. In those days, they did not hand the baby to the mother right away but took him away to be cleaned up first. But at the moment he was being carried away, I called out to him, using his name.

"Samuel."

To the amazement of everyone in the room, he turned his little head and looked directly back at me. He had not turned toward any other voice. But my voice, which he had heard every day from within, he recognized. I remembered reading how Mary looked back at the birth of Jesus, in Luke 2:19, and had this response: "Mary treasured up all these things and pondered them in her heart." I thought, *This is my moment to treasure in my heart, to ponder the birth of my son.*

My son had listened to my voice daily; he recognized and trusted it.

Our Father in heaven speaks to us daily too. Sometimes it's in that still small voice; sometimes it's through others, through circumstances, through the impressions of the Holy Spirit. Always, always, we can hear from him through Scripture. Have you trained your ear to listen to his voice daily? To recognize and trust it even when you're tired and confused and in an unfamiliar and scary situation? He calls out to you. He cares for you, loves you, and desires for you to turn your face toward him when you hear his voice, and then follow him. He will only lead you forward, to light and to life.

My sheep hear my voice, and I know them, and they follow me.

JOHN 10:27, ESV

Abundant Life and Joy

The school year was out, and a friend and I were having coffee. There were clouds over her normally sunny personality. "What's the matter?" I asked. She explained that now that her youngest had graduated, she was looking at a completely empty nest in a few months. "The children were my lifeblood," she said. Another friend had stomach troubles and depression, which hung around her like smog, due to her job. "It steals the lifeblood from me," she said. My ears pricked up. I'd heard that twice now.

In Scripture, blood represents life. In Genesis 9:4-6, God instructs his creation, "You shall not eat flesh with its life, that is, its blood. And for your lifeblood I will require a reckoning: from every beast I will require it and from man. From his fellow man I will require a reckoning for the life of man. 'Whoever sheds the blood of man, by man shall his blood be shed, for God made man in his own image'" (ESV).

For the believer, then and now, blood did not just represent physical life, it represented spiritual life. An animal was slaughtered in the Garden of Eden to cover Adam and Eve's sin. A ram was killed as a sacrifice in place of Abraham's son Isaac. The blood of a lamb was painted on the doorways to protect the Israelites in Egypt. And of course, the ultimate lifeblood came from Jesus Christ, the final sacrifice. First Peter 1:18-19 reminds us, "For you know that it was not with perishable things such as silver or gold that you were redeemed from the empty way of life handed down to you from your ancestors, but with the precious blood of Christ, a lamb without blemish or defect."

That blood purchased our eternal salvation, but also, Jesus tells us in John 10:10, "I have come that they may have life, and have it to the full." Do you feel filled with life in your job, or with your friends, family, or ministry? If not, what steps can you take to make sure that your "lifeblood," that which brings you abundant life and joy, is restored?

The life of the flesh is in the blood, and I have given it for you on the altar to make atonement for your souls, for it is the blood that makes atonement by the life.   LEVITICUS 17:11, ESV

Lessons from the Playground, Part 1

A few days ago, my husband and I watched a TV rerun of a show called *MythBusters*. This episode set out to prove whether a swing could make a 360-degree circle around the swing set if the person on the swing pushed hard enough. We're not big TV fans, but we both stopped what we were doing to watch. "I always wondered that," he said to me. "I tried," I admitted. "But I got scared when it got too high."

The short answer is no: they couldn't make the swing go all the way around, not without causing real damage to the "dummy" they used in place of a person. It was fun to wonder, though, and the next day, on my walk, I stopped at a local park to watch the kids and their parents play. My eyes were drawn to the swings, of course.

A couple of kids ran for those swings, and once there, one kid would hop up on the wide, black rubber seat while his friend would push from behind. Sometimes, a parent would push one kid first and then the other. First, the kid would swing forward just a foot, then two, then soon she was climbing higher and higher with delight. Just like when we were kids, though, these little ones soon caught on to use that helpful push as a running start, as it were, while they used their feet and legs to pump. Soon enough the kids soared on their own without any help from behind.

How like that is life—even well beyond the swing set years? There is no self-made man or woman, and for the most part, people who are given a hand up are not lazy; they are grateful and power through life on their own later. Pride stops us from seeing that on both sides. When I need help, I have not failed; when I offer help, I am not better. We need each other, then and now.

Do you know someone who needs a little help to move forward? Do you need to ask someone for a little push till you can fly on your own? In his loving-kindness, God often provides people to help power us through difficult times.

Don't forget to do good and to share with those in need. These are the sacrifices that please God.　　　　　HEBREWS 13:16, NLT

Lessons from the Playground, Part 2

While out on a walk, I stopped to watch some children playing at a local park. With a smile, I turned my eyes from the swings and looked toward the nearly empty parking lot. There, I spied one little person on a bike. Her dad ran behind her, holding on to the back of the pink bicycle seat as she pedaled.

Do you remember learning to ride a bike?

I do. I had a neon-green banana-seat bike, the coolest bike of them all. Well, it would be the coolest bike of them all once I could ride it. At the back of the banana seat was a metal hoop, which was just perfect for a father to hold on to while his daughter was learning to ride. I was concentrating so hard on learning to ride that I could not feel or sense if my father was still holding on to the hoop at the back. A few minutes into my ride I wobbled and shouted that I was going to fall. Right away, I felt the bike steady as a hand reached out, grabbed that hoop, and kept me upright.

In the park, now, I saw the determined look on the face of the little girl who was learning to ride and then watched as a look of panic flitted across her face when she wobbled. Dad was paying close attention, though, and he did not let her fall. By the time I left the park to finish my walk, she was biking on her own—confident, joyous, feeling empowered.

Our heavenly Father is like that, whether we are trying out something new we desperately wish to master or whether we are wobbling, tired, in a familiar activity. We don't see him, sometimes we don't sense him, but he is always behind us, holding on tight and guiding us. When we wobble, he is there to catch us. But when we can fly? He lets go and lets us skyrocket in joy.

He will not let you stumble. . . . The LORD himself watches over you! The LORD stands beside you as your protective shade. . . . The LORD keeps you from all harm and watches over your life. The LORD keeps watch over you as you come and go, both now and forever. PSALM 121:3, 5, 7-8, NLT

Well Fed

One of my favorite cartoon characters as a kid was Yogi Bear. Yogi was always hungry, ready to poach a picnic basket if need be, and the ranger had to post many signs that read, Do Not Feed the Bears. In real life, in our parks, we are also discouraged from feeding the bears . . . and the birds . . . and the raccoons. If you feed them, they'll be back and bring twenty of their friends.

I was thinking about this as a friend of my husband's battled her cancer. She had traditional treatment, but after, she decided to completely change her diet. She ate nothing processed or with chemical additives, limiting herself to clean, whole foods. Lately, studies have indicated that cutting back on carbohydrates might make the cancer cells "fast" until they die away.

It all comes down to Do Not Feed the Bears.

Most of the bears in our lives live inside us. They might even look like the proverbial seven deadly sins: Lust. Gluttony. Greed. Sloth. Wrath. Envy. Pride. Be certain, Scripture tells us, that all sin is deadly: "The wages of sin is death" (Romans 6:23).

Just like our friend's cancer, when she fought the disease, starved it, it left. God has given us a heart and a mind and a spirit. We are created in his image, and that sets us apart from every other creation. He has given us a will, and we must use it as often as we can to choose to do what is right. Matthew 7:6 admonishes us, "Do not give dogs what is sacred; do not throw your pearls to pigs. If you do, they may trample them under their feet, and turn and tear you to pieces."

Your heart, your mind, your spirit, your health, your holiness—all are sacred, precious. My prayer for me and for you is that we steward them well. The antidote to the seven deadly sins has been, proverbially, the seven opposing virtues: Humility. Generosity. Charity. Kindness. Self-control. Temperance. Zeal.

May we feed them well.

Fear the LORD and turn away from evil. Then you will have healing for your body and strength for your bones.　　　　PROVERBS 3:7-8, NLT

A Benediction for June

June is closing, and July is starting with a shout! In the United States, July is the month when we celebrate freedom; July 4 is our Independence Day. Let's express our delight in our freedom—freedom from the control of sin and evil, freedom from death—by abounding in love for ourselves and others as we seek holiness before God.

Just as each Sunday at church I receive a blessing and a charge for the coming week, I offer you a benediction from the Bible, to encourage you in God's love and equip you to share this love with others in the month to come.

Through these pages and the power of Scripture, I reach my hands out to and over you, as your sister in Christ, and pray . . .

May the Lord make you increase and abound in love for one another and for all, as we do for you, so that he may establish your hearts blameless in holiness before our God and Father, at the coming of our Lord Jesus with all his saints. 1 THESSALONIANS 3:12-13, ESV

JULY

Experiencing the Love of God

Did you recognize anything you struggle with in that list on June 29? *Lust. Gluttony. Greed. Sloth. Wrath. Envy. Pride.* Your sin struggle might be against something entirely different, but while we are in the flesh, we are still able to be tempted. Scripture tells us that even Jesus, both fully human and fully God, was tempted, but he did not sin.

Why not decide today to starve the sin that tempts you? Turn away, don't frequent areas or habits that lead to weakness, ask for accountability. You can do it. God calls us to be holy as he is holy. He would not lead us forward in holiness if it were not possible. He does not assign impossible tasks! How does he lead us? Jesus intentionally took time each day to pray. He withdrew to a private place and prayed. "Submit . . . to God. Resist the devil, and he will flee from you" (James 4:7).

It's been said that it's easier to rid oneself of a bad habit when it's replaced with a good one. So how about feeding one of the doves? *Humility. Generosity. Charity. Kindness. Self-control. Temperance. Zeal.*

Paul says, "What I want to do I do not do, but what I hate I do" (Romans 7:15). But he also says, "I can do all things through Christ who strengthens me" (Philippians 4:13, NKJV).

That is our human dilemma—in our own power, we cannot change. But in the Spirit's power, we can!

Let's do it!

This week I will starve_____.

This week I will feed_____.

The Spirit God gave us does not make us timid, but gives us power, love and self-discipline.   2 TIMOTHY 1:7

God-Sent

I love to play Scrabble, and not long ago I was thumbing through a website that offered a Scrabble dictionary. Being heavenly minded (clears throat here), I noticed that there are a few English words that include the word *god*. The most important one is *godsend*.

A godsend is a blessing, a help, something or someone that arrives just in the nick of time. By including *god* in the word, we mean to recognize that the good that comes our way is initiated or encouraged by the Lord: a check that arrives on time, a friend who texts when we are down, someone willing to serve as a job reference. Often we can sense the supernatural activity behind the timing and will give thanks to God for his moving hearts and circumstances on our behalf.

So, being human-minded as well, I looked up to see how many words had *devil* in them. Not many! The most common is *bedeviled*. If someone is bedeviled, they are, according to dictionary.com, tormented or harassed maliciously or diabolically, as with doubts, distractions, or worries . . . and caused to be confused or have doubt. Those all certainly sound like the work of our enemy, the devil, don't they?

We humans can be used as a godsend—someone the Lord can use to bring peace, blessing, joy, and growth, if we so choose. Alternately, we can be tools that Satan uses, unwittingly most of the time, to bedevil another person with worries, confusion, doubt, or distractions. Often, it all comes down to loving your neighbor as yourself. Doing for others as you wish them to do for you.

In my quest, I found one other popular word that included *devil*. Daredevil. It brought to mind Evel Knievel, the motorcycle-riding bad boy and daredevil I remember watching in my youth who, among other feats, successfully jumped his bike over fifteen cars at one time. You know what? Some people were godsends in his life, and before he died, he accepted Christ. Then Evel was not evil at all!

Will you whisper today, "Here I am, Lord; send me to bless whomever you have in mind"?

I heard the voice of the Lord saying, "Whom shall I send? And who will go for us?" And I said, "Here am I. Send me!"　　　　ISAIAH 6:8

An Early Retirement

This week saw two celebrations: the celebration of a friend who was leaving active work to enjoy her retirement, and the celebration of a friend who had graduated to heaven.

My friend who was retiring had been writing books for decades. Her books were ones that I had read long before I became a writer myself, and her friendship, once we were professional colleagues, was cherished. I could not imagine that she was "hanging up her pen," but she was. She said she'd written all the things she'd felt led to write and didn't have the same passion as she once did. We, her colleagues, would miss her voice, her presence, her wisdom. But we understood her early retirement.

The woman who died was struck down in a minute as she crossed the street. She was a teacher in the church, a woman who was beloved by her family and friends, and who had mentored many young moms. She seemed much too young to be swept up into heaven, but there it was. At the service, it was agreed that while we could not understand how it could be so, the Lord had determined that her work here on earth was done.

Later, as I reflected upon her faithful, fruitful life, I thought: early retirement.

I've heard it said that you're bulletproof until your mission here on earth is done, but when it's done, there is nothing that is going to add to your days. Job 14:5 proclaims, "A person's days are determined; you have decreed the number of his months and have set limits he cannot exceed."

It's so hard when someone dies before what seems to be his or her time. We, the loved ones and colleagues, miss their voices, their love, their presence. And yet God in his goodness and knowledge knows just when our work here on earth is finished and it's time to join him. There wasn't one day that he intended for them that they were unable to live. That number of days allocated for their lives, no matter how shy of perfect it may seem to us, was, in his perfect love and wisdom, the exact and correct number. We miss them, but they missed nothing he intended for them. We don't understand now. But someday, when we meet him face-to-face, all will become perfectly clear.

To me, to live is Christ and to die is gain. If I am to go on living in the body, this will mean fruitful labor for me. Yet what shall I choose? I do not know! I am torn between the two: I desire to depart and be with Christ, which is better by far; but it is more necessary for you that I remain in the body.

PHILIPPIANS 1:21-24

Independence Day

We grow lovely blueberry bushes in our backyard, but as tasty as they are to us, they seem to be doubly tasty to the birds. We don't mind feeding birds—we have a bird feeder that we keep filled with birdseed—but we prefer to keep the blueberries to ourselves. We strung a net over them and then anchored that net with heavy stones.

It did not keep the birds away. They kept on doing what they did naturally, but now they would become tangled and entrapped. One morning I went out, and one of them had made his way under the net but could not make his way out. I lifted the net, and he flew away free.

The next day brought a worse predicament. One of our little friends became entangled in the net and seemed to be nearly upside down. I ran out there with a pair of scissors to cut the net away from her, hoping I was not too late. She made it—barely. After that, I decided that I liked birds more than I liked blueberries, and we took the net down.

The birds did not understand that they could not safely do what they had always done; once trapped, they could not free themselves. The situation reminded me of the Fall in the Garden of Eden. We individually did not cause that fall, but neither can we free ourselves. When I saw their struggle, everything within me was focused on how to safely free those birds. They were so small. They could see freedom on the other side but could not get out.

Our Lord understands our dilemma. We are trapped by many things: oppression, legalism, fear, sin, sorrow, loneliness, and death. I am certain each of us could add to this list. The beautiful thing is, we need not be trapped anymore.

He saw our distress; he saw our dilemma; he knows that we cannot free ourselves, and so he made a way. "God demonstrates his own love for us in this: While we were still sinners, Christ died for us" (Romans 5:8).

What do you need to be freed from, friend? Call out to Jesus.

If the Son sets you free, you will be free indeed.   JOHN 8:36

I Spy

When my kids were little, the I Spy books became popular. Each page held dozens or hundreds of objects on it, and we would give our kids a clue. For example, "I want a drink of water." And they'd find a pitcher. Or "Mom doesn't like these." And they'd find the spider!

Long before there were the books, though, parents have been playing "I Spy with My Little Eye" to keep their kids occupied at restaurants or on long road trips. Sometimes, though, finding the hidden object is difficult. Sometimes the clues are convoluted, or the object is too small, or children are tired, hungry, or thirsty, and the game doesn't seem very fun. And yet, with prompting, the victory is always sweet.

I don't play that game anymore, but I've been led lately to retain and reha-bilitate the discipline. My days are so busy, my circumstances up and down, and often I am hungry, tired, and thirsty, and feeling like life isn't very fun. I've decided to play "I Spy . . . God."

It's easy to do and brings a smile much as the original game did. I spy God in the beautiful sunrise. I spy God in the taste of my morning coffee, which he created. I see both my husband and my Lord in my son's smile. I see God's hand in providing just the right husband for my daughter, in providing a good health-care team even when he doesn't provide the healing I so wish for. Some days it's difficult to spy the good in a sad or fearsome situation, yet I strive to find God's love for me at work, being mindful of the truth that we're to give thanks while presenting our requests (see Philippians 4:6). The good news here is that there are dozens of places we can spy God's love, his handiwork, his attention, in our day-to-day lives. Sometimes we just have to stop, stare, work at it, and sort through the clutter to spy where he is at work in the birds among the blueberries, at the funeral of a dear friend, in a game of Scrabble.

He's there, though, in your home, in your town, in your family, and in your church. Where do you spy him today?

"You will seek me and find me when you seek me with all your heart. I will be found by you," declares the LORD.   JEREMIAH 29:13-14

Pray and Release

Summer is fishing season for many people. The idea of spending a day in the quiet, streamside, deep in nature appeals to many men—and women, too. Although fishing has been a source of food and income for as long as history was recorded (see: the disciples!) my family is interested in recreational fishing, especially fly-fishing.

It's been said that the Romans fly-fished in the second century and that the Bard himself, William Shakespeare, had a fly-fishing partner. Fly-fishing plays a major role in one of my favorite books, *A River Runs Through It*. But mainly, I'm interested in fly-fishing because my husband is interested in fly-fishing. So I won't fish, but I'll keep company and watch. Because he likes to catch fish but not eat them, he practices catch and release—capture the fish for the sport, return them back where they belong.

Fly-fishing is active. The fisherman casts the line out, then pulls it back, casts it out, then pulls it back, so that the synthetic fly appears to the fish, below the surface, to be a tasty insect landing on the water. If the fish is fooled, it snaps at the fly and is caught.

Watching my husband cast the line out, pull it back, cast it out, and then pull it back once more brought a gentle conviction to my spirit. You see, I'd been handing a concern to God all week, or trying to. And then I'd start worrying, and I'd pull it back to consider how I might solve the problem myself. Then I'd decide God could handle it and give it back in prayer. Then "too much" time would go by without an answer, so I'd snatch it back again.

Like the fly that never really rested on the water, I did not let my cares rest with God.

I believe God desires our patience because it is a vote of trust in him, in his provisions, in his goodness. "Lord, I wait for you; you will answer, Lord my God," the psalmist cries out in Psalm 38:15. That's my cry too, even when my hands are shaking to take the issue back into my world as worry. I'm casting it to him for good this time—cast and release.

Cast all your anxiety on him because he cares for you.   1 Peter 5:7

Always on Key

I work in a home office, often with headphones on. While writing this book, I've been listening to praise and worship music—of course! One day, while singing very loudly, I closed the wrong window on my computer, shutting down the music and allowing me to hear my own voice.

"Clanging gong" would be an apt description. So far off-key, it was off the keyboard. I looked at my dog, who usually naps on her blanket next to me while I work. It seemed to me she was nodding her head. "Yes, yes, that's what I must listen to all day, without the benefit of the background music you stream through your headphones to cushion the pain." I'm glad the Lord sees past our appearances—and beyond my off-key singing—and into the heart!

Which is why I'm still not going to stop singing!

Psalm 96:1 tells us to "Sing to the LORD a new song; sing to the LORD, all the earth." Many of the Psalms were written to be sung, so that only seems natural. Ephesians 5:18-19 exhorts us to "be filled with the Spirit, speaking to one another with psalms, hymns, and songs from the Spirit. Sing and make music from your heart to the Lord."

Although I do think it's lovely to literally sing to the Lord, I believe that the key to understanding what he desires from us here isn't necessarily, or only, songs. We are to speak or sing words to one another from the Spirit. What would those be? Ones that express the fruit of the Spirit (see Galatians 5:22-23) might be a good place to start! We're to "make music" from our hearts to the Lord. I'm challenged, too, not to do it the way I've always done it. Singing a new song to the Lord might mean I try a new ministry, reach out to someone new, participate in a new charity, or donate to a fresh cause. This allows me to rely on him for a new adventure, and not on things I may have mastered but that have gone stale.

We should sing—we must!—but we needn't use only song to bring him something new.

I will sing to the LORD, because He has dealt bountifully with me.

PSALM 13:6, NASB

Experiencing the Love of God

You know what can help a mediocre voice? People singing with you! I love listening to duets, and even barbershop quartets when we've had the chance to run across them. My favorite time and place to sing is in my church's sanctuary, filled with so many other people who belong to Jesus; we belong to each other when we worship together.

Not all of us have a ministry in singing (my church is very appreciative of that in my case!), but we can dedicate ourselves to God's people and his creation in a variety of ways. "Through Him then, let us continually offer up a sacrifice of praise to God, that is, the fruit of lips that give thanks to His name" (Hebrews 13:15, NASB). Are you ready to offer your gifts to a new ministry? Perhaps you might join or form one of the following:

Duet: Ask a friend to join you in donating a few hours at a shelter, or making a birthday cake for a charity that provides birthday parties for kids who might not have one otherwise.

Quartet: Join with three others in spending the next month or so assembling backpacks for kids who might not have the school supplies they need when they return to school in a month or so.

Congregation: Investigate which ministries your church supports, and join them in a new way. Perhaps pray for that ministry one day each week, support it financially, or host a furloughed missionary.

It's okay to sing solo, too. Your voice is probably much better than mine. Just sing! Sing! God is active and present in us when we're serving others—whether with others or by ourselves. Philippians 2:13 says, "God is working in you, giving you the desire and the power to do what pleases him" (NLT). How better to sense his love for us than to feel him working in and around us?

I will sing to the LORD all my life; I will sing praise to my God as long as I live.   PSALM 104:33

Miracle Grow

It's the middle of summer, and our lawn has never been greener. Woo-hoo! This is quite an accomplishment because, before now, our lawn was somewhat of a blight on the neighborhood. Although our neighbors kindly said nothing, this year my husband and I decided we needed to tend to it.

The first thing we did was to dethatch it—remove all the dead matter that rested on the soil at the base of the grass, which had been smothering the existing grass and suffocating any new growth. Moss and weeds had to go too. They were competing for the resources the desired grass needed in order to grow.

Next, we aerated. We punched holes into the ground and removed plugs of grass, making space for air, sun, water, and nutrients to go all the way down to the roots, and not just pool on top of the soil.

Once that was done, we fed the lawn with the right fertilizer, watered well, weeded when necessary, and the sun provided lots of shine. Guess what? Miracle grow!

I wanted a vibrant life. Jesus often taught in natural parables, so perhaps years of Bible reading have trained me to look for and see them in the world.

Dethatch: I needed to remove attitudes, habits, and activities that were not healthy or helpful to prepare the ground. Aerate: My schedule, my days, are jam-packed. There is no margin, there is no air. I need to breathe, so I had to take out some plugs of healthy, good activities so I'd have room to do so. I'm drinking plenty of spiritual water from its source, Jesus: "Those who drink the water I give will never be thirsty again. It becomes a fresh, bubbling spring within them, giving them eternal life" (John 4:14, NLT). I'm dining on meat—not quickly digested milk—by attending a challenging Bible study (see Hebrews 5:12-14). And as for the sun—well, we could make that metaphorical, too, with the Son, couldn't we? But honestly, I think I just need more time outside, walking, enjoying nature, not hurrying. Slow growth.

Do you see anything you might adjust to encourage your own miracle growth?

Grow in the grace and knowledge of our Lord and Savior Jesus Christ.
To him be glory both now and forever! Amen.   2 PETER 3:18

Surround Sound

One July, we began the difficult task of preparing our son to leave home as he would start college, five hours away, in a little under a month. I was exceptionally proud of him, of course, but also worried. I started small—would he have a nice roommate? Would he eat well? Would he get a flu shot? Then I moved my worry needle to medium. Would he find a good career? Could we afford schooling? After some brave weeks, I dared consider the biggest questions.

Could he become addicted to something? Become entangled in bad relationships? Worst of all . . . lose his faith?

I prayed about something I could pack with him to take, something that would remind him of what was at stake. He'd take his Bible, of course, and he always wore the cross from his baptism. He loves classical history, though, and I settled upon something fresh that I hoped would be cool enough to hang on his dorm wall. A framed portrait of Odysseus and the Sirens.

The mythological Sirens were beautiful, tempting creatures whose persons and music lured sailors to steer their vessels near the coast, where they would dash on the rocks.

Odysseus was curious to see what the Sirens would sing to him. (First mistake, right?) So he had his sailors plug their ears with wax and then lash him to the mast of his ship, tightly, making them vow that no matter what he said they would not release him. They sailed past the Sirens, and sure enough, the Sirens' song was enough to woo Odysseus to order his men to free him. They did not—instead, they lashed him ever more tightly, and they made it safely through the passage.

To this day, our phrase *siren song* signifies something that is beautiful and compelling, but certain to lead to a bitter end if followed.

Our son understood the meaning. The truth is, we are all Odysseus sometimes, too curious about things that will harm us, and falling into temptation. If we can surround ourselves with people and habits that will lash us firmly to our consciences, our faith, and our commitments, we will sail through without wrecking. As adults, God gives us the autonomy to choose our companions—a symbol of his love for and trust in us, as well as an indication of his desire for us to make good choices of our own volition.

With whom do you surround yourself?

Submit to one another out of reverence for Christ.　　　Ephesians 5:21

No Harm Will Bee-Fall You

My daughter cannot stand to be in the car with a flying insect, so one day while she was driving she had me swatting the little black bug that was pestering but not, in my mind, endangering her. Finally, I shooed it out of the window, but only after she had zigged and zagged across our little country road. I worried she'd be pulled over for suspicion of driving under the influence—under the influence of insectophobia, that is. (It's a real thing!) I mentioned that the real danger came not from the bug but from her response to the perceived harm it could do, causing her to drive a little erratically.

Oh, how those words came back to me! The next week I pulled over to a local park while I returned a business call, and once on the phone I noticed a bee buzzing at the far end of my windshield. I tried my best to keep up the conversation while unbuckling myself to flee from the car. Finally, I made my way out of the car only to discover that the insect was harrying me from the outside of the windshield and had not been in the car at all! I had been safer inside my car.

As Christians, we can spend a lot of time worrying and trying to escape situations that we fear may bring pain or harm. Some of those fears are legitimate, but perhaps some take up an outsized place in our hearts, minds, and prayers. A few might even be on the outside of the windshield—no danger to us at all. I joked with a friend about my "bee-liever's fear," and she teasingly responded, "Oh, Sandra. You know no evil will 'bee-fall' you. You 'bee-long' to Christ." How right she was.

I loved her teasing, but I loved her wisdom even more. We have the security of those who trust in God. I'm not listening any longer to buzzing fears which have no ability to sting. We are firmly inside God's protection.

Be bold, stand firm, don't worry, don't waver, don't flee. You belong to the King. No harm will bee-fall you!

You have made the LORD, my refuge, even the Most High, your dwelling place. No evil will befall you, nor will any plague come near your tent.

PSALM 91:9-10, NASB

He Knows My Name

When I was little, my grandmother purchased a book for me in which my name was substituted for the main character's name. I was delighted. It was a book about me!

We get so used to thinking about the Bible as being good for everyone—and it is—but it is also a personalized book, just for you. Today, to experience how much God loves you, how secure you can be that he will not let anything permanently catastrophic befall you, put your name into the blank spaces in Psalm 91 and read it aloud.

_____, who dwells in the shelter of the Most High will abide in the shadow of the Almighty. She will say to the Lord, "My refuge and my fortress, My God, in whom I trust!" For it is He who delivers her from the snare of the trapper and from the deadly pestilence. He will cover _____ with His pinions, and under His wings she may seek refuge; His faithfulness is a shield and bulwark.

_____ will not be afraid of the terror by night, or of the arrow that flies by day; of the pestilence that stalks in darkness, or of the destruction that lays waste at noon. A thousand may fall at _____'s side and ten thousand at her right hand, but it shall not approach _____. She will only look on with her eyes and see the recompense of the wicked. For _____ has made the Lord, her refuge, even the Most High, her dwelling place. No evil will befall _____, nor will any plague come near her tent.

For He will give His angels charge concerning _____, to guard her in all her ways. They will bear _____ up in their hands, that she does not strike her foot against a stone. She will tread upon the lion and cobra, the young lion and the serpent she will trample down.

"Because _____ has loved Me, therefore I will deliver her; I will set her securely on high, because _____ has known My name. She will call upon Me, and I will answer her; I will be with her in trouble; I will rescue her and honor her. With a long life I will satisfy _____ and let her see My salvation."[7]

As you read this, can you hear the Lord speaking to you through his Word? Do you feel the goose bumps rise as you realize how much he loves you? He does. His love never fails.

Because he has loved Me, therefore I will deliver him; I will set him securely on high, because he has known My name.   Psalm 91:14, NASB

---

7 Based on NASB.

Seeing Clearly

I'm at the age where I'm playing pickup sticks with my glasses. Normally, I wear contacts, but my eyes are aging, and if I want to see close-up, I must pop on a pair of readers . . . if I can find them. When the contacts are out, I must wear the admittedly fashionable distance glasses. I feel like I can see close up half the time and far off half the time, but never perfectly clearly.

There are Christians who believe we are born sinners, and stay sinners, and are constantly subject to the whims of the flesh. Although they feel like we might make a little progress forward, for the most part, they feel our feet of clay are here to stay. I never feel victorious around them. That theology always has me looking for what I'm doing wrong.

Other Christians believe that once we are saved, we are well and truly sinless; they look at the world around them and feel they are doing so much better, living so much more cleanly, that there is no need to count the angels on a pinhead or navel-gaze for sin. I'm not comfortable there, either. I feel like my clay feet might miss the turnoff to the path to holiness if I don't look down once in a while.

What we need are bifocals (no matter how old we are)!

If we can maintain the ability to see close-up the habits and attitudes that still sweat from our flesh, we can repent and mend our ways. If we can maintain the ability to see far off what God intends for us to be, fully, one day, we can reach for the next level of purity. We can change because our ability to do so depends on him, not us.

Our clay is not in our feet. We are both dust and gold, the fragile, clay jars formed in the Potter's hand, in whom he set his great treasure, for both now and later.

We now have this light shining in our hearts, but we ourselves are like fragile clay jars containing this great treasure. This makes it clear that our great power is from God, not from ourselves. 2 CORINTHIANS 4:7, NLT

Sheep Dip

One of my favorite books on experiencing the love of God is *A Shepherd Looks at Psalm 23*, by W. Phillip Keller. Keller was a pastor and a shepherd who used his experiences to help us understand in a deeply personal way how our Shepherd, Jesus Christ, loves us. Keller's explanation is so simple that I can grasp it immediately; his insight is so deep that I'll never forget it. I'd like to share an insight with you that I've drawn from his work.

In his book, Keller describes that when flies harry and harass sheep, the sheep become fearful and sometimes harm themselves to avoid the flies. One way a good shepherd protects his charges is by anointing the sheep with—smearing—an ointment all over their faces and heads. It acts as an insect repellant. The oiliness keeps it on the sheep's fleece, and its scent repels the flies who would do harm—setting the sheep apart from those who would harm them, as it were. Some shepherds, Keller explains, dip their sheep in a vat of the ointment, but a loving shepherd applies the remedy by hand. I imagine that the touch of the shepherd's hand, applying the healing balm, brings as much peace as the ointment itself brings protection and healing. "You anoint my head with oil" (Psalm 23:5).

Scripture tells us that anointing oil is used to consecrate something set apart for God: a building, an altar, or a person (see Leviticus 8). Anointing oil is used to commission someone for service under the hand of the Lord (see 1 Samuel 10 and 1 Samuel 16). We often anoint the sick. James 5:14 tells us, "Is anyone among you sick? Then he must call for the elders of the church and they are to pray over him, anointing him with oil in the name of the Lord" (NASB). I think the fact that the touch of the hand delivers the oil to the one requesting healing means a lot. It's intimate and personal.

If you are a Christian, you, too, are consecrated, set apart by and for the Lord (see Hebrews 10:10), and anointing, both physically and spiritually, is for you today. Jesus can protect you from what harasses you, from what wishes to harm you. I think it likely that he heals more often than we ever realize.

He speaks to you, his little lamb, when he says in John 10:11, "I am the good shepherd. The good shepherd lays down his life for the sheep."

You anoint my head with oil.   PSALM 23:5

Experiencing the Love of God

Olive was the oil discussed most often in the Bible, likely because olives were grown in great quantities in the area. In Leviticus 7:12, olive oil is used as part of a thanks offering; it lit lamps in Leviticus 24; it was good to eat in Deuteronomy 7 and 8 and other places, and was even a part of a miracle in 2 Kings 4. It's often the base oil for anointing.

As a Christian, one of the most beautiful parts of being anointed by oil is the peace that it brings—peace not that the world gives but that Jesus gives (see John 14:27), as the very act recognizes his holiness and sovereignty.

When a person is anointed, he or she is recognized as being under the care, power, and protection of the Lord. Psalm 55:21 talks of olive oil as soothing, and it has long been a healing remedy in the Middle East and countries such as Italy, Greece, and Spain. Anointing with a special, fragrant oil can bring soothing to both body and soul.

Some churches offer anointing; check with your church and see if it does. If not, there is no biblical reason that mature, thoughtful Christians cannot anoint other believers if done with a spirit of respect and dedication to the will and worship of God. It simply offers the person to the Lord, recognizes the situation as under his control, and asks for the Lord's presence, healing, and blessing where the two or three are gathered in his name (see Matthew 18:20).

You can buy anointing oil at a Christian retailer or online, or make some yourself by mixing a few drops of an essential oil (perhaps myrrh) into a flask of olive oil.

Prayerfully and biblically consider how asking for anointing might help you experience the love of God even more deeply.

Moses took the anointing oil and anointed the tabernacle and all that was in it, and consecrated them. He sprinkled some of it on the altar seven times and anointed the altar and all its utensils, and the basin and its stand, to consecrate them. Then he poured some of the anointing oil on Aaron's head and anointed him, to consecrate him. LEVITICUS 8:10-12, NASB

Tool Kits

Our family was watching a mystery movie about a large group of people stranded on an island. One of the island guests was a doctor. We chuckled upon learning that he had brought along his doctor's bag, because many of the items inside were necessary for the mystery. Fictional coincidence, we mused? Perhaps not. I was surprised to learn that many doctors still carry a doctor's bag of sorts with them when they travel.

Doctors are often called upon to help with unexpected emergencies. People know of their skill and knowledge and rely on them to be ready when a need arises. Recently, my husband and I were on a plane when a young woman fainted while waiting for the restroom. Soon enough, the call came over the speaker system asking if there was a doctor present. Doctors must always be prepared.

After we had shut off the TV, I thought about how we as believers must always be prepared. There are hurting people all around us, and we do not know when we might be called upon—or when a situation might arise in which we are needed—to offer the skills we have honed and knowledge we've been given.

What can we do?

Following the Hippocratic writings, "Practice two things in your dealings with disease: either help or do not harm the patient." In our everyday interactions, we must act in accordance with the fruit the Spirit produces in our lives: love, joy, peace, patience, kindness, goodness, faithfulness, gentleness, and self-control (see Galatians 5:22-23).

When we have an opening to share more, we should. "As we have opportunity, let us do good to all people" (Galatians 6:10). And the greatest good we can do for anyone is to share the diagnosis we all have as humans—the sickness of sin and ultimately death—and the antidote, Jesus Christ. "Thank God! He gives us victory over sin and death through our Lord Jesus Christ" (1 Corinthians 15:57, NLT).

Doctors know exactly what to do because they have both the tools and the practice of using them. Will you join me in making sure we do too?

Always be prepared to give an answer to everyone who asks you to give the reason for the hope that you have.   1 PETER 3:15

Deep and Slow

To share the truth is to share Scripture, and to share Scripture we must know it. A few years ago, I fell and needed two kinds of treatments: topical and systemic. First, I needed something to stem the immediate wound—the topical treatment—at the urgent care. After, I needed to visit my doctor to figure out what might be done in the long term to solve the problem underlying the fall. That kind of short-term/long-term treatment is outlined in the parable of the Good Samaritan.

> Jesus replied with a story: "A Jewish man was traveling from Jerusalem down to Jericho, and he was attacked by bandits. They stripped him of his clothes, beat him up, and left him half dead beside the road.
>
> "By chance a priest came along. But when he saw the man lying there, he crossed to the other side of the road and passed him by. A Temple assistant walked over and looked at him lying there, but he also passed by on the other side.
>
> "Then a despised Samaritan came along, and when he saw the man, he felt compassion for him. Going over to him, the Samaritan soothed his wounds with olive oil and wine and bandaged them. Then he put the man on his own donkey and took him to an inn, where he took care of him. The next day he handed the innkeeper two silver coins, telling him, 'Take care of this man. If his bill runs higher than this, I'll pay you the next time I'm here.'" LUKE 10:30-35, NLT

Sometimes I need a quick answer, and I look up a verse or a passage for it. That's not a bad thing. "Timely advice is lovely, like golden apples in a silver basket" (Proverbs 25:11, NLT). In the way that an unexpected injury needs a speedy response, I often look up a verse by a key word or ask a friend for an insight.

To become truly wise, though, I need a systemic, not topical, approach to studying Scripture. I need to learn by reading all the way through, book by book, and not just the "greatest hits" verses, to gain a deep knowledge, to become spiritually healthy, and to help others. My overall health depends on my willingness to tend to my spiritual health regularly and with breadth and discipline.

Are you ready to get healthy? I am!

I did not shrink from declaring to you the whole counsel of God.

ACTS 20:27, ESV

Translation Specialists

When we were in the urgent care waiting to be seen, the intake person had us take a seat. I noticed a flier tacked in front of her desk. It asked in about two dozen languages if patients needed someone to speak in their language in order to make their needs known. There were many people on staff who were bilingual and could help. But if patients spoke a language uncommon to staff members, the hospital would call someone to assist them over the phone. That way their urgent needs would be clearly understood, and they could be immediately and appropriately helped.

The bilingual staff and helpers were, in a very real sense, intercessors. An intercessor is someone who steps up to help another person, to mediate, advocate, and communicate when this person cannot or will not help herself. The Bible is filled with intercessors: Abraham, Moses, and Samuel among them. "As for me, I will certainly not sin against the Lord by ending my prayers for you" (1 Samuel 12:23, NLT).

Our greatest intercessor, of course, is Jesus Christ. "My dear children, I am writing this to you so that you will not sin. But if anyone does sin, we have an advocate who pleads our case before the Father. He is Jesus Christ, the one who is truly righteous" (1 John 2:1, NLT).

Once Jesus made final atonement for us, he was to return to the Father. But he was not leaving us alone to make our way, still broken, wounded, and hurting. No. He said in John 16:7, "It is best for you that I go away, because if I don't, the Advocate won't come. If I do go away, then I will send him to you" (NLT).

We are all called to be intercessors, to step in and advocate in prayer for those we know, for those we love, and even for our enemies. Sometimes we feel for those who are hurting, and we don't know what to say. Don't worry—just pray. The Holy Spirit, our advocate, our intercessor, is right here praying with and for us.

The Holy Spirit helps us in our weakness. For example, we don't know what God wants us to pray for. But the Holy Spirit prays for us with groanings that cannot be expressed in words. Romans 8:26, NLT

Peas and Potatoes

This year we planted peas in our backyard. I bought a tower to support the stalks and planted the peas in the carefully selected soil. I watered. The rain watered. Soon I saw some green sprout up. Victory!

Day after day, week after week, I watched as the pea plants began to spiral around the tower. They sent out long, slender green strands, and I took plenty of pictures of the beautiful green curlicues that would thread their way delicately around the iron arms of the support. But . . . no peas appeared.

Next to the peas, we planted potatoes. They'd sent up green leaves, broad and wide, which soon became somewhat chewed upon by enthusiastic insects. They withered easily and got yellow around the edges. When I had visitors to my garden, no one exclaimed, "My, look at those beautiful potato leaves." I hadn't even put a cute little garden marker declaring, "Potatoes!" next to it like I had many of the other plants. Visitors likely didn't even know there were potatoes planted there.

However, within a relatively short period those potato plants began to bear a crop. We dug them out of the soil with our bare hands and were delighted with their round, promising fleshiness. As I carried a small basket past, I looked at my pretty but barren pea stalks. "Charm is deceptive, and beauty is fleeting," I whispered to them. I don't think they knew that was from Proverbs. I don't think they cared.

I so enjoyed their delicate beauty, and while it was wonderful that the plants grew skyward, I did not plant them for their beauty; I planted them for peas. The lowly, chewed-upon potato plants had not been the focus of praise and admiration, but they produced a large yield. That is what I had hoped for when I planted them.

I determined, then, not to worry so much about how I appeared to others, but to focus on bearing much fruit for my Father, even if the work happened completely out of sight. His love is not dependent on my attractiveness or even on my usefulness. I can therefore focus my efforts on bearing fruit rather than on appearing fruitful to others.

This is to my Father's glory, that you bear much fruit, showing yourselves to be my disciples.　　　　　　　　　　　　　　　　　　　JOHN 15:8

Son-brellas

The dead center of summer has arrived, and with it the quietest of days, and that seems, somehow, to make the sun bear down even more strongly. It's also the time of year when the birds in my town are raising their young. Baby birds have a thin skin that covers their bony little bodies, which have not had time to be fattened up by seed and insects. I think this is one reason why mom and dad birds build nests in places that are sheltered—to be hidden from the sun and from harm.

I have a friend who has many flower boxes, and she specifically plants geraniums because their wide, flat leaves provide cover for the birds' nests. One day I visited her; while we drank iced tea in her backyard, I noticed all her umbrellas were popped out. She must have noticed my quizzical look.

"I rearrange them throughout the day," she said, "moving them as the sun moves, so the nests are sheltered. The geranium leaves weren't enough, but when I place the umbrellas on chairs, it works."

I thought, *How lovely. I'm so happy she's my friend. A busy person with lots of professional and personal responsibilities, yet she has time to take notice of the lowly who count on her*. It brought Psalm 138:6 to mind. "Though the Lord is exalted, yet He regards the lowly" (NASB).

My friend had taken note of how God provides for the birds in the natural world, shading them with flora and foliage, and had copied him. When stronger measures were called for, she stepped in with the umbrellas. How lucky, how blessed, how grateful those birds must have been to have such a defender and provider. She imitated her Master.

How lucky, how blessed, how grateful we as Jesus' friends are to have such a defender and provider. Do not worry when the hot sun beats upon you. "Look at the birds of the air; they do not sow or reap or store away in barns, and yet your heavenly Father feeds them. Are you not much more valuable than they?" (Matthew 6:26).

This is how we know we are in him: Whoever claims to live in him must live as Jesus did.   1 John 2:5-6

Regularly Updated

One year when the technology was still brand-new, I used a GPS to drive my daughter to a birthday party. The party was being held at a skating rink that was not in our hometown. I had no idea where it was, but equipped with my new system, I felt that I could make it there just fine.

We drove and drove, and about five minutes before the party was to begin, we arrived . . . at a gravel pit. There was nothing anywhere near there that looked like a skating rink. I did not have a map, so I humbled myself a few times and asked for directions, and we finally arrived, but very late.

When digital directions became more prevalent, they became more accurate. Still, they occasionally showed thoroughfares where there were actually dead ends. The systems relied on old information when the roads and neighborhoods themselves were constantly changing. Now I subscribe to a service that is updated by satellite every day. My information is current and relevant, and I get where I want to when I want to get there.

I learned a good lesson: when I use a flawed program, it sends me to the wrong place. When I use good information, updated regularly, I go where I am supposed to in order to do what I've set out to do.

Sometimes I find myself relying on well-meaning but worldly based information when making a decision. It often leads me in the wrong direction. Even when I attempt to make decisions based on biblical wisdom, I can sometimes go wrong. Why? I'm relying on maps printed on "old wineskins," as it were. I think I remember what Scripture says about something, but have recalled it incorrectly or not in its full.

God has given us a map that is good for all time. It never needs to be updated; we simply must update ourselves with it regularly. With it, you will always arrive exactly where you're supposed to be and not end up in a lonely gravel pit!

All Scripture is breathed out by God and profitable for teaching, for reproof, for correction, and for training in righteousness, that the man of God may be complete, equipped for every good work. 2 TIMOTHY 3:16-17, ESV

Experiencing the Love of God

I love taking little shortcuts and scenic "longcuts" in my hometown. It's an area I know well, and I don't need a map to navigate it. But if I never go exploring, I don't see anything new.

When I spread out of my little area, I definitely need and want help. I must be willing to use resources such as digital navigation, good maps, and friends who know the area.

Do you have a Bible reading program? They are easy to find online—several Bible search sites will deliver verses to you each day. There are phone apps that will do the same. I'm delighted that you are reading this devotional every day; I'm reading one too. Are you in a Bible study? Do you have mentors or spiritual leaders who can set your feet on the right paths?

To make a change, you must make a decision. What could you decide to do today that will help you map out the biblical way to travel through the rest of the year? Here are some thoughts to get you started:

1. Do you prefer to read your Bible on a tablet or phone or in a hard copy? Both? There are digital Bibles in many versions that are available to download for free.
2. Do you have a copy of the Bible in a place that's easy for you to access, such as next to the chair you sit in when you watch TV or drink your coffee? Do you have an app that's on the home screen of your phone?
3. Do you have a devotional loaded on your tablet or a Bible passage that's delivered to you daily?
4. Are you accountable to anyone for your time in the Word? If not, would you be willing to reach out to someone?
5. Do you have a reward set for yourself when you've completed reading a book of the Bible?

Work hard so you can present yourself to God and receive his approval.
Be a good worker, one who does not need to be ashamed and who correctly explains the word of truth.   2 TIMOTHY 2:15, NLT

VIPs

When I was working on a charity auction committee, we had to call restaurants and ask if they would be willing to donate a gift card. Often, restaurants would say no. But one restaurant said a generous yes; my husband faithfully buys gift cards from them each year as gifts for his cherished volunteers. This restaurant works hard to take good care of important clients.

Similarly, a good friend of mine is working on a project for an important client. She's going to help me with some work inside my house—but not for a few weeks, because this client is her top priority.

James 2:2-4 tells us that we are not to favor the rich over the poor simply because they are rich. We are also to work diligently for our income (see Proverbs 13:4), pay our bills (see Romans 13:7), and be wise (see Proverbs 4:6-7). To do that, we need to work with the primary goal in mind of pleasing the one who pays us, who has hired us to do a task and looks forward to our doing it well.

I realized then that I work for a Very Important Client. Indeed, everyone else I work for is ultimately accountable to him. He has said he has equipped me with everything I am to do (see 2 Timothy 3:17) and will even help me do what I need to get done (see Philippians 4:13). I have other people I work for, of course: publishers, people who contract with me to coach them or edit their work, freelance writing organizations, writing conferences. Ultimately, though, I have only one boss—and he's a good one. The Lord Jesus.

Remember—only you can do the work that God has set aside, from the beginning of time, for you. Work willingly and hard for him, and he will give you beyond what you can ask or imagine (see Ephesians 3:20). That's a promise!

Work willingly at whatever you do, as though you were working for the Lord rather than for people. Remember that the Lord will give you an inheritance as your reward, and that the Master you are serving is Christ.

COLOSSIANS 3:23-24, NLT

Precision Thermometers

My husband is pretty much a meat-and-potatoes man, potatoes optional. Let's just say he's very glad to be the son of a Father who owns the cattle on a thousand hills. So, we bought a thermometer with a long probe that is placed in the center of a roast, anchored by a long, thin cord leading to a countertop thermometer reader. Using it, we can remove the roast at exactly the right temperature. He doesn't want well-done meat. He doesn't want medium meat. He wants medium rare and nothing else.

The meat thermometer broke last year, so of course, we bought a new one. The next time we were roasting an expensive hunk of meat, I promptly inserted the thermometer needle. I left the room and set the alarm to beep when the roast reached the right temperature, and then I went about my business in the other room.

Some time passed . . . too much time, I suddenly realized. By the time I got to the oven, the meat was ruined, which is just about as close to a cardinal sin as one can come in my household. I'd inserted the wrong thermometer, the one that wasn't working. It could tell me nothing at all.

A few days later, I was feeling blue about several life situations. I told Jesus that I thought maybe he didn't care about me, because if he did, why was he letting such and such a thing happen, anyway? He couldn't possibly love me as much as another person I mentioned, whose life seemed to be blessed at every bend in the road.

Then it struck me. I felt convicted, and I smiled at the same time. I was looking at a broken thermometer. Looking at circumstances and my limited, partially blind interpretation of them was not going to give me any reliable information.

Jesus tells us that he loves us as the Father loves him. Do you have any doubt that the Father loves his Son? I do not. Jesus tells me that he loves me in the very same way. His permanence, his sacrifice, as expressed in the Word, give me the right reading, and you and I can trust that whatever he's doing in our lives will turn out perfect every time!

As the Father has loved me, so have I loved you. Now remain in my love.

JOHN 15:9

215

Pet Peeves

I learn a lot from my dog. Or rather, God teaches me a lot through my dog. Now that she is the "only child," as my children have grown up and moved out, she is spoiled. She gets a lot of treats and not so much discipline, but that's okay because she's a pet. Unlike a child, I nurture and feed her but I do not need to prepare her to leave—nor do I want to. I take such good care of her, tend to her needs and desires, and give her attention and affection every day. She'll never want to leave. Why would she?

The idea of a pet, and therefore a pet peeve, came to me when I was irritated at someone recently. I have a friend whose company I truly enjoy, but she is not very good about responding to communications right away, and she's busy on so many levels she sometimes forgets dates we had set.

I like to live by a schedule. The truth is, sometimes the schedule is my boss; I start thinking it's everyone's boss and is, indeed, the right way. And that is my problem. It's a pet peeve to me that people do not respond quickly or keep to a preplanned schedule.

A pet peeve is something that irritates one person regularly but that doesn't seem to trouble others as much. It's a pet because we nurture it and think about it and talk about it and feed it well with more and more examples. Because we feed it well, we wonder why it never wants to leave. Sometimes, though, when we don't let go of the pet peeves, we can, unfortunately, let go of the people behind them.

The Bible tells us that love is not easily irritated. I felt convicted that my friend might be just as annoyed by my adherence to a timeline as I was by her way of operating. My other friends and family might be annoyed by other habits of mine—I'm sure I have a full menu of irritations on offer. But they don't speak up. They love me, and I them, and to be in a community where we honor one another and all our ways of operating, we can nurture only patience and love. Let's show the pet peeves out the door to make room for more love to walk in.

A person's wisdom yields patience; it is to one's glory to overlook an offense.
PROVERBS 19:11

Facing Forward

My husband and I have a friend who is preparing to retire. A few of his friends expressed concerns. "Will you miss it when you're gone? Will you be bored? Will you look back and wonder about things you wish you'd done but didn't?" Our friend has a very practical answer to those questions. He replied, "The day I retire, I am going to dismantle my rearview mirror before leaving the parking lot. Once I drive out, I will not be looking back."

What good advice—for the Christian life too.

So much of our energy goes into second-guessing. What if I would have . . . ? Could I have helped if only I had . . . ? Maybe this wouldn't have happened if only I hadn't . . . Those are not helpful thoughts after the experience is water under the bridge. Perhaps it's not even right to say that events are water under the bridge—*we* are water under the bridge. We are constantly moving forward, passing bridges and events and flowing toward the next thing.

Without a rearview mirror, our friend could see only the vistas ahead. What does God have next? Where can he invest his life for others, for the Kingdom? For us all to remove our mirrors (figuratively, of course), we must trust that if we have made mistakes in the past and repented of them, God can take those mistakes—has taken those mistakes—and made good of them. After all, the working out of God's plan is not dependent upon our acting perfectly. If that were the case, we'd be doomed—or Old Testament law would have been sufficient. No, the working out of God's plan is dependent upon God alone. How glad we are of that! That means, of course, we are free to stop looking in the rearview mirror and wondering, *What if . . . ?*

You may not be retiring yet. But perhaps you're moving on to a new ministry. Maybe your kids are moving into a new grade or moving out of the house. Perhaps you're changing schools or a job. Maybe you've had a divorce. Whatever has happened, has happened. Focus on the horizon just ahead. What's that up there? Something good!

No, dear brothers and sisters, I have not achieved it, but I focus on this one thing: Forgetting the past and looking forward to what lies ahead, I press on to reach the end of the race and receive the heavenly prize for which God, through Christ Jesus, is calling us. PHILIPPIANS 3:13-14, NLT

Never Alone

In Luke 3, Jesus is being baptized, and one of the most powerful sections of Scripture opens up. God speaks audibly to the crowd and says how beloved his Son is to him. The Holy Spirit descends as a dove. Immediately afterward, in Luke 4, the Holy Spirit—note that—leads Jesus to the desert where Satan tempts him. Jesus, of course, does not fall into temptation. At the very end of that passage, though, in verse 13, comes something important that often goes overlooked. "When the devil had finished tempting Jesus, he left him until the next opportunity came" (NLT).

It is true that when we resist Satan, he will flee (see James 4:7). But it is equally true that Satan prowls around looking for whom he may devour (see 1 Peter 5:8). Satan thought there would be an opportunity to tempt Jesus again, so mere mortals like you and I need to, as 1 Peter 5:8 warns, be alert. We are much more vulnerable targets.

What does it mean to be alert? Perhaps it means to know that you are a target for Satan, never more so than when you are working effectively on behalf of the Lord. The more you give yourself to the cause of Christ and Kingdom work, the more of a threat you are to the devil. It is no coincidence that Jesus' tempting came right after his baptism—right after what we call a "mountain-top" experience.

It also means knowing when you are most likely to be tempted, and by what. Jesus was hungry, likely tired, perhaps worn by the elements. He knew he was not meeting people's expectations. He was alone. All of these are times when Satan might find an opportunity to tempt us, too. But notice—Jesus was not left alone to face his temptations. Note, too, that the Holy Spirit led Jesus to that temptation, but nowhere in that passage does it say the Holy Spirit left Jesus during that time. He descended upon Jesus at his baptism and stayed with him throughout the temptation. The Spirit won't leave you, either (see Deuteronomy 31:6).

Be alert—but do not be afraid. When tempting comes, stand strong and know that if your life is a threat to the enemy, it's a benefit to God's Kingdom!

When the devil had finished tempting Jesus, he left him until the next opportunity came.   LUKE 4:13, NLT

Storyteller

An anthology is a collection of works written by a variety of authors but put together as a whole. The Bible might be considered an anthology as it was written over the course of nearly two thousand years, by approximately forty authors from more than one continent. The pieces all work together to be one whole—the Holy Scriptures. Of course, in the case of the Bible, there is truly only one Author desirous of conveying his Word to his people.

Human-driven anthologies also revolve around one theme or purpose. Some might be: clothing in the Tudor era, nature poetry, home canning recipes, or biographies of women in science. Each story adds a unique voice, a new and fresh perspective, that when read together make a complete story.

We, God's children, are an anthology of sorts. We look different, we sound different, we speak different languages, and we live and have lived over the span of thousands of years and in many places. Only when we add our stories together can we see the larger picture of God and what he is doing across space and time.

I joke with the Lord that I hope my story is about someone who wins a large lottery and distributes it for godly purposes. Maybe I can be the one who has the longest-running bestselling book and uses that platform to share about him. Mostly, though, my story and yours are about living life with day-to-day pacing, with one or two shining, blue-ribbon moments, like Eric Liddell (see January 10). Some of us are called to be the chapter of martyrdom, pain, suffering, discrimination, or the long walk of faith during a difficult era. Most of us don't want to be that chapter. And yet, God decides how we add to his story in the most effective way.

Wherever you are in God's story, it is exclusive and important, and the story would not be complete without it. As God's children, we are loved equally by him, but our stories are different. And what a wonderful thing that is! We don't want a duplicate of your neighbor's story, or your favorite musician's or Bible teacher's story. We have that one already. The one we want is yours. His story would not be complete without it.

You saw me before I was born. Every day of my life was recorded in your book. Every moment was laid out before a single day had passed.

PSALM 139:16, NLT

Experiencing the Love of God

I love to read stories of real people who walked the sometimes-thorny path of faith and prevailed. There is nothing like a good biography to help us lift our eyes past our light and momentary troubles (see 2 Corinthians 4:17) and see what God is doing in the long game.

Do you have a favorite biography? Here are a few to begin with. Why not select one for summer reading?

Same Kind of Different as Me—Ron Hall and Denver Moore with Lynn Vincent
Bonhoeffer—Eric Metaxas
A Man Called Peter—Catherine Marshall
Walking on Water—Madeleine L'Engle
The Little Woman—Gladys Aylward with Christine Hunter
The Hiding Place—Corrie ten Boom with Elizabeth and John Sherrill
Tortured for Christ—Richard Wurmbrand
Through Gates of Splendor—Elisabeth Elliot
Chasing the Dragon—Jackie Pullinger with Andrew Quicke
Run Baby Run—Nicky Cruz
Unbroken—Laura Hillenbrand
Fearless—Eric Blehm
First We Have Coffee—Margaret Jensen
God's Smuggler—Brother Andrew with Elizabeth and John Sherrill
Me, Myself, and Bob—Phil Vischer
When Breath Becomes Air—Paul Kalanithi
George Müeller: Delighted in God—Roger Steer
The Heavenly Man—Brother Yun with Paul Hattaway

One of my favorite genres to read is ethnography—stories about people from cultures and backgrounds different from my own. It warms me to know that God has chosen his people from every nation and people and language, and that one day we will all stand together before him. Reading their stories gives me something wonderful to look forward to. How about you?

I looked, and behold, a great multitude that no one could number, from every nation, from all tribes and peoples and languages, standing before the throne and before the Lamb, clothed in white robes, with palm branches in their hands, and crying out with a loud voice, "Salvation belongs to our God who sits on the throne, and to the Lamb!" REVELATION 7:9-10, ESV

Panning for Gold

I was on a long flight recently, and there was a lot of turbulence. Not my favorite way to pass the hours in the sky; not yours, either, I'll bet. Most of us don't like turbulence in general. We wish for "smooth sailing" in the air and life. Yet I have come to believe that the most turbulent times, filled with commotion and unrest, often yield the long-lasting treasures in our lives and society. Just look at the circumstances surrounding most of those biographies listed on July 29!

Once, when my family was flying into a very turbulent area, my young daughter proclaimed that it was as exciting as a roller coaster ride. She didn't know what up or down or twist or turn was just ahead, and it thrilled her. She didn't know there was something to be fearful of—she was confident things would end well no matter what. Her attitude allowed her to enjoy one aspect of an unavoidable circumstance.

Our world is undergoing upheaval in nearly every nation. It's uncomfortable. It feels a bit scary. We don't see where things might lead. Looking back through history, though, much good was wrought during times of instability.

When my kids were little, we took them to a river to pan gold. Gold does not travel far from its mother lode, and it's heavy, so when it does travel, it quickly settles in the sediment of the river. The river must churn, sometimes brought on by a storm, to dislodge the gold from the bottom. If there is no natural storm, gold panners stir up the water themselves with shovels, burrowing them in the sediment to lift the treasure to the surface. Likewise, if you've visited the ocean beach, you know that strong wave activity and pounding surf deliver those beautiful seashells to the shore.

Do not be afraid of the troubled times in the world or in your life. God may be working out things of great value in the turbulence—he can often be the source of troubling the waters to bring about healing. Peace, remember, comes not from our environment or circumstances but from his Holy Spirit, available during turbulent flights or in smooth sailing.

Now there is in Jerusalem by the sheep gate a pool, which is called in Hebrew Bethesda, having five porticoes. In these lay a multitude of those who were sick, blind, lame, and withered, waiting for the moving of the waters; for an angel of the Lord went down at certain seasons into the pool and stirred up the water; whoever then first, after the stirring up of the water, stepped in was made well from whatever disease with which he was afflicted.

JOHN 5:2-4, NASB

A Benediction for July

This part of summer, in the Northern Hemisphere, often brings evening thunderstorms. They are beautiful to watch, but we're aware of their crackling power just the same. Remember, God has the power to control storms, in nature and in life. Without someone bravely considering the lightning once, we would not have electricity. Think how much good has come of that!

I pray for you, my friend, this coming month, as you light your world, and I offer this benediction from Scripture for you, as a reassurance of God's powerful love, infinite care, and ever-present protection. He loves you, you know, no matter the thunderstorms and turbulence that might sometimes suggest otherwise.

Through these pages and the power of Scripture, I reach my hands out to and over you, as your sister in Christ, and pray . . .

Now all glory to God, who is able, through his mighty power at work within us, to accomplish infinitely more than we might ask or think. Glory to him in the church and in Christ Jesus through all generations forever and ever! Amen.　　　　　　　　　　　　　　　EPHESIANS 3:20-21, NLT

AUGUST

Doulas

August always reminds me of children. My daughter is an August baby; our church has the children participate in "big service" in August; and many kids are trying to stretch out one last month of summer before returning to school. This month, a friend is about to become a grandmother for the first time, and her daughter will be cared for by a doula.

Doula means "female servant" in Greek. A doula is wise and experienced. She tends to the mom before, during, and after a baby is born. She's not a midwife or a doctor; she's there to be a support to the mom in nonmedical ways—which are sometimes even more important! A doula provides emotional support, physical assistance, and instruction. She reassures. She tends. She nurtures. Somehow in the process of bringing a cute baby into the world the person doing the work—Mom—is often overlooked. A doula makes sure that doesn't happen.

As important as our physical birth is, Christians understand that the "second birth," that of our spirit, is even more important. Jesus says we must be born of the water—our physical birth—and of the Spirit—our spiritual birth—to enter the Kingdom of God.

I became a Christian as an adult and remember how bewildered I was. A wise and loving woman, Shirley, watched me as I took steps toward Christ. She picked me up for church and didn't ask where I'd been the night before. She reassured and comforted me, prayed for me, and brought me meals. She invited me to Bible studies and made me feel welcome in her home. She rejoiced with me at my new birth. The Holy Spirit led me to salvation, but afterward, I was a tender little calf of a believer. Shirley took me under her wing; as a mature believer, she made sure I was well cared for until my legs weren't shaky anymore. She discipled me. Shirley was, in a manner of speaking, my spiritual doula.

God makes Christians. Christians are to make disciples, and I can think of no better model than a doula. Are you ready to come alongside a new birth and pray, reassure, comfort, and encourage that new believer? With your guidance, their shaky first steps can become sure and steady!

Jesus replied, "Very truly I tell you, no one can see the kingdom of God unless they are born again."
JOHN 3:3

Baby Showers

One of the most exciting times for an almost-new-mom is her baby shower. The people who love her most gather around and help her prepare for all the things she and the new baby will need.

Most new moms don't have any of the necessary equipment, not having had a child before. Mature, experienced moms provide things they'll need—and fun things they'll want, like clothes in sizes up to 3T and books with funny insights for new moms.

In keeping with our understanding of nurturing a believer's brand-new faith, what kind of things could we, mature and experienced Christians, provide for them? A short list might include

- a Bible, of course
- other books by favorite Christian authors
- a list of radio stations that play Christian music
- guidance to a Bible app or a list of favorite verses
- hugs, reassurance, prayer, and love

After a baby is born and the initial excitement fades, the new mom is often left on her own . . . right when she most needs a friend. New babies can be colicky for months. Immunizations are stressful for both Mom and baby. Questions arise at each step of the baby's growth. A great friend, or a grandma or mentor, will stick with the mom long after the shower's party favors have been packed away.

This, too, is a part of the discipleship discussed in yesterday's devotional. Often there is a flurry of excitement after someone accepts Christ, but the busy demands of life get in the way, and the new believer is soon left on her own to tend to her new life of faith. This is often a vulnerable time as she is likely to be distancing herself from bad habits and perhaps bad influences. The most treasured gift I received at a baby shower was a gift of checking-in coffee coupons from an older friend—every month for a year. I knew it came at the cost of her free time, and I treasured it. This is the kind of discipler I want to be too. Do you know anyone who is young or uncertain in her faith, whom you might come alongside?

Be devoted to one another in brotherly love; give preference to one another in honor.
ROMANS 12:10, NASB

Son-Seeking Safaris

August is the month when many churches, including my own, give the Sunday school teachers a sabbatical, which means the kids are in big church for the entire service. Personally, I love it.

Sometimes the kids lead worship, and when they do, I am struck by the purity of the offering of their hearts. Sometimes they are invited to lead prayer or to give a portion of a message. After Vacation Bible School week, they stand on the stage and teach us all the hand motions to the songs they have learned. You haven't lived till you've seen a church filled with people aged eighteen to eighty-eight lifting their hands and repeating the VBS theme-song motions. One week we sat behind a very sad looking young man who smiled after the kids sang. A sixty-year-old woman turned herself around and high-fived the person in the pew behind her. Men worshiped with enthusiasm usually reserved for sporting events.

Don't we all need a little more of that? I know I do!

When did we all start thinking that we need to be serious in church? Of course, we need to be respectful, but the Lord instructs us to make a joyful noise. "Make a joyful noise to the Lord, all the earth; break forth into joyous song and sing praises!" it says in Psalm 98:4 (esv). Sometimes I wonder if a stranger wandering into one of our churches might wonder if he had walked into a funeral service instead of a worship service.

I've resolved to enjoy myself in church, to delight myself in God and all that he has provided: fellowship, music, Scripture, traditions, and teaching. I lean forward. I take notes (digital ones!). I make sure to shake at least one person's hand. I don't dash out the door the moment the service is over. I approach the day with expectant delight.

Isaiah 11:6 says, "and a little child will lead them all" (nlt). Let's raise our hands in praise. Let's sing every song. Let's smile at everyone around us. As for me, I am still whistling the VBS tune "Come on along on a Son-Seeker Safari . . ."

At that time the disciples came to Jesus and asked, "Who, then, is the greatest in the kingdom of heaven?" He called a little child to him, and placed the child among them. And he said: "Truly I tell you, unless you change and become like little children, you will never enter the kingdom of heaven. Therefore, whoever takes the lowly position of this child is the greatest in the kingdom of heaven. And whoever welcomes one such child in my name welcomes me.
MATTHEW 18:1-5

Sweaty Pennies

In the pew ahead of me sat a beautiful little girl with her father. Her dad had come prepared: he had a coloring book, a bag of Goldfish crackers, and a lot of love. She wore a tiara, which sparkled under the ceiling lights. She had on a T-shirt with a rainbow heart decked out in glitter. She had a million-watt smile.

I was close enough to see her father open her hand and drop something in her palm. To me, it looked like four or five coins. She clenched her fist around them and stopped eating the fish crackers as she couldn't maneuver them with one hand. Soon after that, our offering plates were passed, and as her father held one out to her, she unclenched her fist. Those sweaty coins dropped into the plate—all but one, which stuck to her hand. She used her other hand to pry it off and ensure it dropped into the plate before passing the plate along.

She held nothing back. You know why? She didn't need to. Her father had thoughtfully provided everything she'd need, and she seemed to believe without question that she would have whatever she'd need later, too. Her dad had given her the money for a specific reason—not to clutch any of it for herself—but to pass it along to the work of the Lord in our church.

Of course, you and I have more bills to pay and financial obligations than that little girl did. But we share the same Father, do we not? He gives us so much, but he does ask for us to return a small portion to him. I confess, I clench those sweaty pennies more often than I'd like to admit. As the Spirit showed me this, though, I did not sense condemnation. Only encouragement to give . . . and to trust.

I am his little girl. You are too. You get to keep the tiara, as a daughter of the King. Just turn in a few of those pennies somewhere that will do good, in his name.

Where your treasure is, there your heart will be also.   MATTHEW 6:21

Experiencing the Love of God

In yesterday's devotional I shared about a young girl who inspired me by freely giving of the pennies she clutched in her hands—resources given to her by a loving father. Are you, like me, clutching too many coins? Is there something you could do without to give a bit more to your church or another Christian cause? You can start small. I did. Most days, my newspaper goes unread. Canceling that subscription would free up a little money to be donated. I do like coffee better at home, mostly. I can make shoes and coats and other clothing last longer than I have been. I throw away too much food, which is convicting on several levels.

One of the things I loved most about watching that little girl was that she didn't consider it a sacrifice to give. She released freely because, like a funnel, she seemed to understand that resources were simply passing through her. Letting go of a few coins today only made room for more to pass through tomorrow. I want that almost nonchalant faith, trust, and positive anticipation.

Will you make a commitment today to let a few of those sweaty pennies fly?

Not that I am speaking of being in need, for I have learned in whatever situation I am to be content. I know how to be brought low, and I know how to abound. In any and every circumstance, I have learned the secret of facing plenty and hunger, abundance and need. I can do all things through him who strengthens me. PHILIPPIANS 4:11-13, ESV

Good Girl!

One day I popped my toddler daughter and her doll into a shopping cart at a local store. Once inside, I stepped a foot away to pluck something from a shelf, and when I turned back to her, I was horrified. My daughter was sternly talking to her doll. "Bad Baby! Bad Girl!" I turned around to look at the people nearby staring in horror. At me!

I knew what they were thinking, because I would have been thinking it too. Is that the way the mother treats the little girl in the cart? Is that why she is acting it out on the doll? The truth was, I had never told my daughter she was a bad baby, a bad girl, or anything else. She'd picked it up from somewhere else. The ill stares didn't fade away; I had been judged as a parent by the way my child was acting. I wanted to run after these people and assure them that I was a good parent and that my daughter (and her toys!) were well loved and cared for.

We all know what it's like to be misjudged based on someone else's actions, but there are also times when people judge my husband and me positively for the things our children do. Our kids model their father's humor and selfless giving of himself. They model my love of gift giving. Although I credit my children for their own good, I must admit that when people praise me for their good actions, I feel happy that I have poured my heart and soul into them. I worry, too, that when people see them struggle, they might wonder if I've failed along the way somehow.

We Christians are Christ's ambassadors in this world. Rightly or wrongly, the world often judges our faith, and our God, by the way we treat one another. Obviously, we cannot live up to perfection. But we don't want to come across as harsh, either. We can strive to be like Jesus. "Whatever you do, whether in word or deed, do it all in the name of the Lord Jesus, giving thanks to God the Father through him" (Colossians 3:17).

He's a good Father, and I want to show the world I've been well parented! I rejoice in hearing him say, "Good girl!"

Live such good lives among the pagans that, though they accuse you of doing wrong, they may see your good deeds and glorify God on the day he visits us.

1 PETER 2:12

Inner Tubes

We live in a wet climate, a climate that makes mushrooms as happy as clams, and makes clams, who like wet conditions, pretty happy themselves. So, playing outside is not possible for about half the year. Some entrepreneurs came up with a good substitute—playgrounds inside the mall.

When my son was little and we both desperately needed a day out of the house, I took him to one of these indoor play spaces, which was mostly made up of long tubes from ground to ceiling that zigzagged across the room, ending in slides in various places. The play space took up the whole room; I mean a *big* room. A room the size of a small department store. My son crawled way up inside one of those tubes and then . . . he didn't come down.

After a few minutes, I paced the room and called his name toward the high-flying tubes. After a minute or two, he called out, "I'm here, Mommy. I'm stuck."

A kind employee handed over some knee pads, and I scrunched down and climbed into the tube and then up, up, up, to find my son. When I reached him, I found he was not stuck. He was sitting in the center of a tube. "You're not stuck?" I said.

"No," he said. "I was scared. But now that you are here, let's have fun, Mommy!" We made our way across the long tube (several children gave me rather odd looks!) and then slid down together. "That was fun!" my son said. "Let's do it again!"

Well, no. But it was fun—once!

There are adventures presented in my life too, about which I first feel fear. I do not see where the tunnel will end, and the territory I am to cover is unfamiliar. And yet deep in my heart I know that if my Father led me to this adventure, I will be safe. The beauty is, he never leaves me there alone. We, he and I, are always together on our adventures. I can be scared, but when I remember he is with me, I can say, "Okay. Let's have fun!"

Have I not commanded you? Be strong and courageous. Do not be afraid; do not be discouraged, for the LORD your God will be with you wherever you go. JOSHUA 1:9

A Daughter of the King

Buckingham Palace in London is open to the public in August because the queen is at another residence. Hung with portraits and chandeliers, it is as grand and gold as you would imagine. Once when I visited, the tour guide showed us how those beautiful, huge chandeliers are cleaned. I had pictured a tall ladder reaching up, but no. A hidden crank lowered the chandeliers so they could be polished at the level of the mere mortal who spent a day—one whole day!—polishing each one.

I left in a cheerful haze of royal bounty, but I couldn't help but think of Jesus. Along with William Dix, the author of the beautiful Christmas hymn "What Child Is This?" I wondered, "Why lies He in such mean estate?"

The King of kings, when he lived here on earth, was born in a cold barn, without gold or portraits. The chandeliers? Well, there was that one star! He lived in a poor family. He worked as a carpenter. He rode a donkey. And in the end, he was nailed to a rugged cross where soldiers gambled for his clothing.

But then I remember—whence he came, and to where he returned, is a Kingdom richer than any we have yet seen. The cities are made of gold, the gates are made of pearls, and best of all, every creature and being there recognizes his position as King.

You may live in humble circumstances. You may not be esteemed by those around you. I don't have a chandelier, and the portraits on my walls were snapped with my cell phone! But we, friend, are daughters of the King. We must not look here on earth for a lifestyle higher than our King's. "The student is not above the teacher, nor a servant above his master" (Matthew 10:24).

We are children of the King here and must live accordingly, but we will be children of the King in heaven, too, and can live accordingly there as well!

The twelve gates were twelve pearls, each gate made of a single pearl. The great street of the city was of gold, as pure as transparent glass.

REVELATION 21:21

Family Jewels

It's not only the queen who travels; all members of each British royal family are required to travel too, as ambassadors. Recently, one young royal family traveled to Canada with their small, adorable children. Attention is always paid to what the Duchess of Cambridge wears, and on this trip, her jewelry included a maple leaf brooch.

According to reports, the maple leaf brooch, made of diamonds, was given to the late Queen Mother by her husband, King George VI, after a trip to Canada. The duchess's engagement ring once belonged to her mother-in-law, though they never met. She often wears tiaras from the Royal Jewelry collection, which is partly stored in the Tower of London.

These treasures, worth more than most of us can imagine, have been handed down in her family, in her husband's family, for hundreds of years, generation to generation. Many of us have precious treasures we have received from long-gone loved ones, and we intend to pass them on to our children. Once more, though, my mind and heart turn back to the Lord.

Jesus had a crown, of course, but his was made of thorns. It was not given in a moment of joy and admiration, as with human coronation ceremonies. No, it was given to him (along with the royal purple robe he so deserved) in a moment of humiliation. Yet, I propose, this is our blessed, treasured inheritance; it's easier to bear when we understand that he bore it first out of his deep love and his desire for reconciliation with us. We must wear that crown of humiliation in this world; Jesus tells us, "If the world hates you, keep in mind that it hated me first" (John 15:18). It's much the same as picking up our cross—daily—as he did, and following after him (see Luke 9:23).

I am so looking forward to passing along to my children and my grandchildren the few worthy treasures I have collected in life. But mainly, I want to pass along the truth of the Lord and his Kingdom, the most valuable thing I have to share.

The soldiers led Jesus away into the palace (that is, the Praetorium) and called together the whole company of soldiers. They put a purple robe on him, then twisted together a crown of thorns and set it on him. And they began to call out to him, "Hail, king of the Jews!" MARK 15:16-18

Birthstones

When I am tired or busy, and have little time for Bible reading and just want God to give me the answer right now, I identify with the disciples. "Why do you speak in parables?" (see Matthew 13:10). What I'm really asking God is, "Why don't you just make this easier?" Sometimes God gives us immediate and clear directions, but mostly he doesn't.

Why not?

My son lived in Idaho for a short time, and while we were visiting him there one day he mentioned that there was a quarry nearby from which a person could dig out rare star garnets. My ears perked up. "Garnets are my birthstone, and I've never owned one," I said. We decided it would be fun to investigate what would be involved in finding one.

You may remember a few months ago I shared how we'd taken our son to a stocked fishpond when he was a boy—easy fishing (see March 29). Well . . . this wasn't anything like that. The ground was dusty and dirty, and covering it all was mud the texture of mayonnaise. To find a rare garnet would take hours of persistent seeking, digging, rinsing. Then, once the treasure was found, it would need to be carefully handled and polished before it could be used. A gem seeker did not simply stumble into the field, bend over, and pick up something valuable. The principle of discovering and uncovering the Kingdom of God is similar. Proverbs 20 tells us that the one who works, not the sluggard, prospers. That is true for financial and spiritual gain. What we want, we work for; what we work for, we treasure.

When we began our research, we watched a video made by an experienced garnet miner. He said to be successful is to know where to look—for example, clay soil is hard to sift and holds no jewels, anyway. Where do we dig for spiritual treasure? The Word. A solid church. Our intimate prayers. Christian friends with proven spiritual maturity. Christian books. Communion with the Spirit.

Ready to dig?

The kingdom of heaven is like treasure hidden in a field. When a man found it, he hid it again, and then in his joy went and sold all he had and bought that field. MATTHEW 13:44

Strands of Pearls

There is no jewel quite like a pearl—its luminous, moonlight shine is recognized as singular the world over. Pearls, unlike gemstones, are not dug out of the earth. They are harvested from the sea.

Pearls.com explains that a pearl is started when an irritant makes its way into an oyster, mussel, or clam. Interestingly, it's most often not a grain of sand, as we've all been taught, that is the core of a pearl; it's a parasite! The pearl website goes on to explain that layers of fluid are excreted by the shell organism, and this fluid, called nacre, is meant to build up a protective shield around that irritant so it cannot harm the host. It takes many years for a gem-quality pearl to develop.

Natural pearls are rare and beautiful, and therefore, valuable. When my daughter got married, her new mother-in-law passed along some valuable family jewelry to her, including some pearls. Her mother-in-law particularly loves pearls, and on the night of the wedding, she gifted me, too, with a lovely, long strand of them, a gift of deep affection at a dear cost to herself.

A passage in Matthew 13 tells us that to become a subject in the Kingdom of Heaven, ruled by Jesus Christ, we must be willing to give up everything else—its value is worth more than the sum of all that we have. Most of us don't have the financial resources of the rich young ruler (see Luke 18) that we'll have to relinquish. But we all must give up something. Pride? Control of our own destinies? Status? Earthly security? Relationships? Anger?

And yet we know God doesn't ask us to surrender unless it's for our good and the good of his Kingdom. If we surrender our irritants, even our parasites—those who would harm us—to the Lord, he will protect us from harm and even return something valuable to us in exchange. Ask the Lord if there is anything further you need to hand over in return for his Kingdom. You can be sure you're getting something rare, beautiful, and valuable—at a good bargain!

The kingdom of heaven is like a merchant looking for fine pearls. When he found one of great value, he went away and sold everything he had and bought it. MATTHEW 13:45-46

Experiencing the Love of God

I'm a great believer in having physical reminders of emotional and spiritual commitments, of the ways in which God has rescued and saved us. It's a biblical principle laid out in Joshua 4, as well. The Israelites, under the leadership of Joshua, who was following the directions given him by the Lord, had just crossed the Jordan River into the land God had promised them. God miraculously held back the waters for a time so they could safely transport their treasure—the Ark of the Covenant—to the other side.

In order to mark the occasion of this miraculous deliverance and provision, God commanded Joshua to take twelve stones from the places the priestly representatives had stood in the middle of the Jordan River. They were to use the stones to build a monument so the generations that followed wouldn't forget God's miraculous provision. Remembering a previous time God intervened on our behalf helps us have faith that he will act on our behalf again and again!

The past few days I've discussed how having jewels, gems, and other beautiful jewelry sometimes helps me recall God's love and affection for me. Sometimes, faith, which is intangible, is slippery. Having something to remind us of his goodness and provision, whether it's twelve stones in a new land or a raw birthstone, helps keep the eyes of the heart focused. Why not buy for yourself a set of pearl earrings or a strand of pearls? They can be man-made; after all, most of us are *not* rich young rulers, and the idea is to wear something that brings God's Kingdom to mind often. Perhaps you might gift synthetic jewelry, or something with decorative pearls on it, as an encouragement to a believer who needs some hope.

Have you ever owned a piece of jewelry with your birthstone? Why not now? You are precious in God's sight. One woman I knew bought a birthstone from the month of her spiritual birth as a tangible reminder of how precious she is in his sight, and how welcome she is in his Kingdom.

> Joshua said to them, "Pass on before the ark of the LORD your God into the midst of the Jordan, and take up each of you a stone upon his shoulder, according to the number of the tribes of the people of Israel, that this may be a sign among you. When your children ask in time to come, 'What do those stones mean to you?' then you shall tell them that the waters of the Jordan were cut off before the ark of the covenant of the LORD. When it passed over the Jordan, the waters of the Jordan were cut off. So these stones shall be to the people of Israel a memorial forever." JOSHUA 4:5-7, ESV

Dust Devils

We were taking a long drive across the dry, flat agricultural half of our state. I stared into the distance, and something caught my eye. "Is that a tornado touching down?" I asked my husband. "No," he said. "It's a dust devil."

Tornadoes are formed in the air and may eventually touch down. Dust devils are formed on the earth and reach up till they dissipate. Their genesis is in hot ground—a piece of ground hotter than that around it. The air picks up energy and then begins to swirl, collecting dirt and debris from around it, building it into a powerful force. It's only hot air, after all, but the devil has cloaked its identity in whatever muck and filth it can stir up.

Doesn't that just sound like our enemy, the devil, after whom they were named? Stirring up trouble out of nothing, confusing whatever environment he is in, and of course, throwing dirt.

Jesus tells us in John 8 that Satan is a murderer and has nothing to do with truth, because there is no truth in him. Jesus, of course, is the complete opposite. I find it interesting that in English we say, "Tell *the* truth" not "Tell *a* truth." There is only one truth in any situation. There can be many lies about any situation.

Once a lie is told, more lies must be told to support and cover for it. People who won't turn a blind eye to the lie but expose the lie by sharing the truth often become the next victim of the dust devil, the throwing of mud and confusion to cloak what is truly happening.

Satan likes to stir the muck, pointing out things in dry areas of our lives, encouraging us to envy our neighbors, our sisters, our friends. He also looks for heated ground in our lives to stir up strife and anger among coworkers, family, and friends.

Dust devils eventually die out for lack of heat and energy. Although it may sometimes be frightening to speak up to those who lie, God's love for you—and for truth—will give you the confidence to speak up when you need to. Let's commit to bringing only the truth to any situation and disallow envy and contention in our lives, dismantling the confusion the devil likes to bring—in effect, blowing cool air on all that heat.

Where envying and strife is, there is confusion and every evil work.
JAMES 3:16, KJV

No Squawking!

There was a big fight in my front yard this morning. A large gang of characters had gathered, and they were bullying each other. Finally, a few of them gave up and with noisy caws, flew away.

Crows.

But the discontent seemed to have spread to my backyard, too, where the normally mild-mannered and sweet juncos had gathered. One of them had puffed out his little chest and was screeching at another bird who had dared approach the long, cylindrical bird feeder we keep hanging from a mount in a protected section of the backyard. I'd had enough and finally shooed the intimidator away as a little mild discipline. I knew he felt territorial, but after all, this was my territory. I know he was protecting his own, but that was my job. He was concerned about the food, for sure, but I always keep the feeder full, and with access to a freshwater birdbath as well, he needn't be stingy.

But are we very different?

I often wonder if we Christians believe that our faith is a zero-sum game. That is, there are only so many widgets of blessing, let's say one hundred, and if my neighbor gets twenty, and my friend gets fifty, and my coworker gets twenty, that only leaves ten possible widgets of blessing for me. Not at all! God's resources are unlimited (see Ephesians 3:16). Have you heard the phrase "They are printing money"? Our God has no restrictions on the number of blessings he can bestow.

From now on, rather than falling into the temptation of "why her and not me," let's pray, *Thank you for providing for her.* Our Father is rich, friend (see Philippians 4:19). Christianity is not a zero-sum situation; God has enough to give generously to all, to us and through us, and we don't want to descend to the level of squawking birds, even if only in prayer.

Now he who supplies seed to the sower and bread for food will also supply and increase your store of seed and will enlarge the harvest of your righteousness. You will be enriched in every way so that you can be generous on every occasion, and through us your generosity will result in thanksgiving to God.

2 CORINTHIANS 9:10-11

For the Love of a Boy

I know a delightful young man who had some very, very tough years growing up. Although he was rowing in turbulent waters, he had one steady, constant source of comfort—his dog, Oliver. Like many of our pets, Oliver loved this young man completely and without question. He was always near. He was always sympathetic. And he was . . . old.

But he lived on . . . and on . . . and on, many years past his expected life span! I've come to think he was the canine version of the oil and flour provided for Elijah and the widow and her son (see 1 Kings 17). The Lord provided what was most needed, and in the most vulnerable time, in an unusual and unexpected way.

I know that I am often so limited in how I look for and expect God to work. I sometimes look at it as a math equation of sorts, with one definite integer to be provided for a solution. But God is creative and unexpected and uncontrollable. In all that, though, his solutions are perfect and often surprising. "'For my thoughts are not your thoughts, neither are your ways my ways,' declares the LORD. 'As the heavens are higher than the earth, so are my ways higher than your ways and my thoughts than your thoughts'" (Isaiah 55:8-9).

Although this young man would not have chosen to navigate those rough passages in childhood, he understands that they helped to form him and to shape his ministry and his character in ways an easier journey might not have. God did not solve the problems the way my young friend might have wanted them solved. But he provided extraordinary comfort for the journey in the form of a long-lived dog named Oliver.

Let's keep our eyes open for the clever, unanticipated ways our loving God meets all our needs. His ways are not our ways, but his care and compassion, his provisions, never fail.

Praise be to the God and Father of our Lord Jesus Christ, the Father of compassion and the God of all comfort, who comforts us in all our troubles, so that we can comfort those in any trouble with the comfort we ourselves receive from God. For just as we share abundantly in the sufferings of Christ, so also our comfort abounds through Christ. 2 CORINTHIANS 1:3-5

Contagious

I'd always had a great desire to grow lavender. Because I live in a wet area of the country with a lot of trees, the condition for dry-loving, sun-loving plants had not presented itself. Until we moved into this house, that is.

The front of the house faces the water, and there are no trees to block that hot, glorious sun. I planted eighteen lavender plants in all and tended to them carefully. Everything seemed to be going well, until one wilted. All the little purple heads on that bush drooped downward. Thinking I had overdone the dry climate approach and it needed water, I watered it well. Then I took the water wand to each of the other seventeen plants and watered them well too.

Within a week, they were all dying. An expert helped me to understand that the first plant had a fungal disease, and when I had buried the head of the water wand deep within the bush to water it, and then done the same with the other plants, I infected them all. The plants would all need to be ripped out. They could not even be composted; they needed to be burned. Only burning the plants would ensure the disease did not spread to every other plant in my garden—and even to my neighbors'.

One diseased lavender can, and did, infect them all. I loved them, but they had to go, lest they damage the others around them. Is there anything in you—in your habits, in your mind, or in your proclivities—that leads to repetitive sin? Be courageous; rip it out. God is a patient, loving gardener, and he wants us to be healthy. His Spirit is faithful to show us the blights (sin), and then we must take action against our sin. Better to take one, albeit beloved, plant out than to lose the whole garden.

If your hand—even your stronger hand—causes you to sin, cut it off and throw it away. It is better for you to lose one part of your body than for your whole body to be thrown into hell. MATTHEW 5:30, NLT

Feeding the Shepherd and the Sheep

We often think of ministering to others in Jesus' name, or Jesus himself ministering to us. I was surprised, though, as I was recently studying the period just before the Lord's death, when a section of Scripture that I'd read many times before suddenly yielded a fresh insight.

Jesus wants us to minister to him, too.

The night before Jesus was crucified, he asked his disciples to join him in the garden of Gethsemane. "He told them, 'My soul is crushed with grief to the point of death. Stay here and keep watch with me'" (Matthew 26:38, NLT). Unfortunately, Matthew 26:40 reports, "Then he returned to the disciples and found them asleep. He said to Peter, 'Couldn't you watch with me even one hour?'" (NLT).

I feel bad for Peter; all the disciples were asleep, but Peter was called out. Peter's difficulties were not over yet, though. Just a few verses later, before Jesus' crucifixion, we read a now-familiar passage in which Peter denies knowing Jesus. "Peter swore, 'A curse on me if I'm lying—I don't know the man!'" (Matthew 26:74, NLT).

Shortly after his resurrection, Jesus ministered to Peter and commissioned him to minister in his name: "Feed my sheep," he told Peter. Peter never failed Jesus again.

I wondered, am I, as a modern-day disciple, called to minister not just *for* but *to* Jesus? Scripture tells us the answer is yes. In Matthew 25, just one chapter before the Gethsemane passage, the Lord tells us that whenever we offer a hungry person something to eat or a thirsty person something to drink or visit someone who is imprisoned, we are doing it to him.

I don't think he means to limit our actions to those listed in the passage. He tells us that when we encounter someone with a need, whether it be physical, emotional, or spiritual, and we offer them practical comfort and a solution, we are ministering to him.

I know there are times when I have failed my Lord. Like Peter, I know God restores me by grace and offers me the opportunity to minister to him right now, today, this week. I don't want to fail him again.

The King will say, "I tell you the truth, when you did it to one of the least of these my brothers and sisters, you were doing it to me!"

MATTHEW 25:40, NLT

Hall of Famers

I was recently perusing one of my social media feeds when I saw a picture of a friend and her son at the Baseball Hall of Fame. I remembered that he was always interested in baseball. Now he had a career in the sport and visited the place where the greats were listed and honored.

The eleventh chapter of the book of Hebrews is often called the Bible Hall of Fame because it lists many of those recommended, not for their prowess and deeds, but for their faith. In God's Kingdom, faith is the currency that matters. In fact, midway into that passage, Hebrews 11:6 tells us that without faith, it is impossible to please God.

One thing I find truly interesting: there is a so-called Bible Hall of Fame for believers, but there is nothing at all like a Hall of Shame. There is no rundown of those who grew weak, failed a mission, made a bad decision, or even sinned. Who might have been in it? Well, David, perhaps, a murderer and an adulterer. How about Paul—who held the coats of those stoning Stephen, the first Christian martyr? No mention of Peter, either, who, as we read yesterday, would have had reason to be shamed if such a hall existed. There are no bloopers, either: faithful Abraham contrasted with Abraham lying by calling his wife his sister.

Regret and conviction, repentance and remorse, these are God-given emotions meant to help us recognize a wrong path taken and turn around. Shame is a Satan-inspired and man-delivered emotion sent to cripple, paralyze, and humiliate. Have you seen God humiliate anyone in the Bible? Never once.

When we shy away from that painful feeling of shame (the phrase "Shame on you!" rattles many peoples' hearts), it inhibits our willingness to clearly look at our sin. God does not shame us. Instead, when we need correction, he convicts us in love, with clarity and an eye toward wholeness, wellness, and joy.

Put your mistakes behind you, friend, and run swiftly and with confidence toward what lies ahead. You, too, have a place in the Bible Hall of Fame.

Since we are surrounded by such a huge crowd of witnesses to the life of faith, let us strip off every weight that slows us down, especially the sin that so easily trips us up. And let us run with endurance the race God has set before us. We do this by keeping our eyes on Jesus, the champion who initiates and perfects our faith. Because of the joy awaiting him, he endured the cross, disregarding its shame. HEBREWS 12:1-2, NLT

Experiencing the Love of God

If you had a wall upon which you would affix pictures of people in your personal Hall of Fame, whose portraits would you hang? These are people who have helped you, encouraged you, upheld you, led you to faith, or cared for you in a myriad of ways.

Consider posting their pictures (or a list of their names), even tiny ones, on a corkboard in your office or near where you work or often are. Their "presence" will remind you not only of their goodness but the goodness of the Lord who sent them to care for you at just the right moment. If he did that then, he'll do it again!

And then—who would have your picture on their own Hall of Fame board? Don't be shy—you can't encourage yourself to press on to good works if you don't recognize the many ways, big and small, you have already been faithful. If you have difficulty thinking of whom you might have influenced, ask your friends or family. Post those pictures (or names), too, to remind you of the many ways you have stepped out in faith and affection.

Sometimes we don't have a wall in our home where we can post pictures, or if we did, those we wished to honor might not see them. How about posting a photo of someone you'd like to honor on one of your social media accounts? You could complete it with a little insight into how that person has loved and helped you throughout the year.

You might also consider putting a picture of the two of you into a card and popping it in the mail, along with a lunch invitation, if you live nearby. There are lots of ways we can show those we love and honor that they are Hall of Famers to us.

Is there someone you have mentored or guided? Why not follow through by checking in to see how that person is doing today? Not only will your faithfulness honor him or her, it will also honor the Lord, who modeled how we are to love and care for others.

Love each other with genuine affection, and take delight in honoring each other.
ROMANS 12:10, NLT

Mind the Gap

Londoners have a delightful subway system called the London Underground, aka the Tube. They have equally delightful signs to warn riders about the potential danger of the space between the train and the platform: Mind the Gap.

This gap can be a few inches or up to a foot, depending upon the particulars of the Tube station and the train, but can cause the unwary to stumble. Yesterday I had lunch with a wise friend and told her that in this season of my life, I was struggling to trust God deeply in places where I could not foresee the outcome. As we talked, it became impressed upon me that where I struggled was the "gap" between a need I knew I had and my ability to meet that need.

I can do nothing in and of my own power to bridge those gaps. They are completely out of my control, and it's there, then, that I must learn to trust God. God does not tell us we can do all things through discipline, effort, Wikipedia, and human endeavor! Instead, he says we can do all things through him. I shared our immediate financial concerns; he reminded me that he has promised to provide for all my needs (see Philippians 4). I told him I was working hard and growing tired; he reminded me that he has provided a way for me to remain energized if I take him up on it (see Isaiah 41). I shared my hopes and fears for the sales of my books; he reminded me that he delights in blessing those who follow him and that nothing done has been unnoticed or in vain (see Deuteronomy 28; 1 Corinthians 15).

It's not that the answers are not there; it's that I must believe them, not wasting time in worry but choosing to have faith in the certain knowledge that Someone is minding the gap, and therefore I need not. That's the only way to learn to trust deeply. Where are your gaps? He sees them, and he's already got you covered.

"Don't let your hearts be troubled. Trust in God, and trust also in me."

JOHN 14:1, NLT

Neighbors

The home we now live in, the town we now live in, is our forever home (aside from heaven, of course). We are so happy to be here in this small, waterside town and enjoy all that it has to offer. This is one reason I was mortified when I was at the checkout counter in a local store with my husband not long after we moved in.

The cashier had made an error and was not very polite about it. My normally mild-mannered husband made a kind of tart response, and they locked proverbial horns before backing away. After we got into the car, I reminded him, "We're going to live with these people in this small town where news travels fast, forever. We need to be careful how we treat them."

He graciously agreed.

So we keep a neat lawn, and we speak kindly to people (even people whose dogs bark for hours). We leave good reviews for local merchants because they are neighbors and friends, and we want their businesses to prosper. We welcome newcomers with cookies and warm words, and avoid road rage. (Well, mostly. More on that tomorrow!)

I believe that our perspective on heaven might need just that same kind of outlook. Are there Christians who annoy us? Of course there are. Sometimes we want to tell them just what we are thinking. Sometimes we gossip or are short-tempered or unkind or ungenerous. But you know what? We are going to live with one another—literally—forever. Not forever like a couple of decades in a small town. Eternity forever.

I mentioned this to my husband, and he said there would be no problem then, because heaven is sin-free, so everyone would agree with him anyway! He was kidding, of course, and while we're here on earth, we need to seek a solution. Jesus, in John 15:12, says: "My command is this: Love each other as I have loved you." Did you catch that? A command—and we all know what a command means! No other options. Can we do that? Sure we can. He never tells us to do anything we are unable to do without his help!

By this all people will know that you are my disciples, if you have love for one another.   JOHN 13:35, ESV

Training Patience

It's so easy to correct one's husband, so difficult to see fault in oneself.

Not long after I had righteously, though gently (I hoped), rebuked my husband, I found myself on a local road speaking to a driver just ahead of me. "In this state, we use blinkers," I said. "Also known as turn signals."

Luckily, no one else was in the car with me, because, late for an appointment, I continued my unlovely little diatribe at the stoplight. "Green means go," I said. "Are you waiting for a particular shade of green?" A tiny prick plucked at my heart.

I wasn't done yet, though. On Sunday, there was a crying baby a few rows behind me. By sheer willpower I didn't turn around to look, but I did think, *Well, there is a cry room, you know.* I had given my judgmental spirit free rein in church of all places! I felt a much more serious thump of conviction this time and repented.

I've learned it's just as easy to think grace-filled, creative thoughts when I'm annoyed, if I just make an effort. The next time I was held up at a traffic signal I waited patiently behind the woman who didn't gun it the moment the light turned green. When I passed her later, I saw she had a backseat full of little ones. Perhaps she'd been distracted. Was I glad that baby's mother was at church under any circumstances? Of course I was. It was exactly where she needed to be.

Somehow I can give myself a pass on this verse in Matthew 5 if I'm not careful: "[Jesus said,] But I say, if you are even angry with someone, you are subject to judgment! If you call someone an idiot, you are in danger of being brought before the court" (verse 22, NLT).

We're like God when we're kind, tolerant, and patient. Will you join me in seeking ways to be more like him?

You may think you can condemn such people, but you are just as bad, and you have no excuse! When you say they are wicked and should be punished, you are condemning yourself, for you who judge others do these very same things. . . . Don't you see how wonderfully kind, tolerant, and patient God is with you?　　　　　　　　　　　　　　　ROMANS 2:1-2, 4, NLT

Fasting and Feasting

About a year ago, I began a weekly fast. Fasting is a discipline that in Jesus' time was normal and even expected. With few exceptions, though, it has become a practice that is almost unheard of today. Few churches, except for the Orthodox, promote fasting as a normal part of our spiritual disciplines. Discipline is one of the most important reasons to fast.

When we fast, we deny ourselves, something Jesus said we must do if we are to be his disciples. In our era, one filled with plenty, denying ourselves requires a conscious effort. I've learned some things while fasting:

- Denial retrains the appetite. I am not hungry after a few hours, and when I'm finished fasting, I no longer desire the unhealthy foods that may have drawn my attention before a fast. It changes my focus. Somehow, fasting kills my appetite, but eating more makes me hungrier, not only for food, but for almost every other form of consumption.
- Fasting makes me aware that I need much less than I consume. This is true not only for food, but also for the other stuff that makes up our modern lives.
- Fasting sharpens my senses, both physical and spiritual. I hear better, I see more clearly, my thought processes are more focused.

There are many biblical examples of fasting. Jesus taught that some demons could not come out but by fasting and prayer. Both Moses, who brought the old covenant, and Jesus, who fulfilled it and then brought the new covenant, fasted for forty days (see Exodus 34:28 and Luke 4:1-2). Many times in Acts, the early church fasted. Jesus expected that we would fast. In Matthew 6:16 he says, "and *when* you fast" (emphasis added).

As a friend has said to me, fasting is simple, but it isn't easy. No discipline is, to begin with. But do begin. First for a few hours, then for a full day, then perhaps fast once or twice a week (like the Orthodox do). Fasting frees up space when I might be eating or preparing food to instead focus on prayer, meditation, praise, or Scripture reading. With my sharpened senses, I can feast on God's love and leading in a powerful way. You'll soon see physical and spiritual benefits that make you eager for the next fast.

He called the crowd to him along with his disciples and said: "Whoever wants to be my disciple must deny themselves and take up their cross and follow me."   MARK 8:34

A Generous Savior

One year, when my children were very small, I was sick with postpartum depression. In that darkness stood a light: my friend Joye. Nothing was too much for her. She came and picked up the kids and me when I could not drive; she made meals for us. She planned things to make us all feel good and look up and gaze expectantly toward God until I felt better. All of this came at a cost to her. So after I was well and I asked her if she would pick something up for us when she was at the grocery store, she responded, "What? Of course I will!" How could I even wonder if she would do something so small for me when she had already given on such a large level?

I heard a similar story of a man who donated one of his kidneys to his brother. Some time later, his brother asked if he'd be willing to share a bag of chips. You can almost imagine the "Are you kidding me?" look when you think about this, can't you? Having given a piece of himself, what would be even a *case* of chips?

I love to reflect on these stories because they remind me so much of God. The Word tells us in Luke 16:10 that "Whoever can be trusted with very little can also be trusted with much." I believe that works in reverse, too. I had given Joye care over my children and myself at a vulnerable time. Of course she could be trusted with mere groceries! That man had given his brother a precious part of himself, at great cost and pain. Of course he would share in the nonessentials.

When you wonder if God cares about your "small" prayer requests and concerns, remember, he was faithful with the costliest offering, his gift of Jesus Christ for our salvation. He is certainly not going to hold back or be stingy with lesser concerns, having proved faithful with the larger ones. No matter the concern, large or small, you can believe he's interested and is working on your behalf. He who did not withhold much from you will not withhold little either.

Since the world began, no ear has heard and no eye has seen a God like you, who works for those who wait for him! ISAIAH 64:4, NLT

Fresh Fruit

We waited years to have a backyard with just the right amount of sun and space to plant blueberry bushes. Remember that book *Blueberries for Sal?* This was more like Blueberries for Sandra . . . and husband, of course. Even though we bought late-bearing blueberry plants this year, they came early. We did allow the birds to eat some, as I mentioned in the July 4 devotional, but we ate many ourselves. We loved them. But when I walked outside yesterday all I saw on those bushes were tiny, shriveled berries.

I picked and ate them anyway. They were bitter and left a bad taste in my mouth, as I knew they would. It was no longer blueberry season, but I did not let go, because I did not want the season to end.

There are seasons in life that we do not want to end. A honeymoon eventually becomes a marriage, which sometimes becomes a divorce. Babies grow up and move away. Churches close. Friends move. We move. Jobs end. Ministries complete. If these are stages and activities we enjoy, it can be painful and sad to contemplate the end of that stage of life. Wishing it wasn't so doesn't extend the season; it only tempts us to eat the bitter, season-end fruit over and over instead of moving on.

Because my heart had been so set on the blueberries, I hadn't lifted my eyes to see that the blackberry bushes all around me were thick and lush. I had not yet contemplated what I might do with the new, perfumed peaches, taut and sweet beneath their thin skins. They held such promise.

I left the blueberry bushes to the promise of the next year and went to pluck blackberries and buy peaches. So many wonderful ways to use them—so fresh and ripe and ready to be used. Do not be afraid to leave a beloved stage behind, clinging past its season. The Lord has provided many seasons, with their delightful openings and their quiet closings, for us to enjoy throughout the years of our lives. Turn the corner; see what sweet thing is just ahead. There is something beautiful waiting.

For everything there is a season, a time for every activity under heaven.
A time to be born and a time to die. A time to plant and a time to harvest.
ECCLESIASTES 3:1-2, NLT

Experiencing the Love of God

Each of us has a favorite season. Some love winter for its rest and hush; some love spring for the new growth and hope it provides. Summer is a favorite where I live; it stops raining for a little while, and I can meet my friends and neighbors outdoors. Autumn hosts favorite holidays and provides something to look forward to.

We would live poorer lives if we weren't able to experience each of those cycles—in nature and in life. Which of us would like to return to junior high? Not I! I'm content right where I am. In his wisdom and power, God changes seasons, situations, and hearts. When we trust him to usher out the old and bring something fresh and new, we can experience the light of his love in new ways.

Ready for a seasonal late summer recipe? Try this one!

BLACKBERRY PEACH COMPOTE

So easy! This is delicious as the base for a small cobbler or pie, spooned over ice cream or scones, or even lightly spread over grilled salmon.

6 tablespoons quick-cooking tapioca
4 cups fresh peaches, peeled and sliced
2 cups fresh blackberries
1 cup brown sugar, tightly packed

Mix all ingredients in a saucepan and stir together over medium-low heat until tapioca has mostly dissolved and the mixture is thick and holds to a spoon once it's lifted out of the pan.

Daniel answered and said: "Blessed be the name of God forever and ever, to whom belong wisdom and might. He changes times and seasons; he removes kings and sets up kings; he gives wisdom to the wise and knowledge to those who have understanding; he reveals deep and hidden things; he knows what is in the darkness, and the light dwells with him. DANIEL 2:20-22, ESV

Beloved Wanderers

One day, when my daughter was a baby and my son was three years old, I decided to leave my baby at home with a friend and take my son shopping. The department store was in a long strip mall near our house. We'd been there many times before.

I let my son play hide-and-seek in the clothing rounders for a few minutes before we got in line for the return. One moment later I turned around, and he was gone.

At first, I thought he was simply hiding in the rounders again, and I began pulling apart the clothing on them to see if he was hiding inside. My horror and dread grew when it became clear that he was not in any of the rounders. By now, others were helping me look, nearly as alarmed as I was. I began to walk quickly down the aisles looking left and right, and I had made it quite some way when my son walked in through the department store door holding the hands of an elderly couple.

They had found him on the sidewalk outside. I pulled him into my arms and burst into tears. "What were you doing?" I asked.

"I wanted to visit the pet store while you did the boring stuff," he replied, truly confused at my concern. Some people around us celebrated with me. I heard whispers, though, of people wondering how I had possibly let that happen.

You know what? I'm a good parent, but my child had a mind of his own and did what he knew he was not supposed to do, because he was curious and following his own desires. I think of that as I consider the many people we love who have wandered away from Jesus, or just have not yet taken his hand at all. God is not a bad parent, and he allows his children to have a will. There are dear brothers and sisters in Christ right now who have beloved, beautiful children who are wandering.

Let's pray for them and for ourselves and for all who wander. God rejoices when one of his children returns, and so will we.

"This son of mine was dead and is alive again; he was lost and is found."
So they began to celebrate. LUKE 15:24

Owners, Not Flippers

I live in what is called a hot real estate market—one in which values consistently rise, one in which there are many flippers. Flippers buy a house, fix it up with minimal investment, and then quickly sell it at a profit.

There is nothing wrong in making money when honorably done. Proverbs 21:5 tells us, "The plans of the diligent lead to profit." Realize, though, that someone who buys a house to flip it is going to have different goals from someone who is buying a home to live in.

My husband and I derive a certain amount of confidence and comfort from the fact that the couple who sold us our house built it for themselves and their family; they did not cut corners. They invested themselves into the lives of their neighbors, too.

By the nature of their goals, real estate flippers don't put a lot in the house; they don't invest in the neighborhood; and they don't invest in the town. They are interested in short-term gain, not long-term relationships. If the market is no longer immediately profitable, they no longer buy in. They have possession and a title, but they don't really have *ownership*.

Whenever I am considering donating to or becoming a part of a ministry, I ask myself, *Are they in it for the people they serve, or is this simply today's fad or passing idea? Are they ready to bolt if things become complicated? Have they deeply invested themselves before they ask me to invest?*

God invested all when he sent his Son to redeem us. Jesus tells us that he isn't the hired hand—he's with us for the long haul. We aren't simply a resource for him to tend to; we are so beloved that he gave his life to save us. The Holy Spirit is committed to the point that he permanently indwells us to guide, comfort, and convict us.

Looking to invest in tangible goods does not require a hard-and-fast promise to stick with it for the long haul. Pouring into souls does. I want to follow the model of my Lord, sticking with people for the long term, like a good homeowner or a good shepherd.

The hired hand is not the shepherd and does not own the sheep. So when he sees the wolf coming, he abandons the sheep and runs away. Then the wolf attacks the flock and scatters it. The man runs away because he is a hired hand and cares nothing for the sheep. I am the good shepherd; I know my sheep and my sheep know me. JOHN 10:12-14

Pickers and Road Shows

We like to watch the television shows where people bring their antiques in for evaluation to find that the old blanket the dog has been sleeping on is actually a treasure worth hundreds of thousands of dollars. One show usually showcases old trucks and cars—a particular favorite of my husband.

The auto repair shop buys old vehicles and restores them. Occasionally they come upon a beauty, one that has already had its exterior restored. On one episode, after oohing and aahing at the paint job, they popped the hood and lifted it to inspect the engine. Oops. No engine. This car was not going anywhere. We've also seen muscle cars restored with the equivalent of a compact car engine inside it. Not enough power available to do what the car was designed to do.

When Jesus left earth, he gave us all a great commission: *great* because it was most important; *commission* because it was our charge going forward. In Matthew 28:19-20 the Lord tells us, "Go therefore and make disciples of all nations, baptizing them in the name of the Father and of the Son and of the Holy Spirit, teaching them to observe all that I have commanded you" (esv).

This seems like an impossible task. It is an impossible task, as are the rest of his commands in Scripture, if we are working under our own power. We do not have to work under our own power, lawn-mower sized as it may be. Acts 1:8 tells us that we receive power when the Holy Spirit comes on us, and then we can do just what he asks us to do.

First Peter 4:11 exhorts, "If anyone speaks, they should do so as one who speaks the very words of God. If anyone serves, they should do so with the strength God provides, so that in all things God may be praised through Jesus Christ."

If you're trying to get the Lord's work done in your own power, well, no wonder you're tired or going nowhere. But there's tremendous power available to you. Just ask!

You will receive power when the Holy Spirit comes on you; and you will be my witnesses in Jerusalem, and in all Judea and Samaria, and to the ends of the earth. ACTS 1:8

Just Injustice

Our town has a drive-through coffee shop. Because of the way the shops around it are set up, it has two feeder lanes that wind through the parking lot. They funnel directly to the place where orders are given and beverages picked up.

It's not always clear how to funnel into that all-important lane, though, and sometimes people who are not from our town bypass the feeder lanes to directly cut line in front of those who have been waiting. This, as you can imagine, causes some consternation. Sometimes, it provokes outright tantrums!

One day I watched as a man got out of his car, strode up to the bewildered offender, knocked on the window, and demanded that she back out of the line. Another time, the entire pool of waiting cars laid on their horns. The offender had no idea what was going on and drove through anyway. When I got to the front of the line, I mentioned it to the barista. "Oh yes," she said. "We've had people throw rocks and dirt clods at people who cut the line."

What?

God has made us in his image, and 2 Thessalonians 1:6 tells us that he is just, so of course, we are to have a sense of justice and injustice, outrage and unfairness. But what has run amok when our sense of justice is most easily riled by being cut in front of in a coffee line or facing other irritants during a normal day? Where is our outrage at real injustice? Do we act as energetically for the truly harmed, the poor, the overlooked, the needy, and the oppressed? Trust me; I am not throwing the first stone; I need to step it up too.

Recently, a representative for an international justice mission came to our church to talk about how many people are enslaved in this world—more today than at any other time in history—and how we can help. We will help. But we needn't only look around the world; there are needy and poor and oppressed right here in our own country. I had no idea, for example, that the homeless used my local YMCA to shower. They were hidden to me. Now they are not. How can I help? Now that I know, I must. Ask the Lord to show you who in your community might be needy, oppressed, or overlooked, and how you might reach a hand out and up. God tells us what it means to know him in Jeremiah 22:16.

"He defended the cause of the poor and needy, and so all went well. Is that not what it means to know me?" declares the LORD.　JEREMIAH 22:16

A Benediction for August

It's difficult to read about or see the suffering in the world—it's also hard to look at the suffering of those near at hand: our friends, our neighbors, our family, our coworkers, and ourselves. But our world is fallen, and there will be suffering. God allows us to minister to one another in that suffering as he ministers to us. We also have the hope that eventually one season, our time on earth, will turn to another season, a gloriously pain-free season in heaven.

As the seasons change, you might be looking forward to pumpkin spice and warm soups and stews. May you remember that our time here on earth, with its pleasures and its suffering, will soon conclude.

Let me remind you now of God's constant affection, attention, protection, and guidance with this benediction from Scripture. Just as the weekly benediction at the end of my Sunday church service strengthens me for the week ahead and helps me focus on what God has done for me in his love, I hope this blessing will fortify you for the month and season to come. God loves you and wants you to be blessed.

Through these pages and the power of Scripture, I reach my hands out to and over you, as your sister in Christ, and pray you will know that . . .

The God of all grace, who called you to his eternal glory in Christ, after you have suffered a little while, will himself restore you and make you strong, firm and steadfast. To him be the power for ever and ever. Amen.

1 PETER 5:10-11

SEPTEMBER

Nap Rugs

It's the beginning of a new school year, and even though I don't go to school anymore—and don't even have kids in school anymore—I always think about one thing at this time of year.

I want my kindergarten nap rug back. No, really.

Do you remember those little rugs? I don't remember purchasing my own, but I do remember picking out the little rectangle of carpet remnant with each of my kids. When the teacher signaled that it was time to get the rugs out, everyone was cued to yawn and wind down for a little while before attacking the next set of learning and doing.

One of the most powerful lessons the Lord has ever taught me about rest was when I read through this section in Luke 23, just after Jesus' crucifixion: "The women who had come with Jesus from Galilee followed Joseph and saw the tomb and how his body was laid in it. Then they went home and prepared spices and perfumes. But they rested on the Sabbath in obedience to the commandment" (verses 55-56). These women were in deep grief over the seeming loss of the Lord. I'm sure they were filled with emotional turmoil as they prepared the spices and perfumes required for burial. After resting on the Sabbath, early the next morning, they went to Jesus' tomb (see Luke 24:1)—but not before their Sabbath had completed.

I was struck that there is nothing I must do that is more important than what those women had to do, and yet they honored the Sabbath, taking God at his word even while caring for God himself!

I think our need for rest goes beyond the Sunday Sabbath. The word *sabbatical* is familiar; had you realized it uses the same base word as *Sabbath*? It means to take an extended break from work or a task at hand to rejuvenate or learn a new skill. Most of us can't take weeks or months without work, but we can strive to be faithful to that one day. And then, perhaps, we can give ourselves mini-sabbaticals from time to time. One day off to walk in the quiet woods and watch the leaves spiral down—with the phone ringer off. One long weekend to walk on a churning autumn beach. One hour at the end of the day to rest in a comfortable chair with headphones on, listening to uplifting music.

Rest. No rug required.

There remains, then, a Sabbath-rest for the people of God; for anyone who enters God's rest also rests from their works, just as God did from his.

HEBREWS 4:9-10

Experiencing the Love of God

Summer is a season of frenzy and busyness, of making the most of every single daylight hour. Autumn, with its cooler days and longer nights, can signal a slowing down, a time of rest, a period of reflection. A body that never slows down wears out; the mind and the spirit operate in the same manner.

I like to be active, and I like to be busy. But sometimes that busyness is really just a way for me to ensure that what I want to be accomplished will be accomplished. It shows trust all right—trust in me! When I learn to follow the Lord's lead (after all, he often withdrew from the crowds to quiet places) and obey his command that the Sabbath be observed, I'm trusting in him. Trusting that what needs to be done can be done in obedience to the command to rest my body, mind, and spirit. He honors those who honor him (see 1 Samuel 2:30). How better to honor than to obey?

When do you crave rest? What stands in the way of your taking it for yourself? Trust that if you honor God, he will help you make up the time in unusual, clever, only-God ways.

Choose one thing to do to honor yourself, to honor God, with rest, and commit to it for one month. Tell a friend who can hold you accountable—and maybe pull her nap rug out too! Here are some ideas to get you started:

1. Declare some hours and some days screen-free time.
2. Spend some time outdoors, sleeping in a hammock or working the earth with your hands. As you do, free your mind from the cares of the day.
3. Choose a day each week not to prepare and clean up food. You might choose to eat out that day, or perhaps on another day you can prepare double and freeze a portion for another time. Maybe you and a friend could trade the doubles so nobody gets leftovers!
4. Don't do work on Sunday. Just say no.

Jesus said to them, "The Sabbath was made to meet the needs of people, and not people to meet the requirements of the Sabbath." MARK 2:27, NLT

Little Loves, Big Impact

The start of a school year always had us thinking about lunches, too. Hot lunch, cold lunch, a combination of the two? The idea of school lunches was brought powerfully back to mind a couple of years ago in an unexpected way.

Our daughter was working at a local sandwich shop, one that made really, very, extra good sandwiches. Even if she hadn't been working there, we'd have eaten there, but it was especially fun to have her make our sandwiches after so many years of our cooking for her! One day we called in an order for pickup, and my husband ran into the shop to get the sandwiches and bring them home to eat. The sandwiches were wrapped in brown paper sacks, and she had addressed one bag to each of us, with a heart near our names on the outside.

We sat down for a little picnic, and when we opened the paper bags to withdraw our sandwiches, a little note fell out of each one. The notes expressed thanks for us and a word of encouragement for the day. We were so choked up we could hardly eat. We texted her, though. "Thank you for the sandwiches— and the notes! Food for the heart and food for the body." She later texted back to say she remembered all the little notes we had tucked into her lunches during her school days, and how meaningful they were to her as a girl. She thought it would be fun to return the blessing these many years later.

When we love others, it motivates them to reciprocate that love to us. The things we consider "the least of these" among our daily activities often have the longest lasting effect. A word of encouragement spoken, a little note sent, a flower from our garden delivered, a joke shared. The way I loved my daughter was the way she loved me back.

Don't stop doing those little things; you may not learn of the impact you make for God's Kingdom. But undoubtedly, those little things mean more than you'll ever know.

The words of the godly encourage many.   PROVERBS 10:21, NLT

Calming the Storms

I made the project deadline, but the material was not to my boss's liking. She insisted I make changes I did not know how to make, fix things I hadn't believed were wrong. I'd been confident I'd known what I was doing, but just then I was not certain at all.

What was I going to do?

My small group was studying Mark, and I began to read. One day Jesus taught by the lakeshore; that evening, the Lord suggested traveling to the other side of the lake, and his disciples took him. Now, they were mostly fishermen. One owned the family fishing business, and it is safe to presume most had been on the water since they were small boys. It was their area of professional mastery, comfort, and competence. A storm blew up, though, which they felt was beyond their ability to handle, manage, or even survive.

The disciples woke Jesus, who was sleeping comfortably on a cushion in the back of the boat. "Teacher! Don't you care that we're going to drown?" they asked.

I smiled. I, too, have wailed to the Lord, "Don't you even care?" It struck me, then, that the Lord had allowed a storm to blow up in the exact area that the disciples felt they had control. He showed them in the most powerful way that he was with them on the job—their jobs—to handle whatever squalls would blow up.

After he had calmed the storm, they asked one another, "Who is this man?" A few chapters later, Jesus returns that very question to Peter. "Who do you say that I am?" Peter, having not only heard Jesus' teaching but seen it in action, answered correctly. "You are the Messiah."

Our Messiah cares about our workplaces, whether they are on a boat, in an office, in a home, or on a field. He allows squalls so we can see his power and great care for us when he steps in, and so we can build our faith. Without the opportunity to trust, faith cannot increase, a faith that helps us answer difficult questions later.

We are not alone. God is with us in our workplace. He rules it, too.

He asked them, "But who do you say I am?" Peter replied, "You are the Messiah." MARK 8:29, NLT

Autumn Splendor

We live a little ways out of town, and one of the things that makes that long drive pleasurable is to watch the plants change as the seasons do too. There are bunches of crab apples dropping on the lawns nearby, to the delight of the deer. The leaves are beginning to change their colors, transitioning from green to a firestorm of red, orange, and yellow. It struck me that when the leaves begin to die, their most prominent beauty is displayed. Perhaps they, like humans, become wise as they age.

One plant disturbed me, though—a sunflower on a nearby small farm. I could not see the expected bright yellow face, thoroughly freckled with fruitful seeds, though, because its head faced the ground. I thought perhaps a sunnier day would fix things. Nope. I drove by day after day and found the plant still drooping in despair.

Sunflower heads droop for many reasons—sometimes they do not have enough water—the water pressure helps to sustain that long, green neck. Sometimes their roots are not deep enough to support the plant's weight. Sometimes, they are heavy with seeds and cannot lift the weight of their own heads themselves.

Do you ever feel like that? I was so tired the other day that I told the Lord I felt more worn again than born again. A familiar psalm wafted through my mind: "Why, my soul, are you downcast? Why so disturbed within me?" I felt like that little sunflower. Too much weight on my shoulders to hold up my head. Not enough water, not enough strength.

I love that in this psalm, David asks himself what cause he has to be downcast, and he knows the answer. "Put your hope in God, for I will yet praise him, my Savior and my God." But it doesn't happen right away, does it? The next thing he notes is, "My soul is downcast within me."

The way out? "I will remember you." God has not failed us in the past. He will not refuse to help us now.

Why, my soul, are you downcast? Why so disturbed within me? Put your hope in God, for I will yet praise him, my Savior and my God. My soul is downcast within me; therefore, I will remember you. PSALM 42:5-6

Lifter of the Downcast

In yesterday's devotion I talked about a sunflower with a stooped head that I'd seen; its head never raised. It seemed to be in despair. I was still thinking about that sad little sunflower for some time. Maybe because I still felt, *My soul is downcast within me* (see Psalm 42:6). The sunflower became a symbol of how I felt. Then I remembered a gardening friend of my husband's. He'd used smooth wooden stakes to hold up the heads of some of his blossoms until they were ready to let go of some of their seeds. An assist, a help. "He gives strength to the weary and increases the power of the weak," Isaiah promises (Isaiah 40:29).

Life has passages of time in which it seems that our burdens are especially heavy. It is then we must call out to God, honestly, repeatedly, persistently, for help.

I love the story in Luke 11 of the man who goes to his friend's house in the middle of the night, wanting some loaves of bread—because it gives me permission to be a prayer pest. The friend does not give the bread to him at first, but Jesus says the friend will eventually do what the man requests. Why? Verse 8: "I tell you this—though he won't do it for friendship's sake, if you keep knocking long enough, he will get up and give you whatever you need because of your shameless persistence" (NLT).

Jesus says, in verse 9, "So I tell you, keep on asking, and you will receive what you ask for. Keep on seeking, and you will find. Keep on knocking, and the door will be opened to you" (NLT).

Whatever burden you are carrying, friend, ask the Lord to lift it from you—or to support you while you carry it as far as you need to go. Do not be shy in asking over and over. I know when I am tired I feel like I may have energy to ask once, or maybe twice. But ask on your own behalf with the tirelessness you would use in presenting an important request for a friend.

You are worth it. And you will see that he will answer. Perhaps not in the way you want, or perhaps not in this life. But he will lift your head.

I call out to the LORD, and he answers me from his holy mountain.

PSALM 3:3-4

Patient Preparation

I'm not a very patient person. When I rationalize it, I frame it in terms of "I like to be busy" or "I like to get things done." And that's perfectly fine when it's busy and not bossy—meaning "this must happen in my time and not on God's." Then it's a sin. Patience is, after all, one of the fruits of the Spirit.

In seeking to understand a holy way forward, I set out to understand waiting. Passive waiting, I found, was sitting around doing nothing while letting time tick by. There are some places where passive waiting is required and normal: standing in line at the checkout or thumbing through a magazine in the doctor's office. But mostly, the waiting—especially the waiting on the Lord that Scripture talks about—is not passive. It is active waiting.

Just last week, we had an early windstorm. It was predicted to be very strong and was forecast three to four days ahead of time. We spent the time busily preparing. We took in all the patio furniture, made sure the window seals were well caulked, and got gas for the generator. We were waiting on something—an event over which we had no control as to the timing—but doing so productively, so that when the time arrived, we'd be ready!

That, I believe, is the kind of waiting God envisages for us—waiting expectantly for him to act when the time and circumstances are exactly right. Psalm 27 tells us to wait patiently for the Lord; Isaiah 40 promises that when we wait for God we become strong enough for what lies ahead. James 5 uses the example of a farmer. Farmers are not known for doing little or nothing; they work from sunup till past dark.

Do you think this is the kind of waiting you can do—prepare well in anticipation of his good timing? I think it might work!

Be patient, then, brothers and sisters, until the Lord's coming. See how the farmer waits for the land to yield its valuable crop, patiently waiting for the autumn and spring rains. You too, be patient and stand firm, because the Lord's coming is near. JAMES 5:7-8

A Tender Touch

There is nothing so personal as touch. A stroke on the arm, a kiss on the cheek, a ruffling of the hair all convey affection. A slap or a kick or pulling the hair convey anger and abuse. When novelists tell a story, they try to describe all five senses, and the one that is most overlooked is touch. But when it's used—the nubby feel of a blanket on the back of a couch, the silky hair of the spaniel on her lap, the first time a romantic partner takes her hand—it is powerful.

Touch is powerful because it is personal. Touch, especially person to person, makes us both vulnerable and intimate. Many people—more than we can probably imagine—have suffered inappropriate touch, and in a protective reflex they wall themselves off from the appropriate touch that could heal them. It's one further way that Satan has used an abuser to steal something beautiful from them. The right kind of touch can tell them, and everyone, *You are lovable. You are lovely. I want to be near you. All touch need not hurt.*

Touch can heal.

Jesus touched a leper to instantly heal him (see Mark 1:42). A laying on of hands uses touch to directly pass healing from the Holy Spirit through another believer and onto the person who is suffering. Anointing requires one person to touch another—to be, for a moment, the hand that transmits the power of God.

Don't be afraid to reach out and show your affection with appropriate touch—a hug or "air kisses" for good friends, a side hug for brothers and sisters of the opposite sex, a handshake for a colleague. For your kids? A pat on the hair, a hug and a kiss, a high five or fist bump. For your spouse? Aside from normal intimacy, don't neglect back and foot rubs, or a reassuring hand on the arm or shoulder during a difficult time.

If you're coiled when someone trustworthy touches you, let go just a little. If you love such a person, ask permission, and when given, offer a loving touch. Jesus healed through his touch. We can be his hands and offer a loving, healing touch to others too.

When Jesus entered Peter's house, he saw his mother-in-law lying sick with a fever. He touched her hand, and the fever left her, and she rose and began to serve him.   MATTHEW 8:14-15, ESV

Experiencing the Love of God

Touch is so important—it's been said that babies who are not held and cuddled in their first year fail to thrive. I say: I don't think that's limited to babies. We fail to thrive without touch too.

Throughout much of history, people were afraid to touch those with leprosy. The person who touched the diseased person was considered infected too, which meant that no one touched lepers. They became isolated behind rags, separated from their communities. They were untouchables.

Some cultures that sort people by class have castes that are signified as being "untouchable." To be labeled untouchable can often translate as being unlovable, unwanted, or unvalued. Even societies that don't have formalized castes segregate into those we welcome and those we don't.

An honoring touch tells someone, "I'm not afraid of you. I find you valuable. You are wanted. You are lovable."

Today, why not reach out to others for appropriate touch, as mentioned on September 8? Don't be afraid of pedicures, hand or body massage, and scalp treatments. Even offered by a kindly professional and not a family member or a friend, these kinds of touch can activate good feelings too.

Are you afraid of touch? Has someone stolen your sense of well-being and desire for touch? If so, I urge you to speak to someone safe about it. Don't let the thief who harmed you steal one of the strongest ways others have to convey their deep affection for you. Jesus wants to restore you to the fullness of life.

The thief comes only to steal and kill and destroy; I have come that they may have life, and have it to the full. JOHN 10:10

Mountaintops

Our kids are grown, but we come together to eat dinner on Sunday nights. One week our daughter was on a business trip, but we gathered anyway. The food was good, the laughter was there, the fellowship among us was pleasant and enjoyable. Yet we all felt the hole. Things didn't flow as naturally. Some things seemed awkward. We'd turn to ask for her opinion only to remember she wasn't there. The absence of her sweet and zesty spirit created a noticeable vacuum.

The Christian life is an emotional relationship with our Lord. Throughout our journey with God, those emotions ebb and flow, come and go. Our so-called "mountaintop" experiences are when we sense God's presence and have an amazing spiritual victory. Our "valley" experiences are when we are feeling around in the dark for God, who seems to be just out of reach. All Christians experience both.

People will ask, how do I know if I have faith? Sometimes when my faith is vibrant, I distinctively sense it, though mostly it feels like things are operating normally. But sometimes I know I have faith because when it fades for a while, I sense the absence of its vibrancy. In *The Winter of Our Discontent*, John Steinbeck writes, "It's so much darker when a light goes out than it would have been if it had never shone."

There are many reasons why we might not feel God's presence for a time. I had a hard time feeling it when I was deeply depressed—a time I most needed to feel it, which added to my grief. After climbing out of that difficult time, I learned that while God's presence isn't dependent upon my health, sometimes my ability to sense things is. Sometimes we quench the Spirit by sin. Sometimes we are tired or disappointed or angry, and we withdraw to recoup and need to make our way back. His love is always present, though, whether I sense it or not.

It's hard to battle our way back, but we can! Keep praying, keep seeking, keep loving even when it feels like you are calling into the void. Walking uphill is difficult but surely leads to another mountaintop.

Do not banish me from your presence, and don't take your Holy Spirit from me. PSALM 51:11, NLT

Surviving and Thriving

I walked a mile with Pleasure
She chattered all the way
But left me none the wiser
For all she had to say.

I walked a mile with Sorrow
And ne'er a word said she
But oh the things I learned from her
When Sorrow walked with me!

ROBERT BROWNING HAMILTON

There are lessons to be learned in the valleys. To become mature, well-rounded people cast in Christ's image, we cannot avoid lessons that must be learned in dark times. Solomon, to whom God gifted the most wisdom he had given any human ever, said in Ecclesiastes 1:18, "The greater my wisdom, the greater my grief. To increase knowledge only increases sorrow" (NLT).

God clearly meant to bless Solomon, so wisdom was not given as a curse or a rebuke. James 1:5 tells us, "If any of you lacks wisdom, you should ask God, who gives generously to all without finding fault, and it will be given to you." Other Scripture tells us to place a high value on wisdom. "Do not forsake wisdom, and she will protect you; love her, and she will watch over you. The beginning of wisdom is this: Get wisdom. Though it cost all you have, get understanding" (Proverbs 4:6-7). Solomon, who would know, makes it clear that wisdom is not a gift of undiluted pleasure.

As much as we are to take joy in the life Jesus has given to us, one which he says should be abundant, we are not tarrying here on earth only to have a good time. We are here to be conformed to the image of Christ, who certainly walked with sorrow. He was called a man of sorrows who was acquainted with grief (see Isaiah 53:3). He had at least one moment where he felt forsaken by God (see Matthew 27:46), though he of anyone would have known God would not leave him.

Sometimes all we must do is survive in the season of sorrow. The season of thriving will follow. I once realized that while my bright roses don't grow in the shade, lovely moss does. I can see things in the shadows that I can't see in the light. You will too, if you allow yourself to recognize them. Your sorrow will bring wisdom that will last long after God redeems the pain and brings you to the next season of joy. It's coming, friend.

You have turned my mourning into joyful dancing. You have taken away my clothes of mourning and clothed me with joy. PSALM 30:11, NLT

Truth and Circumstance

God uses my dog to teach me so many lessons. I'm not sure if that says something about the Lord's ability to use anything to convey wisdom and insight or my perception level, but in any case, it works!

My seven-pound dog is not afraid of larger animals or people or trucks or anything typical. She is afraid of things that beep. Unfortunately for her, my slow cooker beeps, as does my waffle iron, coffee pot, and kitchen timer. My dishwasher and my washing machine play beeping little tunes. When they do, she leaps onto the hearth as if she needs to head for high ground. I, of course, know that the beeps present no present danger to her. I tell her, "I have never left you in a dangerous situation, and I never will." She remains close, trusting despite her skepticism that I'll protect her if her instincts about the ominous beeps prove right.

More often than I wish were true, I am like my dog. I look around at the circumstances, many of which seem confusing, dangerous, or fearful, and draw my approach from them. Worse, I sometimes draw my understanding of God from them—till I catch myself. I ask myself, What about what happened to so-and-so? They are Christians, and they . . . lost their job . . . underwent a catastrophe . . . lost a spouse . . . lost their life. The truth is, there are any number of catastrophic situations served up to us each day in our personal lives and in the media. I must remind myself that God also provides jobs and sends help in and often averts catastrophes. Not only does he redeem us from death, but the near-death experiences of many believers tell of his powerful presence during their distress.

Here is what I have learned: we cannot look at circumstances to determine truth; we must look at truth to interpret circumstances.

God not only tells the truth, but he *is* truth (see John 14:6). That is how we know we can trust him when he tells us, "[I am] your refuge and strength, an ever-present help in trouble."

God is our refuge and strength, an ever-present help in trouble. Therefore we will not fear, though the earth give way and the mountains fall into the heart of the sea, though its waters roar and foam and the mountains quake with their surging. PSALM 46:1-3

Identity Theft

A couple of years ago, one of my friends had her online identity stolen. The thief then spammed a long reach of contacts, in her name, with violent and pornographic pictures. You can imagine her horror, damage control, and overwhelming desire to let everyone know that she had not sent that despicable material. Most of her friends, of course, knew that she would never be behind something so vile. But new business colleagues, people who didn't know her well, and friends of friends had no base by which to measure her. Others had to speak up in her defense and speak of her character and the truth.

Thieves are after our credit and bank numbers so they can use our good names, our resources, and our credit to buy things for their own pleasure. The digital world has made it easier for us to connect but also easier for people to corrupt.

Bad people attempt to use your good name for their purposes—which are nothing to do with your own goals. Truly, at the core of it, that is what using the Lord's name in vain is—manipulating every good thing his name evokes to cover the words and deeds he did not and would not authorize.

How can we know what theology, what guidance, what statements are true and which might be twisted? First, like with my friend, we must know the Word in order to reject when something presented does not completely align. We ask God's Spirit to guide us. Then we must go a step further. When we hear someone speaking out, saying things we know Jesus does not endorse or participate in (because they are contrary to Scripture), we must speak up. If we do not, those who do not know him may take those false words as truth, leaving them with an untrue impression of our beloved God. Looking at the fruit of the people speaking in his name and comparing it to Scripture to see what our Lord has actually said will help us sort out truth from falsehood.

> *Beware of false prophets who come disguised as harmless sheep but are really vicious wolves. You can identify them by their fruit, that is, by the way they act. Can you pick grapes from thornbushes, or figs from thistles? A good tree produces good fruit, and a bad tree produces bad fruit. A good tree can't produce bad fruit, and a bad tree can't produce good fruit.*
> MATTHEW 7:15-18, NLT

Significant Figures

I am not a fan of math, but I've stayed interested because my son is an engineer who loves math. He said one of his worst days of college was when he realized he'd completed the most advanced calculus class offered. He says math is the language of God. I'm sure glad God speaks in many languages, because I'd never understand him if he spoke only in math.

One mathematical concept caught my attention, though, because I could see the connection between math and God. It's the idea of significant figures. A significant figure, or more precisely, a significant digit, can simply be boiled down to anything that adds some value to the number, any digit that is not zero.

I meditated on this concept because so often we think our contributions must be big to be meaningful. I will tell you there are places I did not donate money or contribute time because I thought I had so little to give, it would not make a difference. There are conversations in which I did not speak up because I thought my one insight would not be worth taking the time to say. I didn't want to pray for something that really mattered to me, because I only had a little confidence and a dab of hope the Lord would bring it to pass.

Do you relate?

Then I remembered Jesus telling his disciples if they had faith as small as a mustard seed they could do great things (see Matthew 17:20). I recalled the touching story of the widow's mite. Remember? Jesus sat down near the Temple's collection box to observe those who gave (if only they knew who was watching!). He praised the widow who gave her small offering (see Mark 12:42-44). God gives us resources—he gave the rich their money; he gave the widow her coins. He gives two talents to some and ten to others (see Matthew 25:14-30). It does not matter how many you are given, whether it be money, insight, time, or whatever. What counts, in Kingdom terms, is what we do with what we are given, little or much.

It's all significant—if what we do with what we are given isn't merely zero!

His master said to him, "Well done, good and faithful servant. You have been faithful over a little; I will set you over much. Enter into the joy of your master."
MATTHEW 25:23, ESV

Wreaths and Crowns

Normally, when we think about crowns we think about royalty. This is why those who were mocking the Lord placed a crown of thorns on his head, mocking his claim to kingship. That is not his final crown, however. Triumphantly, Revelation 19:12 tells us about Jesus' second coming, that "his eyes were as a flame of fire, and on his head were many crowns; and he had a name written, that no man knew, but he himself" (KJV). Jesus' crowns are referred to as diadems—in Greek, the crowns given to royalty.

Excitingly, we Christians can be crowned too.

Second Corinthians 5:10 tells us we will each appear before the Lord to receive what is due for the good and bad we have done while on earth. Dr. Henry C. Thiessen, in his book *Lectures in Systematic Theology*, explains that among other rewards, Christians can earn five kinds of crowns while here on earth:

- The incorruptible or imperishable crown (see 1 Corinthians 9:25), given to those who deny themselves ungodly pleasures, serve others, and live their faith
- The crown of righteousness (see 2 Timothy 4:8), given to those who faithfully discharge their God-given duties
- The crown of life (see James 1:12; Revelation 2:10), given to those who persevere under trial
- The crown of glory (see 1 Peter 5:4), given to willing servants of the Lord, his faithful overseers
- The crown of rejoicing or exultation (see 1 Thessalonians 2:19; Philippians 4:1), given to those who lead others to faith or disciple them

The word the Bible uses to name the crowns believers can earn is *stephanos*, which are more like the laurel wreaths given at the early Olympics. These, too, are signs of honor and merit but are not the royal crowns of the Lord. I treasure that the word *stephanos* is also the name of the first Christian martyr, Stephen, in Acts 7.

When we appear before the Lord, it will be wonderful to have him crown us with rewards so that we may turn around and cast them back before his throne in worship and honor (see Revelation 4:10-11).

Everyone who competes in the games goes into strict training. They do it to get a crown that will not last, but we do it to get a crown that will last forever.

1 CORINTHIANS 9:25

Experiencing the Love of God

Yesterday we learned that each of us will appear before the Lord to receive what's due for the good and bad we've done while on earth, and that will include five different kinds of crowns. I'm a woman who likes to track things, so I mark on my computer calendar the days of the month in which my husband and I expect to be paid for our work. Not only does it help me balance my budget, but when I look at that calendar every day to ascertain what work I must accomplish, it's good to look just a few days or a week ahead to remind myself that I will be paid for it.

Likewise, find a tiny crown, a pretty one, and place it on your desk, near your quiet time reading spot, in the car, or even in your purse. You can find them online (look for ones that might fit on a charm bracelet) and in bead stores. Tiaras can be found at party and craft stores. If you can't find a pretty jeweled or gold one, draw one—or print one out! Maybe you'll like more than one, scattered around (search for crown confetti!), to remind you that the Lord is not negligent toward nor ignorant of the sufferings you undergo or the work you do on his behalf.

Payday is coming! Best of all, we'll be able to turn those crowns back around into wonderful worship.

Be shepherds of God's flock that is under your care, watching over them—not because you must, but because you are willing, as God wants you to be not pursuing dishonest gain, but eager to serve; not lording it over those entrusted to you, but being examples to the flock. And when the Chief Shepherd appears, you will receive the crown of glory that will never fade away. 1 PETER 5:2-4

Boneware

Recently, I noticed that our everyday dishes, which are quite heavy and supposedly sturdy, are crazing: developing tiny little lines throughout due only to the amount of heat offered by the dishwasher. Those crazing lines could eventually go beneath the surface and become faults along which my dishes will crack and leak.

In contrast, my bone china isn't crazing at all, though I have had it for many years. That which I thought would be sturdiest, the stoneware, can tolerate less heat than the fine boneware.

What makes a service piece heat resistant are three things: the materials used to make it, the process by which it is made, and how it is tempered. The ground bone in my delicate, translucent bone china, and the care given to creating it, have made it sturdier than my heavier, clay-based pieces.

Scripture teaches in 2 Timothy 2:20, "In a wealthy home some utensils are made of gold and silver, and some are made of wood and clay. The expensive utensils are used for special occasions, and the cheap ones are for everyday use" (NLT).

I believe you and I are the expensive utensils! We are formed in the image of God using his earth. (Women, we even qualify as boneware!) Our Creator made us by blowing his own breath into us. And finally, he allows us to be tempered by circumstance as well as his own good hand, never allowing the heat to overwhelm us (see Isaiah 43:2).

When the day comes, then, that we are tested, I pray we will know, like three heroes in the book of Daniel, that no matter what heat is placed upon us, our faith, our service, and our confidence will remain unbroken.

Shadrach, Meshach and Abednego replied to him, "King Nebuchadnezzar, we do not need to defend ourselves before you in this matter. If we are thrown into the blazing furnace, the God we serve is able to deliver us from it, and he will deliver us from Your Majesty's hand. But even if he does not, we want you to know, Your Majesty, that we will not serve your gods or worship the image of gold you have set up. DANIEL 3:16-18

À Bientôt

My lifelong friend Jane and I began our journey as writers together. We each had a secret writing dream shared only with each other. Mine was to write a foodie series set in France. Hers was to write books set in the Regency era. What delight when we both were offered contracts to write those books!

And then, Jane got sick.

As our page counts progressed, so did her cancer. By the time our manuscripts were completed, her cancer had advanced to the point where it took her life only a month later. I dedicated my novel to her, ending it with "*à bientôt*." In French, that is the equivalent of "see you soon!"

In John 11, Jesus' friend Lazarus was sick. Jesus was warned about the illness but told his followers, including Lazarus's sisters, that the man did not have a sickness that would lead to death. Later, when the man had been buried, Jesus said that Lazarus would rise again. Both Martha and Mary, Lazarus's sisters, seemed to scold Jesus. Jesus went to the tomb and wept, as a person would at the death of a friend. And then he commanded Lazarus to rise to life again.

I did cry when my friend died, and I miss her still. Not a month goes by that I don't think about something I would like to share with her. And while I cannot do so now, I know that someday I will be able to—Christ has already bid her rise to life again. As Christians, we do not grieve as do people who have no hope. This very knowledge that we will be reunited with our brothers and sisters one day in the company of our glorious Lord helps us to wade through our grief.

Therefore, we need not offer a heavyhearted, formal *adieu* when our loved ones depart. We can say, "See you soon!"

Dear brothers and sisters, we want you to know what will happen to the believers who have died so you will not grieve like people who have no hope. For since we believe that Jesus died and was raised to life again, we also believe that when Jesus returns, God will bring back with him the believers who have died. 1 THESSALONIANS 4:13-14, NLT

The Sweetest Fruit

I was in the grocery store this week, perusing the apple bins. There was an embarrassment of riches, about a dozen or so types to choose from. I noticed that on one bin the price was drastically marked down. Why? The fruit was bruised.

One reason that apples can become bruised is that rather than being harvested by hand, they are shaken from the trees by machines. It's one way to get the fruit off the trees and into the trucks quickly but cannot offer the care of handpicking. Handpicked fruit is gently eased from the tree and lovingly placed into a bucket, which is then carefully emptied into a bin. Those apples remain unbruised.

We live in a world in which appearance means much more than it should. Sadly, that is true not only for fruit but also for people. Apples, and people, are discounted if they don't look perfect. The world has a harsh system. It bruises us, and then it discounts us for being bruised. It sends us situations and circumstances that make it difficult to press on, and then mocks us for not performing perfectly.

We are made in the image of God, and he will never harm us. He handpicked us: "You did not choose me, but I chose you and appointed you that you should go and bear fruit and that your fruit should abide, so that whatever you ask the Father in my name, he may give it to you" (John 15:16, ESV).

I stood in front of the bruised apple bin. The scent was pronounced, so very beguiling, because the bruises had accelerated the ripening of the fruit. It's known that fruit is the sweetest where it's the most tender. I think that's true of us, too. We can offer comfort and love to others undergoing trials and sufferings we ourselves have borne and prevailed over. Empathy is one harvest of suffering. Wisdom is another.

We are all bruised, friend, but not by our Lord. Don't let your wounds stop you from bearing much long-lasting fruit.

A bruised reed he will not break, and a smoldering wick he will not quench, until he brings justice to victory; and in his name the Gentiles will hope.
MATTHEW 12:20-21, ESV

Annual Exams

About a decade ago, I was prescribed a medication that my doctor said I needed to take forever. He initially wrote the prescription for the dose he thought would set me right, but the side effects were intolerable. He changed his methodology and gave me a small dose at first, allowing my body to get accustomed to it and desensitizing me to the side effects. Then he raised the dose a tiny bit every six weeks. My body built up a tolerance, and soon I was at a therapeutic dose.

Building tolerance can be helpful in situations as I've described above. It's a positive character trait when we build up grace and patience toward others and ourselves. But we can also learn to accommodate sin in ourselves and others, bit by bit, a little at a time, until suddenly we find ourselves desensitized with a growing proclivity for acclimating ourselves to sin. It happens just like with my medication, bit by bit, degree by degree.

We are truly free in Christ. We are free from the law—the heavy-handed regulation that Peter says neither Jew nor Gentile is able to bear (see Acts 15:10). Unless something is specifically prohibited in Scripture, we have freedom of practice and the ability to determine for ourselves how to live. And yet, with that freedom comes the responsibility to wield it wisely. We have not, as Paul writes in Galatians 5:13, been given that freedom to satisfy our sinful nature. That is easy to do, degree by degree.

Each year at my physical, or more often if I'm not well, my doctor and I review my habits, my medications, and my overall health. We adjust anything that needs to be amended for optimal health, and he encourages me to make changes that will lead to a fuller life and away from early death. We are truly free to live in Christ, but it might not be a bad idea to undergo regular spiritual checkups, asking the Lord to search our hearts (see Psalm 139:23) and allowing mature Christians and Scripture to speak into our lives too.

Since God's grace has set us free from the law, does that mean we can go on sinning? Of course not! Don't you realize that you become the slave of whatever you choose to obey? You can be a slave to sin, which leads to death, or you can choose to obey God, which leads to righteous living.

ROMANS 6:15-16, NLT

Liberation

While we celebrate our freedom in Christ, it's good to remember that those who are not in Christ are not free at all. Romans 6:17-20 teaches that before we were free in Christ, we were slaves to sin. Slaves, of course, have no autonomy over their own actions—they must obey the master. Furthermore, because of that master's desires, according to Romans 6:20, they are free from the obligation to do right.

It can be difficult, sometimes, for those of us who have had the veil lifted from our eyes, and can now see righteousness and unrighteousness, good and evil with the Lord's eyes. After all, it is no longer we who live, but he who lives within us (see Galatians 2:20). We must guard against the unreasonable expectation—sometimes even demand—that those who are still blinded, and who do not have the freedom we have, make holy choices.

People in shackles cannot run freely—and we would question anyone who was suggesting that they could run a race with equal potential. People who are imprisoned cannot donate time or energy to the needy at the same level as people who have complete autonomy over their will. It's not to say that there are not good people doing good things even though they may not love and know the Lord. It's saying that they are hampered by their slavery, unknowingly or knowingly, to sin. Just like we were before Christ set us free.

I, too, want to see our world turn into a place where peace and justice reign. Perhaps one of the best ways we can do that is to share the Good News of the gospel of Jesus Christ to as many people as we can, in as many clever, heartfelt ways that we can. Only then, when the prisoners have been set free, will they be at liberty to and have the power to do what is right.

Whenever someone turns to the Lord, the veil is taken away. For the Lord is the Spirit, and wherever the Spirit of the Lord is, there is freedom. So all of us who have had that veil removed can see and reflect the glory of the Lord. And the Lord—who is the Spirit—makes us more and more like him as we are changed into his glorious image. 2 CORINTHIANS 3:16-18, NLT

Understanding Down Under

My good friend was about to start a new job, one that was perfectly suited to her, one that she'd seemed to acquire almost without effort. It's not that I wasn't happy for her; I told her I was thrilled, and I was. It's just that I needed a job too. Why wasn't anyone opening the doors I kept knocking on? Did God love her and see her needs, but not love me or see mine? I kept knocking, though, with perhaps less enthusiasm.

My employed friend encouraged me day by day, week by week. And in time, I was hired!

A few years later, her husband told her he was leaving. My marriage was in a steady place, and one night when my husband and I left her company, I saw her looking after us longingly. I understood that longing. We prayed for her on the way home, and I cheered her onward till her clouds cleared.

When we're in a dark place, it appears we are forgotten, overlooked, unloved.

It's easy to feel that we stand alone, an Esau in a field of Jacobs, those whom God loves.

But that isn't true.

As I mulled over this, I thought about another friend, one who lives in Australia—down under! We joke online about our upside-down seasonal differences: when it's summer for me, it's winter for her. When I am planting, she is reaping. We both encounter all four seasons, just not at the same time.

And then . . . I understood, and it made all the difference in my perception of the Lord's affections for me. My summer circumstances often coincide with a stark time in a friend's life. I'll share my sun to give her the warmth she needs, and she'll do it for me, later, when my winter blows in—for a season—just before spring arrives again. That way, we're always dividing the grief and sharing the joy together. He loves us both, and both through each other. That's God's design for friendship.

If two lie down together, they will keep warm. But how can one keep warm alone? Though one may be overpowered, two can defend themselves.

ECCLESIASTES 4:11-12

Experiencing the Love of God

Whether serving a couple, a family, or a large gathering, this recipe is delicious, quick, and easily adaptable to what's on hand. Each friend contributes something different, which makes the whole super tasty and delicious.

The Lord tells us that we Christians will be known by our love for one another (see John 13:35), which means we must not be loners. Hebrews 10:25 exhorts, "Let us not neglect our meeting together, as some people do, but encourage one another" (NLT). Ecclesiastes 4:9 reminds us that "two are better than one" (NLT). Gather together some people you enjoy gathering with, or even a few people you'd like to get to know better, and prepare to eat!

GINI LEE'S CURRY FOR A CROWD

Amounts vary according to how many guests you're serving and personal preferences. Prepare the items below and put into individual serving or side dishes:

Chinese noodles	Chopped peanuts and/or cashews
Cooked, shredded chicken	Chopped tomatoes
Chopped celery	Shredded cheddar cheese
Crushed pineapple	Chopped green onions
Toasted coconut	Cooked jasmine rice

Curry Sauce

1/3 cup finely minced onions	1/4 teaspoon ground ginger
3 tablespoons butter	1–2 teaspoons sugar
3 tablespoons flour	2–3 cups milk (or 2 cups chicken
1 tablespoon curry powder	broth + 1 cup milk)
1 teaspoon salt	

Sauté onion in butter until translucent. Add flour, curry, salt, ginger, and sugar. Stir well. Add milk and/or broth. Stir continually until smooth.

Add any or all of the above ingredients to a serving of rice and chicken. Cover with curry sauce and enjoy!

By this everyone will know that you are my disciples, if you love one another.   JOHN 13:35

Fire Power

My husband and I met in the early autumn at a college retreat in Colorado. The night was snappy with an early chill as is normal in Colorado, and the retreat center had a huge fire pit going in the evening. We sang songs around it and got to know one another better. My new acquaintance—later my husband—and I stayed near that fire talking till well into the night. The camp chaperones stayed nearby, stoking the fire so that we could stay late. I think they noticed something special was "sparking" too!

We've been married more than thirty years now and recently decided to invest in a fire table for our backyard. Now, in the cool early autumns, we sit outside and talk about our days and our fears and hopes for the future. We have propane to keep the fire going these days! But the idea is to keep it burning and keep us together.

In Leviticus 6, the Lord commands his people to keep the fire burning on the altar as a continuous reminder of his power and presence. In Leviticus 9, shortly after God makes the command to keep the fire always burning, Moses and Aaron exit the tent of meeting, they bless the people, and the Lord appears to all of them. Fire comes out of the presence of the Lord to consume the burnt offering. When the people see that, they shout for joy and fall facedown, remembering their love for him.

Fire often represents the Lord in Scripture. God met Moses in a burning bush and led his people in the wilderness through the pillar of fire by night. He is described as "a consuming fire" (Deuteronomy 4:24; Hebrews 12:29), and the Holy Spirit settled upon the believers like tongues of fire (see Acts 2:3). When they saw the fire, God was called to mind.

Our fire table is a way to remind ourselves of our first love and of the power of our commitment. It's a way to "keep the home fires burning."

No matter the chill of the season, find a way to keep your eyes focused on the power and presence of God. He is the same God to us, today, as he was to them, then.

Remember, the fire must be kept burning on the altar at all times. It must never go out.   Leviticus 6:13, NLT

Auctioneer

I am an extrovert in an introvert's job. This can be a bit of a problem because by the time my husband gets home, I have many things to say, all rushing out like a river that has been dammed up after a spring runoff.

One day, I'd been talking for about five minutes ("like an auctioneer!" he teased) when he uncharacteristically broke into the middle of my sentence. "You interrupted me," I said, a little hurt and surprised. "I had to interrupt, dear. You didn't stop talking long enough to listen."

I'm still an extrovert, of course, but I'm careful to listen as much as I talk. James 1:19 tells us that we must be quick to listen and slow to speak. I'm working on that in my relationship with God, too. Do you ever feel like I do, that you run out a long list of thanks and prayer requests to God before rushing off an amen, opening your eyes, and moving on? Scripture shows us that there are times when God will interrupt his people, sometimes drastically if he must, to get our attention.

Think, for example, of the increasingly terrible plagues sent to get Pharaoh's attention. Closer to home for most of us is the fact that many, if not most, of the Jewish people in Jesus' community did not listen to him when he explained, over and over, that yes, he was the prophesied Messiah. He is the Savior. He is God. In those times and at that place, crucifixions were a normal occurrence. And yet, at the moment Jesus released his spirit, God interrupted business as usual in dramatic fashion, with an earthquake, a rending of the Temple's curtain, the opening of tombs, and the resurrection of godly dead. This not only confirmed Jesus' deity to those who were listening, but it also got the attention of many others, like the soldiers present.

Do you make time to listen to our God as well as talk to him? I'm getting better at it every day. I'd rather hear the still, small voice than find frogs in my kneading bowl (see Exodus 8:1-4)!

The Roman officer and the other soldiers at the crucifixion were terrified by the earthquake and all that had happened. They said, "This man truly was the Son of God!" MATTHEW 27:54, NLT

Light Maps

We get some powerful windstorms in our town. The town is heavily wooded, which means that power lines go down often; crews tend to fix the areas that have the most customers first, and we live farther out. So when there is a widespread power outage, neighbors in the dark must depend on one another.

Our next-door neighbors purchased a generator that was more powerful than they needed to keep things lit and warm at their own home. They also purchased extension cords so that they would be able to deliver power to some neighbors' homes. That way, not only were they snug, their neighbors were too.

A few years on, they decided that it was time to move into assisted living, and they sold their home and its contents. The next year, another windstorm threatened. "This is a big one!" the forecasters promised. "What should we do?" I asked my husband. We decided to buy a generator. Once he got it assembled and ready, I texted our new next-door neighbors. "We have a generator now. Come on over if you get cold, or bring your food to our fridge if we lose the lights!"

One of the coolest maps is made possible by the satellites orbiting our earth. It shows, from that long distance, the places where there are lights on—and off—all over the world. The idea is to show us where there is more or less population with access to power and light in the night. It's striking to see how many nations have brightly lit areas, but also how many are dark.

Jesus said that his disciples would receive power when the Holy Spirit came upon them. Who would that be? Everyone who calls upon the name of Jesus for salvation. Think of it—we are perhaps some hundreds of millions of generators scattered all over the world. I feel such joy and contentment in experiencing the love of God that I want to use the power of God in me not only for myself but also for those around me.

Let's light the world!

You will receive power when the Holy Spirit comes upon you. And you will be my witnesses, telling people about me everywhere—in Jerusalem, throughout Judea, in Samaria, and to the ends of the earth. ACTS 1:8, NLT

Barnabas and Saul

A marquee is a large sign outside theaters that announces the name of a current production and its stars. The stars are listed because their names ensure a draw. There is little room on the marquee, though, for lesser known names. This always makes me think of Barnabas and Saul.

It starts out that way, you know: Barnabas and Saul. Saul, because of his persecution of the church (Acts 9:1; Philippians 3:4-6; Acts 22:4-5), is by no means trusted by the church. Acts 9:22 tells us that his preaching is powerful, but the verses that follow make it clear that it is not yet time for his public ministry to blossom in full. To save his life, the church sends him to Tarsus.

Enter stage left . . . Barnabas, a generous man (see Acts 4:36-37). In Acts 11:24-25, Barnabas, "a good man, full of the Holy Spirit and faith," goes to Tarsus to look for Saul. He brings him to Antioch, and for one year (see Acts 11:26) Barnabas and Saul meet with and teach the church.

Saul progresses in his faith, and in Acts 13, the Holy Spirit tells the church to set aside Barnabas and Saul for the work to which God has called them. Throughout their first missionary journey, the duo is referred to as Barnabas and Saul (see Acts 13:4-8). Then, in Acts 13:9, Saul becomes Paul, and in verse 14 we read: "Paul and Barnabas traveled inland to Antioch of Pisidia" (NLT). From that point on, Paul's name is listed first. Paul wrote more New Testament books than any other author. Everyone familiar with Christianity is familiar with his name. Barnabas? Not so much. Paul has become the marquee name.

It's hard to live in a world that values big names over unknowns. It's even harder when we find it in the church. Perhaps it's a comfort to know it has always existed. Each does their part to advance the Kingdom—sometimes it's done in public, and sometimes it's done in secret. That's humbling, but God sees all. Without Barnabas defending, discipling, and mentoring, there may have been no Paul. What task has the Lord awarded to you? What responsibility do you have for this week? It may be small. Next week's may be large. Next year's may be hidden—but God sees. We cannot look for our reward from the world. We must look to the Lord.

True humility and fear of the LORD lead to riches, honor, and long life.
PROVERBS 22:4, NLT

Paul and Barnabas . . . and Timothy

Yesterday we learned that God is not a respecter of persons (see Acts 10:34-35), marquee or no. When Jesus issued the great commission, "therefore go and make disciples of all nations" (Matthew 28:19), it was to every believer, no matter how big a name or how humble the stature. We are all called to be disciplers, and Paul was no exception.

Paul, formerly known as Saul, was a man with an immense knowledge of the Jewish Scriptures, but he was arrogant and proud, zealous in his persecution of the church and the Lord Jesus Christ (see Acts 9:4). Even as a new believer, he preached with power, but perhaps not with a lot of grace. Maybe because he had been discipled and mentored by Joseph (nicknamed Barnabas, which means "Son of Encouragement") with such tenderness and attention, Paul was eventually able to carry out the task we each are called to: discipling in love.

One way I understand mentoring and discipling is via the barrel of monkeys game. Plastic monkeys, each of which has an arm curling left and an arm curling right, pick up other monkeys with one arm while being held from above with the other arm. In that way, the player builds a long chain of monkeys—each one holding on to the arm above and pulling another monkey up from below.

We each are to be mentored by those more mature in the faith. Then we each are to reach out and disciple those who have not progressed in faith to the place we have (see Titus 2:3-5). Paul not only discipled on a large scale, in synagogues and to believers in each town he visited, but he also personally mentored at least one young man, Timothy. He becomes a son of encouragement to Timothy, as shown throughout the entire book of 2 Timothy. In fact, in 2 Timothy 2:1, Paul refers to Timothy as his son.

Isn't that what discipling is all about—helping to love, discipline, encourage, and raise "sons and daughters" in our Lord? It gives me a tangible, huggable, relatable view of God's love for me when he sends someone to guide and encourage me in his name, and then sends me to go and do likewise!

Hold on to the pattern of wholesome teaching you learned from me—
a pattern shaped by the faith and love that you have in Christ Jesus.

2 TIMOTHY 1:13, NLT

Experiencing the Love of God

No monkey business! The great commission is for all of us. Who has reached out in faith to you? Is there someone—or someones—you might reach out to disciple in return? Don't be shy. Sometimes we feel like we know so little, but there is always someone fresher in the faith than we are.

Do you know how to bolster your confidence to disciple others? Be discipled! We are, after all, called disciples. Is there someone you could ask to mentor you if you're not already in that kind of relationship? I've always been so shy to ask, but when I have asked a more mature woman to mentor me, I have never been turned down, and my life, faith, and ministry is immeasurably richer for having asked.

Don't be shy! Pray today about who might be in your barrel of monkeys!

Here are a few people whose faith, life, and love for God I admire—people I might approach to mentor me:

Here are a few people who are young in the faith who could share their enthusiasm with me while I share what God has taught me:

Pray over your lists and give yourself a deadline. Then make that call or text, send that e-mail, or have that conversation!

God is not unjust; he will not forget your work and the love you have shown him as you have helped his people and continue to help them. HEBREWS 6:10

A Benediction for September

I find great peace in seeing people like me—sometimes stubborn, sometimes yielding, always in need of grace—in the Bible. Sometimes I feel like Peter: a hothead who loves the Lord unreservedly. Sometimes I feel like Barnabas, called to encourage others while remaining in the background. It's delightful to know in God's Kingdom there is a place for every kind of personality. It's comforting to know that God sends others to help us understand his heart and mind, to give counsel when it is needed. It's honoring to know he uses us to do the same for others.

It seems right to me to end this month with a benediction drawn from Paul's writings. I offer this prayer of praise to remind you of God's vast wisdom, knowledge, and glory, and to reassure you of his infinite love and grace. Do you sense it? Do you acknowledge it? Receive his blessing as you experience his love in the month ahead.

Through these pages and the power of Scripture, I reach my hands out to and over you, as your sister in Christ, and pray that you will know that . . .

Oh, the depth of the riches of the wisdom and knowledge of God! How unsearchable his judgments, and his paths beyond tracing out! "Who has known the mind of the Lord? Or who has been his counselor?" "Who has ever given to God, that God should repay them?" For from him and through him and for him are all things. To him be the glory forever! Amen.

ROMANS 11:33-36

OCTOBER

Their Daily Bread

Our family recently delighted in a meal of Turkish food—including the most wonderful Turkish flatbread. It was crisp on the outside and steamy-tender on the inside, freckled with lightly browned sesame seeds. We started talking about bread—French bread, Italian bread, Finnish bread, Indian naan bread, Lebanese pitas. Every culture has bread; it's referred to as the staff of life, meaning a basic staple.

When God provided manna for the Israelites, it was a kind of bread: the thing they needed to eat each day. The Lord provided the amount of manna that was needed for that one day alone—and no more. When we live dependent on God day to day, we realize that he alone is our provider. Jesus confirms this powerfully when he teaches us to pray the Lord's Prayer in Matthew 6:11. "Give us this day our daily bread," he models in prayer (ESV). Once we begin to reach too far out, we are tempted to hold on to more and more "just in case," depending on ourselves for provision, for security. And yet Scripture does not teach that.

Acts 2 and Acts 4 relate that when the group of new Christians gathered together, they took an inventory of their possessions. Those who had more sold their extra and shared with the others who did not have as much. (Our friend Barnabas did this!) Do some of us have more than we need? Yes, we definitely do. But was that provided for us to use only on ourselves?

We often hear of people living beyond their means. For believers, perhaps it's better put that we are living beyond our provision. Debt extends our reach beyond what has been provided. Not sharing extends my spending power beyond what was intended. Few of us, with the possible exception of teen boys, would reach across the dinner table and take food from someone else's plate—right? I'm examining my own life to determine if I am consuming what was intended to be someone else's daily bread.

At the present time your plenty will supply what they need, so that in turn their plenty will supply what you need. The goal is equality, as it is written: "The one who gathered much did not have too much, and the one who gathered little did not have too little." 2 CORINTHIANS 8:14-15

Speak Up

I recently read a statistic that said the fear of public speaking, in one form or another, affects 75 percent of all people; more people are afraid of public speaking than are afraid of death! Mostly, when we fear speaking publicly, we are afraid of appearing ignorant, uninformed, or ill prepared. We worry that we'll make a mistake or that people will take exception to our point of view and shame us publicly. Often that fear keeps us from speaking out at all. In our culture, it can be considered rude to speak out about faith, and yet sharing the Good News of Jesus Christ is part of our assignment. "[Jesus] said to them, 'Go into all the world and preach the gospel to all creation'" (Mark 16:15).

I find it comforting to know that the greats, the marquee names of our faith, struggled with this fear too. In Exodus 4:10, "Moses said to the LORD, 'Pardon your servant, Lord. I have never been eloquent, neither in the past nor since you have spoken to your servant. I am slow of speech and tongue.'" Paul knew people were whispering about his abilities when he related in 2 Corinthians 10:10, "For some say, 'His letters are weighty and forceful, but in person he is unimpressive and his speaking amounts to nothing.'"

In Acts 18, Paul had devoted himself to teaching about Jesus to the Jewish people there. Acts tells us that his audience responded abusively, and he wanted nothing more to do with them. Just after he left, though, "Crispus, the synagogue leader, and his entire household believed in the Lord; and many of the Corinthians who heard Paul believed and were baptized" (Acts 18:8). God clearly blessed Paul's efforts.

I'm not going to say, "Don't be afraid to speak up," because often, I am afraid to speak up too. But let's pray for each other that we will have the courage to do so anyway, knowing that God desires and will bless our efforts.

One night the Lord spoke to Paul in a vision: "Do not be afraid; keep on speaking, do not be silent. For I am with you, and no one is going to attack and harm you, because I have many people in this city." ACTS 18:9-10

Sticky Threads

Oh, what a tangled web we weave, when first we practice to deceive.
WALTER SCOTT

At my house, October is spider season. I've found a couple on the inside walls of my home, and I make sure to shake out my shoes in the garage before slipping them on. Yesterday, I wanted to paint a piece of metal art on my fence, and once I started stroking, I noticed my brush was getting completely tangled in spiderweb threads. They were so thin I could barely see them. I saw the spider who spun them, though, skittering away.

It made me wonder, Do spiders ever get tangled in their own webs? No! They have figured out a way to walk alongside the sticky threads, and if they touch them at all, it's only with their sticky-resistant hairs. They do not fall into the trap they have set for their prey and any others, including paintbrushes, that might happen by.

This is not true for the webs humans weave, otherwise known as lies. We do become entangled in them. Lies will always be found out, because they are sin, and all sin will eventually be revealed. Christians, of course, are not supposed to lie. We are commanded not to lie (bear false witness) in the Ten Commandments. And Proverbs 12:22 tells us that the Lord detests lying lips. I do not want to be detestable before the Lord!

And yet the temptation to lie is present before all of us. We want our way. It seems the easier way out. We don't want others to think ill of us. Or, the one that tempts me most often, I don't want to hurt someone's feelings.

The Lord tells us to let our yes mean yes and our no mean no. It's hard to tell the truth all the time, even in small matters, even in matters we can rationalize, even avoiding little white lies. Like any other spiritual discipline, we can do it! Jesus is truth, and living in it is living in him. Knowing that the truth will come out anyway might give us the extra bit of motivation we need!

There is nothing concealed that will not be disclosed, or hidden that will not be made known. What you have said in the dark will be heard in the daylight, and what you have whispered in the ear in the inner rooms will be proclaimed from the roofs.　　　　　LUKE 12:2-3

A Meal with a Friend

We recently had dinner with a group of neighbors. One household invited the others over, and after enjoying a delightful time together, we decided that we should set up a regular dinner club, rotating the hosting from one household to the next.

Tonight, I'm planning for a worship webcast that is being broadcast from church. First, my small group will meet and share a meal together. Then, we will worship together while watching the live stream. After we part ways, if any of us has a need or a praise during the week, we are likely to e-mail, text, or call to share it.

How I socialize with and entertain my friends is very different from, say, how I get together with my banker. Normally, I would not invite my banker to my home; I would go to the bank, conclude my business, and leave. I might not even remember the name on her nametag after I get in my car and drive away. Once we did have a notary from the bank come to our home to sign papers. We were polite, but he was there to transact business. We certainly did not eat together, laugh together, or pray together.

I don't have my doctor over, either. He's pleasant and cares about me, but we would not socialize together. Nor would I invite an employment recruiter in for appetizers.

Sometimes I wonder if we are treating God more like a banker or a doctor than a friend. We ask him to provide for our needs—and he says he wants to. We want him to heal our friends or us. We want him to bring us jobs. But do we want . . . him? Do we want him as a friend?

There are many times in Scripture when Jesus was invited somewhere as a friend. His first miracle was performed at a wedding he attended as a guest. He ate with publicans and tax collectors and sinners, as well as his band of friends. He smiled and laughed. He ate and drank.

I want to say, "Come, Lord Jesus. Come to my house, not just as a banker, doctor, and job arranger. Come and eat with us, laugh with us, and be among us as we worship and pray. Be my friend."

I have called you friends. JOHN 15:15

Courageous Sheep

Scripture tells us that we, Christ-followers in this world, are at war. Not only are we at war (see 2 Corinthians 4:8-9), we are at war with a cunning, experienced, malevolent force (see 1 Peter 5:8).

We, Christ-followers in this world, are sheep! Jesus is our Good Shepherd and takes good care of us (see John 10). But in Matthew 10:16, Jesus tells us, a little frighteningly, "I am sending you out like sheep among wolves."

I'm with Red Riding Hood. I want to hide from the wolves! And yet, I am called to be a disciple of Jesus. I must be like the man in Luke 9:57. "As they were walking along the road, a man said to him, 'I will follow you wherever you go.'" Sometimes that means into battle.

As I began to try to make sense of this, knowing the protective nature of our Savior but also our vulnerability in the world, I came across a most informative quote by Alexander the Great: "I am not afraid of an army of lions led by a sheep; I am afraid of an army of sheep led by a lion."

Alexander the Great, widely known in the ancient world, was "great" as his name suggests. He built and conquered a huge empire and was largely undefeated in battle. So to hear what kind of army he would fear is informative. It's not the followers. It's not the soldiers. It's the commander in chief.

Jesus is unique in history. He was both fully man and fully God. He was sinless and also the ransom for sin. He is both a lamb and a lion. "Then one of the elders said to me . . . 'See, the Lion of the tribe of Judah, the Root of David, has triumphed' . . . Then I saw a Lamb, looking as if it had been slain, standing at the center of the throne" (Revelation 5:5-6).

We need not fear what comes our way in this life, in this constant battle, but not because we are battle hardened and protected by armor. It's because we are cherished and protected by Christ, who has already defeated our enemy.

Having disarmed the powers and authorities, he made a public spectacle of them, triumphing over them by the cross. COLOSSIANS 2:15

Nutritious Recipes

Like many people, I don't have the time available to prepare long, involved meals most nights of the week. I'm not afraid to order out, and meal delivery services are wonderful too. But mainly what helps is simple recipes.

The Bible consists of sixty-six books, perfectly penned over thousands of years. It has much to share, and we are to share it, then, with others. But sometimes, when life overwhelms, it's okay for us to rely on a simple recipe of three basic ingredients for our own spiritual sustenance and to offer to others: faith, hope, and love.

Faith (*pistis*) in Greek is a noun—it is a thing, although we often think it is something we do or feel. It is a conviction of the truth of anything, in this case, a conviction of and firm trust in the truth of God and his Word. "Now faith is confidence in what we hope for and assurance about what we do not see" (Hebrews 11:1). When life feels unsteady, our faith can remain firm because the one in whom it is placed remains firm—steady as the Rock he refers to himself as.

Hope (*elpis*) is the constant expectation of good. To a Christian, it is a joyful and confident expectation of eternity with Christ as well as all the good he promises us in the abundant life he came to bring (see Acts 26:6; Romans 8:22-25; Titus 1:2). Hope is a beloved child looking at a Christmas tree without gifts underneath. She knows that those who love her will not overlook her, and even though she cannot see what is to come, she eagerly awaits what has been prepared, in advance, just for her.

The word in 1 Corinthians we most often translate as "love" is also translated as "charity." We can offer honest charity to anyone, even those with whom we do not have the strong "love" affection we normally associate with that word. "Don't just pretend to love others. Really love them" (Romans 12:9, NLT).

Even when I'm busy and the day is rushing by, I do have time to offer something wonderful, simply prepared. Scripture promises us that those three essentials are eternal.

Three things will last forever—faith, hope, and love—and the greatest of these is love.   1 CORINTHIANS 13:13, NLT

Experiencing the Love of God

Yesterday we learned that it doesn't take a lot of time or extensive teaching to impart God's love and truth into someone's life. Some days, all we need are three simple "ingredients" that convey optimism, trust, and affection in our Lord. Likewise, while there are days when I love making an elaborate recipe, most days I want something simple to prepare but delightful to serve and enjoy. I ran across a video online of a set of three-ingredient recipes, which seemed just the trick. I can mix up three things!

You can do a search for "three ingredients" or "three-ingredient recipes," and many suggestions will pop up, bringing a tasty surprise down to the delicious basics. This one, below, shows up in many places and with good reason—it's fantastic!

THREE-INGREDIENT WHITE CHOCOLATE CHEESECAKE

 9 ounces white chocolate, chipped or broken into chunks
 8 ounces cream cheese, room temperature, in 1-inch square chunks
 6 large eggs, separated, room temperature

Preheat oven to 350°F.

Line the bottom of an 8-inch round cake pan or springform pan with parchment paper; use a sharp knife to make the exact-sized circle. Alternatively, you can buy 8-inch parchment circles—even easier!

Melt the white chocolate in a large glass bowl in the microwave in 15-second intervals, stirring between each interval. When the chocolate is almost but not totally melted, finish melting by simply stirring with no additional heat. Whisk in cream cheese cubes till wholly blended. Add yolks and completely combine.

In a separate bowl, whip egg whites until the stiff-peak stage. Fold egg whites into the chocolate cream cheese mixture and pour into the pan. Place the pan in the center of another pan larger than the one holding the cake. Then pour in hot water until it reaches about an inch up the side of the pan. This is known as a water bath. Put the pan in the oven for about 40 minutes, until just set. Turn the oven off, but leave the oven door closed with the cake inside for an additional 15 minutes. Cool completely before placing into the refrigerator so the cake does not crack. Flip the cake from the pan, and chill in the refrigerator at least 3 hours. Shake powdered sugar over the top for a pretty, lacy effect before serving.

I long to see you so that I may impart to you some spiritual gift to make you strong—that is, that you and I may be mutually encouraged by each other's faith. ROMANS 1:11-12

Holding Hands

I watched two sweet street-crossings last week.

In the first one, a mom held on to her toddlers—twins, I think—one chubby hand in her left hand, and one in her right. The kids were oblivious to the dangers around them, distracted by other activities and each other. Mom held firmly to them, listening for oncoming traffic as they quickly crossed the dangerous road. When they were well out of danger, she let go and let them run in the nearby grass.

The second time, a middle-aged man pressed the "walk" button, and once it began to beep the safety signal, helped an older woman with a walker cross the street. She had to concentrate on the walker and not falling, so he ensured that all oncoming traffic stopped well before it could reach her.

Sometimes I don't know what dangers to look out for. Sometimes I am hobbled by fear or illness or faith fatigue or depression and cannot make the way myself. There are believers who are temporarily blinded by those kinds of things and who cannot see just now. There are those deaf to the promises and call of faith because the roar of difficulty is in their ears. For a moment, they cannot hear the signal saying it's all safe, you can go now. That's where we come in.

Sometimes when people are weary or worried, we can be their eyes to see and their ears to hear, helping them make their way safely until they can, spiritually, do it themselves. We can speak to them about what we, and they, have seen and heard in the past, the mighty works God has done. We can tell of how he has saved us in the past and how he will save us once more, even when the road turns in a direction we didn't want or anticipate or the world is noisy with anxiety-producing situations or we are distracted.

When you are tired, depressed, or unwell, find someone with eyes to see and ears to hear to guide you in Jesus till you're well again. And when you are? Take the hand of someone who needs eyes to see and ears to hear to make it safely through.

I assure you, we tell you what we know and have seen. John 3:11, NLT

Bloopers

A few years ago, several collections of bloopers from church bulletins circulated through group e-mails. My mother-in-law passed some on to us, and we got a good laugh from them. I wondered, though: had they been staged?

Then this year, I received an electronic newsletter from my own church announcing weekend conference topics to help members better live and live together, and stating where the meetings would be held:

Missions meeting held in the Gathering Place
Family in the Boardroom
Finances in the Drama Room
Relationships in the Prayer Chapel

Missions *should* be held in the Gathering Place. When we share our faith in Jesus and his plan for redemption, to those who do not yet know him, it is with the hope and expectation that they will join us in the final gathering place—heaven!

Often boardrooms are places where the people who govern and advise a company meet to assess what is working and what is not. The hope is to discontinue activities and attitudes that do not lead to success for the mission and enhance those that do. What a wonderful idea for a family to do—the whole family—kids included!

Finances in the Drama Room—'nuff said! The apostle Paul shares a wonderful way to defuse that, though, which held true in his world of tentmaking as well as in our world, which is rich with material blessings, or the desires for them. "I know what it is to be in need, and I know what it is to have plenty. I have learned the secret of being content in any and every situation" (Philippians 4:12).

Does anyone know a better place to take concerns and praise over our relationships than to the Lord in prayer? Our relationships, with him and with others, are often the most important things in our lives. They produce the most joy and the most anguish. The hymn "What a Friend We Have in Jesus" encourages us to "take it to the Lord in prayer."

Isn't it wonderful to gather together with others who love the Lord and learn how to live, together?

Let us . . . not [give] up meeting together.   HEBREWS 10:24-25

Homeward Bound

I love to travel, but not quite as much as I love arriving home. One of my favorite parts of returning after traveling overseas is when the border agents at the airport, upon realizing that I am a citizen, reply, "Welcome home!" Yes, I am home, I belong, I am welcomed, and I am among my people.

I'm sure you've all read and heard those Saint Peter at the pearly gates jokes—they center around Saint Peter determining who gets in to heaven and who does not. I love this oldie but goodie:

As soon as a man died, his spirit was immediately whisked to heaven, and he stood outside the pearly gates. As he did, Saint Peter told him that admittance was based on the point system. Peter would ask questions and add up points per the man's answers. Anyone whose answers totaled one hundred points could enter heaven. "Have you given to the poor?" Peter asked. The man said he had, and he earned one point. "Did you tithe?" Peter asked. The man said he did, and he earned one more point. "Did you faithfully attend church?" "Yes," the man said, hoping that was worth quite a bit. "One point," Peter said. At that, the newly deceased burst out, "At this rate, the one way I'm going to get through those gates is by the grace of God!" "Come on in," Peter told him. "That's the only answer that really matters."

You know what? No matter where you travel in life or in this world, whether the roads are dark or light, you have a place at "home." I hope you and I do good and attend church and give generously and help the poor. But that will all be flowing out of a redeemed heart, not the "price of admission." There is only one price of admission, and Jesus tells us what it is: "I am the way, the truth, and the life. No one can come to the Father except through me" (John 14:6, NLT).

You and I may never meet in this life—but we will meet there, for sure. I can't wait till I see you, or if you arrive first, you see me and say, "Welcome home!"

We are citizens of heaven, where the Lord Jesus Christ lives.

PHILIPPIANS 3:20, NLT

Terms and Conditions

We live in a digital world. I love streaming movies whenever I want. I love my word-processing program, and my job is immeasurably easier for it. I don't like that my phone seems to control so much of my time, but I do love being able to text with my friends and family whenever I want, and that my family has a common thread by which we can have an ongoing conversation—no matter where we are.

The cost of all that wonderful digital interaction comes in layers. One I don't often think of is the multipage terms and conditions agreement that accompanies almost every device and digital service I use. I admit—I scroll through the pages and pages and pages till I get to the little box, and then I click to agree. I could take the time to read it, but I don't.

Then, later, I'm outraged to find that they often have access to my contacts and all stored information. Who gave them that permission? Well . . . I did.

I hear similar tales when mentoring people who are younger in the faith. They signed up for salvation—yay—and the abundant life now. What they didn't sign up for, or didn't realize they were signing up for, were the bits about picking up the cross and following Christ, who often travels a difficult road. They didn't realize that suffering and persecution were a part of a believer's package. The terms and conditions agreement to exchange our lives for his? We "signed" it!

The benefits of being a follower of Jesus dwarf the costs and crosses we must bear. He promises to never leave us or forsake us; he tells us he will be with us always, including when we're suffering or undergoing trials. His Spirit lives within us to guide, comfort, and counsel. Still, we need to know that difficulties will come so we are prepared—and so we know whom to lean on.

If I had taken the time to read those multipage agreements, I would have either declined and missed out on the benefits, or have been aware of what I agreed to. It doesn't mean I would have liked the parts I still don't like, but it makes it easier to bear when I recall it was a freely given agreement, and what I receive in return is worth the cost many times over.

If you do not carry your own cross and follow me, you cannot be my disciple. But don't begin until you count the cost. For who would begin construction of a building without first calculating the cost to see if there is enough money to finish it? Luke 14:27-28, NLT

The Editor's Life

As a writer, editing is a part of my life. It is a helpful discipline and one I must invite others into to help me make my work the best. But the truth of it is, editing is painful. When I turn a book in, even though I know there will be multiple changes suggested, or even demanded, I feel I have it right. I must undergo the red "knife," as it were, to help my books be strengthened and expanded so that they may reach into many lives.

Lately, I have heard the word *edit* being used outside of the writing context. People edit their gardens, removing or replacing plants. People edit their habits, switching up a few hours on the couch for an hour at the gym. They edit their contact lists or address books. They audit—and edit—their spiritual practices. Sometimes they edit on their own accord, or at the prompting of the Holy Spirit. Sometimes someone is given a gentle rebuke. These personal changes, too, can be painful.

A friend recently sold her house, and before she did, the realtor told her to remove almost all of her "stuff" and place it in storage because it would not appeal to everyone. After the house was cleared, the realtor had staging furniture delivered, pieces that would appeal to potential buyers. My friend's feelings were hurt. She felt that her own decorations and furnishings were lovely. The realtor finally, gently, asked her: "What is the goal here?" "Selling my house," my friend replied. "Then this is what needs to happen for you to reach that goal" came the response.

That's what editing is—whether it be a house, a manuscript, or our habits. What is the goal here? To be healthy. To grow more in our Christlikeness. To reach others with the word we have been given to share.

Next time you find yourself undergoing the discipline of editing, whether by suggestion or by choice, ask yourself, "What is the goal here?" By focusing on the goal and not the required changes, you can look ahead with a lighter spirit and much anticipation even while undergoing the process.

No discipline is enjoyable while it is happening—it's painful! But afterward there will be a peaceful harvest of right living for those who are trained in this way.   Hebrews 12:11, NLT

Better Bones

I was excited—but also had some trepidation. I'd enrolled in a training program to minister to the women incarcerated in the prison near my home.

The most effective part of the entire program was an illustration offered by the prison chaplain, a devout Christian, at the conclusion. "Do you know how to take a bone away from a dog?" he asked. "If you try to take an old bone from him, he'll just lunge and fight and growl. To take a bone from a dog, you must offer him something better. Then he'll drop it on his own to pick up what's better."

Now, this wonderful man who had given his life to serving the women in prison was not comparing them to dogs. He was a country boy using a country illustration. And it made sense to this city girl. What could I share with these ladies, already in pain, most of them from abusive backgrounds, that would help them drop beliefs that were not working and allow them to see and grasp beliefs founded in the truth?

I thought about their fears. Fear of death. Fear of not being identified with. The reality that they had no autonomy over their lives. Then this came to mind: "Since the children have flesh and blood, he too shared in their humanity so that by his death he might break the power of him who holds the power of death—that is, the devil—and free those who all their lives were held in slavery by their fear of death" (Hebrews 2:14-15).

And then I prayed, *What can I hold out to them that will bring them what they need right now, in their everyday lives in prison?* They are women like I am. No different. They want what I want, and what I want is the fruit of the Spirit in my life every day, in every situation. I didn't have to cajole or plead or argue a case. I only needed to offer them something that we all truly want and none of us has on our own.

The Holy Spirit produces this kind of fruit in our lives: love, joy, peace, patience, kindness, goodness, faithfulness, gentleness, and self-control. There is no law against these things! GALATIANS 5:22-23, NLT

Experiencing the Love of God

Yesterday we discussed that in order to get a dog to let go of a bone it's gripping, we should offer it a better bone so it lets go of the old one on its own. A wise chaplain compared this with offering Christ to those who are gripping old, unworkable habits or faiths other than Christianity. To whom are you offering a new bone?

It might be someone who does not know Jesus. It might be someone who has a baby faith and is not living by biblical truths. It might be someone who simply needs you to display the love and person of Christ in your own life, so she becomes curious enough to ask.

After you identify one person you would love to see freed in some way, ask yourself a few questions.

What would a "better bone" look like to this person? To understand that God's love for us does not depend on performance? To understand that he wants to free them from fear? To know the peace that only he brings? Something else?

Now, have you thought of someone? Have you considered (or prayed about) what might be a compelling draw for them? Name it here.

Great! Now is the time to commit to act. When will you meet up and share, and how?

Which of you, if your son asks for bread, will give him a stone? Or if he asks for a fish, will give him a snake? If you, then, though you are evil, know how to give good gifts to your children, how much more will your Father in heaven give good gifts to those who ask him!　　Matthew 7:9-11

Tuning Out the Jeers

It's football season in the United States. The games are aplenty, and each team has fans.

Sometimes each team's fans (and parents of players!) comport themselves with dignity and sportsmanlike conduct. Sometimes they don't. I have heard cheering from the stands and sidelines, and I have also heard jeers.

The cheers come from those encouraging the players toward determination, perseverance, strategy, and success. The jeers come in when fans of the "other side" speak up, calling out insults, boos, and hisses to try to distract and rattle the other side—giving their side an edge.

No one, no team, is awarded a prize at halftime. Both teams are cheered and jeered till the game is over.

We are on a team, you know—even if we don't play football. We are on God's team, working on behalf of his interests in this world. You can't be on two teams at once. Jesus says those who are not for him are against him. "Anyone who isn't with me opposes me, and anyone who isn't working with me is actually working against me" (Matthew 12:30, NLT).

If you are doing the Lord's work, if you are trying to live a holy life, if you are called to reach out in compassion in the name of Christ, you are going to be jeered. There is no one a sports fan hates more than a player who switches sides to play for the archenemy. When you turned your life back to actively working on behalf of Christ, that's just what you did. Jesus tells us in John 15:18-19, "If the world hates you, remember that it hated me first. The world would love you as one of its own if you belonged to it, but you are no longer part of the world. I chose you to come out of the world, so it hates you" (NLT). It never feels good to be hated or to have people say hateful things about us. In John 16:33, the Lord tells us that in spite of difficulties, we can have peace and take heart because he has overcome this world.

Don't listen to the jeers—they're going to be shouted till you run through the finish line. Don't surround yourself with hecklers! Do surround yourself with those who cheer you on, encouraging you to endure and enjoy. You're going to make it! There's a trophy waiting for you.

Do you not know that in a race all the runners run, but only one gets the prize? Run in such a way as to get the prize.   1 CORINTHIANS 9:24

A Shelter in the Wind

I was listening to the radio the other day, and I heard the announcer say that the phrase "Do not be afraid" is in the Bible 365 times. I did a little digging; we're all supposed to be like the Bereans in Acts 17:11, right? "Now the Berean Jews were of more noble character than those in Thessalonica, for they received the message with great eagerness and examined the Scriptures every day to see if what Paul said was true." It seems that those numbers do not quite add up. Depending on what translation you're using, though, the phrases "Do not be afraid" and "Fear not" do appear somewhere between sixty and ninety times. Not enough for one per day, but enough for one per week—plus. There is something fearsome in my life every week—how about you? And just when I think one circumstance is conquered, resolved, put to bed, another one pops up. And I'm weary.

We are all afraid. God knows that. He remembers that we are jars of clay— that we are fragile and vulnerable physically, emotionally, and spiritually. He understands that sometimes we are a bruised reed (see Isaiah 42:3), a wounded, thin stem that bends under the weight of the wind. He knows that sometimes our wicks sputter in that same wind because we run out of courage and strength.

When I was a young woman, I believed that the circumstances that caused me fear would simply dissolve with time and faith. Now I am not so young, and I see that the circumstances not only do not dissolve, they can sometimes piggyback on each other. When I was young, I thought relief from those circumstances would bring me peace. Now I realize that is not where my peace comes from. "Let the peace that comes from Christ rule in your hearts," Colossians 3:15 (NLT) reminds us. Instructs us. Whispers to us.

The comfort we have, the assurance we have is that our defender, the Creator of the universe, who is omnipotent and omniscient but also *is* truth and love, walks beside us. He will strengthen us. He will help us. He is with us, so we need not be afraid no matter how hard the wind blows this week or next.

Don't be afraid, for I am with you. Don't be discouraged, for I am your God. I will strengthen you and help you. I will hold you up with my victorious right hand. ISAIAH 41:10, NLT

Hostess Gifts

My friend Debbie and I recently threw a dinner party for eight of our friends. We were, in the common language, entertaining them. We thought about what they would like, and how they would enjoy spending their time, and then we set up the evening to do just that. We wanted them to feel comfortable and right at home, and our menu and activities reflected that. We did not invite anyone who would confront or make another guest uncomfortable. We entertained them well, and they wanted to stay and, after leaving, come back.

I thought about that as I was reading through Matthew. In Matthew 9:4, we read, "Knowing their thoughts, Jesus said, 'Why do you entertain evil thoughts in your hearts?'" It would be easy to give myself a pass on this, because the Lord is speaking to self-righteous religious leaders, and I'm not one of those, right? But a few chapters back, in Matthew 5:20 in the Sermon on the Mount, Jesus shared, "But I warn you—unless your righteousness is better than the righteousness of the teachers of religious law and the Pharisees, you will never enter the Kingdom of Heaven!" (NLT).

I am not that righteous.

Furthermore, a few verses on in Matthew he teaches that it is not only doing the deed, like murder or adultery; to be guilty we have only to entertain a sin in our minds.

So what does it mean, then, to entertain evil thoughts? It's not merely to have them appear in our minds. All of us are subject to suggestion, and the flittering of a thought that might tempt us is not sin. To entertain is to do as my friend Debbie and I did. To make it comfortable. Welcome. To ensure that nothing and no one will be able to confront or dislodge it. Perhaps the next step is to rearrange circumstances around these thoughts, or rationalizations.

Next time temptation flits across a screen or a page or in front of your eyes, do not open the door, no matter what kind of hostess gift it comes bearing.

Knowing their thoughts, Jesus said, "Why do you entertain evil thoughts in your hearts?" MATTHEW 9:4

Caged Beasts

We know when tempting or evil thoughts come knocking we're supposed to close the door and not invite them back. But you know, we err—and sometimes we let them into our hearts and minds through mistake, weakness, habit, or willful disobedience. Then what? How do we serve an eviction notice to thoughts that have already made it inside?

Scripture tells us what to do. "We take captive every thought to make it obedient to Christ" (2 Corinthians 10:5). I'm guessing that many who are reading this have heard that verse before, and it kind of glazes over your mind, lightly, like the sugar seal on a donut. But it shouldn't. Taking anything captive is not done lightly or sweetly. It's a strong, almost violent action.

We watch a lot of animal nature shows in our house—my husband is a fan. In many of them, a large animal must be taken captive, either because it is in an area where it threatens human life or itself, or it needs to be transported for safety. Let me remind you: nothing wants to be taken captive. The animals fight back, run away, hide, and are aggressive.

We were warned about how hard it would be to do this. In Genesis 1:28, we learn, "God blessed them and said to them, 'Be fruitful and increase in number; fill the earth and subdue it. Rule over the fish in the sea and the birds in the sky and over every living creature that moves on the ground.'" The Hebrew word translated here as "subdue" can also be translated as "bring into bondage, make it subservient." And once we have the thing subdued? We are to rule over it.

This is the kind of aggressive action a sinful thought, once comfortably at home within our hearts and minds, needs for it to be removed. Confess it to someone (see James 5:16). Declare aloud it has no place in your life. Remove the materials that lead you to succumb (see Mark 9:43). Confess it to God, repeatedly if necessary (see 1 John 1:9). Change the brain channel the moment the thought occurs (see Philippians 4:8). Once you capture the thought, do not free it or give it parole.

You can do it. Be aggressive in taking those thoughts captive, in and through his power (see Philippians 4:13). And once you do, bring them under the complete authority of Christ.

We demolish arguments and every pretension that sets itself up against the knowledge of God, and we take captive every thought to make it obedient to Christ.　2 CORINTHIANS 10:5

Nonstick Christians

There are people who are organized inside their heads, so they don't need their environments to be just so to get to work. Then there are people who aren't so organized inside their heads, like me. I need my environment to be ordered so that I can work well. This has led to some good things, but also some bad—like throwing things away that I shouldn't have, in a tidying frenzy. I threw away my husband's watch. I threw away a paycheck. And last year, I threw away a precious newspaper clipping describing my son's new start-up.

Once I realized it, I panicked. I went digging through the garbage, and thankfully I had placed a folded grocery bag over it, so there was only one tiny, wet corner. After drying off the clipping, I drove to the office supply store and had it laminated. Once it was laminated, it was trash proof! Stain proof! Waterproof and damage proof. No matter what kind of distracted trouble I got into, my treasure was protected.

That night as I made scrambled eggs for dinner, I was reminded of the concept again as my eggs slid right off the coated pan. We believers have a surface like that; we just don't always operate like it. Someone throws an accusation at us, and we let it stick to us rather than letting it slide off. People gossip about us, and we feel bad, owning what they've covered us in.

We know that Satan is our accuser, and those who work for him are too. The great news is, our salvation protects us from those accusations. Revelation 12:10 says, "I heard a loud voice saying in heaven, 'Now is come salvation, and strength, and the kingdom of our God, and the power of his Christ: for the accuser of our brethren is cast down, which accused them before our God day and night'" (KJV).

We need not be oppressed by the enemy's accusations, sometimes shouted publicly and sometimes whispered like a worm in our ears. Our salvation, our strength, and the Kingdom of God has come for us. When we sin—and we will—if we confess to him, he is faithful and just to forgive us (see 1 John 1:9), and he remembers it no more (see Hebrews 8:12).

If he remembers it no more, who should? No one.

There is now no condemnation for those who are in Christ Jesus.

ROMANS 8:1

Followers

Social media has exploded. It has its downsides but allows us to connect with people across the world, reach out to the lonely, share ideas and interests, and even share or deepen our faith.

On social media, we friend or follow people, and they do (or sometimes do not!) follow us back. Some have decried that this kind of friendship is not real—but it can be. We can care for and encourage one another, enjoy discussions, and gain new insights. The flip side, of course, is that sometimes we "friend" people who later turn out to be toxic or harmful to us or our faith.

People worry that social media has replaced "real" life, but truly, it imitates life, and for many is a large part of real life. It can enhance or detract, just like every other relationship. Perhaps it's even taught us a few lessons.

There are many, many places in Scripture where we are taught that large crowds followed Jesus. In those crowds were a mix of people: some wanted to befriend and follow him. "They pulled their boats up on shore, left everything and followed him" (Luke 5:11). Some were simply curious and followed him to learn what he was all about. Some followed him to degrade him, to disrupt or question his ministry. Jesus was never afraid to speak directly to those people—calling them, among other things, a brood of vipers!

I have, after careful consideration, unfriended people on social media. Most of the time they weren't hateful, but they were negative toward me and others and wanted to pull us into their tailspin. I don't think they meant to cause harm or tug others into a negative vortex. But they would not listen to good words pointing them in positive directions, either. I hope that I, and each of us, can be as respectful and kind to our social media friends as we are to face-to-face friends.

I like social media and hope to meet you there. Let's just remember that anyone or anything that consistently keeps us from wholeheartedly trusting and following Jesus, or who removes his joy from our lives, probably needs to be unfollowed.

"Come, follow me," Jesus said.   MATTHEW 4:19

Experiencing the Love of God

Remember on October 12 we talked about auditing and editing our spiritual life? It's a principle that is helpful, I think, to do regularly regarding time spent online, too. My business requires me to self-audit every quarter.

I must ask:

How am I spending my resources?
Am I sticking to the budget I set up?
Is that spending going toward legitimate expenses that will further my
    business goals?

After I answer these questions, I may have to change the way I do things. In your life, and perhaps particularly on social media, are there places you are spending too much time—time that might be trimmed or disciplined? I look at pages that are overall positive even when they discuss difficult issues. I unfollow people or posts that have consistently negative content, including gossip or tearing others down.

Do you have a budget for the time you spend online? Are you sticking to it? I must use social media for some time during the day for my work. However, I compare it to the time I'm doing other work (it cuts my hourly pay rate if I spend too much unpaid time on social media!), as well as other methods of developing my ministry and business. How much time are you online compared to reading good books? Reading the Word? Spending time with friends? There are apps and online timers that will help you manage your time online well.

Do these activities and friendships lead you closer to your personal and spiritual goals, or do they leave you dissatisfied, self-loathing or angry, or losing faith?

Adjust time online, friend or unfriend, follow or unfollow as required. Here's my standard when evaluating the relationships and pages I follow:

The wisdom that comes from heaven is first of all pure; then peace-loving, considerate, submissive, full of mercy and good fruit, impartial and sincere.
JAMES 3:17

Banishing the Black Dog

Winston Churchill called depression the black dog for the way it sat on his lap and haunted him. I've been subject to the black dog twice. Both times were completely debilitating, and I was barely able to care for myself and my children for a few months. I spent all my energy doing just that, though, which left me depleted at the end of the day.

God did not immediately heal my depression, despite my pleadings. He did not forget me though. My husband tended me well, and God sent lovely friends my way. I might not have accepted their care under other circumstances—pride would have prevented me. I had no pride left at this point, though, and their ministrations were necessary and felt good.

One good and loving friend was motivated to care for me in an atypical way. She sat me down and had me close my eyes, and then she left the room. A minute later, she came back with a warm washcloth, and she tenderly washed my face. It wasn't that my face was dirty. It was that it was a very maternal thing to do. Intimate, tender, caring, and refreshing. More than any of the other gifts offered to me during those dark days, this one healed my soul. It was an unexpected gift which cost nothing but provided everything.

I had nothing to give her in return—and she wouldn't have accepted it anyway—except a prayer that the Lord would honor his promise in the book of Luke. "Give, and it will be given to you. A good measure, pressed down, shaken together and running over, will be poured into your lap. For with the measure you use, it will be measured to you" (6:38).

There is a certain love that others, and the Lord, show us when we are down and needy that we don't receive when we are self-sufficient. Look for those ministrations because they may come in unusual ways. Ask God to open your eyes to the many ways others refresh you—and to suggest ways you might refresh them in return.

The generous will prosper; those who refresh others will themselves be refreshed. PROVERBS 11:25, NLT

Peace in the Disruption

Our world seems more chaotic and out of control every day. In the book of Acts, believers feel the world as they've known it is now out of control. This book also shows us just how much good God does when our worlds are upended, and reassures us he will speak to us and clearly guide in ways we can understand.

In Acts 10, we find Cornelius, a Gentile—someone who is untouchable by Jewish standards—but who is also generous and devout. He is a soldier, a commander of many men. When the angel of the Lord appears to him in a vision, the angel speaks to Cornelius in a military manner he understands: commendation for a mission well done, direct instructions on what next to do, who to get to (Peter), and where to find him, with no further explanation.

Cornelius orders three men to find and return with Peter. Meanwhile Peter, hungry and in prayer, also sees a vision: all kinds of foods that have been considered impure to eat under the law are presented to him to kill and eat. Peter, horrified, responds, "Surely not, Lord! . . . I have never eaten anything impure or unclean" (verse 14). God corrects him and sends the vision twice more.

Cornelius's men arrive at the house where Peter is staying shortly after that, and events unfold; Peter understands what God was showing him: faith is not simply for the Jewish person, but also for the Gentile, a new and uncomfortable thought in a world already turned upside down by Christ's death. The vision of the impure and unclean food, clearly understood by Peter in his culture and customs, has been used to show him how he must view the visitors about to knock on his door.

Cornelius is nervous to have Peter appear before him. Peter is uncomfortable presenting these new believers to the church—for good cause (see Acts 11). Enemies are now friends, and friends seemed enemies. Unclean things are made pure by Christ. In these things, normal life is scrambled, but God is on the move.

Do not be afraid when it seems the world is changing in ways difficult to understand. God is at work in the upheaval, but he speaks clearly to his people in ways we understand to reassure and guide us.

Truly, O God of Israel, our Savior, you work in mysterious ways.

ISAIAH 45:15, NLT

No Curse Words

The word *curse* used throughout the Bible does not mean vulgar language; it means to call down the wrath of heaven upon someone, to wish them ill, to have them punished or rebuked. Mostly, it's a cloaked way to ask God to use his power to rebuke and punish our enemies—not his.

The book of James is sometimes understood to have been written by James as a teaching interpretation of Jesus' Sermon on the Mount, directed toward Jewish people who were being persecuted. So this call to love and not curse was directed toward people who would find it a most difficult task. And yet—it was what Jesus required. "I say unto you, love your enemies, bless them that curse you, do good to them that hate you, and pray for them which despitefully use you, and persecute you" (Matthew 5:44, KJV).

This is directly echoed in Luke 6:28 and Romans 12:14 as well. But how do we love our enemies? I think it helps to look at the word used for "love" in the Matthew 5 passage. It means, essentially, to have compassion for the other person's welfare. We can care for the person's physical needs. We can compassionately understand that difficult circumstances may have led to their actions. We do not wish them ill. We share the truth with them. But love in this sense doesn't insist that they become emotional intimates or friends.

Cornelius represented a system that had come against Peter and the Jewish people (see yesterday's devotion). He'd been an enemy until God made him a brother, which was what God desired or it would not have come to pass. Who in this world today is presented as our enemy but may, in fact, be someone God is leading to salvific faith in Christ, or might even be a believer who needs a clearer picture of our faith family and how it operates? What we do and say may bring that about more quickly, or may push the curious away.

Second Peter 3:9 tells us that God wishes none to perish. I want to pray for those who are far off from him to draw near, and I do not want to salt the purity of my language by speaking ill of them while we wait.

With the tongue we praise our Lord and Father, and with it we curse human beings, who have been made in God's likeness. Out of the same mouth come praise and cursing. My brothers and sisters, this should not be. Can both fresh water and salt water flow from the same spring? My brothers and sisters, can a fig tree bear olives, or a grapevine bear figs? Neither can a salt spring produce fresh water. JAMES 3:9-12

Cut the Ropes

My husband and I enjoy watching historical movies, and one of his favorites is *Master and Commander*, the tale of a ship, the HMS *Surprise*, set during the era of the Napoleonic Wars.

The ships are all sail powered, of course, as steam ships are about a decade away. During a storm, one of the ship's topmasts breaks, still connected to the ship by all that rope rigging and a sail. Falling into the sea, it is caught up by the waves. The topmast acts like a sea anchor; it tugs on the ship, causing it to list into the water. And finally, as the broken topmast and sail sink, they'll take the whole ship down with them if the ship cannot be cut free. The crew must cut the ropes holding onto the broken topmast and sails in order to save the *Surprise* and her crew.

It is not an easy decision: a popular sailor is trimming the sails when the topmast breaks and is still holding on when it is cut free. One life has to be sacrificed to save the many.

In watching this, two spiritual threads came clear. First, of course, is that the diligent, innocent sailor, who selflessly works for the benefit of shipmates, is sacrificed so that the many may be saved. It's a clear, poignant picture of the Lord Jesus' sacrifice.

Second, Hebrews 12:1 came to mind. "Since we are surrounded by such a great cloud of witnesses, let us throw off everything that hinders." I had to ask myself, what is holding me back? What ropes are attached to me, holding broken parts of my life to the healthy ones? What habits, or understandings, or sins, or even just unhealthy physical habits or emotional ways of looking at things am I clinging to? They hobble me, for sure. But could they bring me under? Maybe.

Scripture tells us that upon our salvation we are immediately freed to eternal life and salvation and adopted into God's family. It does not say that upon becoming Christians we are immediately untangled from that which hinders us. Grace provides salvation, but God expects us to work alongside the Holy Spirit for sanctification.

What broken bits are holding you back? Let's gather our courage and cut the ropes.

Since we are surrounded by such a great cloud of witnesses, let us throw off everything that hinders. HEBREWS 12:1

Not Afraid of Earthquakes

Only after we bought our house did I become aware of the fact that we lived in an area that is prone to slippage. When you drive across the bridge from the mainland to where we live on a peninsula, you can see large portions of cliffs that have simply slid into Puget Sound. There is a fence on the border to keep people from falling off. Just behind that fence, though, are condos and other houses—not very far from the new slippage zone.

I then looked up a geological map, which showed that our house, only one block away from the Sound, was indeed on a "watch" area for slippage. I should have known! When planting our new garden, we had to amend our beige, sandy soil with dark, loamy earth. Help! Our house is built upon the sand!

Earthquakes are a risk in our area, which is why the slippage fears are real. We cannot stop the earthquakes from coming—nor can we help that the area has sandy underpinnings. But we can bolt our homes to a secure foundation to firmly hold it when the shaking starts. We can remove heavy objects from above our beds, so nothing falls on our heads if the earthquake starts in the middle of the night. We can have three days' worth of food and water ready. We can be prepared. But we cannot stop the earthquakes. Sooner or later, they will come.

Is your house built upon the Rock? Are you bolted to your foundation in Christ? If so, no matter the shaking, you are prepared!

Everyone then who hears these words of mine and does them will be like a wise man who built his house on the rock. And the rain fell, and the floods came, and the winds blew and beat on that house, but it did not fall, because it had been founded on the rock. And everyone who hears these words of mine and does not do them will be like a foolish man who built his house on the sand. And the rain fell, and the floods came, and the winds blew and beat against that house, and it fell, and great was the fall of it.

MATTHEW 7:24-27, ESV

Keeping It Warm on the Back Burner

One day while searching for slow cooker recipes on the Internet, I came across an article on the *Desiring God* website. The author spoke about the wisdom of keeping verses warm, and I have drawn heavily on this article for this devotional because I think it's so wonderful and worth sharing.[8]

Many of us enjoy hosting open houses, where people may drop by as they find it convenient and have time. We often prepare food in advance, or keep it ready in slow cookers or on a back burner, so it will be tasty and warm no matter when our guests arrive.

Let's extend that concept to being prepared to share our faith with people whenever they are ready to receive it. We do not save people; God does, and he knows the timeline in which people will come to saving faith. One way to share your faith is through the beloved "Romans Road" verses, which succinctly share the understanding of salvation.

Romans 3:23—"All have sinned and fall short of the glory of God."

Romans 6:23—"The wages of sin is death, but the gift of God is eternal life in Christ Jesus our Lord."

Romans 5:8—"God demonstrates his own love for us in this: While we were still sinners, Christ died for us."

Romans 10:9—"If you declare with your mouth, 'Jesus is Lord,' and believe in your heart that God raised him from the dead, you will be saved."

Romans 5:1—"Since we have been justified through faith, we have peace with God through our Lord Jesus Christ."

Romans 8:1—"There is now no condemnation for those who are in Christ Jesus."

Romans 8:38-39—"For I am convinced that neither death nor life, neither angels nor demons, neither the present nor the future, nor any powers, neither height nor depth, nor anything else in all creation, will be able to separate us from the love of God that is in Christ Jesus our Lord."

Commit them to heart—or to paper!—and then keep 'em warm!

Preach the word; be prepared in season and out of season; correct, rebuke and encourage—with great patience and careful instruction. 2 TIMOTHY 4:2

---

[8] David Mathis, "Ten Gospel Verses to Keep Warm," *Desiring God*, July 17, 2013, http://www.desiringgod.org/articles/ten-gospel-verses-to-keep-warm.

Experiencing the Love of God

In addition to being prepared to share our faith with those who do not know Jesus, we can minister to people who do, but are hurting, tired, or confused. We never know when that opportune moment is going to appear, but we can be prepared with verses that speak to their situation, and keep those verses ready for them too.

Which verses speak to you in difficult moments? Take a few minutes to jot down three or four and commit them to memory. On someone else's cold day, you'll be ready.

Why not invite friends over to share something warm—perhaps tea or coffee or warmed apple cider with cinnamon sticks, and something tasty from your slow cooker—while you talk and pray?

SLOW COOKER DIP IDEAS

Spinach dip served with triangle-shaped crackers or flatbreads
Pizza dip served with crostini
Barbecue chicken dip served with scoop-shaped corn chips
Queso dip served with tortilla chips
Lasagna dip served with thin bread sticks
Refried beans and salsa dip served with broken taco shells
Fondue dip served with ham cubes and apple slices
Warm chocolate dip served with berries, bananas, or pound cake

Speaking the truth in love, we will grow to become in every respect the mature body of him who is the head, that is, Christ. EPHESIANS 4:15

Joined Together

One cold autumn evening, I was folding laundry and watching a nature show on television. The man on the show was in the equatorial region of the world. The equator, he said, is often used to show where the world is divided into the Northern and the Southern Hemispheres. He did not see much difference on either side of the line—the landscape looked much the same inches, feet, even miles on either side. He said that he began to look at the equator not as where the earth is divided, but as where the two hemispheres are joined.

I loved that. It's not what divides the north from the south; it's what joins them. A few days earlier, our church had been one of many that had celebrated, by telecast, a National Night of Worship. Our congregation plus guests met at church to worship together, with one another and with the hundreds of thousands gathered in their churches across the nation.

The worship sessions were led by praise musicians who were at Madison Square Garden. We got to see not only the musicians but those in the crowd, as the cameras panned around them. In the crowd were Christians of nearly every racial and ethnic background. The congregation in my own church was likewise multiethnic. There were people from many different socioeconomic backgrounds and personal styles. Tattooed and not tattooed. Standing to worship with hands held high, sitting quietly and praising the Lord. Babies in strollers. The aged with their walkers.

It felt like the body. We are all different. We look different and live differently from one another. We vote differently. We worship differently. But these things only mean that we have a wildly, wonderfully diverse family. These things that differentiate us needn't be demarcations that separate and sort us into categories, because Christ is the one who unifies us into one whole.

I appeal to you, brothers and sisters, in the name of our Lord Jesus Christ, that all of you agree with one another in what you say and that there be no divisions among you, but that you be perfectly united in mind and thought.

1 Corinthians 1:10

Flammable

One day I lifted our stovetop espresso maker by the lid—only to find it hot and full. I reflexively released it, spilling coffee into the basin that held the gas burners. The stovetop would not light; I could hear—and smell—gas being released, but there was no spark available to ignite the fire. I had to use a match to light it till it could be restored.

Before Pentecost—the coming of the Holy Spirit after Christ's ascension—the Holy Spirit came upon people for specific divine purposes. Perhaps this is something akin to lighting the fire with an outside flame. When Jesus was nearing the time of his crucifixion, he began to speak more of the Holy Spirit. In John 16:7, Jesus says to the disciples, "Very truly I tell you, it is for your good that I am going away. Unless I go away, the Advocate will not come to you; but if I go, I will send him to you."

After Jesus' resurrection, John 20:22 tells us, "And with that [Jesus] breathed on them and said, 'Receive the Holy Spirit.'" The tense of the word translated as "receive" indicates it was not done at that moment—instead, it was an instruction to do something in the future. We might say the gas was now present, but the flame was not yet lit.

In Luke 24:49, Jesus confirms that and gives the disciples further instruction: "I am going to send you what my Father has promised; but stay in the city until you have been clothed with power from on high." In Acts 1:4, Jesus instructs, "Do not leave Jerusalem, but wait for the gift my Father promised, which you have heard me speak about."

Three days after his crucifixion, Jesus breathed on the disciples, telling them to receive the Holy Spirit later. He then taught them for forty days and ascended. One week later, as related in Acts 2, came Pentecost.

The gas, the power, was now present, and the flame was internally available to light. We have all the power we need now, always accessible, to live a victorious life in Christ as the Holy Spirit indwells us constantly and forever.

They saw what seemed to be tongues of fire that separated and came to rest on each of them. All of them were filled with the Holy Spirit. ACTS 2:3-4

A Benediction for October

In the Northern Hemisphere, October begins to usher us toward shorter, darker days. Maybe we should visit our Southern Hemisphere sisters and brothers, and return the favor in six months! While it may be true the length of days is growing shorter and the shadows deeper, it need not be true in our personal lives. No matter how dark the day or the season, the Holy Spirit indwells us and gives us the power to overflow with hope.

Thinking this month about building on the Rock, I recall the wonderful hymn written by Edward Mote more than two hundred years ago:

> My hope is built on nothing less
> Than Jesus' blood and righteousness;
> I dare not trust the sweetest frame,
> But wholly lean on Jesus' name.
> On Christ, the solid Rock, I stand;
> All other ground is sinking sand.

We have that hope, friend. We have a firm foundation.

Receive this benediction now, as you consider the work God has done in your life this month and look with hope to all that he will accomplish within you in the month to come. He has provided all the power you need to live a victorious life in Christ Jesus.

God loves you and wants you to be blessed.

Through these pages and the power of Scripture, I reach my hands out to and over you, as your sister in Christ, and offer this blessing:

> May the God of hope fill you with all joy and peace as you trust in him, so that you may overflow with hope by the power of the Holy Spirit.
>
> ROMANS 15:13

NOVEMBER

We're All Saints

Today is recognized by some Christian denominations as All Saints' Day. Although Christians don't all follow the same traditions, even those who don't typically observe All Saints' Day might benefit from celebrating it—even if only in a modified manner.

The word *saints* in the Bible comes from the same root word as *sanctified*. To be sanctified is to be set aside for a holy or hallowed use, to be pure. When we become Christians, we are made pure not because of anything we do, but because Christ's righteousness, his holiness, is credited to us. Our salvation is by gift alone: "By grace you have been saved through faith. And this is not your own doing; it is the gift of God, not a result of works, so that no one may boast" (Ephesians 2:8-9, ESV). As believers, then, we are all saints—and it's a wonderful thing to celebrate "our" day.

After our salvation, we partner with God in keeping ourselves pure. "Now in a great house there are not only vessels of gold and silver but also of wood and clay, some for honorable use, some for dishonorable. Therefore, if anyone cleanses himself from what is dishonorable, he will be a vessel for honorable use, set apart as holy, useful to the master of the house, ready for every good work" (2 Timothy 2:20-21, ESV). I think of this often in November and December as I ready the "good china" for holiday use.

This day, one day each year, take a moment to thank the Lord that as a believer in Jesus Christ, you are one of his beloved saints (see Ephesians 1:1; Philippians 1:1). I'm so grateful my salvation is nothing of my own doing; I'm thankful he loves me enough to give this gift to me.

And then, I'm thankful for the conviction of the Holy Spirit, who will guide me to repentance and restoration when I sin, so I may always be set apart, sanctified, and ready to be used for every good work by your Master and mine.

To the church of God that is in Corinth, to those sanctified in Christ Jesus, called to be saints together with all those who in every place call upon the name of our Lord Jesus Christ, both their Lord and ours.

1 CORINTHIANS 1:2, ESV

Miracle Worker

Are there still miracles today?

As with the seventy-two disciples in Luke 10:17, miracles, also called signs, validate the messenger and the message to the recipients. Like street signs, they point the way. Miracles are not limited to being performed by Jesus, though, either in Scripture or in our daily lives.

My friend Jerry recounted a trip one of his colleagues had made to the Philippines. As Jerry's colleague passed through a small village on his way to meet their church-sponsored missionary, a woman in the village came up to him carrying her young child and asked if he was a missionary. He said no, but he was a Christian and was there to meet one of their church's missionaries. She handed him her child and asked him to heal the boy, who had a bent leg that prevented him from walking. Not knowing what to do and with a large crowd gathering around him, he held the child and prayed. While praying, he felt the child's leg move; he looked down and was astonished to see the child's leg was no longer bent! He set the child down, and the child ran to a tree and ran back. The result was that many people in that village came to faith in Jesus Christ.

One of the most humorous passages in Scripture, and an embarrassing one for Paul, is Acts 20:9-11 where Luke records, "Seated in a window was a young man named Eutychus, who was sinking into a deep sleep as Paul talked on and on. When he was sound asleep, he fell to the ground from the third story and was picked up dead. Paul went down, threw himself on the young man and put his arms around him. 'Don't be alarmed,' he said. 'He's alive!' Then he went upstairs again and broke bread and ate. After talking until daybreak, he left."

Which of us has not nodded off in church? Which of us would not perk up if a dead man was brought to life in that same service? Paul was not a trained orator, but God used miracles to validate both his messenger and the gospel message, and he still does today. Sometimes those miracles are large and astonishing. Sometimes they're small, perhaps known only to you as a direct intervention by God in your life or in the life of someone around you. Let's train our eyes and hearts to recognize the love God shows us through his divine interventions, large and small.

"We know that you are a teacher who has come from God. For no one could perform the miraculous signs you are doing if God were not with him."

JOHN 3:2

Seeing Clearly

Last time I was at the eye doctor for my annual exam, he ran me through the usual drills. First, he covered one eye with a cupped paddle and had me read the letters shown on the wall in front of me. I could read some but not all of them. Next, he placed the paddle over the second eye. I could read even more of those, but what was interesting to me was that the wall with the letters on it seemed to shift left simply by covering up one eye.

He placed the ophthalmologic machine in front of me and flipped lenses back and forth, one and two, one eye at a time, and then opened the panels so I could finally see with both eyes. Then it was just a matter of fine-tuning.

I was surprised at how little I could see with only one eye. I tried the experiment on my own, to the same results. Not only were things less clear, but they were obviously skewed to one side or another and left quite a bit out of my field of vision.

So often, that is also true when we examine circumstances and situations in which we must make a choice. I was struck by a medical journal that recounted that eyes prefer to stay open—it's easier—and require muscle effort to remain closed. Therefore, after a person passes away, weights must be placed on his or her eyes, or they must be sealed, because they will naturally open.

I am frail, though. Sometimes I close my eyes to what is going on around me, because I simply don't want to see, or believe, the truth that is before me. I may be afraid of the truth and what it will mean for me or others, or I may be stubbornly ensconced in my own perspective. I might not want to see sin. Sometimes I do keep my eyes open, but because I have only one perspective—mine—my vision is skewed to one side. Then I know I need another perspective. I seek it in the Word—God's perspective. And the Word tells me to look elsewhere, too, to others' counsel.

"Two are better than one," Ecclesiastes 4:9 teaches. Sometimes three or four are even better.

Plans go wrong for lack of advice; many advisers bring success.
PROVERBS 15:22, NLT

Experiencing the Love of God

It's always nice to give something, especially when you are hoping to receive also, whether you hope to receive friendship, insight, or a second perspective. Scripture tells us that wisdom, knowledge, and happiness are gifts from God to those who love him (see Ecclesiastes 2:26). I feel his love when he packages all three of those in the form of a loving, godly friend. I want to be a giving friend too! Life is twice as nice when you share it with a friend, and there's no better way to show affection than to spend time and bring a delicious gift. Prepare two mugs of these simple, tasty cakes and enjoy with a friend or neighbor who needs to be reminded of God's sweet affection—and yours—as you walk through life together. What better gift than warm chocolate?

TWO ARE BETTER THAN ONE FRIENDSHIP MUG CAKES

½ cup self-rising flour
½ cup sugar
½ cup cocoa powder
½ cup hot fudge, softened
½ cup half-and-half
½ cup vegetable oil
2 large eggs

Combine half of each ingredient into two large coffee mugs. Whisk well with a fork until smooth.

Microwave on high for 1 1/2–3 minutes, depending on the strength of the microwave. You'll want the product to be cake like and cooked inside, puffed up on the outside.

Swirl some melted hot fudge, chocolate syrup, or whipped cream on top.

Giving a gift can open doors; it gives access to important people!
PROVERBS 18:16, NLT

A Regular Thanksgiving

Autumn is the season in which many Northern Hemisphere nations bring in their harvest. It is for that reason that Thanksgiving, a holiday celebrated by many countries, is found in the autumn months. I wondered if we might press the concept of thanksgiving beyond the borders of the autumn months, and in my studies was delighted to find we can by celebrating Communion, as the Lord instructed us, regularly throughout the year.

Some traditions refer to Communion as the Eucharist. The word has come to mean, in many denominations, that very solemn remembrance. *Eucharist* is drawn from a Greek word, which the Bible often translates as "thankful." Greek *eucharistia* means "thanksgiving." Another form, *eucharisteo*, is the verb usually translated as "to thank" or "to be thankful" in the New Testament.

Jesus uses this verb when he gives thanks to the Father after collecting the loaves and fishes to serve to his followers (see Matthew 15:36 and John 6:11) and before he serves the Last Supper to his disciples before his crucifixion (see Luke 22 and Matthew 26). He is giving thanks to the Father—offering a thanksgiving—for what the Father has provided for him and for all.

Eucharistia is also the word Paul uses when he echoes Christ in 1 Corinthians 11. Sometimes I wonder if some of us in the church have focused so much on the latter part of the passage, verse 26, which solemnly reminds us that we are proclaiming Christ's death as we partake, that we forget the part about being thankful (see verse 24). God promises to be present where two or three are gathered together in his name. I strongly feel his presence during the sharing of the Eucharist with other believers. Not only are we gathered, we are gathered there in obedience to proclaim his death (see 1 Corinthians 11:26). He tells us to do this together (see 1 Corinthians 11:33). As we do so, we feel thankfulness for what he has done for us and for the brothers and sisters who are gathered with us.

Communion will continue to be a holy time, a moment of reflection of Christ's death for me. But it will now, too, be one where I make sure to offer thanksgiving for all that he has done.

The Lord Jesus on the night when he was betrayed took bread, and when he had given thanks, he broke it, and said, "This is my body, which is for you. Do this in remembrance of me." In the same way also he took the cup, after supper, saying, "This cup is the new covenant in my blood. Do this, as often as you drink it, in remembrance of me." 1 CORINTHIANS 11:23-25, ESV

Loaves and Fishes

Because it is the start of the holiday season—Thanksgiving for many of us and Christmas for all, it is the time when those who serve the poor begin to gear up. Without these services and donors, many would go without a hot meal on the holiday.

I once received a flier that told me how much it would cost to provide a hot meal on each holiday—and then let me multiply that by ten, one hundred, or one thousand if my resources allowed.

In Matthew 15:32, the Lord says to his disciples, "I have compassion on the crowd because they have been with me now three days and have nothing to eat. And I am unwilling to send them away hungry, lest they faint on the way" (ESV). The disciples tell him that there is not enough food to feed such a large crowd. Jesus asks them for what they have—seven loaves and some small fish—and miraculously serves the crowd of four thousand; the food never runs out. Seven basketfuls are gathered, filled with leftovers!

The food given there, as well as in John 6 when Jesus feeds the five thousand with the loaves given by a young boy, is all human provided and Jesus divided. He works in tandem with us. He invites us into his ministry. He could have created bread from stones had he so chosen, but he did not. He includes us in his ministry and left us a pattern to follow.

Perhaps donating to our local missions during this season of celebration is the modern-day division of the loaves and fishes. We give what we can, and he will multiply it through divine intervention and the efforts of our sisters and brothers. Some of us might have more surplus than others, but if we each give what we can, we can gather basketfuls to share. Scripture tells us that we are to become Christlike (see Romans 8:29), which means being like Jesus. Jesus gave wisely and freely out of goodness and charity. Perhaps we can experience God's love in a fresh way when we divide what we've been given and share it with others, both imitating and joining him in this most rewarding way.

I do not mean that others should be eased and you burdened, but that as a matter of fairness your abundance at the present time should supply their need, so that their abundance may supply your need, that there may be fairness. As it is written, "Whoever gathered much had nothing left over, and whoever gathered little had no lack." 2 CORINTHIANS 8:13-15, ESV

Not for Display

On a recent vacation, my husband and I visited a historic home, which had a collection of many hundred years' worth of battle armor. It was wonderfully displayed—easy to see and even touch in some instances. We marveled at the workmanship of the armorers who had created and maintained the pieces.

Some of the armor was thin, light, and beautifully wrought—it had nary a nick in it but was not intended for battle. Some armor was tougher, thicker, heavier, and marked up. You could clearly imagine the wiped-off blood. That armor was not for show; it was for protection. It had plates that overlapped one another, and chain mail so the tip of a sword could not find a vulnerable gap and make a deadly way through.

My husband has a military background, and he has displayed his parade sword in our homes over the years. The dress, or parade, sword is exclusively for ceremonies, parades, and dress uniform. It looks the part—it's shiny and showy—but is not a combat weapon. The blades can be made with cheaper metals and are often hollow or stamped and not heat treated; the blades are lightly bolted to the grip, resulting in a weak connection.

By contrast, a real sword is a forged blade; its finished form is sharpened, polished, tempered steel. Its blade provides strength and power. It's meant to defend and to attack when required. Its blade is one with its tang, providing strength and power.

Do you have gaps in your armor, friend? Seek out where you are most vulnerable—any enemy wants to exploit that. Perhaps you think you do not need armor and so do not put it on. Maybe loneliness or bitterness or sorrow or disappointment has made gaps large enough for the enemy's weapons to reach your heart.

Is your sword battle ready? We are not called to be parade ground Christians with pretty yet powerless armor and useless swords. Our faith is not just for show or light fencing; if we wholeheartedly follow Christ, we will certainly be called into spiritual battle.

Take up the shield of faith, with which you can extinguish all the flaming arrows of the evil one. Take the helmet of salvation and the sword of the Spirit, which is the word of God. EPHESIANS 6:16-17

Bread of Life

When Jesus is teaching his disciples, then and now, how to pray, we find this important phrase: "Give us *today* our *daily* bread" (Matthew 6:11). It reminds us twice in six words that we are dependent upon God day by day to give us the sustenance we need.

This truth runs clear through the Bible. In 1 Kings 17:6, we are told how God provided bread for his servant Elijah: "The ravens brought him bread and meat in the morning and bread and meat in the evening, and he drank from the brook." It came daily.

When the children of Israel left Egypt and were in the desert, Exodus 16:4 tells us, "The LORD said to Moses, 'I will rain down bread from heaven for you. The people are to go out each day and gather enough for that day.'" God would provide, day by day.

That daily provision of bread, their sole provision for life, was found only in God.

Then in the New Testament, God provides us eternal life in Jesus, the Bread of Life. He calls his body the bread, when he breaks it for our eternal spiritual sustenance (see Matthew 26:26). So then what does he mean when in Matthew 4:4 he teaches, "People do not live by bread alone, but by every word that comes from the mouth of God" (NLT)?

We know he means himself—he is the Bread of Life and he is the Word of God. "In the beginning was the Word, and the Word was with God, and the Word was God" (John 1:1). Jesus teaches in John 3 that in order to be saved we must be born both physically and spiritually. All of us are flesh and must regularly eat to sustain our physical bodies. If we are born again, we must partake of the Bread of Life to sustain our spirits as well.

I had an insight the other day. I do not lack for food. But every day I wake up yearning for a word from God. Something just for that day, just for me. To guide me, to help me remember that he loves me and is attentive to my concerns and my voice.

Why not? Why wouldn't I expect that he will provide my daily bread—the bread that is him—every day? Each morning, now, I must go out and expectantly look for it in Scripture, gathering what I need for the day, believing in faith that he will give me what I need for that day and return the next morning with what I need for it, too.

Jesus declared, "I am the bread of life. Whoever comes to me will never go hungry, and whoever believes in me will never be thirsty. JOHN 6:35

Proper Protocols

One day one of my newly adult children came to ask me for a small loan. The reason behind the loan made sense, and my children are loving and responsible. Still, I thought it was a good idea this time, for a good "teachable moment," to ask my child to show me on a spreadsheet what their current financial situation looked like and how they expected to repay the loan. They looked at me, bewildered, and said, "I feel like that is an inefficient use of my time." I raised my eyebrows but then explained that when you ask someone else for something, you must follow the procedure that person has set up through experience and wisdom—or walk away from the request.

A few days later, I was praying for something that was dear to my heart. Imagine my surprise when I heard myself tell God that I had been praying about this so long that I was about done. I actually said, "I don't want to waste any more time with this if you're not going to answer." It wasn't exactly the language my child had used with me, but it was close.

When we come to God with a request, he does ask us to go through a proper protocol, and his reasons are sound. Philippians 4:4-7 (NLT) says:

- Always be full of joy in the Lord. I say it again—rejoice!
- Let everyone see that you are considerate in all you do. Remember, the Lord is coming soon.
- Don't worry about anything; instead, pray about everything. Tell God what you need, and thank him for all he has done.
- Then you will experience God's peace, which exceeds anything we can understand.

I often do not take the time to rejoice before prayer. I don't always make time to ensure that my actions are considerate before asking God for consideration in a matter. I'm learning to put thanksgiving in every prayer that includes a request, which is, let's face it, most of them! He is discipling me into not waiting for the resolution of the circumstance that led to the prayer to gain peace, but to gain peace knowing he is able and he cares, and I have lifted my concerns to him.

Do not be anxious about anything, but in every situation, by prayer and petition, with thanksgiving, present your requests to God. PHILIPPIANS 4:6

A Happy Melt-Off

One November not so long ago, there was a historic snow and ice storm in my town. The home we lived in then backed up to a thickly wooded area with both fir and deciduous trees, and as the snow fell prettily and landed on the branches, we enjoyed the rare sight. As the storm continued, we watched the fir trees become slowly enrobed in snow. Icy rain fell next, and the deciduous trees became, twig by twig and branch by branch, sheathed in ice. A fascinating thing about this process is how weightless a solitary snowflake or a drop of water is, and yet how much damage can be wrought when there are hundreds, thousands, tens of thousands of them piling up on one another.

Within a few days, the mighty trees began to weary. The deciduous, bereft of the ability to bend and yield, became brittle, and their branches and limbs shattered at the least blow of the wind. Whole branches abruptly snapped off, leaving my backyard a hilly forest of amputees. The firs, more flexible, held up better, but they also were more generous in catching and collecting snow. After a certain weight, those branches that had not been able to throw off their snow cracked and fell too. The trees that seemed to make it all right were those that could take their pressing weight and lean into a mightier tree nearby, resting until the wind and snow stopped and the sun melted away their great load.

I was reminded of our Christian faith. We are not exempted from the ice that suddenly delivers many tiny, stinging troubles, which pelt and pile upon us till we are ready to snap and break. Nor are we excused from heavier loads—snow dropped quickly and all at once—the ones that seem to be our own personal bough breakers. After all, this is not heaven yet. But we are given a promise: we have Someone upon whom we can lean and rest, and to whom we can transfer the weight of our cares and sorrows. He props us, as it were, till the stormy cycle passes (and it always does) and our burdens melt away, allowing us to stand true and straight again.

Come to Me, all who are weary and heavy-laden, and I will give you rest.
MATTHEW 11:28, NASB

Experiencing the Love of God

Although we all have burdens, I admit there are some that I undertake that are not mine to carry. I am not responsible for others' decisions or their outcomes, though I can be present to counsel and comfort and celebrate. I do not need to fix everyone—or anyone—or any situation other than myself. Even then, I need not do it alone. Matthew 11:28-30 instructs us to come to the Lord with our burdens. Sometimes I forget that means I can deliver the burdens I carry for others to Jesus as well as handing over my own.

Your Father is waiting to help you shed some burdens and shoulder others till the storm passes. Below, write down five burdens—your own or others'—that you will give to him today. They may be ones that you can step out of completely, or they may be ones you are asking him to help bear for a time.

1.

2.

3.

4.

5.

How can you find rest today? Turn off the phone for a few hours? Take a long bath? Take the day off from cooking? Read a book in a soft, warm chair? How about letting go of a burden that wasn't meant to be yours? In his love for us, he wants to ease our load.

Today, I will rest for at least one hour by:

Come to me, all you who are weary and burdened, and I will give you rest.
MATTHEW 11:28

An Enveloping Hug

One day, while cleaning out a closet, I came across a pencil sketch of Jesus cradling a girl to himself, kissing her temple in a loving, fatherly way. I looked at that girl and saw myself in her. I felt it, deep in my heart, him holding me, his child.

My own children had some struggles that week. I could close my eyes for a moment and imagine Jesus pulling each of them close, as children, as teens, as the adults they are now, and kissing them on the temple in protective affection. Could I imagine him doing that for me? I could. I did. He loves me.

That sketch reminded me—we are God's children. Our children are God's children. The kinds of things you and I hope for our children, or our nieces and nephews, our godchildren, the children and grandchildren of our friends— God has those desires for us, his children, too. We worry for our children—and we take them to a God who understands.

He, too, has sick children, worried children, suicidal children, tempted children, lost children, floundering children, and he loves them all, just like we do.

He is strong enough to create and rule the world, yet gentle enough to sing lullabies over them and us. "The LORD your God is with you, the Mighty Warrior who saves. He will take great delight in you; in his love he will no longer rebuke you, but will rejoice over you with singing" (Zephaniah 3:17). He disciplines them and us. "The LORD corrects those he loves, just as a father corrects a child in whom he delights" (Proverbs 3:12, NLT). He gets angry with them and us. He returns to them and us.

When you feel lost and afraid and confused and do not know what lies ahead, lean into the arms of Jesus, because he tenderly cares for you. When you are fearful for your children and have no power to step in and help, place them in the arms of Jesus, because he cares for them, and will draw them into a protective embrace.

See how very much our Father loves us, for he calls us his children, and that is what we are! But the people who belong to this world don't recognize that we are God's children because they don't know him. 1 JOHN 3:1, NLT

Lessons of a Quiet Garden

The weather report showed a blessed two days of autumn sun, and I decided to capitalize on it by spending some hours outdoors finishing up my prewinter garden tasks.

First, I plucked off some suckers that were already growing on a couple of amputated tree limbs. The limbs had been cut down because the tree had been shaped for its best health and growth, and some disease had been pruned away. "If your right hand causes you to stumble, cut it off and throw it away" (Matthew 5:30). Sometimes when we rid ourselves of a sinful habit, it tries to make its way back into our lives. The tree suckers warned me to be alert to that possibility and pluck them off as soon as they appeared.

The coldest portion of the season had not yet appeared, so despite several strong windstorms, many of my deciduous trees still had leaves clinging to them. Ordinarily, I would let them remain until they fell off on their own. In the case of my medium-sized witch hazel trees, though, I hand-plucked those dead leaves off one by one. Witch hazel trees bloom in early winter, and if I did not remove the dead leaves, they would hide and smother the winter blossoms. "He cuts off every branch in me that bears no fruit, while every branch that does bear fruit he prunes so that it will be even more fruitful" (John 15:2). I removed everything that was not producing any longer, to make way for the health and glorious display of those that would.

Last, I noticed that a young tree we'd planted had grown crooked. It's easier to see the bend when a tree is bare. I pointed it out to my husband, who braced it straight. It's easier to fix something heading in the wrong direction when it's just started. If we wait till years in, the plant will be more firmly entrenched in the wrong direction, more difficult to turn in the right direction. "Repent and turn to me again" (Revelation 3:3, NLT).

God teaches me while I work in his creation. How about you?

The heavens proclaim the glory of God. The skies display his craftsmanship.
Day after day they continue to speak; night after night they make him
known. They speak without a sound or word; their voice is never heard.
PSALM 19:1-3, NLT

Seedlings

After finishing up the work in the front yard, I went around to the backyard. One of my sacred responsibilities is to keep the bright yellow bird feeder in the back cleaned and filled. Because my area gets so much rain, if I don't clean the feeder often the seeds mold. Because the little birds are hungry and there isn't much around just now, if I don't keep the feeder filled they go hungry. In the planting season, too, providing birdseed ensures the birds don't eat my garden seeds!

I unhooked the feeder and noticed the scattered seed on the ground below it, which always brings back the powerful parable Jesus tells in Matthew 13. The farmer, God, went to plant some seeds. He scattered them, but not everything took root. Birds ate some, and some fell on poor soil. Some fell among thorns, and finally, some took root and grew into what he'd hoped they would be.

I take cheer in that story because sometimes it feels like the ministries I am involved in are not growing as I wish they would. Sometimes they never get off the ground, or they start and falter, or personality conflicts spoil things. But sometimes everything is working just right, and I see people blessed, people come to Christ, people's faith restored in God and in humanity.

I continued watching the birds and was encouraged to see that, even when no seed was present in the feeder, making for an easy meal, they didn't give up. They rooted under fallen leaves, looking for bugs and worms, and checked for what might have been scattered in the sleeping garden. They didn't give up in their pursuit of fruitfulness, even when it didn't come easily.

Don't be afraid to get involved in ministry. Even God seems to experience the thwarting of his efforts, and yet we know he does not. Don't lose heart. In the end, if we don't give up, we will harvest a good crop (see Galatians 6:9).

Listen! A farmer went out to plant some seeds. As he scattered them across his field, some seeds fell on a footpath, and the birds came and ate them. Other seeds fell on shallow soil with underlying rock. The seeds sprouted quickly because the soil was shallow. But the plants soon wilted under the hot sun, and since they didn't have deep roots, they died.

Other seeds fell among thorns that grew up and choked out the tender plants. Still other seeds fell on fertile soil, and they produced a crop that was thirty, sixty, and even a hundred times as much as had been planted! Anyone with ears to hear should listen and understand. MATTHEW 13:3-9, NLT

Spiritual Therapy

The day was cloudy, so I settled into my office to do some paperwork. My office faces our street, though, and midway through the day I watched as one of my neighbors, an older man, made his way up the street very slowly. He'd recently had his hip replaced and after a month of physical therapy was learning how to walk again.

The day after, he was back at it, and the day that followed that. Day by day he regained his mobility and flexibility, and I had no doubt that by Christmas he'd be walking well again.

My neighbor's hip replacement helped me recall the passage in Genesis 32 when Jacob spent the night wrestling with someone—seemingly winning—until the being he wrestled with touched Jacob's hip and wrenched it out of its socket. In verses 26-28, "Jacob said, 'I will not let you go unless you bless me.' 'What is your name?' the man asked. He replied, 'Jacob.' 'Your name will no longer be Jacob,' the man told him. 'From now on you will be called Israel, because you have fought with God and with men and have won.'"

I love that story for two reasons: first, it's okay to wrestle with not only man but with God. Sometimes life is difficult, and sometimes our walk with him is not easy or clear. And second, God always wins!

I remember when my children learned to walk. First, they pushed themselves up off the ground, and next, they toddled. Eventually, they walked and ran. Injuries and age can sometimes slow us down; we can heal, and with persistence, it is often possible to get back on track.

That's how it is with our walk through life, too. Sometimes we can't run, or we are injured or tired or feel old. Don't give up. One day at a time, just take a few steps forward. It's okay to wrestle with life, with man, and with God. Just keep walking forward, and soon enough your wound will heal and perhaps even become a blessing.

I will walk among you; I will be your God, and you will be my people.

LEVITICUS 26:12, NLT

Always Listening

I'm preparing to attend a study group I enjoy. The people are wonderful and kind and thoughtful, and the studies are always good. There is just one thing that troubles me. At the end of our time together, prayer requests are taken. As a group, we pray. But I've noticed there are times when my or others' prayers aren't "picked up" by someone else in group prayer. I'm left hoping the leader will remember to include me in the final wrap-up. Sometimes they do, and sometimes not. It's a little awkward afterward. It kind of feels like people are choosing teams and at the end of siding up, neither side chose you.

Was my prayer request not important enough? Do I ask for prayer too often? Were people simply busy and rushing to complete? I always assume the best motives because of the kindness of the members. It does make me hesitant to offer a prayer request the next time, though.

I spoke with the Lord about it on the way home after the last meeting. He did not give me an answer to any of the above questions, but still warm in the glow of the Spirit that follows a Bible study, I could clearly sense his voice. "It's all right," he reassured me. "I'm always listening to you, whether anyone speaks up with your prayer request or not."

It reminds me the Lord has placed wonderful people in our lives—Jesus himself says other believers are our true mothers, brothers, and sisters (see Mark 3:33-35). Our friends and family are blessings. But they, and we, are human. We forget. We are busy. We have so much on our minds; we forget important things we mean to remember for people we love. Even in our best intentions, we are sometimes frail.

God is not frail. He is never too tired, too overwhelmed, too busy to care. He is always with me—he indwells me—so we are never apart. I still love bringing my prayers to my church family; we are commanded to pray for one another (see James 5:16) and told it does much good. But even so, when others cannot or forget, God never will.

God did listen! He paid attention to my prayer. Praise God, who did not ignore my prayer or withdraw his unfailing love from me.

PSALM 66:19-20, NLT

Leave It Up to Him

Last week in the grocery store I stood in line behind a very pregnant woman with a toddler in her cart. Her toddler was patting her mommy's tummy, and her husband unloaded the cart so she would not have to lift anything. When we talk about a woman who is with child, we use the word *expecting* and not *hoping* or *wishing*. She may be hoping that things go well and that the baby is healthy, but she is not hoping or wishing to have a baby. She's expecting to. Everyone is just excitedly waiting for it to happen.

Do we hope that the Lord will answer our prayers, do we wish that he would, or do we offer our prayers to him and wait expectantly? We expect him to answer us; we are certain that he will, though we do not know how everything will play out.

My friend Anne recounted that she does not always pray specific requests and results for people in her prayer life. She simply holds them up to the Lord and asks for his best in their lives and situations. Then she sits back to wait for it to happen.

This approach reminds me of a beloved concept in Japanese cuisine: *omakase*. This is a phrase that can be translated as "I'll leave it up to you" and means that the diner is entrusting the choice to the chef. The chef, knowing what is freshest that day, what his best skills are, and who the customer is, prepares something unique to delight the diner. The diner leaves the decision in the hands of a trusted provider.

Anne's insight has given me a new lease on my prayer life. Sometimes, I *do* present my specific requests to God and ask him for an exact, desired conclusion, recalling Philippians 4:6 as I do: "Let your requests be made known to God" (ESV). But sometimes I also simply say, "My request is for your best in this situation, with this person, Lord. I'll leave it to you. I entrust my hopes and wishes and fears and concerns to you because your ways are perfect." And then I wait expectantly.

Listen to my voice in the morning, LORD. Each morning I bring my requests to you and wait expectantly.   PSALM 5:3, NLT

Experiencing the Love of God

Do you more often offer a menu of solutions to the Lord in your prayer requests, or is it easy for you to pray, "Not my will, but yours" (Luke 22:42)?

What would you serve to your favorite people if you were selecting a menu for them? My menu would change depending on whom I served: my vegetarian daughter? My crab-loving son-in-law? My urban-eater son? My meat-and-potatoes man? I'd adjust, too, for the season, as well as hope to delight and surprise them. Would your selection change depending on whom you were serving?

The special menu you would prepare for a meal with those you love:

What specific prayer requests do you have for some beloved people in your life?

I delight in taking special requests from my family, and I'm always happy to prepare that special request if I can. But I also love when they say, "Just make something good—you always do!"

A delightful treat or meal only someone who knows you would bring for a special occasion:

A prayer you would like to write and then pray, for one specific person, asking God to provide his best for this person:

I'm committed to opening my heart and my hands and trusting the Lord, taking him at his Word and allowing him to shape my heart by seeing him work with the fears and hopes I entrust to him—in faith. I'll pray for specific circumstances and people I love but with an open heart should he choose to answer differently, according to his will. Will you join me?

"Abraham believed God, and God counted him as righteous because of his faith." The real children of Abraham, then, are those who put their faith in God.   GALATIANS 3:6-7, NLT

Sense and Spiritual Sensibilities

One day I was caught up in discussion with someone who does not believe in God. She asked me, "Don't you find it the least bit odd that you order your life around someone you've never met?"

We amicably closed our discussion, and then I left the social event and drove home. As I was driving, I thought, *You know, it would seem odd to others.* I've considered this before, but I mused on it anew. My choices in who I married, which careers and ministries I've pursued, how I raised my children, who my closest friends are, and how I order my day—and my life—all center around Someone I have never met in the flesh.

And yet, there are many important things in life that are undetectable to our senses. We cannot see or sense oxygen, and yet we need it minute by minute for life. I cannot touch heat, but I can sense it. Whenever the atmosphere changes, people who suffer from migraines or arthritis sense it immediately, though it is not detectable to the human eye or ear. Emotions cannot be taken in with the five senses but are a critical part of our lives—we feel them, strongly.

The book of John tells us about Jesus' appearance to Thomas:

The doors were locked; but suddenly, as before, Jesus was standing among them. "Peace be with you," he said. Then he said to Thomas, "Put your finger here, and look at my hands. Put your hand into the wound in my side. Don't be faithless any longer. Believe!" "My Lord and my God!" Thomas exclaimed. Then Jesus told him, "You believe because you have seen me. Blessed are those who believe without seeing me" (20:26-29, NLT).

We have not seen the Lord face-to-face, though we know we will. We sense him in the world around us, in the arranging of circumstances, and the way the Holy Spirit quickens within us as he is teaching or leading us. We feel his presence almost like atmosphere, especially when we are gathered with other believers; we "hear" his voice deep in our spirits in prayer and in the Word. We believe and are blessed.

You love him even though you have never seen him. Though you do not see him now, you trust him; and you rejoice with a glorious, inexpressible joy.
1 PETER 1:8, NLT

Fetching the Bone

My husband's friend knew someone with a young dog that was a nuisance. The puppy killed a pet chicken, making the owner's daughter cry, and trapped their neighbor in a garage. My husband's friend, a strict disciplinarian, heard of the trouble and took on the challenge of the pup, adopting the dog from the original owner.

This adoptive "pet dad" loves to collect sheds—the antlers bucks shed each year. He had old, unmatched antlers lying around and let the dog chew on one. Next, he called one of those old antlers "the bone" and used it to play with the dog, rewarding the puppy with affection, and sometimes treats, for fetching "the bone."

One day while playing outdoors, the dog ran up with a brand-new shed—something it had found on its own. This started a new and exciting life for the dog. Man and beast spent companionable time together searching for antler sheds, and the dog was a natural. One day it found an awe-worthy matching set—from a very large buck—which must have earned the dog quite a lot of praise.

Why wouldn't that dog bring in sticks or real bones—or dead chickens!—instead of antlers? It was not rewarded for them! As the dog's owner knew, you get more of what you reward.

Like that pup, I have had many loving mentors who trained, guided, coached, and loved me during my Christian life. They told me they were proud of me, and they thanked God for me in my presence, which was warmly affirming. They prayed for me. With their love and affection, they affirmed and rewarded me when I was doing right, and because of their efforts I continued to grow in wisdom and insight under their tutelage.

Who has the Lord entrusted to your care? What are you charged with teaching them, encouraging them to do? Remember—you get more of what you reward with praise . . . and the occasional treat!

Ever since I first heard of your strong faith in the Lord Jesus and your love for God's people everywhere, I have not stopped thanking God for you. I pray for you constantly, asking God, the glorious Father of our Lord Jesus Christ, to give you spiritual wisdom and insight so that you might grow in your knowledge of God. EPHESIANS 1:15-17, NLT

Great and Good

God is great; God is good;
Let us thank him for our food.
By his hands we all are fed,
Give us Lord our daily bread.

This was the little prayer I prayed each evening before eating my dinner when I was a girl and not yet a Christian, nor in a Christian family. And yet it encapsulates almost everything we want to consider each day, doesn't it?

God is great. *God is great* means he is mighty, powerful, impressive, distinguished. *Great* denotes having the ability to bring about situations and solutions others may not be able to by their own power and resources. God is great—he can do whatever he pleases and is equipped to care for our every need. "Once God has spoken; twice have I heard this: that power belongs to God" (Psalm 62:11, ESV).

God is good. *God is good* means that he is righteous; he is pure. He always does what is right in every circumstance. He is excellent and virtuous. "God is light; in him there is no darkness at all" (1 John 1:5).

Because he is good, he personally feeds us with his loving hands, as a father hands good food to his child. Because he is great, he can give us what we need each day.

Whenever we wonder if we should turn to God with a concern, we are asking, is he able? Is he willing? The fact that he is both great and good answers that.

What are you struggling with, friend? Can you hand it over to the Lord, the one who is both able and willing? In Matthew 8, a leper appeared to Jesus, and, suffering, called out to him: "Lord, if you are willing, you can heal me and make me clean." He believed in the Lord's ability; the leper did not know if Jesus was willing. Verse three tells us, "Jesus reached out and touched him. 'I am willing,' he said. 'Be healed!' And instantly the leprosy disappeared" (NLT).

God is great and God is good. God is able and God is willing. Trust him.

How great is the goodness you have stored up for those who fear you.
PSALM 31:19, NLT

A Place at Our Tables

Over the course of my life, there have been years of plenty and years of little. A cursory read of the Bible shows that to be true for almost every generation— and, as Jesus tells us, the poor will always be with us. It's hard to understand sometimes: the Lord could provide for the hunger and other needs we have as humanity. Perhaps he has—but we have mismanaged the resources. Proverbs 27:20 tells us, "Just as Death and Destruction are never satisfied, so human desire is never satisfied" (NLT). No matter how much he gives us, individually and collectively, we always want just a little more.

Thanksgiving is a time to remind ourselves to be grateful for what we do have, little or much, in each year. The concept of a tithe, 10 percent, is a great equalizer. Rather than asking for a particular amount, the Lord simply asks for a portion back, and it's not always money.

I wonder what percentage of my time I allow him? Of my thoughts and hopes and desires? How many activities do I undertake with his goals and Kingdom in mind? Parsing activities and gifts down to a percentage can seem legalistic, but perhaps it was set in place to counterbalance the truth of Proverbs 27:20.

Startlingly, one of the tithes that might be described as a "Thanksgiving tithe" in the Old Testament instructs that we should take 10 percent of our yield, gathered at harvesttime, and buy a feast. In your head, calculate what 10 percent of your annual income is, and imagine spending that entire amount on a feast! What would you buy? Once we purchase the finest food, the Lord asks us to eat it in his presence, at the place he chooses, where he dwells.

He wants a place at the table, to share in his bounty at our generous Thanksgiving. Will you invite him to the feast and then thank him for what he has done?

You shall tithe all the yield of your seed that comes from the field year by year. And before the LORD your God, in the place that he will choose, to make his name dwell there, you shall eat the tithe of your grain, of your wine, and of your oil, and the firstborn of your herd and flock, that you may learn to fear the LORD your God always. DEUTERONOMY 14:22-23, ESV

The Best of Times

It was the best of times, it was the worst of times, it was the age of wisdom, it was the age of foolishness, it was the epoch of belief, it was the epoch of incredulity, it was the season of Light, it was the season of Darkness, it was the spring of hope, it was the winter of despair, we had everything before us, we had nothing before us, we were all going direct to Heaven, we were all going direct the other way.

CHARLES DICKENS, *A TALE OF TWO CITIES*

Although this was written almost two centuries ago, it can also be aptly applied to the times in which we live. There are wondrous things taking place across the world while there are also heinous crimes occurring. In our own lives, we may find circumstances that bring us great joy in the same week we hear heartrending news. The Lord has been teaching me, though, that I may freely celebrate the best of the times or minimize the worst of the times no matter what is going on, depending on my mind-set. The times themselves must be interpreted by me.

Whenever I find a place of joy, I find the joy thief, too: fear. I call it "interfear-ing" because fear gets in the middle of whatever I am trying to take pleasure in. It warns me that the good times won't last or that something troubling is just around the corner. This robs the best of times from me. When I worry about what may happen in the times to come, I am ensuring that it is always the worst of times. I experience anxiety when nothing bad is going on, draining me of energy and resources I'll need whenever difficulties do arrive.

The Lord commands us to let the peace that comes from Christ rule in our hearts. *Rule* is a strong verb. It has final say. It determines the outcome. Letting something, or someone, rule us is hard. We much prefer the idea of self-determination or perhaps reasoning to a compromise. But that isn't the model God works under. He is divine, and his answer is final. His final say, though, is based in his goodness, his greatness, and his power. Giving the peace of Christ final say means we aren't ruled by whims, worries, anxieties, or worldly compromise. Isn't that good news? Like any discipline, submission isn't easy to do, but it allows us to harvest the peace we so want (see Hebrews 12:11).

When I choose, in both pleasant and painful situations, to let the peace of Christ have the final call, the worst of times will be lightened, and the best of times can be enjoyed without concern.

Let the peace that comes from Christ rule in your hearts.

COLOSSIANS 3:15, NLT

A Beautiful Bride

I spent the day rearranging my storage areas and came across my carefully wrapped but completely underused wedding dress. My daughter was already married, and the sight of the dress called to mind a ministry my friend and cousin-in-law Becky serves with. Perhaps I might harness my unused dress for good?

Each summer, Becky's team serves former Rwandan street kids who are now young adults. They teach them English and help them with job training. A heartfelt personal need is that many of these young adults want to get married, but their poverty makes it very difficult to afford everything required for a traditional celebration.

Becky asked how many couples were planning on getting married the following summer, as she would make wedding cakes for them during her annual trip. She was informed that there were eight couples. In her words, "I began to think about ways to help them, and I thought about bringing wedding dresses over for them." Becky's beloved sister had recently passed away, and her brother-in-law asked if she might want her sister's dress for the ministry, especially as Becky had made the gown. She continues, "As I took the dress out of the box, I was flooded with many precious memories, and it hit me that I could keep those precious memories boxed up, or I could give this dress to a young gal who couldn't afford to get married. The wedding gown represents a new life, new beginnings, and hope."

She told others, and suddenly the idea caught fire. Two hundred pounds of dresses were packed up, and she took them over to those young brides. The enterprising Rwandan women not only used the dresses for their own weddings, but they also rented them out, providing income for themselves and beautiful dresses for other brides.

Becky finishes, "These brides, now businesswomen, were so very touched by the love of people they will never meet. The renewal of life was very real to them since many of them were orphaned. Before the ministry, they didn't have much chance of having a decent life. Now they are married, some have babies, and they are living a dream they always thought was for someone other than themselves."

Most of us have been given so much. And because we see how God loves us, we give to others to share his love with them too. What will happen in return? More will be given us so we may give yet again.

The Spirit of the Sovereign LORD is upon me, for the LORD has anointed me to bring good news to the poor.   ISAIAH 61:1, NLT

Experiencing the Love of God

In the spirit of Thanksgiving, do you have anything around your house that might be harnessed for good? Almost anything can do. My friend Anne cleaned up 150 pairs of used and donated running shoes to be given to the women's prison. You can do an Internet search for "donate wedding dress" and find many good places where your beautiful memories can live on in the lives of others. How about donating Bibles or Christian books to your local Little Free Library? Maybe you can give a "loaf and a fish" for a shelter or mission outreach to divide. In this way, mysteriously, the Lord divides our small offering and multiplies it so it might be of use to many people.

I recently saw a challenge by the Salvation Army to take a plastic bag and, each day for a month or more, place in the bag something you don't use that someone else might. This is a hand-me-down of the best order. It helps us organize our environment, freeing time from caring for items we don't use. It helps employ people at the stores that sell secondhand goods. It gets affordable items into the hands of people who need them. And it provides money to continue funding ministries. Many pieces from one small loaf!

You might already be giving to the poor, and if so, that is wonderful. Well done! If not, you might consider offering yourself to the Lord to anoint you to bring good news to the poor. As you reach out with his hands and his heart, you will be blessed as much as, or more than, you bless others.

Give, and it will be given to you. A good measure, pressed down, shaken together and running over, will be poured into your lap. For with the measure you use, it will be measured to you. LUKE 6:38

Chicken Noodle Soup

My son-in-law and I were speaking of the practical ways we see God at work in our lives, when he recounted this story to me.

"My first year in school, I had very few benefits. I was living with a roommate in very poor circumstances, and we had no financial margin. I could scrape together rent and just the barest amount for food. However, my school was having a food drive for Thanksgiving, and I wanted to participate in some way. I was embarrassed by the little I had to offer—I didn't have enough for myself—but I knew I could give a can of soup. I love chicken noodle soup, so that is what I gave."

He continued, "The teacher in charge had put together a significant number of donors, and so the boxes of food grew and grew. We left that week happy that we all could contribute something. I, however, still had no idea what I would be eating for Thanksgiving.

"Imagine my surprise when my teacher drove up and delivered all those Thanksgiving boxes. She knew what my circumstances were and had been planning all along that I would be the recipient of the boxes. I gratefully unpacked every one—the food would last me long beyond the one-day feast. When I came to the final box, I plucked out the can of chicken noodle soup. I had donated it as an offering of the highest cost to me, and God sent it back to me many times over."

As he told me that story, my first thought was, *Thank you, Lord, for bringing this man as a husband to my beloved daughter.* And second, *How good you are, Lord, to show us your love, attention, and generosity in such tangible ways.*

"Do not forget to do good and to share with others, for with such sacrifices God is pleased," Hebrews 13:16 reminds us.

Do not be ashamed of what little you might have to offer God in thanksgiving this month, or any other. He knows our circumstances and honors our sacrifices while delighting in showering us with bounty.

Whatever you give is acceptable if you give it eagerly.

2 Corinthians 8:12, nlt

All Things New

Following the financial and epicurean indulgences of the holiday season, which stretches from Thanksgiving to the start of January, often brings a firm commitment—or a commitment to making ourselves firm! It often brings a lengthy scroll of promised to-dos, do-overs, or makeovers. No more cheese corn. No more cheesecake. Hey—no more carbs at all!

The beauty of a Monday in each week, or the first day of a month, is the opportunity to start fresh. But sometimes in our zeal to begin again, we reach too far, too fast, or have expectations not in line with what we can accomplish. We are a "doing" culture, and when we fail to meet our new goals, we fall off the wagon and, discouraged, tuck away the scroll of good intentions and slide back into old habits. But the Good News of Christianity has always been the good news that we don't have to—in fact, we cannot—regenerate ourselves.

We couldn't do it spiritually at the start—we had to be born again by the Spirit—and we can't continue or provoke new growth along the way. Only God can do that. And he will if we step aside and let him lead. He says, "I am the vine; you are the branches. If you remain in me and I in you, you will bear much fruit; apart from me you can do nothing" (John 15:5). He says, "Forget the former things; do not dwell on the past. See, I am doing a new thing! Now it springs up; do you not perceive it? I am making a way in the wilderness and streams in the wasteland" (Isaiah 43:18-19).

Here is the freedom offered: if we remain in him, God will bring the fruit. If we remain in the Word, he renews the mind—the essence of any person—and will change us, as God always does, from the inside out. If we watch and yield, we will observe that he is doing the new things, not us. We simply need to open our eyes and see them and then follow his leading. He brings new life and change, not only in simple cases, but also to stubborn, long-lasting problems: wilderness, wasteland, places many of us have given up on as year after year our human endeavors fail to bring the peace and success we hoped for. Victory lies just ahead!

Behold, I am making all things new.　　　　　REVELATION 21:5, ESV

Magic Erasers

My husband and I were planning to refinance our mortgage, and the appraiser was scheduled to visit in just a few days. We got all the big stuff done, and then I went room to room with an evaluative eye. As I did, I noticed all kinds of things I ignore every day, for example, the white trim.

When we bought this house, I loved that white trim—the doors, the floorboards, the crown molding, the chair rails, the shutters, the fireplace. White, white, white, nice and light and bright. But, man—did it show every scratch and smudge. I did not have time to paint them all. I bought an eight-pack of a trusted cleaning friend: the Magic Eraser.

It is magic; I do not know how it works. You dampen the little white sponge and apply it to any surface—metal, painted walls, sneakers, even magic marker on the face of a kid—and it removes the smudge without harming the surface. Within a few hours, all my white surfaces were smudge and smear free, and I loved that white trim once more.

As I worked, I thought about the Lord, who speaks this to us in Isaiah 1:18: "'Come now, let's settle this,' says the LORD. 'Though your sins are like scarlet, I will make them as white as snow. Though they are red like crimson, I will make them as white as wool'" (NLT).

I cleaned a windowsill that we had painted the year before; we had not applied a primer, and the previous color bled through the white. Paint only covers up; Magic Erasers remove. We can cover our sins, to others and perhaps even to ourselves for a time. But that does not remove them, and eventually, they will bleed through into our lives. Not so with forgiven sins. Psalm 103:12 promises, "He has removed our sins as far from us as the east is from the west" (NLT).

It's not magic, of course, but it is miraculous. It's redemption bought by the blood of Jesus, and we are now white as snow . . . or perfectly cleaned trim!

I, even I, am he who blots out your transgressions, for my own sake,
and remembers your sins no more.   ISAIAH 43:25

Bus Stops

One day, while on vacation, my husband and I were tempted by the smell of coffee and a rhubarb custard crumble displayed in a shop window. The problem? We had very little left in our daily budget. If we were going to indulge in the dessert, we would have to take the city bus back to where we were staying, not a taxi. Ordinarily, that would not be a problem, but we were in a foreign country. It would be navigating new terrain.

But gazing at the crumble, we were emboldened to take the bus. After all—how hard could it be? So, after indulging in the treat—totally worth it, by the way—we walked up the road and stood in front of the bus stop. We could not make sense of the bus guide, but thankfully someone helpful saw our bewilderment and offered direction. "You will never get where you want standing here," she said. "You are on the wrong side of the street. The buses here go in the opposite direction of the one you're looking for."

We crossed the street, and soon enough the right bus arrived. A thought came to me as we traveled out of town. We must be on the right street—and on the right side of the street—to get where we want to go in life. If we are not standing smack in the center of where the buses run, we will never board. If we are on the wrong side, we may be headed in a direction we do *not* want to go!

As Christians, we do not know what the future holds. Jesus tells us to be dependent upon him day by day—for our daily bread—and in Matthew 6:34 he reminds us, "Therefore, do not worry about tomorrow, for tomorrow will worry about itself. Each day has enough trouble of its own."

If we stay in the center of his will, day by day, we will be exactly where we need to be to get exactly where we want to go, every day. Make sure you are headed in the right direction, friend!

Always be joyful. Never stop praying. Be thankful in all circumstances,
for this is God's will for you who belong to Christ Jesus.

1 THESSALONIANS 5:16-18, NLT

A Benediction for November

As the month turns from November to December, I hope we can keep the warm spirit of Thanksgiving alive, blowing on its embers as we head into Advent. Advent is, of course, the four weeks before Christmas, leading up to the celebration of the birth of Jesus, and marking the beginning of a month of feasting, giving, and reflection.

My prayer for you is that this final month of the year will be its highlight. That you see Christ in each day's activity, every gathering of friends and family, every gift offered and received. That you deeply know and experience God's love for you, morning and night, at the close of one month and the start of a new one.

God loves you and wants you to be blessed.

Through these pages and the power of Scripture, I reach my hands out to and over you, as your sister in Christ, and offer this exhortation as you enter a season of celebration:

> *I pray that God, the source of hope, will fill you completely with joy and peace because you trust in him. Then you will overflow with confident hope through the power of the Holy Spirit.* ROMANS 15:13, NLT

DECEMBER

A Sweet Perfume

Although retailers would have us start planning for Christmas in early September, the beginning of December often kicks off the delightful Christmas countdown. We plan for meals and travel, gifts and festivities. For many of us, it is the time when we pull our decorations from storage. I love how festive and welcoming they make my home look, but more importantly, I love how each and every one recalls Jesus Christ, ushering him into each room.

My grandmother gifted me with a ceramic tabletop tree whose tiny branches are alight with birds when I plug it in. It reminds me of Jesus' words in Matthew 6:26: "Look at the birds of the air; they do not sow or reap or store away in barns, and yet your heavenly Father feeds them. Are you not much more valuable than they?"

In the center of our dining room table is a wooden Advent candle wreath— it's always a wreath, a circle, to signify the unity of the Trinity and the continuity of God. Often the four candles placed in the wreath are purple to signify the royalty of Jesus, and the pillar candle in the center is white to signify his purity. Each Sunday, for four Sundays before Christmas, one of the purple candles is lit to anticipate hope, love, joy, and peace. The white, center candle is lit on Christmas Day, to symbolize the coming of Christ—the Light of the World (see John 8:12).

When my children were younger, we would press cloves into oranges, piercing the skin to make a pomander ball, a Colonial American tradition. We'd then attach a red ribbon by which it might be carried or displayed. The oranges represent the world and the cloves the nails that pierced Jesus, while the red ribbon represents his cleansing blood. The beautiful scent it spreads recalls 2 Corinthians 2:14: "Thank God! He has made us his captives and continues to lead us along in Christ's triumphal procession. Now he uses us to spread the knowledge of Christ everywhere, like a sweet perfume" (NLT).

Which of your Christmas decorations bring sweet thoughts of your Savior as you celebrate throughout the month?

When Jesus spoke again to the people, he said, "I am the light of the world. Whoever follows me will never walk in darkness, but will have the light of life."   JOHN 8:12

Experiencing the Love of God

One of my favorite traditions as a kid was opening the little Advent calendars that had hidden chocolates inside. A few years ago, I bought a wooden box with twenty-five compartments. Each year, we fill it with the best-quality chocolate for each day plus a little strip of paper with a Scripture on it. In the evening, before bed, we enjoy both kinds of treats. If you don't have such a box, simply buy a box of chocolate and read verses!

There are many traditional Advent verses; here are the ones we use.

Day One: Genesis 3:8-21
Day Two: Genesis 22:1-8, 13
Day Three: John 1:29-36
Day Four: Jeremiah 33:14-21
Day Five: Isaiah 9:2-7
Day Six: Psalm 89:1-4
Day Seven: Isaiah 11:1-10
Day Eight: Malachi 3:1-4
Day Nine: Isaiah 40:9-11
Day Ten: Isaiah 40:1-5
Day Eleven: Mark 1:1-3
Day Twelve: Isaiah 52:7-9
Day Thirteen: Luke 1:5-13

Day Fourteen: Luke 1:14-17
Day Fifteen: Luke 1:18-25
Day Sixteen: Luke 1:26-35
Day Seventeen: Luke 1:36-38
Day Eighteen: Luke 1:39-45
Day Nineteen: Luke 1:46-56
Day Twenty: Micah 5:2-3
Day Twenty-One: Isaiah 7:10-14
Day Twenty-Two: Matthew 1:18-25
Day Twenty-Three: Luke 2:1-20
Day Twenty-Four: Luke 2:21-35
Day Twenty-Five: Matthew 2:1-11

The angel said to her, "Don't be afraid, Mary; God has shown you his grace. Listen! You will become pregnant and give birth to a son, and you will name him Jesus. He will be great and will be called the Son of the Most High. The Lord God will give him the throne of King David, his ancestor. He will rule over the people of Jacob forever, and his kingdom will never end."

LUKE 1:30-33, NCV

A Beautiful Tree

Washington is nicknamed the Evergreen State, and there is no better time to appreciate our evergreen glory than December. Shortly after Thanksgiving, the U-Cut farms begin to advertise their wares, and we head off, ax in hand. Some years I select a majestic noble fir for the long arms that allow my ornaments to be freely displayed. I'm also fond of the douglas fir. Its bushy green beard and pinched pine scent fill the room. I love, too, the grand fir; its gray under-needle is sophisticated and vintage. Each has a unique beauty.

Despite that, once the tree is home, a decision must be made. Which side will face the wall?

Usually, it's the side that appears a little thin or misshapen or has an unsightly hole or a dry patch. Sometimes branches hang so awkwardly that I can't tie them back with twine to fake lushness. The side that I perceive as weakest or least attractive is pushed toward the wall, hidden from view. The best branches must face out.

I've recently realized that I sometimes present myself to the world, and to the Lord, in the same manner. I do the emotional equivalent of a tree-branch comb-over; I take my best, healthiest bits and use them to hide my bald spots. And if necessary, I use a wall to my advantage. I don't want others to see my unsightly habits or where I have been singed or where I'm spiritually dry. I want to be loved, and I mistakenly think I'll find that by being lovely.

Artificial Christmas trees are perfectly lovely, but they are plastic. Even the best always seem a little unreal. Charlie Brown's Christmas tree is the iconic unchosen leftover. Yet the reason we love his tree so much is that in its weakness, its vulnerability, its smallness, its beauty is found.

It is real. And so are we, you and I.

God sees your bald spots; he understands your weaknesses. He made you just as you are, and as the saying goes, he doesn't make mistakes. There is no side of you that needs to face the wall. You are beautiful and beloved from every angle.

I praise you because I am fearfully and wonderfully made; your works are wonderful, I know that full well.　　　　PSALM 139:14

Childlike Delight

We often say Christmas and the season itself were meant for children—perhaps what we mean is that we enjoy the childlike delight they seem to take in it. (More about that in a few days!) Once we are no longer children, we must work through the season—there is no long school break to enjoy—and we must pay for the attendant gifts and feast.

On the other end of the age spectrum are our elderly friends and family members. They, too, often have fewer responsibilities, but the passage of time may have dampened their ability to enjoy the season. Physical restrictions might be easier to accommodate than the intellectual and memory limitations many of our loved ones live with. And yet—with a little planning, we've found they may have as much delight as a child!

God gave us five senses with which to enjoy and understand our environments, and even when mental processing is diminished, the senses can recall the joy of Christmas for those who struggle with memory issues. Here are a few ideas to use all the senses to invoke the holiday:

- Bake something with a special meaning; for example, cinnamon rolls in the oven may bring back the time when they made this treat for their family, or their own mother did.
- Sing the Christmas carols they sang when they were younger. Nothing brings people of all ages together quite like caroling!
- Talk about their favorite Christmas stories, and look through a picture album with them of times gone by.
- Buy presents together—even gifts meant for them! They will delight in choosing something at the time and be delighted again in a few weeks when they open it, likely not remembering the first wonderful trip out.
- Don't feel the need to be 100 percent candid about people who have passed on. Just like we sometimes tell kids the truth but not the whole truth, depending on what they can handle emotionally, we can simply respond, "I haven't seen her for some time" if a beloved elder asks about someone long since passed away.

Most of us go to great lengths to make Christmas enjoyable for our children; let's do the same for our beloved elders.

Stand up in the presence of the elderly, and show respect for the aged.
LEVITICUS 19:32, NLT

No Playing Favorites

There isn't a kid alive who doesn't count the presents under the tree as they begin to stack up. There's likely not a kid alive who doesn't also count the number of gifts his or her siblings have under the tree, keeping a careful tally. Even children who know they're loved worry—do Mom and Dad love him or her more than they love me? In the mind of a child, tallying the offerings is one way to make that answer clear.

Sibling rivalry is as old as humanity—consider Cain and Abel (see Genesis 4:1-8), Jacob and Esau (see Genesis 27), the sons of Jacob (see Genesis 37), the Prodigal Son (see Luke 15:11-31), and even Martha and Mary (see Luke 10:38-42).

It's our nature, patterned after God's, to desire to be loved and wanted. It's our human nature, derived from Adam and his family, that leads us to envy, discouragement, depression, and the desire to come out on top when compared with our brothers and sisters. This isn't limited to our blood relations—we can be as envious of and competitive with our brothers and sisters in the faith as the ones in our families.

The problem is, everyone has something we wish we had, and if we aren't careful we can interpret that as favoritism. Good parents, however, do not show favoritism. We have always told our children: we spend the same amount of money on each of you, even though one of you may have a greater number of gifts than the other.

This reminds me of the wisdom of a friend. When they were remodeling their home, she, in charge of the budgets, said, "You can have anything you want, but you cannot have everything you want."

Our Lord is a loving parent who looks upon us without favoritism. After all, he clearly teaches again and again in his Word the dangers of favoring one child over another. If the Lord has chosen one gift for your sister and another for you, he has taken as much care as any good parent does in selecting that which is just right for each. Do your best not to "count the gifts under the tree" whether it is December or not, and look upon each one as carefully selected and wrapped in love especially for you!

God does not show favoritism.   Romans 2:11

A Tiny Tuxedo, Part 1

Late on the fourth day of our hospital stay, I willed myself to lay my baby down. They said I needed to leave the hospital for a few hours. I took out a brush and pulled my dull hair into a ponytail. My eyes looked old.

Before leaving, I wandered back to the crib and touched the sterile steel rails jailing my son. No mobile playing a soothing lullaby. No bumper guards. No happy bunny wallpaper. Instead, cold fluorescent lights and antibacterial cleaners. My husband stood beside me, and fear, the ultimate stealth weapon, sneaked into the room unseen. It wrapped its evil arms around us both. *Something might happen while I am gone.*

I lifted Sam's tiny hand, his fingers limp and light in mine. He slept; blue veins crisscrossed eggshell eyelids. Thin IV tubes rushed medicine through the vein in his skull. I stared at it, remembering the afternoon the doctor slipped that needle in, and adrenaline chilled my blood.

"I'm sorry." The doctor had been agitated as well. "The veins in his hands and feet are too small. They keep collapsing. We'll need to put the IV into his head." One member of the IV team had stretched a large rubber band over Sam's skull, the veins throbbing angrily as the baby screamed in pain and confusion. My husband had held Sam down, taking his tag-team turn; I felt guilty about that.

I should have been there.

"I guess I'll go now," I mumbled, returning to the present. I stretched my arms into my jacket sleeves. "Where are you going?" my husband asked. "I don't know. Not back to the house," I said. I didn't want to face the happy bunny wallpaper in silence. "Shopping, maybe." The hallway echoed with the clomping of my boots as I walked toward the elevator. There were other sounds too. The creak of wheeled cribs from treatment rooms to recovery rooms. The crunching of ice from a dispenser into the glass of a woman trying to keep her fluid levels up so she could nurse her daughter when they left the hospital. *If they left.*

It is so hard to face what seems like the end of the world. But be strong and courageous! Our God always has something redemptive in mind, no matter how dire the circumstances may seem!

Surely I am with you always, to the very end of the age.   Matthew 28:20

A Tiny Tuxedo, Part 2

My infant son had been in the hospital for four days, and I needed to get out. Once I got into my car, it was a short drive to a little strip mall. Christmas lights twinkled in each window, pooling their reflections into the puddles on the ground like impressionist watercolors. I wandered around in a few stores and bought a bear that flashed red lights and played Christmas carols when you squeezed its paws. *Sam will like that when he wakes up.*

Next door was a children's clothing store. I hadn't bought many clothes before Sam's birth. People had said the baby might be big, that I'd have too many clothes that wouldn't fit. They were right; Sam was big. It was a good thing, too. Big babies have a better chance of recovery. And he was only four weeks old.

As soon as I walked in, I saw it. A little velvet tuxedo—tiny, soft, and roomy. Festive. The salesclerk saw my longing. "Would you like this?" she asked. "It's the only six-month size left." "I don't know," I said, backing out of the store. I headed for a bench and sat down, its planks cool against my thighs. An outdoor sound system softly piped in Christmas carols, which surrounded me like a soothing cloak. What if I bought that tuxedo and Sam died? What if I had to take it home, unworn, and stare at it in the happy bunny room? *O Jesus, can I trust you with my son?*

The hopes and fears of all the years are met in thee tonight . . . As if on cue, perhaps God's cue, unseen carolers sang that familiar line through the sound system. Faith thawed my heart, flash-frozen by fear. I knew it was my answer.

Giving birth was the beginning of a joyous and precious and difficult and faith-requiring journey. As a mother, I saw that life offers both hope and fear. And both are met by the one whose birth into this world—as a fragile baby—would be celebrated soon.

My family would celebrate, I decided in faith, placing all my hopes and fears into God's good hands, with Sam in his new tuxedo.

Do you have hopes and fears this Advent season, friend? Do not hesitate to put them all in Jesus' good, strong, kind, and capable hands.

Don't let your hearts be troubled. Trust in God, and trust also in me.
JOHN 14:1, NLT

No Child Left Behind

My husband has the blessing, though he has not always regarded it as such, of sharing his birthday with the Lord. Yes, he was born on December 25. While it's true that no one will ever forget the date, it has also been true that many don't remember that date also belongs to him. He told me parts of his story.

"Even though people tried," he said, "My birthday was always eclipsed by Christmas. One year, I think when I was in the fifth grade, sums it up. It was a difficult time when I had few friends as we had recently moved to a new small town. We went over to my aunt's house for a Christmas visit. While we were there, my older cousin arrived with his little kids. I was in another room but could hear everybody talking excitedly in the kitchen and dining room. I heard talk about having a birthday cake and singing 'Happy Birthday.' Of all the family, I was the only one with a birthday, right? I grew excited.

"They called everyone together and said we were going to sing 'Happy Birthday' and enjoy a birthday cake for the celebration. I walked in behind everybody—expectant and excited. And then my aunt said, 'Isn't it so sweet one of my granddaughters wanted a birthday cake for Jesus?' She next said we were all going to sing 'Happy Birthday' . . . to Jesus."

When he heard that, he was hurt. Of course, he was very happy to be celebrating Jesus, but as a young boy who wanted a celebration of his own, he was sad that it was never the time to celebrate his birthday too. The continual expectation of something positive that was often overlooked gave the Christmas holiday dark shadows for him for many years.

Much time has gone by, and my husband has had happier celebrations. But the wounds inflicted upon us, even innocently, as a child, remain with us for a lifetime and do affect how we think about others and about God. This Christmas, let's each seek out a child who has little—and provide a gift to chase away the dark shadows that can come when the holiday seems to arrive for everyone but him or her. Let's show them that Jesus notices them, too!

Jesus said, "Let the little children come to me, and do not hinder them, for the kingdom of heaven belongs to such as these." MATTHEW 19:14

Experiencing the Love of God

While the focus of December is always on Christmas and the celebration of Jesus' birthday, my husband's memory about being overlooked each year as a child on his December 25 birthday is a good way for us to recall how special birthdays are to children. I recently read that there are more than a hundred thousand kids in the United States in foster care waiting for permanent adoption. Additionally, our local shelters are filled with parents and children who are struggling to feel safe, warm, fed, and loved.

We often experience God's love most strongly when we extend it, in some way, to others. What better way to celebrate Jesus' birthday than to help a child celebrate his or her birthday, no matter in which month it may fall? My daughter and I are involved in a local charity that provides birthday dreams to children in shelters, in conjunction with their parents, who desperately want a way to help their children celebrate. As for me, I would like to bake many more cakes than my aging body should eat—this is a wonderful way to have the best of both worlds! There may be such an organization near you.

You might consider coming alongside a foster family in your community or church to help provide a birthday celebration, or even help a family or child within your circle of family or acquaintances. I love this verse: "One who is gracious to a poor man lends to the LORD, and He will repay him for his good deed" (Proverbs 19:17, NASB).

Who among us wouldn't want to lend to the Lord and wouldn't be eager to see how he would repay?

You and your mixer, or your shopping skills, or your treat-bag-packing cleverness can be put to excellent and *fun* Kingdom work!

> *The King will say, "I tell you the truth, when you did it to one of the least of these my brothers and sisters, you were doing it to me!"*
> MATTHEW 25:40, NLT

Heavy-Duty Tractors

A few years ago, we had a big December storm that rained ice. When I finally dared to drive, I backed slowly out of the driveway and into the road. It didn't take long before I was slipping all over the street. I pointed my car toward the curb and stayed there until conditions became safer. What made the road safe again wasn't the melting of that ice—that would take some time. It was a truck that came and spread sand all over the road. That sand provided grit so I could gain traction, move forward, and control the car once more.

A couple of months later we were staying in a nearby mountain town, which is used to receiving heavy snow loads. Our SUV was trapped, and we were so relieved to see a local man driving up and down the street in his tractor. Not only did he use the tractor to clear the snow from the road, but he also harnessed the power available to him to help those with spinning wheels who could not free themselves.

Our way in life often proves slick and slippery—and sometimes we feel like we are fearfully spinning out of control. Satan would like us to believe that, but God tells us things are very much in our control. Second Timothy 1:7 encourages, "God gave us a spirit not of fear but of power and love and self-control" (esv). No matter what circumstances are rained upon us, we have power and control, friend. Sometimes we just need to remind ourselves to apply a little old-time grit to the situation.

Then sometimes, we really are stuck in the snow . . . or the circumstances. Not to fear. That man in a tractor who came to help us? He was a pastor! God will send heavy-duty help in the most unlikely situations. God loves you, and because of that love, he promised to come to your aid. Remind yourself, "I can do all things through him who strengthens me" (Philippians 4:13, esv).

"Because he loves me," says the LORD, "I will rescue him; I will protect him, for he acknowledges my name. He will call on me, and I will answer him; I will be with him in trouble, I will deliver him and honor him. With long life I will satisfy him and show him my salvation." PSALM 91:14-16

Christmas Movies, Part 1

The Christmas movie that most moves me to prayerful thoughts and forward action each year is *A Christmas Carol*, based on the book by Charles Dickens. In the story, the spirits of Christmas past, present, and future visit Ebenezer Scrooge, offering him the opportunity to review what has been, what is now, and what may be. Christmas is a perfect time for each of us to do that.

When the first spirit shows Scrooge his past, he recalls, sometimes with sorrow, the things he had once hoped for but had since let go of. The spirit gently unveils the bitter life circumstances that had been visited upon Scrooge, through no fault of his own, which had discouraged him from the love, dreams, and hopes he once had for his future.

Each year when I put the Christmas ornaments on our tree, I revisit the years and decades in which they were purchased. Some say, "Baby's first year" or "First house." Others may recall a dream for a vacation or a hoped-for career that did not come to pass. Sometimes the ornaments remind me of happier times with people who are no longer in my life, or of faith that felt so vibrant in the early years but can flicker, now and again, in the older ones. Some remind me how blessed I really am.

At the end of his time with the spirit of Christmas past, Scrooge tries to place a cone over the light these reflections into the past shed. Dickens writes, "But though Scrooge pressed it down with all his force, he could not hide the light, which streamed from under it, in an unbroken flood upon the ground."

Sometimes examining Christmases past can be painful. Dreams may have been shattered or not pursued; people we loved are now gone. But the light that Christ brings does not cause pain, but brings healing and hope. Your Christmases past, for all their special joys and unique difficulties, are just that—past—but they have helped make you who you are, and that's something to be celebrated. The best is yet to come! First Corinthians 2:9 promises, "No eye has seen, no ear has heard, and no mind has imagined what God has prepared for those who love him" (NLT). Perhaps God makes Christmas preparations too!

Forgetting what is behind and straining toward what is ahead, I press on toward the goal to win the prize for which God has called me heavenward in Christ Jesus. PHILIPPIANS 3:13-14

Christmas Movies, Part 2

The second spirit to visit Ebenezer Scrooge is the one who shows him Christmas present. Many of the activities that unfold in this section of A Christmas Carol focus on the difference between Ebenezer Scrooge, an old man with many resources but bitterness and loss of faith, and Tiny Tim, a young, crippled boy with few resources and a dim future but unwavering faith and hope.

Bob Cratchit, Tim's father and Scrooge's employee, recalls to his wife their young son's words on the way home from church. "He told me, coming home, that he hoped the people saw him in the church, because he was a cripple, and it might be pleasant to them to remember upon Christmas Day, who made lame beggars walk, and blind men see."

Scrooge's problem is that he has always been planning—he has taken no time to live in the present. Tim's problem is the one all of us have, though few of us acknowledge: we are not promised tomorrow or next Christmas.

By the end of his time with the spirit of Christmas present, Scrooge is beginning to realize all he has lost by mourning the past and putting off today's pleasures. Tim, on the other hand, enjoys each day no matter what it brings. The simple pleasures of walking in the snow, eating a pudding, or sharing time with his siblings delight him.

What wonderful things have you been blessed with this Christmas season? A new child or grandchild? A new son- or daughter-in-law? Perhaps a ministry that brings you great pleasure or the time to bake cookies or an unexpected friendship? Have you had a health reprieve? Or friends who rallied when you did not? Celebrate them—*this* is the day (and the year and the Christmas) that the Lord has made. We will rejoice and be glad in it (see Psalm 118:24)!

I have noticed one thing, at least, that is good. It is good for people to eat, drink, and enjoy their work under the sun during the short life God has given them, and to accept their lot in life. . . . To enjoy your work and accept your lot in life—this is indeed a gift from God. God keeps such people so busy enjoying life that they take no time to brood over the past.

ECCLESIASTES 5:18-20, NLT

Christmas Movies, Part 3

I'm a fan of praise music; my husband is a fan of hymns. One day I caught him singing a portion of "Come, Thou Fount of Every Blessing." He sang, "Here I raise my Ebenezer." As I came into the room I told him, "I have raised all the children I intend to raise, so there will be no Ebenezer!" Except for *A Christmas Carol* and that hymn, Ebenezer (as in Ebenezer Scrooge) is a name with which most of us are unfamiliar.

In 1 Samuel 7:12 we read, "Then Samuel took a stone and set it up between Mizpah and Shen. He named it Ebenezer, saying, 'Thus far the LORD has helped us.'"

In this portion of Scripture, the Israelites had messed up again—against the Philistines.

In their despair, there was an unexpected help. God! As an honor and a monument, Samuel raised that stone, the Ebenezer, which when translated means "the stone of help." God's help brings us hope for the future, hope that when we choose poorly, the Lord rescues us, his beloved, and brings about the victory.

In the end of *A Christmas Carol*, Ebenezer Scrooge grows into his name. He becomes the help that the people around him need. He donates generously to the collection for the poor that his colleagues are gathering. Even better, he shares his love with Tiny Tim, whose faith and love first changed Ebenezer's heart. Tiny Tim helps Ebenezer. Ebenezer helps Tiny Tim.

Dickens writes, "'A merry Christmas, Bob,' said Scrooge, with an earnestness that could not be mistaken, as he clapped him on the back. 'A merrier Christmas, Bob, my good fellow, than I have given you for many a year. I'll raise your salary, and endeavor to assist your struggling family. . . .' Scrooge was better than his word. He did it all, and infinitely more; and to Tiny Tim, who did *not* die, he was a second father. He became as good a friend, as good a master, and as good a man as the good old City knew, or any other good old city, town, or borough in the good old world."

God loves us, you and me. And he helps us to reclaim our past, live our present, and have hope for future Christmases and beyond!

Behold, God is my helper; The Lord is the sustainer of my soul.

PSALM 54:4, NASB

Christmas Movies, Part 4

Of all the Christmas movies I enjoy as an adult, *The Nativity Story* is my favorite. I love the honest emotions that each of the actors conveys—they remind me these were real people thrust into supernatural situations. In that culture, Mary might have been stoned to death for her out-of-wedlock pregnancy. Her family was ostracized. Joseph was seen as a man who was cheated on by his young fiancée. And yet, during the darkest times leading up to the brightest day, they persevered.

We often ask the Lord, why do you not make life easier for us? Smooth our paths, smite our enemies. As Scripture teaches and the movie brings brilliantly to life, Jesus did not make circumstances easy even for himself. He was born in poor, uncomfortable conditions, persecuted from the outset. He and his parents had to flee to safety in Egypt, the same land his ancestors had fled from hundreds of years before. I don't know if that teaches that there is value in suffering or simply that the world is a difficult place to live. In either case, he did not exclude himself from affliction.

Mary, likely a teenager, was presented with what was an impossible situation from a human perspective. Yet she bore up under the weight of it with admirable grace and determination. How do I bear up under the circumstances the Lord requires of me? With grace and faith?

Meditate on the fact that the angel did not appear to Joseph at the same time he did to Mary. Mary had only the Lord to rely on for a time. Perhaps that cemented her faith and centered her before Joseph became a strong ally. There were no angels sent, either, to convince the people that Jesus was the Messiah. He would do that on his own, in his own time.

Part of the significance of Mary, a virtuous woman of no worldly remark, having been chosen as the mother of Jesus is that she shows us how we, virtuous people of no worldly remark, can respond when called to step up for God in difficult times. Part of the takeaway for us, too, is to trust God to reveal his truth in his timing—even when it's difficult.

Mary trusted God and never looked back.

Mary responded, "I am the Lord's servant."　　　　　Luke 1:38, nlt

Christmas Movies, Part 5

Of all the Christmas movies I enjoyed as a child, my favorite was *The Little Drummer Boy*.

The story behind the movie comes from an old Czech tale and song called "The Carol of the Drum." In both, there is a young boy who is poor and has very little, perhaps nothing, to offer the newborn baby Jesus. In the movie, the young boy's parents were killed, and he has not been able to let go of his unhappiness and bitterness. In fact, he cannot even smile—he must paint one on to appear happy in the times and places he is expected to be happy. Many of us can relate to that, can't we? We're supposed to be happy, especially at Christmas, but we're just not. So we fake it.

And yet this little drummer boy is given the opportunity to be presented before the glory and holiness of the newborn Jesus, the King of the world, our Savior. In the presence of the wise men's wealthy gifts, he feels he has nothing to offer. But God has made him able to create music with his simple drum, and that is what he gives, the talent and gift God has given him offered back in a song of praise. Each of us can, as Psalm 96:1 exhorts us, "Sing to the LORD a new song," even though most of us won't be offering a literal song. We can play our best for Jesus by offering our God-given talent back to him in a new way, a heartfelt way.

I would posit that the wise men gave four gifts. The traditional three we think of often: gold, frankincense, myrrh. But was the fourth present the gift of worship? Many of us have little or none of the first three to offer, but all of us can richly give of the fourth.

We can duplicate, replicate, invest, and offer whatever talents God has given us. And we can worship. When we do, in the Spirit and truth (see John 4:24), for a moment, an hour, a week, a month, or more, we will find we no longer need to paint on that smile!

Ascribe to the LORD the glory due his name; worship the LORD in the splendor of his holiness.   PSALM 29:2

Experiencing the Love of God

What unique gifts, talents, skills, resources, or abilities do you have to offer the Lord in worship? When I reflect on the Little Drummer Boy, I realize his talents were often called upon when he didn't want to use them. But then when he had the opportunity to freely give his song and his gifts, it was done with a completely new attitude.

Maybe your special gifts are so often asked for that you feel used. If you have financial resources, it might seem like people are always asking you for money. You might cook for everyone who seems busy—but you are busy too. Maybe you're asked to care for children often, even when you are tired. Maybe you're an accountant and people ask you many tax questions, so the idea of donating your time pro bono seems wearying. Perhaps you have the gift of organization or cheerfulness or hospitality.

I do know that God has uniquely gifted all of us. How can you offer your gifts to him in worship? Write a poem to him? Sing a song for him? Prepare a meal and commune with him (and others) while you eat it? Serve him by offering professional skills to your church? My favorite kind of Christmas tree is one that has many different kinds of wrappings holding a wide variety of gifts. How dull would it be to have just one kind of wrapping paper? How boring to have people open the same gift over and over! Instead, our diversity is beautiful. What do you have to offer? It's something beautiful and unique. Give what you'd like to, not because you must (see 2 Corinthians 9:7). Freely given without compulsion or pressure, these gifts will shine with life!

There are different kinds of gifts, but the same Spirit distributes them. There are different kinds of service, but the same Lord. There are different kinds of working, but in all of them and in everyone it is the same God at work.

1 CORINTHIANS 12:4-6

Starry Adventures

One of my husband's favorite books is *Undaunted Courage*, the story of Lewis and Clark's journey across the United States to find out what was there—and map it. A poignant portion is when the Corps of Discovery reached what they thought would be the tributary providing the all-water, transcontinental route, connecting the Atlantic to the Pacific. Instead, as they expectantly crested a ridge they looked upon a terrifying sight: craggy, giant Rocky Mountains for as far as the eye could see. They were not only *not* at the end of the journey; it had just grown much longer and more difficult. They faced a new and fearful unknown far removed from their highly anticipated expectations. But they had to go on.

Our biblical forebears faced many similar situations. God simply told Abram to "go." In Genesis 12:1, "The LORD had said to Abram, 'Leave your native country, your relatives, and your father's family, and go to the land that I will show you'" (NLT). Abram did as he was told, trusting God but having no idea where he would end up, how long the journey would take, or how difficult it might be.

When the Lord freed the Israelites from Egypt, he led them in a supernatural way. "The LORD was going before them in a pillar of cloud by day to lead them on the way, and in a pillar of fire by night to give them light, that they might travel by day and by night" (Exodus 13:21, NASB).

With Moses, they went where God led them without knowing where it would lead.

This week, I've heard songs, watched movies, and read Scripture that included the three wise men. They set off from their lands, educated and literate, one supposes, but not relying on maps. Instead, they relied on a star. Matthew 2:9 tells us, "The star they had seen in the east guided them to Bethlehem. It went ahead of them and stopped over the place where the child was" (NLT). Once they found him, they worshiped him. Wise indeed!

In two weeks, we'll be stepping into a new year. Where will God lead us? Let's be brave and adventurous enough to follow!

The LORD is the one who goes ahead of you; He will be with you. He will not fail you or forsake you. Do not fear or be dismayed.

DEUTERONOMY 31:8, NASB

Gold, Frankincense, and Myrrh

I spend a great deal of time thinking about Christmas gifts for my children and other loved ones, and I'll bet you do too. What are they interested in? What would they like to try but cannot afford? What challenges lie just ahead for them? Then I marry my budget with their desires.

We are told that the wise men, the magi from the east, brought gold, frankincense, and myrrh to the young Jesus and his parents. As soon as those wise men left, the little family had to flee. Matthew 2:13 tells us, "When they had gone, an angel of the Lord appeared to Joseph in a dream. 'Get up,' he said, 'take the child and his mother and escape to Egypt. Stay there until I tell you, for Herod is going to search for the child to kill him.'" How could they provide for themselves, the costs associated with the journey, and the expenses they would surely find once they arrived? Thanks to the magi—and the God who led the wise men by the star—they had cash on hand.

Gold as a liquid asset needs no explanation—long before Jesus' birth and right up to this day gold has been useful in almost every society as a ready currency. Myrrh is, and was, an essential oil and resin that is valuable for its medicinal and perfume properties.

Frankincense has a truly interesting history. It's very valuable as it is grown primarily in one place—Oman—which is close to Persia, whence the wise men came. Frankincense was used by the Greeks, Romans, Israelites, and Egyptians for burial and other religious services. It is said that the emperor Nero, who was to persecute Christians shortly after Jesus' death, used an entire year's harvest at the funeral of his mistress. Frankincense was valuable indeed.

I felt so encouraged to learn of the clever, thoughtful, and complete manner in which God provided for his Son. What gifts and provision God supplied for his child, Jesus! What will he provide for us? No matter where the Lord calls you to journey this next year, he will ensure you have everything you need to be well cared for.

If you then, who are evil, know how to give good gifts to your children, how much more will your Father who is in heaven give good things to those who ask him!　MATTHEW 7:11, ESV

Cheerful Receivers

Throughout the months of this devotional, we've talked about ways we can reach out in love and affection to others: our friends and family, other Christians, strangers. For most of us, giving to others is a pleasure, a way to share the love of God, and the Lord Jesus has said, "It is more blessed to give than to receive" (Acts 20:35).

Most of us would agree with that. There is no better way to experience the love of God than by giving as he does . . . except, perhaps, by receiving. So why is being the recipient so much more difficult than being the giver?

I have been blessed to be a giver many times in my life. I have also been the recipient of gifts during times in our lives when we were down and out, either financially or emotionally. There were times people generously offered just what we needed and allowed us to keep our dignity while accepting help. However, we were once "adopted" by a family who was to deliver desperately needed groceries for Christmas to seminary families. When they arrived at our small rental house, we were apparently better off than they expected, because the mother whispered to her children that she wasn't going to bring in the rest of the food because we didn't need it. Oh, but we did.

In most cases, though, the attitude most needing adjustment was mine. It's hard to be in need. It's hard to take and receive. What does that say about me if I expect others to have periods of need, but not me? Do I expect to graciously give but not graciously receive? "As each has received a gift, use it to serve one another" (1 Peter 4:10, ESV). Am I saying I am willing to serve in the name of the Lord but not be served in that same name?

Lord, forgive me my pride.

This Christmas, it may be you or me who needs to reach out and ask for help. Maybe the kids need others to provide gifts, or there isn't enough for groceries, utilities, or rent. Maybe we need a place to celebrate and people to rejoice with. It's okay. We're family here.

Be thankful in all circumstances, for this is God's will for you who belong to Christ Jesus.　　　　　　　　　　　　　1 THESSALONIANS 5:18, NLT

No Ugly Sweaters

My daughter and son-in-law were doing some quick shopping the week before Christmas—not unusual—but what they were looking for were ugly sweaters. Her employer was having an "ugly sweater" party, and prizes were to be given for the ugliest sweaters worn. They finally found some at a local used clothing store and, after laundering them, stopped by our house to show us.

"You two are the cutest people in the least attractive wrappings I have seen in a long time," I told them. They left, and I went back to wrapping gifts—something I do not do very well. In fact, my husband is the designated gift-wrapper in our house because my paper edges do not ever line up. I use too much paper, which leaves an unsightly bulge, or not enough, which leaves a gap. I overuse tape. Every gift under the tree is beautifully wrapped—except for his, because I've wrapped them!

I do buy good stuff for the inside, though, and that's important.

Thinking the concept over, I realized that there have been many times in my life when I have received gifts that, at first glance, I did not want, because they were wrapped in unappealing covers. I received an unwelcome diagnosis, but once it was received, I took much better care of my health and now am healthier than I have been in years. As a writer, I am subject to many public praises and criticisms of my work. Some of the words used are hurtful—but useful—if I am willing to see beyond the "packaging."

Sometimes the wrapping isn't ugly, it's just that it gives no hint to the value of what lies within. I received a lovely, valuable piece of jewelry whose box was wrapped in newsprint. I've received large checks that arrived in plain envelopes.

In our world, in which everything is packaged to have maximum eye appeal, let's be careful to look beyond the bling, the ribbons and bows, and the package presentation to test the worth by what we find inside. After all, the costliest, most valuable gift ever given came wrapped in strips of cloth.

You will recognize him by this sign: You will find a baby wrapped snugly in strips of cloth, lying in a manger. LUKE 2:12, NLT

Favorite Christmas Carols, Part 1

Do you know the thing I most love about Christmas carols? They are some of the few songs that can be played in public arenas—in grocery stores, malls, and restaurants—that speak openly and clearly about the Lord Jesus Christ.

My second favorite thing about carols is they are a wonderful way to recall and replant spiritual truths. While we are baking, wrapping, working, shopping, and eating, the truths of Jesus are filtering in through our ears and rooting in our hearts and minds. We join with others and joyfully sing them to God—perhaps the only songs we sing year after year throughout our lives. Because carols play such an important role in our Christmas experience, let's look at the theology in a few of them so we may deeply understand and offer even more sincere worship this season.

Although I love the song "Away in a Manger," this line has always struck me as odd: "But little Lord Jesus, no crying he makes." Every mother, upon giving birth, is holding her breath until she hears the first robust cry from her child, announcing that he is alive. Jesus was, of course, the perfect human, but he was human, and fully so, so that he could become our great high priest (see Hebrews 2:17-19). I'm so glad—and I'm guessing he cried!

"Oh come all ye faithful, joyful and triumphant, oh come ye, oh come ye to Bethlehem," another carol implores us. By this time in December, we are rounding home plate to the completion of another year. It has likely brought happiness, sorrow, challenges, discouragement, and victories. Completing the year by celebrating Jesus' birth is the perfect way to reorient ourselves before the start of a new one. Because we are faithful to him, we share in his joy and triumph, confidently and fearlessly facing anything in front of us (see Psalm 112:8).

"What Child Is This?" That is the question each of us must answer for ourselves during our earthly lives. The song, of course, offers the truth of who the child is and what he is here for: "The King of Kings salvation brings, let loving hearts enthrone Him. This, this is Christ, the King" (see Revelation 19:16).

I will shout for joy and sing your praises, for you have ransomed me.

PSALM 71:23, NLT

Favorite Christmas Carols, Part 2

"God rest you merry, gentlemen, let nothing you dismay," we are exhorted. I love that we are named merry right off—and why not? "Merry Christmas" is our holiday greeting—may this season, this day, be jolly, cheerful, happy, lively, and celebratory. We, both gentlemen and ladies, can be merry because God has rested us—given us peace and reclaimed us. When and by whom? "For Jesus Christ, our Savior, was born upon this day." Then we are reminded of our deepest need, and the reason Christ was born at all: "To save us all from Satan's power when we were gone astray," as we all do (see Romans 3:23). "O tidings of comfort and joy" because our sins can now be washed away (see 1 John 1:7).

That washing away of our sins is done by redeeming grace (see Ephesians 1:7). "Silent Night" tells us that this is the start of it all. "Son of God, love's pure light; radiant beams from thy holy face with the dawn of redeeming grace, Jesus, Lord, at thy birth."

What is the appropriate response to the knowledge that we are now merry, free from the painful consequences of sin, and that his redeeming grace has freed us? I hope we will, like many of our Bible brethren, fall on our knees. First Corinthians 14:25 says, "So they will fall down and worship God, exclaiming, 'God is really among you!'"

"O holy night," indeed.

Once we realize what love the Father has lavished upon us (see 1 John 3:1) our response will be to extend that love to others. "Truly, He taught us to love one another; His law is love, and His gospel is peace." "Love each other. Just as I have loved you, you should love each other," Jesus tells us in John 13:34 (NLT), "with your feet fitted with the readiness that comes from the gospel of peace" (Ephesians 6:15).

Once we start walking, we know what to do next. Shout it! Whisper it! Whatever it takes. "Go, tell it on the mountain, over the hills and everywhere; go, tell it on the mountain that Jesus Christ is born!"

Teach these new disciples to obey all the commands I have given you. And be sure of this: I am with you always, even to the end of the age.

MATTHEW 28:20, NLT

Experiencing the Love of God

We can deepen our celebration of Christmas when we experience it through all five senses. Christmas carols remind us how much faith, hope, love, and celebration we can take in through our ears; when their theology is sound, they help us understand the Son of God. We are bathing our minds in the joy and hope that Christmas brings. "We know also that the Son of God has come and has given us understanding, so that we may know him who is true" (1 John 5:20).

Do you have a favorite Christmas carol? Why is it your favorite, and how does it remind you of Jesus?

Do you have a favorite Christmas scent? Perhaps a candle or some baked good? The piney scent of a tree? What does that favorite "perfume" recall to mind about Christmas?

What is your family's traditional Christmas meal? Does each dish point to a cultural tradition or favorite person?

The sights of Christmas are all around us. Do you have a favorite—perhaps something on your tree, or poinsettias, famously shaped like the star of Bethlehem?

Touch is the sense we most overlook, both when describing things to others and when we're thinking of something ourselves. But touch brings comfort and memory in a unique way. Do you remember licking icicles as a kid—and maybe having a stuck tongue? Do you tuck yourself into a soft, warming blanket while reading Advent stories or this devotional? Does the touch of your pet's fur beneath your hand soothe you at the end of the busy day?

What are your favorite Christmas sensations, and how do they recall the glory of the Lord's story to you?

When I see _____, it reminds me of the Lord's love for me.

When I smell _____, it reminds me of God's care for me and others.

When I taste _____, it brings to mind a time when I ate it with others who love me and love the Lord.

When I listen to _____, I'm reminded of God's care and provision.

When I touch _____, it brings back a memory of God's ongoing concern for my feelings and well-being.

Taste and see that the LORD is good; blessed is the one who takes refuge in him.
PSALM 34:8

Swan Song

There is an ancient tradition that a swan, which may not make any noise during most of its life, will sing sweetly just before its death. This may or may not be true, but it lives on in the common imagination: a person's best and most beautiful work is offered shortly before they retire or die. It's where we get the phrase *swan song*.

The myth of the Thorn Bird tells of a bird that spends its life flying around looking for a thorn bush. When it finds one, it lands and is impaled on a thorn as it does so, but that is its singular purpose—what it was born to do. It sings the most beautiful song as it dies.

Tomorrow marks the celebration of the birth of Jesus Christ—the most important birthday in all of humanity. His birth was a gift to us, the ultimate Christmas gift, as it were. Behold what manner of love the Father has for you (see 1 John 3:1)! And yet the traditional green and red of Christmas recall both the beginning, the green life, and the end, the death and shedding of Christ's red blood.

Jesus was born to be crucified as atonement for the sins of mankind, and to be resurrected to life, as we will be in him. We read in Matthew 27:29-30 that hours before he died, "They wove thorn branches into a crown and put it on his head, and they placed a reed stick in his right hand as a scepter. Then they knelt before him in mockery and taunted, 'Hail! King of the Jews!' And they spit on him and grabbed the stick and struck him on the head with it" (NLT).

His death was history's most beautiful swan song, which could not have been possible without his birth. He was the Thorn Bird who came for one reason only, and having completed it, died with the thorns of his crown and nails driven into his hands and feet, causing him pain and misery. But his death song is an overture of spiritual life for you and me and all who call upon him.

Everyone who calls on the name of the Lord will be saved.　Romans 10:13

Our Way Maker

In the Old Testament, the people of Israel carried around the Tabernacle, in which God dwelt among his people. It was portable so it could travel with them. God wanted to be with his people wherever they were, wherever life took them. When it came time for the hundreds of prophecies foretelling of Christ to be brought to a glorious culmination with his birth in Bethlehem, the most prized, resonant truth is that now he is not only among us, but *with us* and *in us*.

Immanuel. God is with us.

"He came into the very world he created. . . . So the Word became human and made his home among us. He was full of unfailing love and faithfulness. And we have seen his glory, the glory of the Father's one and only Son" (John 1:10, 14, NLT).

I love the story of a swallow that flew into a burning barn. Other swallows were inside, and there was only one tiny hole at the top of the eaves from which to escape. Because of the smoke the birds could not see a way out, until the new swallow—who looked just like them—entered through the hole to guide them to safety. Jesus came to be *with* us where we live so he could guide and lead us. Fully God and fully man, as his birthday proves.

Better, even, than living among us, with us, is that Jesus made way for God to live *in* us. His atoning death made us holy enough for God to indwell us in the form of the Holy Spirit. No further need for a traveling tent—God goes with us wherever we go. "Don't you know that you yourselves are God's temple and that God's Spirit dwells in your midst?" (1 Corinthians 3:16).

This day, let's take a moment and wholeheartedly thank God for loving us so much that he not only made a way for us to be with him, eternally, he made a way to be with us right now, every day, wherever we may go in the here and now. Merry Christmas!

Look! The virgin will conceive a child! She will give birth to a son, and they will call him Immanuel, which means "God is with us." MATTHEW 1:23, NLT

Thank-You Notes

I had a grandmother who was a fair stickler about thank-you notes. She gave lovely gifts at Christmas and liked to hear that we enjoyed them. I will say, in contrast to many of the other adults I was familiar with at the time, she also took the time to write thank-you notes to us kids for our little offerings too. She not only taught me the fine art of showing my thanks, but she also practiced what she preached. Those lessons have been valuable to me throughout my life.

Today, it's a rare thing to receive a handwritten, mail-carrier-delivered anything, much less a thank-you note. That must be why I am so thrilled when I receive one. I'm still very happy to receive a call or a text or even a message on social media thanking me for a gift or for reaching out to help someone in any way. Truthfully, I am more likely to extend myself a second or third time for someone who expresses thanks than I am for someone who does not.

When we forget to say thanks, I don't believe it's because we're not grateful. I think we are just so busy. That's not an excuse; it's a fact. Our world has sped up every year that I've lived, and the demands placed upon us are greater, sometimes, than our resources to deal with them.

I love the biblical understanding of giving thanks—it is a sacrifice. "Giving thanks is a sacrifice that truly honors me," Psalm 50:23 (NLT) tells us. Scripture elaborates in several places about what a sacrifice of thanksgiving is and when it should be offered. Like any sacrifice, it takes away resources—finances and time—that we might spend elsewhere. But it is so important.

This year, I am determined to show thanks in creative ways to the people who gift me with their time, their treasure, and their love. Will you join me? Let's start with the Lord, the giver of all good things (see James 1:17).

One of them, when he saw he was healed, came back, praising God in a loud voice. He threw himself at Jesus' feet and thanked him—and he was a Samaritan. Jesus asked, "Were not all ten cleansed? Where are the other nine?"
LUKE 17:15-17

Opening Bible Bookend—Genesis

Bookends are, of course, sturdy and reliable objects that hold the row of books between them steadily upright. In conversation, the word can also mean a support placed at the beginning and end of a conversation. In the Bible, then, our bookends would be Genesis and Revelation.

We've spent this year discovering the many and varied ways we experience the love of God. A careful reading of Scripture will bring alive the ways God loves us, and he starts to reveal that right from the start, in Genesis.

I was with some friends last weekend, and we took a few pictures of ourselves. We were careful to ask one another for permission to post them online, as all of us are cautious, and perhaps protective, of our public images. I recently took a "selfie" at a monument for a work purpose, and it did not go public until I had cropped it and run it through a filter. I'm also careful about what I say and how I present myself, not only for my own image, but for how I represent my employers, my family, and most importantly, my Lord.

I find it incredibly trusting, then, that God made us in his own image. What we bear forth into the world tells everyone we meet something about him. He is spirit, and therefore while we might believe that our physical features could in some way represent him, it's our spiritual, emotional, and intellectual characteristics that best call him to mind.

When a baby is born, parents spend time trying to distinguish whose nose he has or whose smile she has inherited, because they are so pleased and proud to be identified with the new baby. Adoptive and foster kids can take after their parents too, in those most important ways—character, affection, ethics, and faith. Even those we teach or mentor can partly be, in some good ways, "made in our image."

God shows us how much he loves us in that when he made us, human beings alone, he made us in his image. He wants to show us to the world and say, "Hey, look! My kid!"

God created mankind in his own image, in the image of God he created them; male and female he created them. GENESIS 1:27

Closing Bible Bookend—Revelation

Most of us receive a name at birth and don't change it except at marriage, adoption, or divorce. It's a parent's prerogative to name a child, and it's done with great care and forethought.

When God made a covenant with Abram to honor him and make him the father of many nations, God changed his name to Abraham (see Genesis 17:2-5). When Jacob wrestled with God in Genesis 32, his name was changed from Jacob, which means "deceiver," to Israel, which means "strive with God."

Jesus changed Simon's name the moment they met. In John 1:42, Jesus looked at him, and said: "'You are Simon the son of John; you shall be called Cephas' (which is translated Peter)" (NASB). *Simon* means "listen," but *Peter*, *Cephas*, means "rock." In Matthew 16:18, the Lord expands on that, after Peter declares Jesus to be the Messiah: "Now I say to you that you are Peter (which means 'rock'), and upon this rock I will build my church, and all the powers of hell will not conquer it" (NLT).

After his conversion, Saul (a Hebrew name), was called both Saul and Paul, a Latin name, which fits neatly with the fact that he preached the gospel to both Jewish and Gentile people. Perhaps most importantly for you and me, we began to be called Christians in Acts 11. *Christian* means "Christ-follower." I pray we live up to the name!

In our family, we have pet nicknames based on inside family information and affection. My husband always refers to our daughter as "peat-swee," rather than sweet pea, because of her desire to be different. I'm certain you have terms of endearment that you use with your beloveds, and they with you.

God has engraved our names on his hand (see Isaiah 49:16) and will also give us a new name after the final judgment, when he makes all things new. It will be something personal and private, a reward given in love. Because he changes names with affection and commission, I cannot wait to find out what my new name will be. Can you?

To everyone who is victorious I will give some of the manna that has been hidden away in heaven. And I will give to each one a white stone, and on the stone will be engraved a new name that no one understands except the one who receives it.
                                        REVELATION 2:17, NLT

Speak Gently

In one closet is a stack of scrapbooks and a tower of boxes that hold photos and bits of paper that whisper from the past. As I sorted through them one day, I came to a tiny cache of photos of myself as a baby, a child, and a teen.

The photos show me in many emotional phases: happy, joyful, worried, self-conscious, and with my teenage eyes darkly shadowed by trouble. Suddenly, I didn't feel like I was looking at myself. I felt like I was looking at a girl, a young woman, who was dear to me but needed someone to reach out and hug her, to tell her it was all going to be okay.

What would you say to yourself if you could speak to the girl or boy, young woman or man you once were?

If anyone heard the noise in most of our heads, the words would often not be ones we would say to others. Often there are accusations of failure or ugliness; sometimes we hear voices of shame—a parent or a teacher or others speaking down to us. We echo the unwelcome words of abusers.

Those are not loving actions. And yet loving ourselves is what we are expected to do! It's supposed to be the assumed norm. "Love others as you love yourself" (see Matthew 22:39) implies that we will naturally love ourselves, and yet we don't always.

We have the chance, now, to change what we're saying to ourselves. We can change what we say to ourselves about what happened and what we did or did not do. We can speak gently to ourselves as surely as the Lord would speak compassionately to us. "As a father has compassion on his children, so the LORD has compassion on those who fear him" (Psalm 103:13).

We determine, from this day forward, we will only speak to ourselves, inside our heads and out loud, those things that build up and do not tear down (see Ephesians 4:29).

Jesus replied, "'You must love the LORD your God with all your heart, all your soul, and all your mind.' This is the first and greatest commandment. A second is equally important: 'Love your neighbor as yourself.'"
                                                            MATTHEW 22:37-39, NLT

Experiencing the Love of God

Take a quiet moment today, when no one else is around, and close your eyes and pray. Then ask yourself:

What kind things would God have you say to your younger self? Can you speak them aloud to yourself now? Remember, he has said, "I have loved you with an everlasting love." Those "everlasting love" kinds of words are what he would speak to you and have you speak to yourself.

If you could say one thing to your current self, something said in love and encouragement and affection, what would it be? Say it aloud now.

If you have your calendar nearby, sit down and write or type one encouraging thought to yourself and about yourself for each month next year. You might write things such as:

You are an admirable person who always gives her best effort.
People like to be around you because you are funny and kind.
You are diligent even when no one is looking.

Think of twelve legitimate compliments to give yourself and place one in each month. Go ahead—don't *say* you'll do it. Just do it. Next year you will be blessed by your own words!

I have loved you with an everlasting love. JEREMIAH 31:3

A Benediction for December

As we close the year, I want to take a moment to thank you, dear reader and fellow believer, for sharing this year of understanding and exploration with me. I pray that you will experience the love of God in new, powerful, and fresh ways each year you journey with him.

Please accept my benediction over you for the near new year, drawn from a passage in Scripture in which the Lord tells one of his followers to bless the others.

God loves you and wants you to be blessed.

Through these pages and the power of Scripture, I reach my hands out to and over you, as your sister in Christ, and pray . . .

The LORD bless you and keep you; the LORD make his face shine on you and be gracious to you; the LORD turn his face toward you and give you peace.

NUMBERS 6:24-26

About the Author

After earning her first rejection at the age of thirteen, bestselling author Sandra Byrd has now published fifty books.

Sandra's series of historically sound Gothic romances, Daughters of Hampshire, launched with the bestselling *Mist of Midnight*, which earned a coveted Editor's Choice award from the Historical Novel Society. The second book, *Bride of a Distant Isle*, was selected by *Romantic Times* as a Top Pick. The third in the series, *A Lady in Disguise*, was published in 2017. Sandra is excited to continue writing Gothic romance and will be adding books to that genre beginning in February 2019.

Check out her contemporary adult fiction debut, *Let Them Eat Cake*, which was a Christy Award finalist, as was her first historical novel, *To Die For: A Novel of Anne Boleyn*. *To Die For* was also named a *Library Journal* Best Books Pick for 2011, and *The Secret Keeper: A Novel of Kateryn Parr* was named a *Library Journal* Best Books Pick for 2012.

Sandra has published dozens of books for kids, tweens, and teens, including the bestselling *The One Year Be-Tween You and God: Devotions for Girls*. She continued her work as a devotionalist, this time for women, with *The One Year Home and Garden Devotions* and *The One Year Experiencing God's Love Devotional*.

Sandra is passionate about helping new writers develop their talents and their work for traditional publishing or self-publication. She has mentored and coached hundreds of new writers and continues to guide developing authors toward success each year via novelcoaching.com.

Please visit www.sandrabyrd.com to learn more or to invite Sandra to your book club via Skype.

Do-able. Daily. Devotions.

START ANY DAY THE ONE YEAR WAY.

For Women

The One Year®
Home and
Garden
Devotions

The One Year®
Devotions for
Women

The One Year®
Devotions for
Moms

The One Year®
Women of the
Bible

The One Year®
Coffee with God

The One Year®
Devotional of Joy
and Laughter

The One Year®
Women's
Friendship
Devotional

The One Year®
Wisdom
for Women
Devotional

The One Year®
Book of Amish
Peace

The One Year®
Women in
Christian History
Devotional

CP0145

For Men

The One Year®
Devotions for
Men on the Go

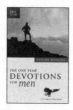

The One Year®
Devotions for Men

The One Year®
Father-Daughter
Devotions

For Families

The One Year®
Family
Devotions, Vol. 1

The One Year®
Dinner Table
Devotions

For Couples

The One Year®
Devotions for
Couples

The One Year® Love
Language Minute
Devotional

The One Year® Love
Talk Devotional

For Teens

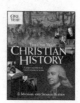

The One Year®
Devos for Teens

The One Year®
Be-Tween You
and God

For Personal Growth

The One Year®
at His Feet
Devotional

The One Year®
Uncommon Life
Daily Challenge

The One Year®
Recovery Prayer
Devotional

The One Year®
Christian History

The One Year®
Experiencing God's
Presence Devotional

For Bible Study

The One Year®
Praying through
the Bible

The One Year®
Praying the
Promises of God

The One Year®
Through the
Bible Devotional

The One Year®
Book of Bible
Promises

The One Year®
Unlocking the
Bible Devotional

TheOneYear.com

OTHER BOOKS BY
SANDRA BYRD

HISTORICAL FICTION
Daughters of Hampshire
Ladies in Waiting

CONTEMPORARY FICTION
French Twist

TEENS & TWEENS
London Confidential
Secret Sisters
Forever Friends
Hidden Diary

DEVOTIONALS
The One Year Be-Tween You and God
The One Year Home and Garden Devotions
The One Experiencing God's Love Devotional

CP1291